A TREASURY
OF BIBLE
Illustrations

A Treasury of Bible Illustrations

Compiled by
Ted Kyle and John Todd

AMG
PUBLISHERS

Chattanooga, TN 37422

A TREASURY OF BIBLE ILLUSTRATIONS

ISBN 0-89957-227-8

Contents

Admonition

1 Going Too Fast

A number of years ago, a Navy jet fighter plane shot itself down over the deserts of Nevada while testing a new cannon mounted on its wing. The plane was flying at supersonic speeds, but the cannon shells were subsonic. What happened was crucial. The fighter actually ran into the shells it had fired seconds before. The jet was traveling too fast.

Sometimes we travel too fast for our own spiritual good. God speaks and we are going too fast to hear Him.

Don't be guilty of traveling so fast with your life that you run past the sound of the Word of God. Be in the center of His will.

2 See Only Christ

You are familiar, no doubt, with one of the most famous paintings ever done by any artist: *The Last Supper* by Leonardo da Vinci, that classic portrayal of Christ and the twelve apostles at the table.

Many students of art history believe that the painting, when first created, was somewhat different from the version which we now see. There was initially, it is believed, an exquisite lace border on the tablecloth. When, immediately upon completion, da Vinci invited a group of art students to view his masterpiece, they were immensely impressed by the delicate design of that lacework. They studied it intensely and praised it highly.

Upon seeing the reaction of these young men, the artist took up a brush, dipped it, and made a few long strokes across the canvas, obliterating the lace. Then, with uncontrollable feeling, he shouted, "Now, you fools, look at the face of Christ!"

3 The Mind Has No Garbage Disposal

In describing one of the new movies of the day, a critic wrote, "The plot moves rapidly down the sewer." It would not be so damaging to those who watch such trash if the mind could be equipped, like your kitchen sink, with a garbage disposal. Then you could flush away all the filth and be done with it, but the mind does not work that way. It stores up impressions for a lifetime. The only way to protect the mind is to expose it to only the best!

4 The Burning Torch

Among ancient Greeks the runner who won the race was not the man who crossed the line in the shortest time, but the man who

1

crossed it in the least time with his torch still burning.

We are so often so busy with life's activities that we are in danger of allowing the torch of our spiritual life to become extinguished.

A good woman once said that in the rush and hurry of her life she felt in danger of being "jostled out of her spirituality." There is a real danger of being too busy to be good, of running too fast to keep our torch burning.

5 Tracing Character to Its Source

During a thunder storm that contained high winds, a giant oak tree was blown down. The tree was thought to be in perfect health; that is, from outward appearance it seemed to be in good health since it was almost perfectly shaped and full of green leaves. However, the massive tree could not withstand the stress of the high wind because of deterioration on the inside. What started as a tiny corruption at the center of the tree had spread until that tremendous tree was so weakened that it was toppled by the wind.

One may reach a point where he forsakes God altogether. It is because he (like the tree) has decayed on the inside. Perhaps the deterioration started with a little lie or one small drink of beer or forsaking the assembly to go fishing or camping. Long before our feet carry us where we ought not go, and our hands do what they ought not do, the desire

is in our hearts (Ps. 119:9-11). With pure hearts we will be able to stand the stress of temptation and the stress of everyday living.

6 Extremes

Many times we are caught in the trap of running to extremes. God's will has been revealed and needs to be understood the way God intended it to be.

The Pharisees had this problem. They even had everyday life defined to the point where it was hard for a person to live. On the Sabbath day, they had problems with different concepts such as "work." On the Sabbath you were to cease from work, and the Pharisees decided to define what God intended by this. Here are a few examples:

1. You could not turn over in bed more than seven times or that was considered work.

2. If you wanted to borrow something from your neighbor, you could not put your hand through the threshold of the door to receive it, nor could the neighbor do that. This would be considered work. If you both met halfway, it was not considered work.

Jesus said in Matthew 15:6, speaking to the Pharisees, ". . . And thus you invalidated the Word of God for the sake of your tradition." For the sake of their definitions which they had made law, their extremes, they made void the Word of God. We laugh at the Pharisees and wonder how they could have been so ignorant. But if Jesus were here physically today, what would He say of us? Let us not run to extremes; let us seek what God intended and do it. Either extreme of a truth is no longer truth.

7   Ten Mistakes to Avoid

1. *Remorse* over yesterday's failure.

2. *Anxiety* over today's problems.

3. *Worry* over tomorrow's uncertainty.

4. *Procrastination* with one's present duty.

5. *Resentment* of another's success.

7. *Criticism* of a neighbor's imperfections.

8. *Impatience* with youth's imperfection.

9. *Skepticism* of our nation's future.

10. *Unbelief* in God's providence.

8   Committed, Now Complacent

There is a tiny harbor town on the ocean shore where many ships have crashed on the rocks in violent weather. This town became well-known because of a dedicated rescue team which aided mariners in distress. The rescue team would rally to the sound of the siren and rush to the scene of the accident, risking life and limb to save the sailors from drowning. As time went on, the citizens of that tiny town raised enough money to build a rescue station close to the shore. While this greatly facilitated the operation, it softened the dedicated team as well. As time went by they added some of the comforts and conveniences that other rescue stations had. Through the years the rescue station became a social club where the town's people gathered to have fun and relax. Ships would still crash upon the rocks, the alarm would still sound, but eventually no one responded. They were reluctant to leave their comforts because their commitment to rescue the miserable mariners was no match for their complacency.

9   A Successful Shock Treatment

A young military officer was traveling by train from Newark to New York City. He constantly introduced profane language into his conversation as he conversed with another passenger beside him. His profanity greatly annoyed a young lady who sat not far away.

At last, unable to tolerate his language further, the offended passenger leaned over and inquired politely, "Sir, can you converse in a foreign language?" "Yes," was his reply in a slightly surprised manner, "Then," she continued, "if you wish to swear anymore, you would greatly oblige me—and, no doubt, the rest of the passengers—if you would swear in another tongue."

Astonished at her suggestion as well at her audacity, the young officer was speechless momentarily. However, he finally resumed his conversation; he did not swear again—neither in a "foreign language" nor in English.

10 Decision Without Procrastination

During the early days of the ministry of Dwight L. Moody, the great evangelist launched a series of meetings in Chicago with promise of the largest crowds that he had ever addressed up to that time. He was speaking of the life of Christ, and on the first Sunday night, October 8, 1871, he took as his topic the trial before Pilate. As he came to the end of his message, he turned to Matthew 27:22, "What shall I do then with Jesus, who is called Christ?" He concluded, "I wish you would take this text home with you and turn it over in your minds during the week, and next Sabbath we will come to Calvary and the cross, and we will decide what to do with Jesus of Nazareth."

It may have been an artistic device. But speaking of it in later years, Moody called that conclusion to his morning's address the greatest mistake of his life. Even while Mr. Sankey was singing the final hymn:

> Today the Savior calls;
> For refuge fly;
> The storm of justice falls,
> And death is nigh—

the fire engines began to sound on the street on their way to their first contact with the great Chicago fire in which Moody's hall was laid in ashes, and in which it is estimated that over a thousand persons lost their lives. Moody never saw that congregation again, and some of those to whom he spoke on that night doubtlessly died.

11 Is the Church a Zoo?

Some church members are as stubborn as a Missouri mule about doing church work, but as sly as a fox in their own business deals; as busy as a bee in spreading the latest gossip, but as quiet as a mouse in spreading the gospel of Christ. Many are as blind as a bat to see the needs of others, but have eyes of a hawk to see the faults of a few. Some are as eager as a beaver about a barbecue, but as lazy as a dog about the prayer meetings. Some will roar like a lion when things do not go just to suit them, but they are as gentle as a lamb when they need the preacher of the church. Some are as noisy as a blue jay when calling on the church for advice, but as timid as a kitten about talking to the lost and as slow as a snail about visiting absentees and shut-ins. Many are night owls on Saturday nights, but "bed bugs" Sunday mornings and as scarce as hen's teeth on Wednesday nights.

12 Whose Fault Is It?

A preacher and an atheist barber were once walking through the city slums. Said the atheist barber to the preacher: "This is why I cannot believe in a God of love. If God was as kind as you say, He would not permit all this poverty, disease, and squalor. He would not allow these poor bums to be addicted to dope and other character-destroying habits. No, I cannot believe in a God who permits these things."

The minister was silent until they met a man who was especially unkempt and filthy. His hair was hanging down his neck and he had a half-inch of stubble on his face. Said the minister, "You cannot be a very good barber or you would not permit a man like that to continue living in this neighborhood without a haircut or a shave."

Indignantly the barber answered: "Why blame me for that man's condition. I cannot help it that he is like that. He has never come in my shop; I could fix him up and make him look like a gentleman!"

Giving the barber a penetrating look, the minister said: "Then do not blame God for allowing these people to continue in their evil ways, when He is constantly inviting them to come and be saved. The reason these people are slaves to sin and evil habits is that they refuse the One who died to save and deliver them."

13 How Much of the Gospels Is Occupied by the Death of Christ?

Nearly one-third of the four Gospels is devoted to accounts of the death of Christ, the incidents leading up to it and following it. A writer has reminded us that the other two-thirds of the four Gospels are given up to a preparation for the account of Christ's death.

If the men who gave us the record of Jesus' life thought His death was an event of such importance as to justify giving it so large a portion of their attention, is it not possible that we have erred in understanding the comparative importance of the cross?

14 Simplicity of Living

During the Revolutionary War in America, a few British officers, the bearers of a flag of truce, were invited by the general of the Insurgents to stop and dine with him. As a result of this courtesy, they were ushered into a tent where an officer was roasting some potatoes on a camp stove. Expecting an elaborate table, the British officers were astonished when the officer preparing the meal wiped away the ashes from the potatoes, and placed them on the table as the dinner for the general and his company.

When the British officers returned to their own camp, they contrasted the American soldiers' fare with their own expensive fare. They justifiably reflected on the difficulty of their self-indulgent habits and their need of contentment under all circumstances.

15 The Blind Man and the Lantern

A blind man was discovered sitting at the corner of a city street with a lantern beside him. When he was asked why the lantern was there since light and darkness were the same to him, he replied, "I have it so that no one may stumble over me."

What a message for Christians who have the light!

16 Word Camouflage

The footnote in the New International Version at 2 Kings 18:4 is most interesting. When Hezekiah found the children of Israel worshiping the brazen serpent made by Moses in the wilderness, he destroyed it. Hezekiah called the serpent "Nehushtan." The footnote explains the meaning of the word as "a serpent made of brass."

We wonder how such an idol could have existed for so long. It would seem that it would have been destroyed in one of the reformation movements of one of the judges or kings. In my opinion, it lasted so long because it apparently was not recognized as an idol. Perhaps the children of Israel justified the worship by not calling it an idol. Hezekiah, however, came and called it what it really was—a brass image of a snake.

How often we justify sin by either ignoring it or calling it a different name! Some call adultery "a meaningful relationship." We excuse covetousness by calling it "prudence" or "economy." A life of sensual pleasure is "living with gusto."

In answer to a critic, Abraham Lincoln asked, "How many legs does a cow have?" "Four," was the reply. "If you call her tail a leg, how many does she have?" "Five," was the answer. "No," Lincoln said, "just calling a tail a leg does not make it a leg."

Have we made a similar mistake? Do we think that sin is not sin just because we do not call it by the right name?

17 It Only Takes a Minute

Charles Dickens once wrote: "Reflect upon your present blessings, of which every man has many; not on your past misfortunes, of which all men have some." It only takes a minute to begin reflecting on our present blessings: the gift of life itself, the warmth of friendships, the riches of good health, the power of love, the glory of a sunrise, the privilege of prayer, the joys of music, the satisfactions of work, the treasures of books, the beauty of art, the miracle of spring, and the grace of God. Be more grateful and you will become more joyful!

18 Lincoln Speaks

Abraham Lincoln spoke about the legacy the people of his time were leaving, and he clearly is speaking to us today as well.

"We have been the recipients of the choicest bounties of heaven; we have been preserved these many years in peace and prosperity; we have grown in number, wealth, and power as no other nation has ever grown.

"But we have forgotten God. We have forgotten the gracious Hand which preserved us in peace and multiplied and enriched and strengthened us, and we have vainly imagined, in the deceitfulness of our hearts, that all these things were produced by some superior wisdom and virtue of our own.

"Intoxicated with unbroken success, we have become too self-sufficient to feel the necessity of redeeming and preserving grace, too proud to pray to the God that made us."

19 Saints in Wrong Places

The sins committed by ancient Israel were recorded "for our admonition" (1 Cor. 10:6, 11) that we might not make the same mistakes. Many great men have failed God because they were found in the wrong places. In the form of a question, we introduce several of the "wrong places" where some great servants of God failed.

Are you on the slippery path of DISHONESTY, as was Abraham when he went down to Egypt (see Gen. 12:10-20)? Since his wife, Sarah, was such a beautiful woman, Abraham feared that the Egyptians might kill him in order to have her. To prevent this, Abraham deceived them by telling them she was his sister. It was only a "half-truth" for Sarah was Abraham's half-sister (Gen. 20:12). We have a modern name for what Abraham did: "situation ethics," the philosophy which says that one's ethics are determined by the situation in which he finds himself. According to this concept, there is no absolute standard of morality, no objective basis for conduct. Thus, one may lie, cheat, commit immorality, etc., if the situation "calls for it." However, God has always abhorred the practice of dishonesty (Deut. 25:13-16), no matter who was involved. Christians are to "provide things honest in the sight of all men" (Rom. 12:17).

Are you giving way to IMPURITY as did David when he walked upon the housetop (2 Sam. 11, 12)? David yielded to his lower and baser instincts when he saw the beautiful Bathsheba bathing. The immorality led to further sin—murder! It all began when David was at the wrong place at the wrong time. The Christian, whose mind should be on things above (Col. 3:2), would do well to avoid people, places and literature which tempt him to yield to unholy passions.

Are you sitting under the juniper tree of DISCOURAGEMENT as did Elijah (1 Kgs. 19:1-18)? Elijah's great victory at Mt. Carmel was followed by despondency when he learned that Jezebel was out to kill him. He sat down under a juniper tree and prayed that God would let him die. Despondency frequently comes after a mountain-top experience, doesn't it? When it happens we want to crawl under our "juniper tree" and let the rest of the world pass us by. Remember, God is still on His throne and rules the world (cf. Ps. 42:5).

Are you sailing on the ship of DISOBEDIENCE as did Jonah when he fled to Tarshish (Jon. 1:1-17)? Jonah's prejudice prompted him to disobey God when he was told to preach in Nineveh. Is it possible that you are "on the way to Tarshish" when you should be "on the way to Nineveh?" Did you obey the Lord in becoming a Christian, but you have now boarded the ship of disobedience and are fleeing away from your Redeemer?

Saints in the wrong places! Maybe we can learn something from them and avoid their mistakes.

20 The Door That Goes Nowhere

Have you ever been caught in a revolving door? It just keeps on going around and you cannot get out. Some people are like that, they have no direction as to where they are going. You may ask someone, "Where are you going?" The person will answer, "I don't know." Then how will you know when you get there? Besides its common use as the entrance to a house or building, this word is used metaphorically as the entrance to anything. Jesus said that He is the door, the entrance, into the kingdom (John 10:7-9). The door of faith is the opportunity of belief offered to the Gentiles in Acts 14:27. Elsewhere it means opportunity.

Paul refers to a great door opening to him in 2 Corinthians 2:13. Revelation 4:1 says, "I looked and a door was opened." Do we have the ability to see the open doors, and if so, do we go in and avail ourselves of the opportunities that await us? Jude talks about people who have no direction, driven about by winds first one way then another. This accomplishes nothing. Ephesians 4 speaks of being carried about by every wind, again depicting no direction.

Some brethren show no more direction after being a Christian for thirty or forty years than they did when they first obeyed. This is the door that goes nowhere. They have gone through the door but stopped, so in essence it has taken them nowhere. Paul relates to this when he says, "By reason of time you ought to be teachers, you have that need that someone teach you again what be the first principles" (Heb. 5:12).

21 Keep Your Eye on the Sparrow

"Are not two sparrows sold for a penny? And not one of them will fall to the ground without your Father's will (Matt. 10:29 RSV).

We worry too much. We follow the example of our earthly father Adam when he confessed to God, "I was afraid . . . and hid" (Gen. 3:10). We have become a fearful people, even though most of our fears are often unfounded or just plain silly, because we do not have our eyes on the sparrow.

One of the renderings for the term sparrow in Hebrew referred to small birds, and in Matthew the word probably refers to a small house sparrow. The birds were well known in Syria; they were small, tame and found everywhere. Because of their great number they were sold cheaply; five would go for one and one-half cents. The idea is that if God cares for something so inexpensive and small, then certainly He will care for and protect us!

Jesus always gives us the assurance, "I am with you always" (Matt. 28:20). Yet we continue to be afraid: Nuclear war, loss of health, serious accident, job loss, and a thousand other things.

The lesson of 1 John 4:18, "There is no fear in love; but perfect love casts out fear," should teach us something: that either we do not love God as we should, or we do not believe Him when He says that He loves us. Think about the following:

"Worry comes through human interference with the divine plan."

"You cannot change the past, but you ruin a perfectly good present by worrying about the future."

"Why worry when you can pray?"

"Worry is interest paid on trouble before it is due."

The story is told of the ship that was trapped in a severe storm at sea. All were preparing to abandon ship, all except one young lady who was playing with her dolls. When asked if she were not afraid, she calmly replied, "No, because my father is the captain."

When the storms of life seem to trap us, let us learn to keep our eyes upon the sparrow and to say, "I am not afraid because the Captain is my Father!"

22 Forward through Goals

A person without goals in his life is like a ship without maps and a compass. He will drift aimlessly from day to day hoping to arrive at the nebulus port of "somewhere." His voyage though life will be left to chance. Without goals life is uninteresting and without challenge. Goals are decisions to action. Goals are maps which give the routes to distant ports in life. Goals help a person know where he is going and how he is going to get there. A goal is more than a dream; it is a dream being acted upon. It is more than an "Oh, I wish I could." A goal is a clear statement of "This is what I am going to do." Goals are not fanciful doubts; they are declarations of faith.

14 REASONS FOR SETTING GOALS

Do you have a list of goals that you are working on at this moment? If you do, congratulations, because it places you in a small group of achievers. If you do not have goals for your life, let me share some basic reasons why you need to set goals.

1. Goals will give your life purpose. They help you to specifically know where you are going. They provide a clear target for your life.

2. Goals will help you develop a plan of action for reaching your goals.

3. Goals are exciting because they keep you active. Work is a sure way to success and happiness.

4. Goals are biblical. Paul said, "I press toward the mark for the prize of the high calling of God in Christ Jesus" (Phil. 3:14).

5. Goals produce results. They are not just exercises in futilities.

6. Goals help keep you young

and interested in life. There is hope and expectation in the future.

7. When you work on your goals you help to encourage others to do the same.

8. Good goals help you know where you are at each month. You have planned your journey in life. You have a map to check each action by.

9. When you set meaningful goals you are following the pattern of all great leaders who have gone before. They work.

10. Goals are essential if you are going to accomplish things in life. Whether on the job, in the home, or in the church, goals are vital to success.

11. Goals get us involved in the *present*. The steps to accomplishment must be taken today.

12. Goals provide a procedure for doing things decently and in order. It eliminates the "hit-and-miss" approach to life.

13. Goals provide a framework for evaluating our progress.

14. Nothing will happen until you set some goals for your life. This is the major advantage of failure: you do not have to do anything to achieve it.

23   Belief in Action

The world is full of nominal Christians—but how many are Christians in deed? The Bible makes it clear that mere belief is not enough.

A United States Senator recently quoted a very moving, yet indicting poem, "Listen Christian!" (by Bob Rowland), which reads as follows:

I was hungry,
and you formed a humanities club
and discussed my hunger.
Thank you.

I was imprisoned
and you crept off quietly
to your chapel in the cellar
and prayed for my release.

I was naked
and in your mind
you debated the morality of
my appearance.

I was sick
and you knelt
and thanked God
for your health.

I was homeless
and you preached to me
about the spiritual shelter
of the love of God.

I was lonely
and you left me alone
to pray for me.

Christian,
you seem so holy;
so close to God.
But I am still very hungry,
and lonely,
and cold . . .

This poignant poem is an obvious modification of the words of Jesus Himself as recorded in Matthew 25:35, 36: "For I was hungry and you gave me food, I was thirsty and you gave me drink, I was a stranger and you welcomed me. I was naked and you clothed me, I was sick and you visited me. I was in prison and you came to me."

Age

24 Now Is the Time

A pioneer preacher was called to conduct the funeral for a man who never entered the church building while he lived. As the pallbearers neared the meetinghouse door, the old preacher stood in the doorway and beckoned saying: "Gentlemen, I have never taken an undue advantage of any living person, and I am not going to begin imposing on the dead. If this man were living he would not enter this building. Put him down right there and let us respect him enough to finish his earthly pilgrimage as he lived it."

The service was conducted from the doorway, with the casket resting on the church-house lawn. Perhaps the preacher was a bit "hard," but he certainly had a point. Better think about dying and eternity while we live.

25 Attitude

Several years ago a man encountered the idea that we should live our lives in such a way that when we die even the undertaker will be sorry that we are gone!

The saying is that life begins at 40. It really begins when we want it to begin!

At age 71 an agent turned down Jack Benny thinking he was washed up. Jack found another agent and fulfilled twelve million dollars more in bookings before he died at the age of 81.

Moses was 80 when he received the Law.

Aaron was 83 when he began to perform miracles and plagues in Egypt.

Joshua was 85 when he led Israel into the promised land.

Will Durant sold a series of television programs at the ripe young age of 91.

Frank Lloyd Wright created the magnificent Guggenheim Museum at 89.

Colonel Sanders was in his 60s when he sold his first Kentucky Fried Chicken franchise.

A University of Wisconsin study says that if we are physically well, and keep active as we get older, we can enjoy people, laugh at ourselves, and get as much out of life at 90 as we could when we were 40!

26 What, Not When

Some time ago the United Technologies Corporation published in the *Wall Street Journal* a full-page message entitled, "It's What You Do, Not When You Do It." The message contained a listing of many eaglelike people who soared at various ages in their lives.

Ted Williams, at age 42, slammed a home run in his last official time at bat.

Mickey Mantle, age 20, hit 23 home runs his first full year in the major leagues.

Golda Meir was 71 when she became Prime Minister of Israel.

William Pitt II was 24 when he became Prime Minister of Great Britain.

George Bernard Shaw was 94 when one of his plays was first produced.

Mozart was just seven when his first composition was published.

Now, how about this? Benjamin Franklin was a newspaper columnist at 16 and a framer of the United States Constitution when he was 81.

You are never too young or too old if you have talent. Let us recognize that age has little to do with ability—and, age has NOTHING to do with dreams and determination and vision.

27 Reaction

It is now believed that a man reaches his peak mentally around the age of 35 and that this peak is maintained even past 70 years of age.

It has also been proven that the old saying, "You can't teach an old dog new tricks" is untrue. The learning power at 70 is about the same as it is at 17.

As one authority put it, we do not become old through the passing of years, but rather by our reactions to the circumstances of life.

28 Attitude and Opportunity

In the central place of every heart there is a recording chamber. So long as it receives a message of beauty, hope, cheer, and courage— so long are you young. When the wires are all down and your heart is covered with the snow of pessimism and the ice of cynicism, then, and only then, are you grown old.

29 All Times Are His

Our times are in His hand
Who saith, "A whole I planned.
Youth shows but half; Trust God,
See all, nor be afraid!"

For age is opportunity, no less
Than youth itself, though in another dress,
And as the evening twilight fades away
The sky is filled with stars, invisible by day.

30 Because of the Remnant

"He that sows to his flesh shall of the flesh reap corruption; but he that sows to the Spirit shall of the Spirit reap life everlasting" (Gal. 6:8).

One need not look far today to see that most of society does not want to be bothered with things that are spiritual; they have no time to look at, or reflect on anything spiritual; rather they seem to be primarily concerned with the economy and the temporal things of this life. So much that we used to hold dear—the historical ideals of conduct that were associated with the

Judeo-Christian heritage—seem of little importance. Even our TV screens portray homosexuality and loose morals as simply another lifestyle and nothing to be worried about.

Paul refers to this at length in the first chapter of Romans, and we can see that these are the very things that seem to be creeping into the fabric of society all around us. The only thing that has probably stopped God's judgment on the human race thus far is the fact that He still has a remnant; a people that seek to serve the Lord Jesus Christ, and be a light in the midst of increasing darkness. May we ever be on our guard as we journey onward, in order that the truth of the gospel will continue to influence the people around us, and ultimately people around the world.

31 Old but Still Useful

"He shall be like a tree planted by the rivers of water, that brings forth his fruit in his season; his leaf also shall not wither" (Ps. 1:3).

An article out of *Choice Gleanings* reads as follows:

"As one approaches the three-score-and-ten age, thoughts as to future usefulness to the Lord often occur. Walking through a nearby forest, I spotted a strange sight. An old, gnarled tree had been broken, but green shoots were still proceeding from it. It was also supporting a fallen tree. We can still be useful at three-score-and-ten and beyond."

32 Old Age

Old age is a privilege.
You cannot buy it.
You cannot sell it.
You cannot earn it.
You cannot inherit it.
You cannot merit it.
So if you are fortunate enough to have it, for heaven's sake enjoy it; and do not complain about it.

Remember, if you were not old—you would be dead.

33 Born Old

Elderly Christians tend to be thoughtful, kind, patient and loving. Through years of imitating Christ they have grown more and more into his image. Physical health may be failing, or the eyesight growing dim, the hearing failing, but there is no reason to lose heart. Why? "The inner nature is being renewed every day." And these saints are more lovely than they have ever been.

For those who resent the passing years, an interesting possibility has been suggested by Charles L. Allen. He writes, "Just suppose the process were reversed. You would start living at an old age and every day be a little younger. Now that would be terrible. Every day you would know a little less than you knew the day before. You would start off with your grandchildren but in a few years they would all be gone. Your family, instead of growing, would constantly be diminishing. You would eventually get to the age where you start to college.

You would start off a senior and end up in the first grade. Now, little first graders are cute with their short pants or little pink dresses, but I would hate to think I would have to be one again.

"Tottering old age has its drawbacks, but being a tiny baby is a lot worse. If you were getting younger, you would have to look forward to losing everything and end up by being a helpless baby with a bottle. Finally, you would just fade away into nothing. Babies do not have a previous existence, so complete oblivion would be the end."

When it is put like that, it is easy to see the advantage of growing older rather than shrinking younger. In the spiritual realm, who would want his faith to grow weaker day by day? Who would want to see his Christ-like qualities diminish with the passing of time? Who would want to give up the personal experiences where God has proven His faithfulness time and again in one's own life? Not me!

Experience is a great teacher. We are confident that:

> They who wait for the Lord
>   shall renew their strength,
> they shall mount up with wings
>   like eagles,
> they shall run and not be weary,
>   they shall walk and not faint.
> (Is. 40:31)

34 Remembering

Just a line to say I'm living,
    that I'm not among the dead,
Though I'm getting more forgetful
    and mixed up in the head.
I got used to my arthritis,
    to my dentures I'm resigned.
I can manage my bifocals,
    but God, I miss my mind.
For sometimes I can't remember
    when I stand at the foot of the stair,
If I must go up for something
    or have I just come down from there.
And before the fridge so often
    my poor mind is filled with doubt.
Have I just put the food away or
    have I come to take some out?
And there are times when it is dark
    with my night cap on my head,
I don't know if I'm retiring, or
    just getting out of bed.
So, if it's my turn to write you
    there's no need getting sore,
I may think that I have written
    and don't want to be a bore.
So, remember that I love you
    and wish that you were near,
But now it's nearly mail time
    so I must say goodbye, dear.
There I stand beside the mailbox
    with a face so very red,
Instead of mailing you my letter,
    I have opened it instead.

Attitude

35 *No Root, No Fruit*

Have you ever wondered why you do what you do?

One former Navy pilot tells how he was living a wilder life than he knew he should live. He decided his problem was that he was being led astray by his friends in flight training. So he arranged to finish his work in the program early and be transferred to another field nearby. Yet, it wasn't long, he said, before he was back in the same old bars, with the same girls, just with different friends. One night out-on-the-town he wondered, "Why do I do this?" And he realized, "Because I like to."

Before a person becomes a Christian—I mean a real Christian, not just someone who says he is—his "want-to" is broken. He is not interested in God. He is bored by church and by reading his Bible. He cannot "make" himself "want to" do right and he cannot "make" himself "want not" to do wrong. When a person is born again, God repairs his "want-to." Even though he still feels the pull of temptation, he will have a new set of desires. He will love God and want to talk to God in prayer and see what God has to say to him in His Word, the Bible. He wants to be around other people who love God; church attendance becomes meaningful. There is a new desire to obey God.

Why do we do what we do? The answer is simple: we do what we do because of what we are. It's like fruit trees. Apple trees bear apples, pear trees produce pears, peach trees grow peaches. The fruit is the natural result of the nature of the tree. I suppose you could tie apples to a peach tree, but that would not make it an apple tree. In the same way, adding religious activities to one's schedule doesn't make one a Christian. Just as the fruit of the tree naturally flows from the nature of the tree, even so the attitudes, words, and actions of our lives reveal the true nature of ourselves.

Jesus said, "Even so, every good tree bears good fruit, but a bad tree bears bad fruit. . . . Therefore, by their fruits you will know them" (Matt. 7:17, 20).

36 *A Choice Each Day*

Charles Swindoll said: "The longer I live, the more I realize the impact of attitude on life. Attitude, to me, is more important than facts. It is more important than the past, than education, than money, than circumstances, than failures, than successes, than what other people think or say or do. It is more important than appearance, giftedness or skill. It will make or break a company, a church, a home. The remarkable thing is we have a choice every day regarding the attitude we will embrace for that day. We cannot change our past, we cannot change the fact that people will act in a certain way. We cannot change the inevitable. The only thing we can do is play on the one string that we have, and that is our attitude. I am convinced that life is 10 percent what happens to me and 90 percent how I react to it. And so it is with you. We are in charge of our attitudes."

37   A Time to Laugh

In William Barclay's daily devotional *Daily Celebration*, appears this little story:

"There was a little Indian girl at school today," announced my son proudly.

"Does she speak English?" I asked.

"No," came the quick reply, "but it doesn't matter because she laughs in English!"

Laughter is the universal language. You can laugh in any language and it will be understood. Keep laughing!

If you can laugh at it, you can live with it. Laughter is to life what salt is to an egg. Laughter is the cheapest luxury man has. It stirs up the blood, expands the chest, electrifies the nerves, clears away the cobwebs from the brain, and gives the whole system a cleaning rehabilitation.

38   Sight

"Wouldn't you hate to wear glasses all the time?" asked a small boy of his playmate. "No-o-o," the other boy answered slowly, "not if I had the kind grandma wears. She sees how to fix a lot of things, and she sees lots of nice things to do on rainy days, and she sees when folks are tired and sorry, and what will make them feel better, and she always sees what you meant to do even if you haven't got things just right. I asked her one day how she could see that way all the time, and she said it was the way she learned to look at things as she grew older. So it must be her glasses."

39   A Changed Attitude

It was Napoleon Bonaparte who, early in his life, said, "God is on the side of the biggest artillery." Years later, when he was exiled on an island, he reversed his opinion, and conceded, "Man proposes, but God disposes." Napoleon learned the attitude of "If it is the Lord's will" the hard way. May we learn it now.

40   Future Hope

Not only does the Bible contribute to our belief in the best is yet to be, but the things of our daily lives reveal that this is true, too. It is this belief that keeps the scientist, inventor, and researcher busy.

* The best car hasn't been developed.
* The final cure hasn't been discovered.
* The safest plane hasn't been produced.

* The best song hasn't been written.

* The best product is not on the market.

* The best church hasn't been grown.

* The best sales presentation has not been perfected.

* The best class hasn't been taught.

* The best way hasn't been found.

* The best . . . is yet to be.

The phrase "The best is yet to be" is a positive affirmation that gives life direction. It provides hope: there is more to come in life. It's the spirit of expectancy: good things are going to happen. It is seen through the eyes that look for opportunities that will be greater than ever. It is received through proper planning and work. Desire is the fuel that makes it a reality. THE BEST IS YET TO BE!

41 Resignation

Not everyone is ready to accept the fact that the best is yet to be. This is true for a number of reasons.

1. Some are content to live in the past. They delight in the "good old days."

2. Many are content to live mediocre lives. They are content to drift from day to day.

3. Insecurity hinders many persons from believing that the best is yet to be. They want to hold on to their position or things. They will never know the excitement of

launching out by faith, or waiting for the great things of tomorrow.

4. Negative thinking guides the decisions and attitudes of many people. They choose to accept the premise that the worst is yet to come. They will get what they wish for if they are not careful.

5. Scores have no goals for their lives. They don't know where they are going today, much less tomorrow.

6. A few think they don't have any needs. They are pleased with the way things are in their lives (cf. Rev. 3:17). There is always room for improvement in everyone's life.

7. Fear is always a major enemy to progress. It also hinders a person from becoming excited about the future (cf. 2 Tim. 1:7).

42 Barriers

At a coastal aquarium, a savage barracuda quickly tried to attack the mackerel but was stopped by the partition. After bumping his nose repeatedly, he finally quit trying. Later, the partition was removed, but the barracuda would swim only to the point where the barrier had been and stop. He thought it was still there! Many people are like this. They move forward until they reach an imaginary barrier, but then stop because of a self-imposed attitude of limitation.

43 When Everything Material Is Lost

Dr. G. Campbell Morgan tells of a man whose shop had been burned in the great Chicago fire. He arrived at the ruins the next morning carrying a table. He set it up amid the charred debris and above it placed this optimistic sign, "Everything lost except wife, children, and hope. Business will be resumed as usual tomorrow morning."

44 Thankfulness

When Matthew Henry was robbed, that very night he prayed:

"I thank Thee, first, because I was never robbed before; second, because although they took my purse, they did not take my life; third, because although they took my all, it was not much; and fourth, because it was I who was robbed, and not I who robbed."

45 You Find What You Look for!

It is said that two kinds of birds fly over the California deserts: the hummingbird and the vulture.

All the vulture can see is rotting meat because that is all he looks for. He thrives on that diet. But the hummingbird ignores the carcasses and the smelly flesh of dead animals. Instead, he looks for the tiny blossoms of the cactus flowers. He buzzes around until he finds the colorful blooms almost hidden from view by the rocks. Each bird finds what it is looking for.

What are you looking for? Better still—what are you finding? What you are finding tells what you are really looking for. Your expectations of life will determine your outcome.

46 Sacrifice

A chaplain was speaking to a soldier on a cot in a hospital. "You have lost an arm in the great cause," said the chaplain.

"No," said the soldier with a smile. "I didn't lose it—I gave it."

In that same way, Jesus did not lose His life. He gave it purposefully. "He died that we might be forgiven and go at last to heaven."

47 Christian Contentment

As an elderly Christian lady with arthritis sat by her front window watching the traffic go by, she said, "I don't know what I'd do without that traffic to keep me interested."

Later on she was moved to a room in the rear where she could no longer see the traffic from the window. She conceded, "I like this better. I can watch the sweetest little children next door playing in the backyard."

At last she was moved to the slums of the city. To a friend she said, "Come and see my beautiful view—my beautiful view of the sky!"

48 Adjustment

During World War II General Creighton Abrams and his command were surrounded by the enemy to the east, west, north and south. General Abrams said, "Gentlemen, for the first time in the history of this campaign, we are now in a position to attack the enemy in any direction."

What has you surrounded, tied down, fenced in? All of us have limitations in life. Some we will have to bear with while others the Lord wants us to break through! It will only happen if we give ourselves an attitude adjustment.

49 Adventurous Boldness

Somebody said that it couldn't be done.

But he with a chuckle replied,
"Maybe it couldn't, but
he would be one
Who wouldn't say so till he'd tried."
So he buckled right in
with the trace of a grin
On his face. If he worried he hid it.
He started to sing as he tackled the thing
That couldn't be done, and he did it!

50 Trials and Tribulations

Take a piece of wax, a piece of meat, some sand, some clay, and some shavings, put them on the fire and see how they react. Each of them is being acted upon by the same agent, yet . . . the wax melts, the meat fries, the sand dries up, the clay hardens, the shavings blaze.

Just so, under identical influence of circumstances and environment one man is made better, and he becomes stronger, and another becomes weaker, while another withers away.

This explains why one hears the Word of God and is made better. Still another hears the same thing and is made angry. Not so much what is done to us, but what we do, determines our destiny. Take heed how you hear and act.

51 Sour Grapes

There is a fable concerning a fox who kept leaping up at some inviting looking grapes. Unable to reach them despite his best efforts, he came to the conclusion that they did look rather sour. He walked away without pangs of covetousness.

Be as smart as a fox if you want to be happy. Consider the things that you cannot obtain as "sour grapes."

52 Getting Along Without It

A nurse was showing a patient to his room. "Now," she said, "we want you to be happy and enjoy yourself while here, so if there is anything you want that we haven't got, let me know and *I'll show you how to get along without it.*"

53 Spiritual Sight

The hymnwriter Fanny Crosby gave us more than 6,000 gospel songs. Although blinded by an illness at the age of six weeks, she never became bitter. One time a preacher sympathetically remarked, "I think it is great pity that the Master did not give you sight when He showered so many other gifts upon you." She replied quickly, "Do you know that if at birth I had been able to make one petition, it would have been that I should be born blind?" "Why?" asked the surprised clergyman. "Because when I get to heaven, the first face that shall ever gladden my sight will be that of my Savior!"

One of Miss Crosby's hymns was so personal that for years she kept it to herself. Kenneth Osbeck, author of several books on hymnology, says its revelation to the public came about this way: "One day at a Bible conference in Northfield, Massachusetts, Miss Crosby was asked by D. L. Moody to give a personal testimony. At first she hesitated, then quietly rose and said, 'There is one hymn I have written which has never been published. I call it my soul's poem. Sometimes when I am troubled, I repeat it to myself, for it brings comfort to my heart.' She then recited while many wept, 'Someday the silver cord will break, and I no more as now shall sing; but oh, the joy when I shall wake within the palace of the King! And I shall see Him face to face, and tell the story—saved by grace!'" At the age of 95, Fanny Crosby passed into glory and saw the face of Jesus.

That's the sure hope of every child of God!

54 Like Pharoah, or Job?

What can make the difference in how we face our everyday trials, even our little ones, is our attitude. We can have the attitude of the Pharaoh of Egypt, who, when confronted by Moses and the ten plagues from God, grumbled, and griped, and became stubborn, causing more woes to come upon him. Or, that of Job, who at the loss of all his possessions, even his own health, succumbed to the will of God and remained faithful. That type of commitment to Christ will give us eternal life, happiness and joy.

Remember: "I can do all things through Christ who strengthens me" (Phil. 4:13). "And we know that all things work together for good to them that love God" (Rom. 8:28).

55 The Importance of Attitude

A Scotsman was an extremely hard worker and expected all the men under him to be the same. His men would tease him, "Scotty, don't you know that Rome wasn't built in a day?" "Yes," he would answer. "I know that. But I wasn't foreman on that job."

56 Peace

Among the students at a college was a young man on crutches. Although not a handsome fellow, he had a talent for friendliness and optimism, and he earned many scholastic honors as well as the respect of his classmates.

One day a new student asked him what had caused him to become so badly crippled. "Infantile paralysis," replied the genial young man.

"With a misfortune like that," exclaimed the other fellow, "how can you face the world so confidently and so happily?"

"Oh," replied the polio victim, "the disease never touched my heart."

57 My Future

Someone said, "My past is gone; my present is passing; my future is arriving."

The best thing about the future is that it comes upon us by degrees, a day at a time. We can manage that! Whatever it holds, my future is mine: if it be fair weather, let me bask in the sun; if it be storms, let me bend with the wind.

The future belongs to those who can make adjustments.

"Sanctify yourselves against tomorrow" (Num. 11:18).

58 Zeal

The Bible provides a sound basis for enthusiasm. Here is how the Apostle Paul states it: "And whatsoever ye do, do it heartily, as to the Lord, and NOT unto man" (Col. 3:23); "always abounding in the work of the Lord" (1 Cor. 15:58); "zealous unto good works" (Titus 2:14); "Your zeal hath encouraged many" (2 Cor. 9:2).

In Revelation the Apostle John commanded the Laodiceans to be "zealous, therefore, and repent" (Rev. 2:19).

It is interesting that "zeal" and "zealous" come from a Greek word which means "to boil; seethe." An enthusiastic person boils inside; it spills over to peak performance.

The wise man stated it in these words, "Whatsoever thy hands findeth to do, do it with all thy might" (Eccl. 9:10).

Some people verbalize their inability to be enthusiastic. I don't believe there is a person who hasn't been excited or enthusiastic about something. A raise in salary, an award, vacation, promotion, birth of a child, opportunity, or some other event in life creates zeal by its very nature. What we need in the church is enthusiasm for the mission God has given His people. This guarantees peak performance.

Bible

59 Tunnel Lights

"He hath done all things well" (Mark 7:37).

Some Bible verses are like lanterns. They were made for dark places and dark hours. Did you ever hear about the little girl in the train? She couldn't understand why the trainman was going through the car lighting the lamps. She said, "Mother, it is the middle of the day and the sun is shining, why is he turning on those lights?" The mother smiled, and said, "Wait a bit and you'll see what the lights are for." In a moment or two the train plunged into a long, dark tunnel, and then the little girl saw the wisdom of the lamplighting process.

Dear friend, that Bible of yours contains thousands of verses that seem very ordinary and unnecessary. You can't see why God has gone to all the trouble of lighting those lamps of truth, but some day you're going into the tunnel of bereavement, or the tunnel of temptation, or the tunnel of suffering, and then you will value and appreciate the verses that appear to be commonplace today.

60 Get What You Can!

Some folks do not read the Bible because, they say, there are so many things in the Book that they cannot understand. It is said that these things which cannot be understood trouble them. Of course these are excuses.

What does one do when he sits down to a Southern-fried chicken dinner, and finds there are bones in the chicken which he is unable to chew? Does he excuse himself, and say, "I can't chew the bony parts of the chicken, therefore I won't try to eat any of it?" Hardly. He merely puts the bones to one side and enjoys the edible part of the chicken. Why not put at least this much effort into Bible reading?

One rescued sinner said, "The fact that I am alive and on my way *somewhere* really caused me anxious moments, until I found the answer in the Bible. When I found it, it prompted me to let the shed blood of Christ cleanse me from my sins. God saved me and gave me the assurance of it, and I began to study the Bible, digesting the parts God's Holy Spirit led me to understand, and setting the rest aside, until He opened my eyes to the Truth therein. As God showed me the answers, my worship of Him increased naturally. Oh, indispensable is the Book of books!"

61 Forgiveness

Testimony of a former Soviet prisoner: One time I was put in prison in Siberia. I was taken to a cell in the middle of the night. There were about 20 prisoners already there. None of them were sleeping, even though it was after midnight. They were all upset about something.

When the door was locked behind me, immediately they surrounded me and their first question was, "How many men did you kill?"

I said, "Well, I didn't kill anyone. I am a Christian."

They said, "You are lying. In this cell there are only murderers. Everyone here has killed at least three men. Some of us have killed four or five. So prove you are a Christian. Let us see your Bible."

You can't have a Bible in a Soviet prison. It would be confiscated. But hidden away in my things I had a miniature Gospel of Mark that I used to read secretly. I showed it to the prisoners and immediately they said, "Let us read it." So I did.

The next morning I awoke late, and I found that none of the other prisoners had been sleeping. They were all sitting in a circle, and one was reading the Gospel of Mark aloud. They had gotten to the last chapter. They were having a kind of Bible study—trying to discuss what it all meant. Those men had never heard the gospel before, had never read a portion of God's Word. But when I awoke, their first questions showed me that they understood what the gospel meant.

Their first question was this, "Can God forgive us?" That meant that they understood the meaning of the gospel, what salvation is. I explained that yes, God can forgive you. Jesus Christ forgave the thief on the cross next to Him.

I spent a week in that cell, and we talked a lot about God, but then I was to be transported to another prison. They wanted me to give them my Gospel of Mark. I remember one of them said, "Your God will send you many more Bibles, many more New Testaments. We'll never have another portion of God's Word in this prison." That Gospel was very precious to me, but I gave it to those men. And it is still there with them.

62 Guidance

The Word of God *corrects* us. That is a particularly interesting word. When flying to Florida, it seemed to me like a pretty straight shot from Chicago to Fort Lauderdale. But in the cockpit of the airplane is a fine-tuned radar mechanism. All during the trip, the plane is flown on automatic pilot, which continually yet imperceptibly *corrects* the course of the plane to keep it on track. That's what God's Word does for us. It nudges us to keep us on course. It keeps affecting the way we think, the way we draw conclusions, and the way we make our daily life decisions.

63 Man's Testimony

How important is it to read the Bible? Here is the answer of some of

America's historically prominent men:

Andrew Jackson said, "That book, sir, [the Bible] is the rock on which our republic rests." *George Washington* put it this way: "It is impossible to righteously govern the world without God and the Bible. . . ." *Charles Dickens* stated, "The New Testament is the very best book that ever was or ever will be known in the world." *Horace Greeley* asserted, "It is impossible to mentally or socially enslave a Bible-reading people." Finally *President Woodrow Wilson* urged, "I ask every man and woman in this audience that from this day on we realize that part of the destiny of America lies in their daily perusal of this Book [the Bible]."

Reading the Bible and following its instructions will enable you to find Christ as your all-sufficient Savior. Further, regular reading will *minimize your anxieties*, decrease appetite for lying, cheating, stealing, immorality, and all manner of sin. *You will realize* real peace, joy, and love in your life.

64 God's Principles Are Nails; His Word Is the Hammer

Have you ever watched a little boy learning to use a hammer? The lad grasps the hammer near the head of the shaft and is merely able to go "tap, tap, tap," hardly working the nail into the wood. He has the right tool but no power.

Compare the craftsman carpenter as he holds his hammer down at the bottom of the shaft gaining all the leverage he can. His arm goes "bam, bam, bam," driving nails home using a few swift hard strokes without damaging the surface of the wood. He holds the tool to get the power.

65 Knowledge

The Bible must always be at the heart of our preaching, teaching, and way of living. If the Scriptures do not guide our lives, we have no guide better than ourselves. No human document can compare in the least with the Word of God.

Woodrow Wilson is reported to have said, "We have deprived ourselves of the best there is in the world if we deprive ourselves of a knowledge of the Bible." There is no comparison: the Bible is the best guide, and the believer's life is the best guided. Don't be deprived of the Bible's rich blessings. Read it daily. Study it often.

66 All Sufficient

When I am tired, the Bible is my bed;

Or in the dark, the Bible is my light;

When I am hungry, it is vital bread;

Or fearful, it is armor for the fight.

When I am sick, 'tis healing medicine;

Or lonely, thronging friends I find therein.

If I would work, the Bible is my tool;

Or play, it is a harp of happy sound.

If I am arrogant, it is my school.
If I am sinking, it is solid ground.
If I am cold, the Bible is my fire;
And it is wings, if boldly I aspire.

Should I be lost, the Bible is my guide;
Or naked, it is raiment rich and warm.
Am I imprisoned, it is ranges wide;
Or tempest-tossed, a shelter from the storm.
Would I adventure, 'tis a gallant sea;
Or would I rest, it is a flowery lea.

Does gloom oppress? The Bible is a sun,
Or ugliness? It is a garden fair.
Am I athirst? How cool its currents run!
Or stifled? What a vivifying air!
Since thus thou givest of thyself to me,
How should I give myself great Book to thee!

67 *Just Use Me*

Most of us resent being "used," but here is something which could change the world, and it is crying out to be used:

Just use me—I am the Bible.
I am God's wonderful library.
I am always—and above all—the Truth.
To the weary pilgrim, I am a good strong staff.
To the one who sits in gloom, I am a glorious light.
To those who stoop beneath heavy burden, I am sweet rest.
To him who has lost his way, I am a safe guide.
To those who have been hurt by sin, I am healing balm.
To the discouraged, I whisper glad messages of hope.
To those who are distressed by the storms of life, I am an anchor.
To those who suffer in lonely solitude, I am a cool, soft hand resting on a fevered brow
O, child of man, to best defend me, just use me!

If you have not yet discovered that wonderful book we call the Bible, it's time you did. In the words of Samuel to Saul, "Stop here yourself for a while, that I may make known to you the Word of God" (1 Sam. 9:27).

68 *A Tool*

The best carpenter in the county was asked, "Which is your best tool?" Instead of pointing to a costly power saw or drill, he picked up a simple square and said, "This is the best tool; it makes all the others work."

Let us not overlook our best tool; the simple gospel (Rom. 1:16). In this verse, Paul gives four reasons why the gospel is our most effective weapon:

First, it is *power*. The original word is similar to our word for dynamite.

Second, it is *of God*. Though Rome with her imperial power was great, the power of God was greater. However sincere the motive, any alteration or substitution of that power only weakens it.

Third, it is *unto salvation*. In addition to being a past event and a future hope, salvation is a present reality. It can turn hate into love, despair into hope, and defeat into triumph.

Fourth, it is *for everyone*. The saving power of the life, death, and resurrection of Jesus Christ is for all!

69 *Reach*

REACH!—meaning "to stretch." It implies an inconvenience. It involves movement. You can't lean back, relax, get comfortable—and then reach, without giving up some of the comfort (at least for a moment). Reaching involves a little extra effort to get to something you want. How much extra energy you are willing to spend depends on how badly you want what you're reaching for. The more it means to you, the farther you are willing to stretch (even if it hurts).

It's not convenient to "reach" up to God to find the hand He lovingly extends to us; or to reach out to other people who so desperately need to know someone cares. It's not even easy to reach within ourselves to find our true feelings and values. But there is no more important way for us to spend our energy than to reach for a life that is pure, clean, and faithful to God. It may seem like a lot of trouble—but it's worth it!

70 *Multitude*

A Christian traveler was once packing his suitcase when he remarked to a friend, "Well, I still wish to pack a guidebook, a lamp, a mirror, a telescope, a book of poems, a number of biographies, a bundle of letters, a hymn book, a sharp sword, a small library containing 66 volumes. . . ."

"But," his friend interrupted him, "you've only got about six inches left in one side of your suitcase. How are you ever going to manage to get it all in?" The Christian smiled and his eyes twinkled, "That will be very easy," he said. "You see, all I have to do is put my Bible in the suitcase, for it is all the things that I have mentioned."

71 *Healing*

Some years ago a woman went to consult a famous New York physician about her health. She was a woman of nervous temperament. She gave the doctor a list of her symptoms and answered his questions, only to be astonished at his brief prescription at the end: "Go home, and read your Bible an hour every day; then come back to me a month from today." And he bowed her out before she could protest. At first she was inclined to be angry; then she reflected that the prescription was not an expensive one. She went home determined to read conscientiously her neglected Bible. In a month she went back to the doctor's office a different person, and asked him how he knew that was just what she needed. For answer the physician turned to his desk. There, worn and marked, lay an open Bible. "Madam," he said, "If I were to omit my daily reading of this Book I would lose my greatest source of strength and skill."

72 Power

A physician went to hear D. L. Moody. Although he had not thought of such a result, he was converted. When asked the reason for his change of heart, he said, "I went to hear Mr. Moody with no other idea than to have something to laugh at. I knew he was no scholar, and I felt sure I could find many flaws in his argument. But I found I could not get at the man. He stood there hiding behind the Bible and just fired one Bible text after another at me till they went home to my heart straight as bullets from a rifle. I tell you, Moody's power is in the way he has his Bible at the tip of his tongue."

73 Doctrine and Interpretation

A New York enthusiast had a good collection of paintings, one of them being the *Leaning Tower of Pisa,* which hung over his writing desk.

For a long time he noticed that it persisted in hanging crooked despite the fact that he straightened it every morning. At last he asked the housekeeper if she was responsible for its lopsided position each morning that he came to his office.

"Why, yes," she said, "I have to hang it crooked to make the tower hang straight."

Does that sound strange? That is exactly how a lot of people read the Bible. Many people twist the Word of God in order to justify their own opinions or actions, or doctrine to make them all appear right. Let us not twist the Scriptures to suit our own fancy. Let us be sure to hang the picture right!

74 The Wonder of the Bible

1. The wonder of its *formation*—the way in which it grew—one of the mysteries of time.

2. The wonder of its *unification*—a library of 66 books, yet one Book.

3. The wonder of its *age*—the most ancient of all books.

4. The wonder of its *sales*—the best-seller of all time, far ahead of any other book.

5. The wonder of its *interest*—the only book in the world read by all classes of people.

6. The wonder of its *language*—written largely by uneducated men, yet the best book from a literary standpoint.

7. The wonder of its *preservation*—the most hated of all books, yet it continues to exist!

75 Out of Tune

Some years ago, musicians noted that errand boys in a certain part of London all whistled out of tune as they went about their work. It was talked about and someone suggested that it was because the bells of Westminster were slightly out of tune. Something had gone wrong with the chimes and they were discordant. The boys did not know there was anything wrong with the peals, and quite unconsciously they had copied their pitch.

So we tend to copy the people with whom we associate; we borrow thoughts from the books we read and the programs to which we listen, almost without knowing it.

God has given us His Word which is the absolute pitch of life and living. If we learn to sing by it, we shall easily detect the false in all of the music of the world.

76 *Palm Oil*

Fred W. Cropp, president of American Bible Society, received a letter asking a question: "What do you recommend for keeping the leather on the back of Bibles from getting stiff, cracking and peeling?

The reply was, "There is one oil that is especially good for treatment of leather on Bibles. In fact it will insure your Bible will stay in good condition. It is not sold, but may be found *in the palm of the human hand.*"

77 *Familiarize Yourself With Your Weapon—the Bible*

In spiritual warfare as in physical warfare, the effectiveness of any weapon is directly proportionate to the efficiency of the one operating it. For this reason, during a late, great war, the U.S. Army assigned a new recruit one rifle which he kept throughout his training. It was called his "piece," and it became a part of him. The recruit handled the piece continually, disassembling and reassembling it. He cleaned it. He conducted basic maintenance. He carried it 12 hours a day. When crossing rivers or streams his head might have gotten wet, but his piece had to stay dry.

Six months later in the heat of battle, the soldier knew every inch of it—every mechanism. He understood things that could malfunction and how to remedy them. He could break it down and reassemble it in just seconds, blindfolded. Man and weapon had become a synchronized and deadly, efficient fighting machine.

The spiritual warrior's proficiency with his basic weapons should be no less remarkable. But quite sadly, if believers had to rely on their own Bible familiarity in life and death situations, the majority would helplessly perish.

78 *Who Is on Trial?*

There is no city in the world, perhaps, where the treasures of art are more appreciated than Florence, Italy. It is told that an American visitor to the Pitti Palace, after viewing some of the paintings there, said to his guide: "Are these the great masterpieces that everyone tells me about? I don't see much in them to arouse such enthusiasm."

"It is not these paintings that are on trial sir," the guide answered, "but it is you who view them."

So it is with the Word of God.

Sometimes we run across scoffers, men who sneer at divine revelation, who say that they cannot feel much enthusiasm about the Bible. But the Bible is not on trial. Whether men believe it or not, it is the Word of God, "which liveth and abideth forever" (1 Pet. 1:23).

79 God's Laser

Scientists have discovered a variety of uses for the laser beam. We once thought it a design of science fiction. Now lasers are used for many industrial, medical, navigational and communicative purposes.

The difference between lasers and a light from an ordinary bulb is direction. A regular bulb diffuses light in all directions. A laser sends powerful parallel beams.

God's Word is like a laser. It can pierce into the very heart and soul of everyone on earth. It can separate the soul from the spirit. It can discern the highest and lowest thoughts. It can speak to our attitudes and intentions.

Are you allowing God's laser, His Word, to work in you?

80 A Touch of His Presence

It is said that the Eastern shepherd, as he brings his sheep back to the fold each night, stands at the door and counts each one. As he does so, he puts his hand on the head of each animal. He makes a habit of touching each one of them. If he were to grow careless and neglect to habitually touch his sheep, it would soon turn its head away when it heard his voice! This, of course, could be very serious, for with such a broken habit would follow the animal's actually ignoring the warning shout from the shepherd and subsequently could be disastrous for the sheep.

If we are experiencing the Shepherd's touch daily in our lives, then we will recognize His voice when He warns of impending danger. This will mean "practicing His presence" daily. It we do not practice *His* presence then we have probably been practicing the presence of our enemy. Our Lord awaits the moment to "touch" our day with His presence.

81 Come On

A little boy who for the first time saw the sign "Common," in Boston at the entrance of the great park known as Boston Common, called out joyfully, "It doesn't say, 'Keep Off the Grass'; it says, 'Comm on'!"

The New Testament was written in the common language of the people so that everybody could understand that the great sign reads, "Come on!"

82 Did the Jews Make a Mistake?

A Hyde Park orator was denouncing the feeble efforts of the Jews to resist the Roman oppression in the first century of the Christian era, and suggested that if they had appealed more to the sword and less to the sacred writings, they might have fared much better.

One in the crowd asked, "But where are the Romans today?"

"Nowhere," was the quick answer.

"And where are the Jews today?"

"Everywhere," was the sarcastic but true reply—to the evident appreciation of the hearers.

83 Reading for Eye Specialist

Have you heard about the little fellow in their group who was working diligently on his ABC Memory Book? He always looked like a little professor. His mother took him to the eye specialist, who had the young chap sit on the chair for examination. He placed the card with the letters on the wall in front of him and said, "Will you read it for me, please?"

Sure enough, the boy did not hesitate for a moment and said distinctly, "A—All we like sheep have gone astray, we have turned everyone to his own way."

84 How Men Hate and Fear the Bible

Only one book is banned from the government schools of America, though once it was in every classroom on the teachers' desks and read daily to the students.

Only one book is hated and feared by Communists, humanists and other atheistic groups. They claim that it is only a book of myths and legends, but they cannot tolerate it.

A religious liberal years ago was attacking the Bible in his weekly column in a local newspaper. He said that the Bible was full of errors, contradictions, superstitions, folklore and mythology. We requested permission from the newspaper to answer him week by week, line by line.

In our answer, we asked him why, if the Bible was only a man-made book of legends, he could not let it alone. Why the weird bent to discredit it?

When 10,000 Bibles were sent from America to the people of Romania, Communist Director Nicolas Ceausescu accepted them in order to get favored-nation status from the United States Congress. He then shipped them to a paper mill to be recycled into toilet paper. They were so poorly recycled that Bible words such as Esau, Jeremiah and God remained visible (*Reader's Digest*, July, 1990, p. 84).

The wicked Communist leader eventually met a horrible death as his regime was toppled by the people he had persecuted. The anvil of God's Word had broken another little human hammer that beat upon it.

The enemies of God's Word will be judged by the Word which they reject, despise and hate. The redeemed will be saved by the Word which they accept and love.

85 You Gotta Look at It!

A man was seated on a park bench when a little chap of about five sat down beside him and started winding what appeared to be a most prized possession—a watch. "My, what a pretty watch," remarked the man. "Does it tell you the time?"

"No sir," replied the boy; "you gotta **look** at it."

God's Truth is everywhere, but you must look for it and at it to see it.

86 As People Grow Wiser, They Talk Less and Say More

Recently, 50 of America's leading citizens selected the Bible as the number one piece of literature.

America is great today because our forebearers believed in this Book, and established the foundation of our country upon its precepts. Most American presidents have been ardent students of the Bible.

The survival of our nation today, in this hour of world crisis, will be due to the faith of our citizenry in the Bible, and in the God of the Bible.

87 What They Said about the Bible

"Make it the first morning business of your life to understand some part of the Bible clearly, and make it your daily business to obey it in all that you do understand"—John Ruskin.

"I cannot too greatly emphasize the importance and value of Bible study—more important than ever before in these days of uncertainties, when men and women are apt to decide questions from the standpoint of expediency rather than on the eternal principles laid down by God Himself"—John Wanamaker.

"It is impossible to mentally or socially enslave a Bible reading people. The principles of the Bible are the groundwork of human freedom"—Horace Greeley.

"If I am asked what is the remedy for deeper sorrows of the human heart, I must point to something which in the well-known hymn is called "The old, old, story," told of an old, old Book and taught with the old, old teaching which is the greatest and best guide ever given to mankind"—William Ewart Gladstone.

88 Thoughts on America

William Arthur Ward wrote these moving words:

"I believe in America.

"I believe it became great because of its faith in God, its hope for independence, and its love for freedom.

"I am grateful for America's glorious past; I am awed by its unbelievable present; I am confident of its limitless future.

"I am not ashamed to take my hat off and to stand at attention when Old Glory passes by. I do not apologize for the lump in my throat when I repeat the Pledge of Allegiance. I am not embarrassed by the tears in my eyes when I hear 'The Star Spangled Banner.'

"Like millions of Americans, I want a free choice, not a free handout. I prefer an opportunity to prove my abilities on the job rather than a license to demonstrate my frustrations in the street.

"I am an old-fashioned American with a new-found determination to do my part to make democracy work."

89 Missing the Point

Orville and Wilbur Wright were excited. On December 17, 1903, they had finally succeeded in keeping their homemade airplane in the air for 59 seconds. Immediately they rushed a telegram to their sister in Dayton, Ohio, telling of this great accomplishment.

The telegram read, "First sustained flight today fifty-nine seconds. Hope to be home by Christmas." Upon receiving the news the sister was so excited about the success that she rushed to the newspaper office and gave the telegram to the editor. The next morning the newspaper headline read, "Popular Local Bicycle Merchants To Be Home For Holidays."

One of the greatest stories of the twentieth century was missed because an editor missed the point.

But who has not made the same mistake in reading the Scriptures? If one is too casual about it, he might learn some truth but miss that which is most important. For years Charles Hodge has been saying, "Familiar Scripture should be read more closely." That advice is well worth heeding, but all Scripture should be read more closely to let the deep meaning sink into your heart.

The Book of Revelation is probably the least understood book of the Bible. We have not been able to see the forest for the trees. We become so entangled with living creatures, seals, horsemen, dragons, numbers, marks and trumpets that we miss the point.

Revelation is a book of imagination. It is built with symbols and vivid imagery. But behind it all is a great truth. God is ruling on His throne. He's in control. And Christians do not have to worry in the midst of persecution and death. We have been given a vision of victory!

Read the Bible. Read it carefully. And don't miss the point.

90 The Anvil

Last eve, someone passed beside a blacksmith's door, and heard the anvil ring the vesper chime.

Then looking in, he saw upon the floor old hammers, worn with beating years of time.

"How many anvils have you had," he asked, "to wear and batter all these hammers so?"

"Just one," said the blacksmith, and then added with twinkling eye, "The anvil wears the hammers out, you know."

Just so, the anvil of God's Word, for ages skeptic blows have beat upon.

Yet though the noise of falling blows was heard, the anvil is unharmed—the hammer's gone!

Christt

91 Incomparable Carpenter

Socrates taught for 40 years, Plato for 50, Aristotle for 40 and Jesus for only 3 1/2 years. Yet the influence of Christ's ministry infinitely transcends the impact left by the combined years of teaching from these greatest of philosophers.

Jesus painted no pictures, yet some of the finest artists such as Raphael, Michelangelo, and Leonardo da Vinci received their inspiration from Him.

Jesus wrote no poetry, but Dante, Milton and scores of the world's greatest poets were inspired by Him.

Jesus composed no music; still Haydn, Handel, Beethoven, Bach and Mendelssohn reached their highest perfection of melody in the music they composed in His praise.

Every sphere of human greatness has been enriched by this humble Carpenter of Nazareth.

92 Would You?

Once there was a well-trained carpenter who never asked for union wages; who never owned a home that he could call his very own; a brilliant young teacher who never asked for an increase in salary; a great physician who healed the sick and afflicted and never asked whether they had Medicare or insurance; a good neighbor who always tried to show His love and was never unfriendly.

He traveled all over the country trying to help somebody everywhere He went; and often fed large numbers of people when He found them hungry whether they had money or not. He was so wrapped up in trying to help people that He often wept over their pitiful condition. Yet, they crucified Him, and some of the very people He tried to help joined the senseless mob who mocked Him and spit in His face!

93 He Gave Up His Place

When the government phased out its surplus commodity food program, one man went early to the last distribution to secure a place in line before the foodstuffs ran out.

A few hours later, he was near the door where the cheese, butter, dry milk and peanut butter were handed out. He saw a friend walking by and called him by name.

He knew the man. Neither his wife nor he had any work for some time. They had four children. The man confirmed that his prospects were poor.

The man in line knew the food would run out soon, but he told the unemployed family man to take his place in the line. The poor man did so and the other went back to the end of the line.

Within a short time the distribution ended and the one who gave up his place had also given up his food.

This is like Jesus Christ, who drew us into His place, while He stepped in ours, taking upon Himself all the consequences of our failures.

94 Wounded for Me

During World War I the Prince of Wales visited 36 severely wounded men in a hospital in the outskirts of London.

The Prince and his escorts went through the main ward and shook hands with most of them. As preparations were made to leave, the Prince indicated that he had only seen 30 men. "Where are the other six?" Although he was informed that the six others were extremely severe cases and in a different section of the ward, the special visitor demanded to see the others.

Five other maimed and bruised men were viewed. "But where's the last one?" again the Prince inquired. Although the Prince was told that the grotesqueness of the man's appearance would be unbearable, the Prince insisted on seeing him.

The Prince stood silent for a moment, and then moved toward the man and stooping down, kissed him! With a breaking voice the Prince of Wales was heard to say, "Wounded for me."

"But He was wounded for our transgressions. He was bruised for our iniquities: the chastisement of our peace was upon Him; and with His stripes we are healed" (Is. 53:5).

95 Anxieties Like Iron Filings

Joel C. Gregory recalls that when he was in junior high, "we did an experiment with iron filings on a piece of paper. When we poured the filings on the paper they fell into a disheveled pile. Then we put a magnet under the paper and, as if by magic, the iron filings lined up . . . and followed the magnet's shape and force of direction."

All our anxieties are like so many iron filings poured out on the surface of our lives. Jesus says, "Put My presence and My kingdom underneath your life, see Me as a habit, and you'll find that your worries will line up and take My shape." The greater gift is given, and the lesser ones will be taken care of."

That's His promise, and our choice.

96 Backsliders Do Not Bid Jesus Goodbye

Mr. Moody once said, "A rule I have had for years is to treat the Lord Jesus Christ as a personal friend. When I go away from home I bid my wife and children goodbye; I bid my friends and acquaintances goodbye, but I never heard of a poor backslider going down on his knees and saying, 'I have been near you for ten years; your service has become tedious and monotonous; I have come to bid you farewell. Goodbye, Lord Jesus Christ.' I never heard of one doing this. I will tell you how they go: they just run away!"

Deity

97 *The Seamless Robe*

There is one item in the account of the crucifixion and resurrection of the Lord Jesus Christ that is seldom, if ever, referred to in any depth, namely, His seamless robe. In John's Gospel it says, ". . . the coat was without seam, woven from the top throughout" (John 19:23).

In the Bible, garments speak of conduct or of a display of character. A good example is "be clothed with humility" (1 Pet. 5:5). What precious truths about Jesus can we learn as seen in His seamless robe?

Our Lord was flawless and absolutely beyond reproach in His character. He is "holy, harmless, undefiled, separate from sinners, and made higher than the heavens" (Heb. 7:26). There is no seam dividing His meekness from His anger, His gentleness from His firmness, His authority from His winsomeness, or His mercy from His sincerity. He is uniquely beautiful in His character. The robe is all one piece!

We see Him compassionate, but inflexible; full of truth, yet full of grace; come to save, yet come for judgment; eating in the upper room, yet sitting at the table with publicans and sinners.

All is done with uniform consistency. Nothing is ever out of perspective. Power is without pride, knowledge is without superiority, and authority is without arrogance. Yes, His robe is woven on the loom of eternity.

John last saw that seamless robe in the hands of gamblers near the cross. How he must have been stirred when he was in the Spirit on the Lord's Day and saw Jesus "clothed with a garment down to the foot" with the name upon it "KING OF KINGS, AND LORD OF LORDS" (Rev. 1:13, 19:16).

As we, His redeemed, are "clothed . . . with the garments of salvation" and covered "with the robe of righteousness" (Is. 61:10), let us fall at His feet during this time of resurrection remembrance to worship, praise, and cry out to God for an experience of "the power of His resurrection" in order that we might be genuine reflectors of the wondrous character of our Lord Jesus Christ.

98 *The Birth of Christ*

An artist once drew a picture of a wintry twilight, the trees heavily laden with snow, and a dreary dark house, lonely and desolate, in the midst of the storm. It was a sad picture indeed. Then, with a quick stroke of yellow crayon, he put a light in one window. The effect was magical. The entire scene was transformed into a vision of comfort and good cheer. The birth of Christ was just such a light in a dark world.

Remember the words of John William Hart: "In Him was life; and the life was the light of men." That Light is more than enough to lend comfort and direction to your life!

99 Christianity and Its Three Great Pillars

The Reverend Charles H. Spurgeon once said, "Christianity rests on three great pillars, the Incarnation, the Crucifixion, and the Resurrection of the Lord Jesus Christ. Incarnation alone could not redeem sinful men. But apart from the Incarnation there could be no propitiatory sacrifice that would avail to put away sin. God became man in order to die. We cannot, therefore, make too much of the mystery of the union of the human and the divine in Him who was both Son of God and Son of Mary. In Him we have the Daysman for whom the patriarch Job longed, one who can lay His hand upon both God and man (Job 9:33) because He combines the natures of both in one glorious Person. Bethlehem, Calvary, and the empty tomb, all alike should stir our souls and draw our hearts out to God in wonder, love, and praise.

100 Our Matchless Christ

To many, Jesus Christ is only a grand subject for a painting, a heroic theme for a pen, a beautiful form for a statue, and a thought for a song; but to those who have heard His voice, who have felt His pardon, who have received His benediction, He is music, warmth, light, joy, hope and salvation, a Friend who never forsakes, who lifts us when others try to push us down. We cannot wear Him out; we pile on Him all our griefs and troubles. He is always ready to lift us; He addresses us with the same love; He beams upon us with the same smile; He pities us with the same compassion.

There is no name like His. It is more inspiring than Caesar's, more musical than Beethoven's, more patient than Lincoln's. The name of Jesus throbs with all life, weeps with all pathos, groans with all pains, stoops with all love. Its breath is laden with perfume.

Who like Jesus can pity a homeless orphan? Who like Jesus can welcome a prodigal back home? Who like Jesus can make a drunkard sober? Who like Jesus can illuminate a cemetery plowed with graves? Who like Jesus can make a queen unto God out of a lost woman of the street? Who like Jesus can catch the tears of human sorrow in His bowl?

There is no metaphor with which to truly express Jesus. He is not like the bursting forth of an orchestra; that is too loud and it may be out of tune. He is not like the sea when lashed into a rage by a storm; that is too boisterous. He is not like a mountain wreathed in lightning, canopied with snow; that is too solitary and remote.

He is the Lily of the Valley, the Rose of Sharon, a gale of spices from heaven.

Foundation

101 The Touchstone

A painter of landscape scenes always kept in front of him on his easel a number of precious stones—emerald, sapphire, ruby. Asked why, he replied, "To help me keep my colors true. In course of time, without some constant reference, my eye might lose its perception of color tones, and the colors I choose may not be right, may not be what they once were."

So it is with us, in the requirements of our ongoing life. Lest we wander astray, we need occasional exposure to some unchanging and unfading standard. Unless we are in touch with some constant reference, we can deviate and scarcely know it. We need some touchstone to test ourselves by, one that is worthy of what life is, one by which our lifetones can be safely set—the only perfect unchanging Lord.

102 Christ, the Cornerstone

In Mark 12, Christ calls Himself the measuring stone, or, as it is translated in our Bibles, the cornerstone. The cornerstone, in the minds of most Americans, is the stone that tells that a building was erected at a certain time, when a certain person was mayor, and so on. It is merely an exaltation of man.

But when the Bible refers to a cornerstone, it refers to the first stone laid for the foundation. The builders would get a stone from the quarry and chisel it carefully to

get as near a right angle as possible. They would measure the placement of all the other stones against that cornerstone, that first measuring stone. It was the standard by which all the walls of the building were determined.

When Jesus Christ is called the cornerstone, God is saying, "I measure everything by Jesus Christ."

103 How Hard One Strikes Depends on One's Foundation

A short man wanted to drive a nail in a wall to carry a big picture. He stood on a chair, but it was not high enough. His wife set out a small box and, balancing himself precariously, he began to give the nail hesitating taps with the hammer. His wife said, "Why don't you give a brave blow or two, and settle it?"

He replied, "How can a man give a brave blow or two when he is standing on a foundation like this?"

That settles the question of certainty or uncertainty. It depends upon the foundation upon which the person is standing. The Hebrew prophets never sounded a note of uncertainty, for God Almighty was their Foundation, and they knew that He stood behind their "Thus saith the Lord."

Mediator

104 Christ Is Our Mercy Seat

In the Tabernacle Holy of Holies, the light of God's glory was present between the cherubim, telling Israel that God was in her midst. The mercy seat was the place appointed where God met once a year the blood of the sacrifice of atonement. The blood of atonement was sprinkled there. It was not an appeasement. God does not have to be appeased. He is merciful, compassionate, and full of lovingkindness, but He will not hold man guiltless without an atonement. When the blood was sprinkled, there was satisfaction. Sin was covered. The offering for sin was made.

The One whose soul was made an offering for sin is Messiah Jesus. He is the Mercy Seat where the justice of God and the satisfying sacrifice meet, bringing peace to all who believe.

Power

105 Jesus' Authority

In a football game, the power of big, strong, muscular men is ruled by a man with a striped shirt and a whistle. The referee alone has ultimate authority in the game. He alone has the power to stop the game and even throw rebellious players off the field. That's the type of authority Jesus claims for Himself. In spite of Satan's attempts to control the universe and the affairs of men, Jesus wears the striped shirt and carries the whistle. He controls the field of play. If we are going to accomplish His mission, we must operate under His authority.

106 In the Hands of a Champion

One man used to play tennis quite a lot. He wasn't very good, but he was always open to anything that could help him. One day he was watching a match on TV, and saw a commercial advertising the Wilson T-2000 metal racquet. It showed Jimmy Connors making a lot of fancy shots while a hidden narrator said, "If the Wilson T-2000 could win Wimbledon and Forest Hills, it could certainly handle my little matches."

So he played with one all that summer. And he lost all summer. That racquet didn't do anything for him. The truth is, the Wilson T-2000 didn't win Wimbledon or Forest Hills. Jimmy Connors did—using the Wilson T-2000. When the fans walked away from the match that day, they didn't talk about what a great racquet the Wilson T-2000 was; they talked about what a great player Jimmy Connors was. And the prize check was made out to Jimmy Connors and not to you-know-what.

Now in tennis, a racquet is essential—but it isn't the racquet that wins. It's the champion who wins, using the racquet. In the doing of works and greater works, Jesus is the champion and we are the racquet in His hands.

Provider

107 Jesus Left:

His purse to Judas;
His clothes to the soldiers;

His body to Joseph of Arimathea;
His mother to John;
His peace to His disciples;
His supper to His followers;
His gospel to the world;
His presence with God's children.

108 "Korban"—Offering

The one Hebrew word, *Korban*, which is most often translated as "offering," generally speaks of the remarkable fact that access to God is gained by means of the offering. The word appears almost 70 times in this respect. The New Testament counterpart, the Greek word *prosphero*, appears in the book of Hebrews 19 times, referring to the sacrificial sense. Hebrews 9:14 tells us that Jesus Christ offered Himself as a sacrifice without blemish, and verse 28 says, "So Christ was once offered to bear the sins of many." He is the way to God.

109 "No, But I Do Know Where It's Safe"

It was a dark and stormy night when a lady was on a boat crossing Lake Michigan. The lightning, thunder, and rain made her very nervous. She saw jagged rocks jutting above the surface of the lake. In fear, she asked the captain, "Do you know where all the rocks are out there in the lake?" "No," the captain replied, "I don't, but I do know where it's safe."

As you "sail" through life, you are going to see lots of "rocks" out there. Some you will know how to avoid, others will come upon you as a surprise. The important thing to know is "where it's safe." Jesus knows the safe way; follow Him.

110 Never Again

Never again will I say, "I can't," for "I can do everything through Him who gives me strength" (Phil. 4:13).

Never again will I admit lack, for "My God will meet all your needs according to His glorious riches in Christ Jesus" (Phil. 4:19).

Never again will I fear, for "God did not give us a spirit of fear, but of power, of love and of self-discipline" (2 Tim. 1:7).

Never again will I harbor doubt and lack of faith, for "The Lord is my light and my salvation—whom shall I fear" (Ps. 27:1).

Never again will I allow the supremacy of Satan over my life, for "the One who is in you is greater than the one who is in the world" (1 John 4:4).

Never again will I admit defeat, for "God always leads us in triumphal procession in Christ and through us spreads everywhere the fragrance of the knowledge of Him" (2 Cor. 2:14).

Never again will I lack wisdom, for "If any of you lacks wisdom, he should ask God, who gives generously to all without finding fault, and it will be given to him" (James 1:5).

Never again will I be worried and frustrated, "Casting all your anxiety on Him because He cares for you" (1 Pet. 5:7).

Never again will I be in bondage, for "Now the Lord is the Spirit, and where the Spirit of the Lord is, there is freedom" (2 Cor. 3:17).

111 Why Did God Come Into the World as a Baby?

A missionary in India spoke near a fountain on the subject, "Jesus, the Water of Life." A Muslim interrupted, "Your religion is like this little stream of water, but Islam is like a great ocean!" "Yes," said the missionary, "but there is this difference: When men drink ocean water they die of thirst. When they drink the water of life which Christ gives, they live forever!" The stream is small, but it can satisfy your thirst. Jesus Christ came into the world as a little baby that He might show that no one is so little or so insignificant that the great God will not come to dwell within him.

112 He Has Raised Up a Horn of Salvation

Salvation is the fruition of redemption. Redemption purchases salvation, salvation realizes redemption and brings it into our actual experience. Zechariah speaks not so much of salvation as of the "horn of salvation." This bold figure, perhaps, originated in primitive times when mighty hunters, like Nimrod, returning from the chase, loved to grace their tents with the splendid horns of the animals that they had slain: the antlers of the deer, the tusks of the elephant, and the horn, perhaps, of the mighty rhinoceros. And so the word "horn" came to be the figure of beauty, power, and dominion. It has passed into the imagery of inspired prophecy and song, so that we find the earthly powers described by Daniel and John as horns upon the head of the beast.

And so we find the psalmist speaking of God as his Horn of Salvation and his High Tower. In speaking, therefore, of Christ as a Horn of Salvation, Zechariah meant to emphasize the glory and beauty of the Savior, His supreme and universal dominion and His infinite and divine power. It is coronation, singing, "Bring forth the royal diadem, and crown Him Lord of all."

Savior

113 Christ Abides With Us

When the first missionaries went to St. Thomas, they could not get near the suffering and degraded slaves until they took part in their bondage and asked the masters to make them slaves also. Then they were received with perfect confidence and were able to bring multitudes of the poor suffering ones to Christ. They trusted them when they saw that they had become identified with their very own lives and lot. "Praise be to the Lord the God of Israel, because He has come and has redeemed His people" (Luke 1:68).

But He comes closer. These missionaries could work by the side of the slave, but they could not come into their hearts.

114 Important Because Imported

The physician was going to operate on a very rich man who always wanted the best of everything. "I don't think there will be any problem," said the doctor, "This operation is routine. We can even use a local anesthetic."

"No," shouted the millionaire. "Don't use a local. Get something imported."

That's what Jesus is— "something imported"; or Someone imported. A hymn puts it like this: "There was no other good enough to pay the price of sin; He only could unlock the gate to heaven and let us in."

His birth was miraculous, the only one of its kind in history. It was prophesied in Isaiah 7:14, 700 years before it happened. But even more startling than that is John's declaration, "The Father sent the Son to be the Savior of the world." That meant one thing—that Jesus was born to die.

The virgin birth of Jesus gave to us a divine Redeemer whose life became a ransom for sin. A Jesus born in sin or subsequently guilty of sin couldn't have atoned for sin. The Lord Jesus Christ will never be understood by those who don't see Him as the Savior. And Christmas is an empty thing unless the Christ of Christmas is your Savior. Why not receive Him as your Savior now?

115 It Makes All the Difference

On a crowded street of one of our large cities, a young man was snatched from the path of a speeding truck, his life saved by a venerable-looking man. Still breathless from fright, the youth thanked the one who saved his life and then was lost in the crowd.

Two weeks later in a crowded courtroom, an anxious young man stood in the prisoner's box to be sentenced for murder.

"Young man, have you anything to say before the sentence of death is passed upon you?" "Why! Yes! Yes, Judge," the youth responded, "you know *me*." A silence moved like a shock wave over the courtroom. "I'm sorry. I cannot place you."

"Yes. Surely you remember. Two weeks ago. At Main and Seventh Streets, you saved my life. Surely, Judge, you can do something to save me now." A silence pervaded the courtroom. "Young man, now I *do* remember you. *But that day I was your savior. Today I am your judge.*"

Today the Lord Jesus Christ wants to be your Savior. If you refuse Him and His grace, one day He will be your Judge.

116 Beware! Satan Is Aboard! It Is a Hijack!

The human race is aboard a hijacked jet flying through time. God Himself directed its takeoff from the divine control tower. The initiator of all evil, whom we call Satan, managed to get a boarding pass. When cruising height was reached, he produced his weapons, threatened the pilot, and took control of the jumbo jet and all of its passengers. So it hopped on uncomfortably through history from airport to airport till it was caught on the tarmac at Jerusalem, an outpost of the Roman empire, in the reign of Tiberius Caesar, where the Son of God offered Himself as sole hostage in exchange for passengers and crew. The further you push the parallel the more fanciful it seems. But the basic idea of the human race aboard a hijacked jumbo flying through time is sound enough. The passengers must keep a wary eye on the hijacker, induce the pilot to take his directions from God's control tower, and be ready to accept rescue through the sacrifice of the willing Hostage. That is their only escape route.

117 Christ, a Threat to Man's Religion

When Bishop Hurst was in Poona, India, he went out to the great temple of Parvati, and there watched the worshipers. He asked the ancient Brahman priest, who for many years had received the offerings there, "Are there as many people coming here to pray as formerly?"

"No, there are fewer every year." "How long will this worship last?" was the next query. "God knows," he sadly replied. "What will bring it to an end?" "Jesus Christ," the Brahman answered.

Those who promote human religions are indeed afraid of Christ because He puts an end to human religion by introducing the promise of heaven.

118 Could Anyone Fill Jesus' Sandals

Some years ago, a college student took a psychology course in which another student tried to argue that Jesus was not greater than other men. The student stated that he could probably do everything Jesus had done. As a public service to those who have such lofty aspirations, we are publishing a partial list of things which you MUST do if you think that you can do everything that Jesus did.

1. Feed five thousand unexpected guests, and then have your amount of garbage exceed the amount of food with which you began.

2. Have a raging storm stilled at your command, and the wind and the waves stop simultaneously.

3. Become such a threat to a significant portion of the religious establishment that they demand that you be executed. (You must do this by what you say. You are not allowed to use demonstrations, riots, card-burnings, or picket signs, or any form of violence.)

4. Rise from the dead after you have been executed and pronounced dead.

That is enough of the easy things. Now let's look at some requirements which are more exacting. (By the way, you need not accept the Bible in order to KNOW that

Jesus accomplished these things.) By 1900 years after your death (from which you rose), you must have accomplished the following:

1. Every week, millions of people must gather in thousands of places for the sole purpose of telling about what a good person you were.

2. Thousands of hospitals and schools must have been built and be operating in your name.

3. The calendar, used in most of the world, must be dated from the time of your birth.

4. Men must still consider it worth their time to prove that you were a fake. (If you really were a fake, you would have been forgotten long before now.)

5. Your life must be considered to be the standard and ultimate goodness for a large portion of the world, and even for those who claim no association with the entity you founded to honor and serve you.

6. MOST IMPORTANT OF ALL, YOU MUST HAVE ACCOMPLISHED ALL THIS IN 3 1/2 YEARS.

119 The Hands of Christ

When our Lord was here on earth, He frequently ministered to man's needs with His hands. He broke the loaves and the fishes to feed a hungry multitude. He made clay and rubbed it on the eyes of a blind man to give him sight. He touched an unclean leper in the act of cleansing him. He said to Thomas, "Behold My hands." One day we, too, shall behold them.

The story is told of a young girl whose mother was very beautiful—all except her hands, which were shriveled and scarred and hideous. Although the child was long reluctant to speak about them, the time came when she asked her mother how her hands became so marred.

The mother told her how their house caught fire when the girl was very little. The mother rushed upstairs to the room where the girl was sleeping in her crib, and with the help of the Lord was able to carry the babe downstairs and outside without being harmed. But in doing so, the mother's hands were terribly burned.

This brought sobs to the child as she said, "O Mother, you know I've always loved you—especially your face, your smile, your eyes. But better than all, now I love your hands."

The One who left heaven's glory and became flesh for us bears in His compassionate hands the scars of His sacrifice on our behalf. His hands will be an eternal reminder of His love.

120 When He Waited the Longest

When Leonardo da Vinci painted *The Last Supper* on the wall in Milan, Italy convent dining room, the monks began to have many questions about his ability, and his integrity. The picture was merely a copy of the dining area in which it was being painted. The table, the linen, even the dishes used by the monks, were all identical to those in the picture.

Some of the monks thought da Vinci was taking advantage of his contract to paint this picture. They were resentful of his long periods of inactivity, when da Vinci would stand for hours without touching his brush to the wall in front of him.

When they asked da Vinci about this apparent inactivity, he replied, "When I pause the longest, I make my most telling strokes with my brush."

No other event in the life of our Lord has been painted more often, but none can match the one painted by da Vinci nearly 500 years ago.

In like manner, God paused, the world waited, "But when the fullness of the time was come, God sent forth His Son. . . ." (Gal. 4:4).

121 What the Artist Cannot Paint

An artist can *paint* the physical hands and feet of our Lord, *but he cannot paint* the healing power of those hands and the godly walk of those feet. He can paint the outward suffering, but not the inward cause; the cursed tree, but not the curse of the law; the bearing of the cross, but not the bearing of the sins of His people; the cup of vinegar, but not the cup of wrath—the derision of His enemies and the forsaking of the Father.

Where is the artist who can paint one hand of Christ nailed to the cross and the other hand claiming an inheritance of believers?

Or who can paint our Lord bruising the serpent's head, conquering sin, death and the grave?

The artist can only portray blood and water flowing from Christ's side, but he cannot paint what the eye of faith sees in that blood: salvation and pardon.

Second Coming

122 Welcome Back

A farmer had an old hound dog that he cherished. One day the dog disappeared, and several weeks passed without his return. In spite of this, the farmer continued to set out fresh food for the dog every day.

Finally, in curiosity, one of the farmer's neighbors asked why he continued to set out food for the dog when he obviously was not returning.

"He will be back," replied the farmer. "Because he knows I am here waiting for him. And when he gets here I want him to know he is welcome back."

Today we wait for Christ's return with great expectancy. We do not know the day nor the hour of His return, but we are confident that He *is* coming back.

As we wait for Christ's return, we prepare ourselves each day to meet Him.

123 The Promise of the Second Coming

Both the Old and New Testaments are filled with promises of

the second coming of Christ. Someone has reported that there are 1,845 references in the Old Testament alone and a total of 17 books that give it prominence.

Of the 260 chapters in the entire New Testament, there are 318 references to Christ's second coming. That averages one out of every 30 verses. Furthermore, 23 of the 27 New Testament books refer to this great event. That leaves only four books that do not refer directly to the Second Coming. Interestingly, three of these four books are single-chapter letters which were written to specific persons on a particular subject.

Christianity

124 Which Is Your Choice?

If you want your father to take care of you, that's **Paternalism**. If you want your mother to take care of you, that's **Maternalism**. If you want Uncle Sam to take care of you, that's **Socialism**. If you want some dedicated Communists to take over the government and take care of you, that's **Communism** (we would say slavery). If you want and are able to take care of yourself, that's **Americanism**. If you surrender all to Christ, and want God to take care of you, that is true **Christianity.** Of course, you'll be called a "square" or an "extremist," or a "crackpot," but you will have the best for time and eternity.

125 How to Start a Religion

Someone said to Bishop Talleyrand, one of the most astute men who ever lived: "The Christian religion—what is it? It would be easy to start a religion like that."

"Oh, yes," replied Talleyrand. "One would only have to get crucified and rise again the third day."

126 In Tune

Have you at sometime watched a symphony orchestra as a performance is about to begin? The musicians sit and stand about, strumming on strings, blowing into horns, beating on drums. There is a lot of noise, but no music. Then the conductor enters. He walks to his podium and steps up onto it. His eye sweeps the scene before him—all the musicians and all their instruments. He lifts his baton, pauses there for a moment, then he gives the downbeat. Instantly there is music; all instuments blend into one harmonious whole.

Our human spirits are a lot like symphony orchestras. Within us there may be discordant elements, warring factions that pull this way or that, and we are out of focus, out of tune—we are just not together within. As an orchestra needs a master control, so do we. When we turn the whole focus of our attention to our Lord and acknowledge that He is in command, our lives will give forth harmonious music.

127 Back to the Basics

It probably wouldn't work, but somebody ought to start a movement back to the basics. And again, it might be just novel enough to not only catch on, but to flourish.

How long has it been since you walked into a store without seeing "New" or "Improved" written on every bottle? And toothpaste? There's a new ingredient added every week. If you don't have FL-7, Amalgam-58, ammoniate, fluoride, chlorophyll, etc., your teeth are sure to fall out before you finish reading the label. Regardless of how faithful you have been in brushing your teeth in the past, that doesn't count if you have missed out on the latest ingredient.

It's a wonder people ever got their clothes clean in the past. Just think of it! They actually used non-miraculous soap, and often with "non-purified" water. What a world!

Do you recall what happened to Coca Cola when they wasted multi-millions of dollars bringing out the "New" Coke? Improvement went too far and irate customers wouldn't drink the new stuff. Coca Cola almost immediately decided the old drink wasn't so bad after all. This time they returned to the old formula, but gave it a new name (Classic). What a world!

Given the state of our times, it's hardly any wonder that there are countless preachers out trying to sell a "new" and "improved" Christianity. Let us pray that it will have the same success Coca Cola enjoyed.

128 Today It's "Frozen" Not "Chosen"

It has been suggested that the mark on many church people today is not that they are "chosen" but that they are "frozen."

129 Finish It

The life of a Christian can be described in one of four ways: as a journey, as a battle, as a pilgrimage, and as a race. Select your own metaphor, but the necessity to finish is always the same. For if life is a journey, it must be completed. If life is a battle, it must be finished. If life is a pilgrimage, it must be concluded. And if it is a race, it must be won.

Christians

130 What Kind Are You?

Some Christians are like wheelbarrows, not good unless pushed.

Some are like canoes, they have to be paddled.

Some are like kites, if you don't keep a string on them, they fly away.

Some are like kittens, they are more contented when petted.

Some are like balloons, full of wind and likely to blow up unless handled carefully.

Some are like trailers, no good unless pulled.

Some are like buzzards, they "get wind" of a foul smell and come quickly.

Some are filled with the Holy Spirit, and thank God for these!

131 A Nobleman's Legacy

In a certain mountain village in Europe several centuries ago, a nobleman wondered what legacy he should leave to his townspeople. Finally, he decided to build a church for a legacy.

The complete plans for the church were kept secret until its completion. When the people gathered, they marveled at the church's beauty and its completeness. Following many comments of praise, an astute observer inquired, "But where are the lamps? How will the church be lighted?"

Without answer, the nobleman pointed to some brackets in the wall; he then gave to each family a lamp to be carried to the worship service and hung on the wall. "Each time you are here, the area where you are seated will be lighted," the nobleman explained. "Each time you are not here, that area will be dark. Whenever you fail to come to church, some part of God's house will be dark."

132 Value by Association

An American tourist in Paris who purchased an inexpensive amber necklace in a trinket shop was shocked when he had to pay quite a high duty on it to clear customs in New York. This aroused his curiosity, so he had it appraised. After looking at the object under a powerful magnifying glass, the jeweler said, "I'll give you $25,000 for it." Greatly surprised, the man decided to have another expert examine it. When he did, he was offered $10,000 more!

"What do you see that's so valuable about this old necklace," asked the astonished man.

"Look through this glass," replied the jeweler. There before his eyes was an inscription: "From Napoleon Bonaparte to Josephine." The value of the necklace came from its identification with a famous person.

As Christians, we are in union with one who is far more important than any human being. It is from this union that the Christian finds his true identity and worth.

So in an age when man is searching for his past and discovering his potentials, the Christian can rejoice that his true worth comes from God and his identity is found in Jesus Christ.

133 It Is Better to Be Late Than Pass by One Who Needs You

Charles Harvey, Good Samaritan of Grand Prairie, Texas, felt a bit nervous as he was driving to an important job interview. He was fifteen minutes late and in a hurry when he passed a middle aged woman stranded with a flat tire. "My conscience made me stop," he said. "I changed her tire and headed to the interview, thinking I could just forget about getting the job now."

But he filled out the job application anyway, and went to the Personnel Director's office. Did he get the job? He sure did. The Personnel Director hired him on the spot. She was the woman whose tire he had just changed.

134 How Permanent Is What You Build

"And the rain descended, and the floods came, and the winds blew,

and beat upon that house; and it fell not; for it was founded upon a rock" (Matt. 7:25).

The permanence of any building depends upon three things: the materials used, wisdom exercised in its construction, and its foundation. Inferior materials, though skillfully assembled, cannot stand for long against the elements of nature. Nor will superior materials, if carelessly put together, be able to stand. A combination of sound materials and wise direction in assembling is necessary if the building is to endure, also it is very important that it be built upon a solid foundation. The same truths apply to the building of a life. One must choose his materials carefully and work them into the structure of his life wisely. He must be positive that it is built on a good foundation. In the sermon on the mount, Jesus challenges each one of us *to build for eternity!* Jesus urges men to cast aside such material as selfishness, hypocrisy, lust, and hatred. These can only lead to failure and ruin.

Christ prescribes the materials that will stand throughout time and eternity. He stresses humility, meekness, righteousness, mercy, and purity. The quality of this material has been tested and tried through the centuries.

We must heed the instructions of the Master Architect. *Build with Christ—Build for eternity!*

135 Are You God's Wife?

Sometimes we lead in ways that we don't realize are bringing others closer to God. Recently I read an incident that occurred when a man was working in a shoe store in Nova Scotia. The man said that he noticed a barefoot little boy outside the baker's shop next door to the shoe store. The boy was trying to keep warm by standing on a hot air register outside the bakery. The man watching was uncertain about what to do about the little boy when a middle-aged lady came by. She spoke to the child and then brought him into the shoe store where she purchased shoes and socks for him.

The child asked the lady, "Are you God's wife?"

She replied, "No, son, I'm just one of His children."

"Well, I knew you must be some kin to Him," he remarked as he thanked her and left. That unknown lady was a leader for the cause of Christ, and the little boy and the man watching were able to recognize some Christ-like qualities in her.

136 Christians Are to Be Different

During World War II a 15-year-old boy managed to enlist in the Navy and eventually joined the crew of a destroyer escort in the North Atlantic. After the ship left port, he gave himself away by being so frightened and homesick.

Even though the safety of the ship was at stake, the youth had to stand his watch. The bo's'n assigned to him the midnight to 4 a.m. watch

on the bow. A lanky cowboy from Texas named Cogswell had the preceding duty at the dangerous and important post.

Fearing the worst, the captain stayed on the bridge during the "graveyard watch." About 1 a.m. he looked out through the starlit night to see how the novice sailor was faring. To his amazement, he recognized the tall frame of Cogswell.

The next morning, the skipper asked the bo's'n, "Did you know Cogswell took the kid's place last night and stood eight hours straight duty?"

"Yes sir, I did," he replied. "Well," replied the captain, "what do you think about it?" "Sir, I didn't think anything about it. Didn't you know? Cogswell's a Christian!"

137 Hammer Christians

What we need are more Christians who quietly but effectively do their jobs like a hammer. A hammer keeps its head; it doesn't fly off the handle; it keeps pounding away; it finds the point quickly and drives it home; and perhaps more important, it is the only knocker in the world that accomplishes anything worthwhile!

Consider the hammer, and follow its example in your daily walk with Christ.

138 What Do You Offer?

Men today want to know, How much does the job pay? What do you offer?

The story is told that when Garibaldi set out to liberate Italy, he saw some young men standing at a street corner, and he asked them if they would like to enlist in his cause. "What do you offer?" they said.

"Offer?" replied Garibaldi. "I offer you hardship, hunger, rags, thirst, sleepless nights, footsores in long marches, privations innumerable, and finally **victory** in the noblest cause that ever confronted you." Young Italy did follow him!

Our Lord says, "If any one would come after Me, let him take up his cross and follow Me" (Mark 8:34).

139 How Is the Christian Different?

The Christian sees through kinder eyes—like Jesus.

He gives from a bigger heart—like God.

He speaks with a purer tongue—like Christ.

He serves with more willing hands—like Jesus.

He walks with a greater faith—like his Lord.

He loves with *agape* love—like the Father in heaven.

He thinks with a spiritual mind—like Christ.

He sees the needs of others with a compassionate view—like Jesus.

He heals the wounds of others with love—like the Master.

The Christian is different only when Jesus rules his life.

140 True Riches

A tax assessor came one day to a poor minister of the gospel to determine the amount of taxes he would have to pay. "What do you possess?" he questioned.

"Oh, I am very wealthy," replied the minister. "List your possessions, please," the assessor instructed.

The man of God replied, "First, I have everlasting life—John 3:16. Second, I have a mansion in Heaven—John 14:2. Thirdly, I have peace that passeth understanding—Philippians 4:7. Fourth, I have joy unspeakable—1 Peter 1:8. Fifth, I have divine love that never faileth—1 Corinthians 13:8. Sixth, I have a faithful, pious wife—Proverbs 31:10. Seventh, I have healthy, happy, obedient children—Exodus 20:12. Eighth, I have true, loyal friends—Proverbs 18:24. Ninth, I have songs in the night—Psalm 42:8. Tenth, I have a crown of life awaiting—James 1:12."

The tax collector closed his book and said, "Truly, you are a very rich man, but your property is not subject to taxation."

141 Christians Are Members of the Body of Christ

A lady accepted Christ as her Savior late in life and found in Him such joy that she could not keep still about it; she was praising God and talking about it all the time. One day a friend said, "You seem pretty confident about this salvation of yours. I would not be too sure if I were you; suppose the Lord should let you slip through His fingers?" "But," said the elderly lady, "I am one of the fingers."

142 A Christian Should Be:

A MIND through which Christ thinks,

A VOICE through which Christ speaks,

A HEART through which Christ loves,

A HAND through which Christ helps.

143 Abiding in Christ

An English woman illustrated what it means to have Christ between us and danger. She said she was wakened by a very strange noise of pecking. When she went to the window, she saw a butterfly flying inside the window pane in great fright; outside a sparrow was pecking at the pane and trying to reach the butterfly. The butterfly did not see the glass pane and expected every minute to be caught; the sparrow did not see the glass and expected every minute to catch the butterfly. All the while the butterfly was safe because the glass was between it and the sparrow.

So it is with the Christian who is abiding in Christ. God's presence is between His child and every danger.

144 Parable of the Deadly Wound

Have you heard the story about Satan's attack upon a certain Christian? First, he shot a poisonous dart at his heel, but the Christian was unharmed because he had his feet shod with the preparation of the gospel of peace. Satan's next attempt was at his loins, but the Christian repelled this because he had his loins girt about with the truth. Unsuccessfully the devil tried a shot at his breast, the breastplate of righteousness. The Christian knocked away another arrow. But the devil, still not discouraged, slipped around behind the Christian and shot him in the pocketbook, and killed him dead as a hammer.

145 More Than a Conqueror

Alexander the Great subdued the world about him, but he was conquered by his own lusts; he died in a drunken stupor. The Christian conquers his own lusts in order to subdue the world within him. Through Christ, we are more than conquerors (Rom. 8:37).

146 Defeatism Grieves God

Christian defeatism grieves God. We must refuse to stand as mere spectators while the godless dismantle our nation.

Believers through Christ are to be the overcomers, not the overcome. Have we forgotten how those first century believers, working against even greater odds, "turned the world upside down"? Have we become so mesmerized by the coming "tribulation" that we have forgotten Christ's order to "occupy until I return"?

Once again Christians must become the nation's salt, its preservative, and put the reins into the hands of righteous leaders. No longer can be we mere "hearers" but through God "doers," if the nation is to survive.

147 How You Can Be a Peacemaker

Carl and Sam were at odds with each other. They could not even remember the initial cause of friction . . . but their hostility had festered through the years. A deeply concerned deacon prayed that God would use him as a peacemaker.

He called on Carl. "What do you think of Sam?" he asked. "He's the sorriest guy in town!" "But," countered the deacon, "you have to admit that he's a hard-working man." "No one can deny that," said Carl. "I've never known a person who worked harder."

Next the deacon visited Sam. "Do you know what Carl said about you?" "No, but I can imagine his lies," he responded angrily. "This may surprise you," said the deacon, "but he said he's never known a harder worker." "He said that?" Sam was stunned. "What do you think of Carl?" asked the deacon. "It is no secret that I have absolutely no use for him." "But you must admit he's honest in business," said the deacon. "There's no getting around that," said Sam. "In business he's a man you can trust."

Later the deacon met Carl again. "Do you know what Sam said about you? He claims you're absolutely trustworthy in business, that you are scrupulously honest." "Well, how 'bout that," reacted Carl with a smile.

Soon the peacemaking deacon noticed Sam and Carl would cautiously nod in a friendly sort of way. Before long they were shaking hands, talking, even visiting in each other's homes. Today they are best of friends.

Many people, even church folk, seem to delight in promoting a fight by carrying news of ill-will. Rip this page from a deacon's peacemaking notebook. It's a worthy example to follow.

148 Help Yourself by Helping Others

The story is told of two men riding on a sleigh during a blizzard. Almost frozen and afraid that they would not reach warmth and safety, they came upon another traveler who had fallen in the snow and was near death from the terrific cold. One suggested that they stop and help. The other refused, saying that to stop might keep them from reaching safety. He insisted on going on.

However, the first man decided to stay and help. He set himself to the task of massaging the man's body to restore circulation. After long hard work, the man responded and was saved. The traveler's work in helping another helped keep himself warm and alive. The one who refused to stay and help was found some distance ahead, frozen to death.

149 Rejoicing Always

A saintly woman who had suffered for weary months from a

painful illness said to her pastor, "I have such a lovely robin that sings outside my window. In the early mornings as I lie here, he serenades me."

Then a smile brightened her thin features as she added, "I love him because he sings in the rain."

That is the most beautiful thing about a robin. When a storm has silenced every other songbird, the robin sings on. That is what the Christian who is with Christ may do. Any one can sing in the sunshine. You and I should sing on when the sun has gone down, or when clouds pour out their rain, for Christ is with us.

150 The Need to Remain Useful

The great violinist, Nicolo Paganini, willed his marvelous violin to Genoa—the city of his birth—but only on condition that the instrument never be played. It was an unfortunate condition, for it is a peculiarity of wood that as long as it is used and handled, it shows little wear. As soon as it is discarded, it begins to decay.

The exquisite mellow-toned violin now has become worm-eaten in its beautiful case, valueless except as a relic. The moldering instrument is a reminder that a life withdrawn from service to others loses its meaning.

How well Jesus' strong emphasis upon service is illustrated! In order to retain our value and our worth and not degenerate into a

worthless relic, we should serve and remain active.

"But whosoever will be great among you, let him be your minister. And whosoever will be chief among you, let him be your servant" (Matt. 20:26, 27).

151 A Precious Stone

In a box in a jewelry store there were precious stones, sapphires, and diamonds; the beryl and the amethyst; and many others. Right in the center, according to the story, was a common looking pebble, and a man said to the clerk, "Why do you have that pebble there? If you saw it on the floor you would pick it up and throw it out the window." The clerk took the stone out of the box and said, "You do not know the beauty of this stone"; he held it and in two or three minutes you could not see the stone, but instead, all the colors of the rainbow, moving in such rapid succession they would almost dazzle you; but when the stone got cold the colors would vanish. You might place that stone on the windowsill on the hottest day and it would have no effect on it, but it would respond to peculiar moisture of the human hand to bring out its beauty.

That is what happens when we lie passively in the hand of God. All the beauty that is in us shows.

152 How's Your Interior Decorating?

Warren W. Wiersbe relates that one day he was scanning the shelves in a bookstore in Cincinnati, Ohio, when he discovered a volume out of place. It was in the "Religion" section, but the title of the book was *The Art of Interior Decorating*. He started to remove the book, but then it dawned on him that the volume was just where it belonged. For, after all, isn't that what the Christian faith is all about—interior decorating?

"I can't think of a better description of the Christian life than 'interior decorating,' " he commented. "You see, the Bible emphasizes the fact that each of us has an 'inner man'—the real person down inside. The body may change and decay and even die, but the 'real you' down inside will live forever."

153 Pleasing Christ

A desire to please Christ is not something extra for the Christian. It is basic to Christian sanctity. It is not a dessert, but the main course—not a sideshow, but the main tent. It is not a motive to which we can resort to when convenient; it is a controlling force to which we have committed our lives. We have abandoned everything else. In time, applause and pleas of the world have a hollow ring. We are marching to a different drumbeat. His smile is singularly our greatest delight! This is the lifestyle of love.

154 The Cross and the Crown

"The highest joy to the Christian almost always comes through suffering," said Alexander Maclaren. "No flower can bloom in Paradise which is not transplanted from Gethsemane. No one can taste of the fruit of the tree of life, that has not tasted of the fruits of the tree of Calvary. The crown is after the cross."

155 Frequent but Not Common

Bill Smith. There may be no name more common in the English language. In a seminary class, one professor related an event that happened his first day in college.

His teacher professed an uncanny command of the English language. It seemed that he always pulled out the most appropriate word for the occasion. On this, the first day of school, he was calling the roll. After recognizing each student he made some pertinent comment about his name—its history, meaning, or some historically related story. Finally, he came to Bill Smith. He said with a pause and in a reflective tone, "Bill Smith . . . that is a common name." Stirred from within, Bill arose from his seat and said in a loving but firm tone, "Sir, Bill Smith may be frequent but not common."

Who among us has not lived under the teacher's philosophy? Thinking there is nothing special about ourselves, we have concluded that we are common, everyday, ordinary. Let us continually remind ourselves that each one of us is a chosen person, a royal priest, a member of a holy nation, a person that belongs to God (1 Pet. 2:9).

156 Tested!

The WEATHER Test—Are you a sailboat Christian, making progress in the Lord only if the winds are favorable and things go your way? Or are you a tugboat Christian, plowing right ahead according to God's Word even though the gales are against you? (Rev. 2:10).

The WORRY Test—If you trust, you do not worry; if you worry, you do not trust as you should. Haven't you found that "He keeps him in perfect peace whose mind is stayed on Him" because he trusts in God? (Matt. 6:28; Luke 12:27).

The WORLDLINESS Test—Do you think as the world thinks, go where the world goes, act as the world acts? Does your life give evidence of having your affections set on things above, not on things of the world? (Rom. 12:1).

The WALLET Test—What proportion of your income last year was turned over for the work of the Lord? Was it at least as much as the tithe which the Jews paid before the grace of God was revealed in Christ? (Lev. 27:30; Neh. 12:44).

The WORK Test—How much of your energy is being given to the work of the Lord, and is it a reasonable portion of what you are expending in the day-to-day task of making a living? (John 9:4).

The SOUL-WINNING Test—Are you by life and lip presenting Christ so that He is attractive to those who do not know Him as their Savior and Lord? (Matt. 12:30; Rom. 15:5, 6).

157 I Missed Church . . . But God Understands!

Quite often, when people are encouraged to put aside whatever is preventing them from attending services regularly, they will say: "Well, I really should be there, but I think God understands!"

God has gone on record in Hebrews 10:25 as saying, "Not forsaking the assembling. . . ." He does not understand why some of His people willfully hold to habits of forsaking the assembly! God does understand that we need to meet to praise Him and study His Word. God understands that others need the encouragement of our presence, we are a family that He put together. He does understand group fellowship, the power of people meeting together for mutual strengthening.

But do we understand those things? Many times we do not—and that is why so many allow Satan to bring one little excuse after another into their lives until they are separated from our God and His assembly.

Let us pray that God will help us to understand the need, the purpose and the power of attendance to Bible classes and worship services whenever the doors are open. And let us pray for the courage to do our part in making the gathering of the saints a time of love, praise, and spiritual growth! It is a matter of spiritual life and death, really, not only for us, but also for others whom we are influencing. Think about it!

158 Trees

"And he shall be like a tree planted by the rivers of water" (Ps. 1:3).

Who shall be like a tree? The good man, anyone who loves God, and loves his Bible and loves to do right.

The trees can teach us many lessons:

1. *Grow straight and beautiful.* Live a life so you will have a good reputation; do not let any sin make you grow crooked and full of knots and gnarls.

2. *Be sound of heart.* Some beautiful trees are rotten-hearted, hollow-hearted. They are dying trees, they are hypocrites, the lumber man cuts one down and it cannot be used. Be honest, be true, be sincere, be what you want people to think you are.

3. *Be strong.* Do not let any little wind of temptation blow you over. Overcome evil with good. Sometimes the winds topple even live trees in the forest, but God is better to His children than trees. "Ye shall not be tempted above that ye are able."

4. *Keep growing.* Last winter was cold, last summer was hot, but every live tree grew a little; it added one more ring to the trunk, a few more twigs to the branches. Do not let trouble keep you from growing in faith; do not let hard work keep you from growing in love; keep growing every year.

5. *Give help to others.* All live trees are of some use—shade, timber, nuts or fruits. Every Christian can be of some use in the world. Find your work and do it well.

6. *God cares for all.* For every tree there is a place to grow, plenty of air, light and rain. There is also for you all that you need. God cares for all His children. He never has forgotten one; He will never fail you nor forsake you.

7. *Be contented.* No tree ever worries, fusses, or grumbles. Does it grow in a wilderness? It may yet be a part of a city palace. Is your life lonely or sad? Some day death will transplant you into the great city of heaven.

The trees look in at your window, they smile down upon you along the streets. Learn the lessons that they teach, and you may be like a tree planted by the river of water.

159 Totality

I must have a whole Christ for my salvation;

I must have a whole Bible for my staff;

I must have a whole church for my fellowship;

I must have a whole world for my parish.

—Augustine

160 Salt of the Earth

In his early remarks during what we call the Sermon on the Mount, Jesus describes His disciples as "the salt of the earth." Notice this verse carefully:

"You are the salt of the earth. But if the salt loses its saltiness, how can it be made salty again? It is no longer good for anything, except to be thrown out and trampled by men" (Matt. 5:13).

Jesus takes it for granted that all understood the uselessness of salt that is incapable of preserving and flavoring. "Throw it away!" is His advice for useless salt. The application to Christians is clearly seen. God put us here to preserve and flavor His world. If we are not doing that, what good are we to Him or others?

In A.D. 252, a killing plague swept through the North African city of Carthage. The heathens threw the dead in the streets and fled the city in fear for their lives. Cyprian, leader of the church in Carthage, marshaled the saints and they began burying the dead and nursing the sick. Their action saved the city and thrust the church into prominence in the minds of its citizens.

Good people are salting the earth and preserving the creation of God. They are lighting the world and glorifying the God who made it.

I have a question: If we are not salting this earth and lighting this world, then why are we here?

161 Things You Will Never Be Sorry For:

For telling the truth;
For living a pure life;
For your faith in Christ;
For acknowledging your sins;
For doing your best;
For thinking before judging;
For forgiving your enemies;
For helping a fallen brother;

For being loyal to the church;
For standing by your principles;
For being courteous and kind;
For money given to he Lord's cause;
For being honest in business.

162 Be a Doer

If you have a gift—bring it.
If you have a song—sing it.
If you have a talent—use it.
If you have love—diffuse it.
If you have sadness—bear it.
If you have gladness—share it.
If you have happiness—give it.
If you have religion—live it.
If you have a prayer—pray it.

163 A Friend Is . . .

A push when you're stopped,
A guide when you're searching,
A song when you're glad,
A word when you're lonely,
A smile when you're sad.

164 What Do You Do for Fun?

Several years ago a Christian girl told me about an incident with a young man who had been asking to date her. He was not a member of the church, and they just didn't have anything in common. She had turned him down twice and now she had said "no" to attending a rock concert with him. In a kind of mock exasperation, the young man asked, "What do you do for fun? You don't dance, you don't drink, you don't attend rock concerts, what do you do for fun?"

To the young man she replied, "For fun I get up in the morning without feeling embarrassed, ashamed and guilty about what I did the night before."

The young man had nothing more to say. She was right; it *is* fun not to feel guilty for your actions the night before.

Come to think of it, there are many things in life that are fun. For example, that Christian girl is now married to a fine Christian man. They have a little girl and are building an outstanding Christian home together. I am thrilled thinking about the fun she is having!

She is having fun every day living without the affliction of deep scars of fornication, drugs or alcohol, and regrets from her past. It's fun getting ready each afternoon to receive a husband home from work, knowing that he won't be stopping off at a local bar for a few drinks with the boys. It is fun knowing that while he is away from her, his Christian conduct won't allow infidelity or even flirting. It's fun watching him hold his little girl on his lap with loving, protecting arms. It's fun knowing that her little girl will never see her father in a drunken stupor or experimenting with drugs. It's fun living with assurance that the home will be led by a spiritual leader who will guide each family member toward heaven.

The list of fun things for Christians is endless; what do you do for fun?

165 Can Man Be Just a Christian?

At times it appears that in our "Christian world" man is converted to a church rather than to Jesus Christ. Loyalty to a body of believers seems to have priority over allegiance to the Lord Jesus. Although each religion claims faith in the same Bible, because of certain doctrines peculiar to various denominations they separate themselves from one another. Frequently each denomination is divided into a number of sects.

Is it possible for man simply to be a "Christian"? Must he separate himself with some denominational name as Baptist Christian, Methodist Christian, etc.? God doesn't divide believers into various denominations—man does. Even with his own church choice, man is frequently at variance with his brother over some biblical understanding. Also, world Bible scholars differ in matters pertaining to Scripture understanding.

What authority does one believer have in saying, "I am right and you are wrong," or "I am more honest than you." Certainly the Bible is right, but does it necessarily follow that I am the one who has perfect understanding? Do you ever differ with members of your family over some conviction? Does it mean that you are no longer a member of that family? If there can be no unity in diversity, there is simply no possibility of unity, for we all differ in many things.

166 Short and Long Term Survival

Here is a spiritual insight from Charles A. Lindbergh: "Short term survival may depend on the knowledge of nuclear physicists and the performance of supersonic aircraft, but long term survival depends alone on the character of man. We must remember that it was not the outer grandeur of the Roman but the inner simplicity of the Christian that lived on through the ages."

167 *Something Larger*

"Bad will be the day," said Phillips Brooks, "for every man when he becomes absolutely contented with the life that he is living, with the thoughts that he is thinking, with the deeds that he is doing, when there is not forever beating at the doors of his soul some great desire to do something larger, which he knows that he was meant and made to do because he is still, in spite of all, the child of God."

Christmas

168 The Silent Authors of "Silent Night"

Only by happy coincidence did the names of the true authors of the song "Silent Night" come to light—thirty-six years after they wrote it.

The story begins in 1818 in a church in the little Austrian town of Oberndorf. Shortly before Christmas Eve, a mouse ate a hole in the leather bellows of the church organ, effectively silencing it. The itinerant organ mender was not due in town for months, and music was needed for the Christmas Eve service. In three and one-half hours, Franz Gruber, the organist, composed music for a poem written by Josef Mohr, a priest. It began "Stille Nacht, Heilige Nacht" ("Silent Night, Holy Night"). On Christmas Eve, the two men sang their composition accompanied by a guitar and children's chorus. They were a great success.

The following May, when the organ mender turned up, Gruber gave him a copy of the song, which the man then circulated in his travels. By 1831, thirteen years later, the Strasser family quartet was billing "Silent Night" one of their numbers, as a Tyrolean folk song by "authors unknown."

Time went by, and soon the now-popular song was being attributed to several famous composers. In 1854, the leader of the king's orchestra in Berlin wrote to the choir director of the Benedictine school in Salzburg, asking for a copy of "Silent Night" by Michael Haydn, brother of the more famous composer Franz Joseph Haydn. The choir director asked a student—who just happened to be Felix Gruber, Franz Gruber's son—to find a copy. And you can guess the rest.

169 A Strange Birthday Celebration

If the following story were not true, it would surely be unbelievable. It is true, however, as you yourself will agree when you have read it.

There was once a great king. His love for his people knew no limits. Although the kingdom was very large, the king knew every person by name. Everything the people of the kingdom had was a gift freely given by the loving king.

So, to show their love and appreciation to the king for all he had done for them, the people decided to have a great celebration to honor his birthday. Everyone agreed it was a marvelous idea. Preparations for the celebration were very elaborate. No expense was spared by the people. They adorned their homes with lights, decorations, and expensive ornaments. There were parties, dinners, and celebrations throughout the kingdom.

All the people brought gifts for their friends and family. Many of the gifts which the people gave each other were quite expensive, involving considerable indebtedness. In fact, the people spent more on the birthday celebration than they spent at any other time of the year.

Many who were not citizens of the kingdom, and who did not even know the king, joined in the celebration. Their celebration of the king's birth was marked by excessive drinking. Since they did not know the king, they invented a good-natured, fat fellow in a red suit. He laughed a lot, but never said anything. But that didn't matter because they were too busy celebrating to listen anyhow.

The great day of celebrating his birth finally arrived, and some of his people did come bringing gifts and thanking him for his goodness to them. But to his dismay, most of the citizens never came to his house at all on the day of celebration. And the gifts brought to the king by those few who came were very meager when compared with the gifts they had given themselves.

For the most part the people said they had been so busy with all the celebrations and personal plans that they had forgotten about the king.

Several said they had thought of him, but really could not work it into their schedules or budgets to come see him or bring a gift. A few were known to be quite put out when it was suggested that going to the king's house or remembering him with a gift was important.

Those people who did come to his house and who brought their loving gifts were welcomed and blessed by the king. But when they had gone and he was alone again, the king fell to thinking of the vast numbers of his people who had forgotten and forsaken him. How could they have forgotten? Had he not loved them all? How could so many of his beloved people who had found the time and money for shopping and feasting and partying and decorating and all sorts of celebrations—how could they possibly be so thoughtless, so ungrateful or selfish? Did they not know that he, too, had feelings? Was not the purpose of the birthday celebration originally planned to honor him?

When the king was alone, pondering these questions, he felt the tears well up in his eyes. And in his loneliness, he wept.

One thought brought some hope and consolation. Even though they had forgotten him, he had not forgotten them.

170 Immanuel

Two missionaries were captured and imprisoned in the same cell but forbidden to speak to each other. Christmas came.

One of the missionaries, shivering and silent, sat on the floor covered with hay. As he was playing with bits of hay around him, he thought that he discovered a silent way of communicating with his friend. He spelled out the word Immanuel. As soon as his friend saw the word, immediately he lit up with joy. They were captives, but they both believed that God was with them and that ultimate triumph would be theirs.

This Christmas let us find a variety of ways of showing to others that God is indeed Immanuel, God with us.

171 Keep Christ Central in Christmas

It is a principle of art that in the composition of a picture, all the parts shall be so arranged as to lead the eye inevitably to the central figure or feature. Whatever prevents this is a capital defect. Accessories are only important as they help this end.

When Varelst, the Dutch painter, made his tulips so glorious that they drew attention away from the face of James II, in whose portrait he had placed them, he violated this canon. So did Haydon when, in his picture of Christ's triumphal entry into Jerusalem, he made the figure of the beast on which the Master rode more attractive than the person of Christ.

So does the theologian or the metaphysician or the logician, who fascinates by his argument and rhetoric, or the preacher and liturgist, who stresses his forms of worship and symbols of religion.

It is not the swaddling-clothes of ceremonialism, but the Christ of the simple gospel story consistently lived, that shall span the continents with love and make Christmas perpetual in the heart of man.

172 Christmas Is Costly

It cost Mary and Joseph the comforts of home during a long period of exile in Egypt to protect the little Babe.

It cost mothers in and around Bethlehem the massacre of their babies by the cruel order of Herod.

It cost the shepherds the complacency of their shepherds' life, with the call to the manger and to tell the good news.

It cost the wise men a long journey and expensive gifts and changed lives.

It cost the early apostles and the early church persecution and sometimes death.

It cost missionaries of Christ untold suffering and privation to spread the good news.

It cost Christian martyrs in all ages their lives for Christ's sake.

More than all this, it cost God the Father His own Son—He sent Him to the earth to save men.

It cost Jesus a life of sacrifice and service, a death cruel and unmatched in history.

173 The Shoemaker's Dream

One of the most beautiful of all Christmas stories was told by the

American poet, Edwin Markham, about a cobbler, a godly man who made shoes in the old days. One night the cobbler dreamed that the next day Jesus was coming to visit him. The dream seemed so real that he got up very early the next morning and hurried to the woods, where he gathered green boughs to decorate his shop for the arrival of so great a Guest.

He waited all morning, but to his disappointment, his shop remained quiet, except for an old man who limped up to the door asking to come in for a few minutes of warmth. While the man was resting, the cobbler noticed that the old fellow's shoes were worn through. Touched, the cobbler took a new pair from his shelves and saw to it that the stranger was wearing them as he went on his way.

Throughout the afternoon the cobbler waited, but his only visitor was an elderly woman. He had seen her struggling under a heavy load of firewood, and he invited her, too, into his shop to rest. Then he discovered that for two days she had had nothing to eat; he saw to it that she had a nourishing meal before she went on her way.

As night began to fall, the cobbler heard a child crying outside his door. The child was lost and afraid. The cobbler went out, soothed the youngster's tears and, with the little hand in his, took the child home.

When he returned, the cobbler was sad. He was convinced that while he had been away he had missed the visit of his Lord. Now he lived through the moments as he had imagined them: the knock, the latch lifted, the radiant face, the offered cup. He would have kissed the hands where the nails had been, washed the feet where the spikes had entered. Then the Lord would have sat and talked to him.

In his anguish, the cobbler cried out, "Why is it, Lord, that Your feet delay. Have you forgotten that this was the day?" Then, soft in the silence a voice he heard:

"Lift up your heart for I kept My word.
Three times I came to your friendly door;
Three times My shadow was on your floor.
I was the man with the bruised feet.
I was the woman you gave food to eat,
I was the child on the homeless street."

174 Christmas Spells Peace

Amid the horrors of World War I, there occurred a unique truce when for a few hours, enemies behaved like brothers.

Christmas Eve in 1914 was all quiet on France's Western Front, from the English Channel to the Swiss Alps. Trenches came within 50 miles of Paris. The war was only five months old, and approximately 800,000 men had been wounded or killed. Every soldier wondered whether or not Christmas Day would bring another round of fighting and killing. But something happened: British soldiers raised "Merry Christmas" signs above the trenches, and soon carols were heard from German and British trenches alike.

Christmas dawned with unarmed soldiers leaving their trenches, though officers of both sides tried unsuccessfully to stop their troops from meeting the enemy in the middle of no-man's land for songs and conversation. Exchanging small gifts, they passed Christmas Day peacefully along miles of the front. At one spot, the British played soccer with the Germans, who won 3-2.

In some places, the spontaneous truce continued the next day as neither side was willing to fire the first shot. Finally, the war resumed when fresh troops arrived, and the high command of both armies ordered that further "informal understanding" with the enemy would be punishable as treason.

175 Hark the Herald Angels Sing

Charles Wesley of England was without doubt one of the most productive hymn writers and preachers of all time. Yet, strangely enough, Wesley was able to get only one hymn poem into the Church of England's Book of Common Prayer, and that one by error!

An eighteenth century printer didn't know that the "established Church" of England frowned with disapproval upon Wesley's hymns.

Since he needed material to fill an empty space in the new hymnal, he took it upon himself to insert a Christmas poem called, "Hark, How All the Welkins Rings!" by an Anglican clergyman named Charles Wesley. When the error was discovered attempts were made to have it removed, but it proved so popular that it was allowed to remain.

It was written in 1738, but is still very moving today.

"Hark the herald angels sing.
Glory to the new born King.
Peace on earth, and mercy mild:
God and sinners reconciled."

176 At Christmas Is Christ Happy Over Us?

"Mommy," asked Jane, "what makes everybody so happy at Christmas?" "Well, because it is the Lord Jesus' birthday . . . and because we love Him . . . and because we are happy about His coming to this world."

Jane thought a minute and then said, "Then is the Lord happy about you?" "Oh, little girl, what a question you have asked!"

Is the Lord Jesus happy about us on His birthday? Is he really happy because He sees within our hearts a deep, true love for Him? Does He see a satisfying love and not just a seasonal affection stirred up by the festivities of Christmas? What He wants more than anything else on His birthday is the love of our hearts.

177 Do You Recognize Christ in Christmas?

Not long ago, a professor of psychology in one of our great universities gave a word suggestion test to his class of 40 students. He instructed them to write the word "Christmas," and all the class did so. "Now," said the professor, "right after the word 'Christmas' write the first thought that flashes through your mind regarding that day." When the papers were turned in, such answers were given as "tree," "holly," "mistletoe," "presents," "turkey," "holiday," "carols," and "Santa Claus," but not one had written, "the birthday of Jesus."

As there was no room for the baby Jesus in the inn, there is no room for Him today in the celebration of Christmas.

178 Do Not Weep Over What You Do Not Have But Decorate What You Have

One Christmas Eve, as late Christmas shoppers hurried along the street, a crippled newsboy stood on his crutches offering his papers to the passersby. He looked happy, and his crutches were decorated with evergreens.

One man greeted him with a cheerful smile, "My boy, you surely have the Christmas spirit."

The boy replied "What's the use of putting on a sour face? Sure, I am poor and lame, but that's no reason for looking glum. I won't get presents like other boys at Christmas, but I can have fun, too.

So I decorated my crutches just to make them seem special for Christmas."

If we go out to seek joy, it will elude us. If we go out to impart joy, we will find it. This Christmas, whether you have little or much, it makes no difference. It is your attitude that counts.

179 A Christmas Prayer

Then let every heart keep
        Christmas within—
Christ's pity for sorrow,
Christ's hatred for sin,
Christ's care for the weakest,
Christ's courage for right.
Everywhere, everywhere,
        Christmas tonight!

180 When Christmas Comes

Have you any old grudge you'd like to pay,
    Any wrong laid up from a bygone day?
    Gather them all now, and lay them away
    When Christmas comes.

Hard thoughts are heavy to carry, my friend,
    And life is short from beginning to end;
    Be kind to yourself—leave nothing to mend—
    When Christmas comes.

181 Some Christian Reminders

May the Christmas *cheer* remind you of Him who said, "Be of good cheer."

May the Christmas *bell* remind

you of the glorious proclamation of His birth.

May the Christmas *carols* remind you of the song the angels sang, "Glory to God in the highest."

May the Christmas *season* remind you in every way of Jesus Christ your King.

182 Open the Gift Package

There was a gift for each of us left under the tree of life 2,000 years ago by Him whose birthday we celebrate today.

The gift was withheld from no man. Some have left the packages unclaimed. Some have accepted the gift and carry it around, but have failed to remove the wrappings and look inside to discover the hidden splendor. The packages are all alike: in each is a scroll on which is written, "All that the Father hath is thine. Take and live!"

183 The Xmas of Christmas

Someone has written that people use Xmas and it means Xhaustion, Xcuses, Xchanges, Xcesses, Xtravagances, Xasperations, Xhibitions and worldly Xcitement. How much better to make the Lord the very center of our Christmas observance. Keep Christ in Christmas!

Church

184 Forward-Moving Christianity

When I think about the kind of offensive strategy God expects from His church, I think about the San Francisco Forty-niners. They were the team of the eighties. Their greatness was due to their ability to make an offensive impact. They controlled the ball, thereby controlling the game. Their offense was almost always on the field, so other teams rarely had an opportunity to score. Even if the other teams did score, the Forty-niners almost always came back and scored again.

God doesn't expect Satan to "control the ball" in his battle against the church. God expects the church to be on the offensive, executing His game plan. Satan's defense is to be kept on the field while God's offense scores the touchdowns. When Satan's team does have the ball, the church ought to be causing fumbles so the right offense gets back on the field. The church isn't in the game just to keep Satan from scoring. God has called His people to be forward-moving Christians.

185 The Church's Responsibility

Like many Christians today, the disciples had a faulty view of the future. They focused on Christ's future kingdom rather than on their responsibility to occupy enemy territory and represent His kingdom until He returns (Luke 19:31). The church's responsibility to occupy the world can be compared to what happened in 1983 on the island of Grenada. Due to the rise of Communist insurgency, the U.S. President ordered troops into Grenada. In just eight hours, the battle was over. However, many of the Communists would not accept defeat. Rather than surrender, they sniped at our troops from behind cars, buildings, and trees. So our troops remained there until the victory was secured and a new government was installed.

When Jesus died on the cross and rose from the dead, He was victorious over all God's enemies. He clearly won the victory. However, Satan and his followers have not accepted defeat and still try to claim victory. Thus, the victorious Christ has established His troops—the church—to secure the victory until He returns to set up His new government. The church is God's occupational force until He comes again. Rather than focusing on their future rule with Him, therefore, Jesus wanted the disciples to focus on their impact in the world and be ready to receive God's power through the Holy Spirit.

186 Safety Tips

1. Do not ride in an automobile (or get in the way of one), as automobiles cause 20 percent of all fatal accidents.
2. Do not stay at home; that's where 17 percent of all accidents occur.
3. Do not walk across the street; pedestrians are victims of 14 percent of all accidents.
4. Do not travel by air, rail or water; 16 percent of all accidents are the result of these activities.
5. Only .001 percent of all fatal accidents occur at church and almost none of these during worship and Sunday School.

Obviously, the safest place to be is in worship and Bible Study with your family and fellow Christians. I hope to see YOU in Bible Study and worship this coming Lord's Day!

187 Who Flew the Kite?

"I did," said the sticks. "I did," said the paper. "I did," said the boy. "No, I did," said the wind. But they all flew the kite together. If the sticks had broken, the tail caught in a tree, the paper torn or the wind has lulled, the kite would have come down. Each had a part to play. The application is inescapable. We each have a work to do. If the work of the Lord is to be a success, then all parts must be played by every member of the church. We have the work of visiting, giving, preaching, and countless other jobs to do to

make the church and its work successful. We must all work together and each do what he can to help. It is a matter of teamwork (1 Cor. 3:6-9).

188 Fourteen Ways to Kill a Sunday School

1. Attend only when convenient.
2. When you do attend, arrive late.
3. Grumble about having to attend.
4. Criticize the officers and teachers in front of your family and friends.
5. Refuse to accept any responsibility in the Sunday school. If you ever do accept any, do it grudgingly and neglect it often.
6. Never study your lesson.
7. Always show your lack of interest in the lesson.
8. Appear relieved when the class is over. Act as if you have wasted your time.
9. Refuse to welcome visitors; make them feel that you belong and they don't.
10. Criticize every new idea that is suggested.
11. Dominate discussions; always insist that your opinion is right.
12. Regard the teachers of your children as upstarts and busybodies.
13. Show your distrust or disapproval of teachers when they call in your home.
14. Never sacrifice for the Sunday

school; leave that to somebody else.

189 The Oldest Company

It happened at the noonday luncheon of the local Rotary. The dishes had been cleared away, and the meeting had been called to order. After the reception of new members and the introduction of visitors, the chairman asked who of those present represented the oldest company in the community.

A young man in the back of the room hesitated a moment, then arose and said: "I believe I do, sir. I am a minister of the gospel. The company I represent was founded some 1,900 years ago. And I am happy to say that it is still flourishing." His announcement was greeted with applause, for none of those present was inclined to contradict him. He did, indeed, represent "the oldest company" in the community.

It was 19 centuries ago that the Founder of this "company" had said: "Upon this rock I will build My church, and the gates of hell shall not prevail against it" (Matt. 16:18). How true the intervening centuries have proved His startling prediction to be! On every continent and on the islands of the seven seas, from East to West, from North to South, the company of Christ's redeemed have carried the message of salvation.

It was that "company" that the young minister represented—indeed, the oldest, grandest, and the largest to be represented at the meeting, a "company" that you can belong to by simple faith in Christ the Savior. We are "fellow" citizens with the saints and of the household of God, and are built upon the foundation of the apostles and prophets, Jesus Christ Himself being the chief Cornerstone (Eph. 2:19, 20).

190 Fishing and Wishing

While some are wishing for the church to somehow grow, others are preparing themselves to be instruments of God in church growth as "fishers of men" (Mark 1:17).

191 From My Heart

"It is written, 'My House is the house of prayer, but you have made it a den of robbers' " (Luke 19:46).

The week preceding Jesus' crucifixion is one of the busiest recorded in Scripture. The reason would seem to be that Jesus knew His time was drawing near. For this reason, everything He did was for a purpose—from the riding on the donkey to the cursing of the fig tree; from the breaking of the bread to the cleansing of the temple.

The Temple of Jerusalem was a major attraction for visitors. The temple was also, unfortunately, a major place of business. The merchants sanctioned by the temple abused their business privileges. They also used special temple currency which was exchanged at unfair rates. However, this was only a small part of what upset Jesus.

The temple was divided into several courtyards. The outermost courtyard was the one designated for the Gentiles. They could not go any further into the temple, so that was their place for prayer.

Here there was buying and selling, hordes of people talking, and animals all over the place, which made it hard to focus on fellowship with their heavenly Father. Not only that, but God was being robbed, too.

Today we face a similar problem in our churches. They have become social centers where we come to catch up on the latest gossip or to be seen by the masses. And when we casually approach worship, we hinder someone else in the process. They are hurt by our gossip or they can't focus on God because of our distraction.

Now let's take it the next step toward personal application. Is my body the "temple of the Holy Spirit?" Everything I do with my body, I do it to God's temple. Am I robbing Him or is my body truly a house of prayer?

Dear Jesus, Come examine your temple and cleanse me of **all** that distracts me from You. Amen.

192 Mystery Doesn't Bother Us in the Dining Room

Did you ever raise a radish? You put a small black seed into the black soil, and in a little while you return to the garden and find the full grown radish. The top is green, the body white and almost transparent, and the skin a delicate red or pink. What mysterious power reaches out and gathers from the ground the particles which give it form and size and flavor? Whose is the invisible brush that transfers to the root, growing in darkness, the hues of the summer sunset? If we were to refuse to eat anything until we could understand the mystery of its creation, we would die of starvation—but mystery, it seems, never bothers us in the dining room; it is only in the church that it causes us to hesitate.

193 Remedy for a Prune Face

Under a caption in the *Detroit Free Press* appeared a new prescription for retaining beauty. It continued with the following: "Ladies, do you want to stay young? Then join a church choir. Women who sing stay younger looking. A singer's cheek muscles are so well developed by exercise that her face will not wrinkle nearly so soon as the non-singer."

This is the article we have been waiting for. Now women and men, if you do not want to look like a prune, *join the choir!*

194 Why Sit Near the Front?

There is a tendency to "spread out" and leave vacant pews in the front of the auditorium. I have come to the conclusion that you will never be motivated to sit toward the front until you convince yourself of the value of doing so. Here are some of the reasons for sitting up front that you might consider.

1. *Because it is considerate of other people*. People who come in

late, especially visitors, want to be seated as quickly as possible. If they have to walk to the front of the auditorium to find a seat it is quite embarrassing.

2. *There are fewer distractions during worship.* By sitting toward the front, I avoid a lot of distractions that disrupt my concentration during worship. I do not see the latecomers filing in, nor the darling baby perched on mother's shoulder. My mind is clear to marvel at the cross of Christ during the Lord's Supper and to sing with "understanding!"

3. *The singing is more enjoyable.* Sitting up front means that all the voices are pointed in your direction. You are surrounded by the sound of harmonious voices singing praise to God. I am stirred to sing more enthusiastically myself.

4. *The preaching is better.* I am serious. You miss a lot in the back of the auditorium. The expression on the face of the speaker (and the song leader) adds depth to the message being communicated. I feel more a part of the message, as if the speaker were talking directly to me.

5. *It makes a positive statement about my interest and involvement in what is happening.* Question: When you buy a ticket to a concert, theater or a sporting event, do you ask for the seat farthest away? When visitors see rows of empty pews at the front, what impression does that make on them as to our involvement in worship and our excitement about the Lord?

195 Making Simple Things Hard

We are great planners. We like to spend many hours drawing up complex organization charts, carefully constructed diagrams, and in-depth plans for building the church. Most of these never come to fruition. Many are just "pipe dreams."

Would you be interested in a simple, yet profound, plan that will help you build the church? Listen to the simple formula for a growing church set out by Mack R. Douglas in his book, *How To Make A Habit of Succeeding:*

1. Set a Goal. That's logical. You can never know if you've arrived at the place you wanted to go unless you first had your target pinpointed. Right?

2. Get a Plan. Planning is drawing a map as to how you are going to reach your goal. Ever have someone try to tell you how to get to someplace and have them say, "Get me a piece of paper." He draws you a map that tells you how to get from where you are to where you want to be. That's what we mean by planning.

3. Go to Work. Somebody always has to foul up a good idea. This is our biggest stumbling block. We've got lots of goal setters and planners, but are short on workers. But this is where the "rubber meets the road." No church is going to grow unless we've got people working! Jesus felt this pain during his ministry, "The harvest is plentiful, but the workers are few"

(Matt. 9:37). Douglas then adds this fourth point: "Don't be discouraged by anything or anybody."

196 Some Don'ts for Church Attenders

Don't visit: worship.

Don't hurry away: speak and be spoken to.

Don't dodge the preacher: show yourself friendly.

Don't dodge the collection plate: contribute what you are able.

Don't sit in the end of the pew: move over.

Don't stare blankly while others sing: join in.

Don't wait for an introduction: introduce yourself.

Don't criticize: remember your own frailties.

Don't monopolize your hymn book: be neighborly.

Don't stay away from church because you have company: bring them with you.

Don't stay away from church because the church is not perfect: how lonely you would feel in a perfect church.

197 Is the Church Costing Too Much?

On June 2, 1940, a little girl was born. She cost money from the moment she was born. As she grew from babyhood to girlhood, she cost even more. Her dresses and shoes were more expensive as well as the doctor through all those childhood diseases. She was even more expensive during her school and teen years. She needed long dresses to go to parties. When she went to college, it was discovered that all college expenses are not listed in the catalog. Then after graduation she fell in love and married. She had a church wedding, and that, too, cost a lot of money.

Then, five months after her marriage she suddenly sickened and within a week she was dead. She has not cost a penny since the day the parents walked away from her grave.

As long as the church is alive she will cost money, and the more alive a church is, the more money she will cost. Only a dead church, like a dead child, is no longer expensive!

198 What Do You Get Out of Church?

Have you heard the story of Jim Smith and Ron Jones? Jim went to church one Sunday morning. He heard the organist miss a note, and he winced. He saw a teen talking when everyone else was praying. He felt certain the usher was watching to see what he put in the offering plate, and it made him boil. Five times, by actual count, he caught the preacher in slip-of-the-tongue mistakes. During the invitation, he slipped out the side door, all the while muttering to himself, "What a waste of time!"

Ron went to church, also. He heard the pianist play an arrangement of "A Mighty Fortress Is Our God," and he was stirred to worship by the majesty of it. A special missions offering was received, and he was glad his church was doing what they could for people around the world. He especially appreciated the sermon that Sunday; it really spoke to a need in his life. He thought, as he shook the preacher's hand and left, "How can anyone come here and not feel the presence of the Lord?"

Both men were in the same church the same day. Each found what he was looking for. It has been said that churches and banks are much alike in one respect: "What one gets out is, for the most part, dependent upon what one puts in."

199 A Church Garden

Three Rows of Squash
1. Squash indifference.
2. Squash criticism.
3. Squash gossip.

Four Rows of Turnips
1. Turn up for meetings.
2. Turn up with a smile.
3. Turn up with a visitor.
4. Turn up with a Bible.

Five Rows of Lettuce
1. Let us love one another.
2. Let us welcome strangers.
3. Let us be faithful in duty.
4. Let us give liberally.

200 Make Church Your Starting Place

A traveler stopped in a small town and asked of the people, "What is this place noted for?" The reply from the people was, "This is a very important place. It is the starting place for any place you want to go.

You can start from here and go anywhere you wish."

What is so important about this church? Your home? Your class? You can start from there and go any place you wish to be. You can go to the town of forgiveness, the mountain of faith, the island of eternity, the community of friendliness. The church is important because you can start there and go anywhere you wish.

201 Flying Together

Have you ever wondered why the Canadian geese fly only in the V formation? For years specialists in aerodynamics wondered the same thing.

Two engineers calibrated in a wind tunnel what happens in such a V formation. Each goose, in flapping his wings, creates an upward lift for the goose that follows. When all the geese do their part in the V formation, the whole flock has a 71 percent greater flying range than if each bird flew alone. Each depends upon the other to get to its destination.

Something else—When a goose begins to lag behind, the others "honk" it back into place.

Now, let us learn from God's animal creation. The church needs to fly in a spiritual V formation, "honking" one another into steadfastness. And it must be at least 71 percent easier to live the faithful Christian life flying with the flock as opposed to going it alone. "Let us consider one another, to provoke unto love and to good works" (Heb. 10:24).

202 Someone Else

The church was bowed in grief this week to learn that one of our most valuable members, Someone Else, passed away. This death creates a vacancy that will be difficult to fill. Someone Else has been with us for many years. During all these years, he did far more than a normal person's share of the work. Whenever leadership was mentioned, this wonderful person was looked to for inspiration as well as results.

Whenever there was a job to do, a class to teach, or a meeting to attend—one name was on everyone's list: "Let Someone Else do it."

Someone Else was also among the largest givers of the church. Whenever there was a financial need, everyone just assumed that Someone Else would make up the difference.

This beloved church member was a wonderful person, sometimes appearing superhuman; but a person can only do so much. Everyone expected too much of Someone Else.

Now Someone Else is gone. Who will pitch in to do the things that Someone Else has done? If you are asked to take a job in church, we hope you won't reply, "Let Someone Else do it." Now we need you to pick up where Someone Else left off.

203 One by One

A young man, walking along the beach at dawn, noticed an old man ahead of him picking up starfish and flinging them into the sea. Catching up with the man, the youth asked what he was doing. The answer was that the stranded starfish would die if left until the morning sun.

"But the beach goes on for miles, and there are millions of starfish," countered the young man. "How can your effort make any difference?"

The old man looked at the starfish in his hand, and then threw it to safety in the waves. "It makes a big difference to this one," he said.

The attitude of many, in today's churches, is, "since we cannot completely deal with the problem, we will not do anything."

204 Even God Cannot Get Into Some Churches

For more than a year a little old charwoman who lived on the wrong side of the tracks had been trying to join a fashionable downtown church. The preacher was not eager to have a seedy looking person in faded, out-of-style clothes sitting in a pew next to his rich members. When she called for the fifth time to discuss membership, he put her off for the fifth time.

"I tell you what," said he unctuously, "you just go home tonight and have a talk with God about it. Later you can tell me what He said."

The poor woman went on her way. Weeks moved into months, and the preacher saw no more of her, and his conscience did hurt a little. Then one day he encountered her scrubbing floors in an office building, and felt impelled to inquire, "Did you have your little talk with God, Mrs. Washington?" he asked.

"Oh, my, yes," she said, "I talked with God, as you said."

"Ah, and what answer did He give you?

"Well, preacher," she said, pushing back a wisp of stringy hair with a sudsy hand, "God said for me not to get discouraged, but to keep trying. He said that He himself had been trying to get into your church for 20 years, with no more success than I have had."

205 How Far Is God From Your Church?

A stranger who once visited a church where the service proved to be formal, prayed so loudly, the usher bent over him and whispered, "You don't have to pray so loud—God is not deaf!"

In response, the stranger whispered softly to himself, "God isn't deaf, but He is a long way from this place."

206 This Is My Church

It is composed of people just like me.
    It will be friendly if I am.
It will do a great work if I work.
    It will make generous gifts to many causes if I am generous.
It will bring others into its fellowship if I bring them.
    Its seats will be filled if I fill them.
It will be a church of loyalty and love, of faith and service.

If I who make it what it is, am filled with these,
Therefore, with God's help, I dedicate myself to the task of being
All these things I want my Church to be.

207 Dusted or Cleansed

He was only a boy of four, so there was nothing unusual about the fact that he did not like soap and water. One day his mother, endeavoring to reason with him, said, "But surely you want to be clean, don't you?" "Yes," the boy replied through his tears, "but can't you just dust me off?"

This is amusing when coming from a boy of four, but pathetic when grownups are content with a once-a-week spiritual dusting. (And some only let the duster be applied a few times a year.) The inner filth goes undisturbed in their lives and they seem content to have it so.

208 What God Can Do, and Does

Someone has estimated that the average member of the church has heard 6,000 sermons, 8,000 congregational songs and saved *zero* sinners! Here is the way the problem stacks up:

200 total membership
20   too old to work
180 left to work, but . . .
18   too timid to accept much responsibility
162 left to work, but . . .
12   work out of town or away for school
150 left to work, but . . .

25 work long hours six or seven days a week

125 left to work, but . . .

20 tied down with children

105 left to work, but . . .

20 handicapped by poor health, aches and pains

85 left to work, but . . .

35 are unfaithful—do not attend—indifferent

30 left to work, but . . .

20 attend, but refuse to work

10 left to work, but . . .

8 are very tired and ask to be relieved

2 left to work. You and I . . . But I'm too busy with other things, so you do the work.

209 The Church

The church is never a place but always a people; never a fold but always a flock; never a sacred building, but always a believing assembly. The church is we who pray, not where we pray. A structure of bricks or marble can no more be a church than one's clothes of serge or satin can be he. There is in this world nothing sacred but man, no sanctuary of God but the soul.

210 Uninvolved Church Members

Someone once called a preacher to say he wanted to place church membership. But, he went on to explain that he did not want to worship every week, study the Bible, visit the sick, or serve as a leader or teacher.

The minister commended him for his desire to be a member, but

told him the church he sought was located in another section of town. The man took the directions and hung up.

When he arrived at that address, the man came face to face with the logical result of his own apathetic attitude. There stood an abandoned church building boarded up and ready for demolition.

211 The Church Is a Trading Post

During the century of westward migration in America, the trading post was a familiar landmark in every frontier town. To the trading post came the hunters, trappers, miners, and homesteaders with such things as furs and gold, and these they traded for things they needed more—food, tools, weapons, clothing.

In a very real way, the church is a kind of trading post. Here some things may be put down and left, and others may be picked up and taken. We may bring our cares and fears, our sins and guilt, and we may take forgiveness, joy and peace.

212 Can a Person Be a Christian Without Joining the Church?

Yes, but it is like a soldier without an army; a student who will not attend school, a salesman without a customer, a sailor without a ship, a bee without a hive, an author without a reader, or a baseball player without a team.

These situations might exist, but they would not be very satisfactory.

213 They Won't Miss Me!

Try to imagine how unattractive our church building would be if bricks in the wall were missing. Not only would it be unattractive, but it would also be weakening to the rest of the structure. If our building were missing bricks, we would get busy and correct that situation immediately.

Simon Peter tells us that the Lord's spiritual house (the church) is made up of "lively stones." But often we observe numerous stones missing from the worship assembly. The result is a most unattractive and weakened structure.

Even as every brick in our church building is needed, so every living stone in the spiritual house is needed. How unfortunate when some member has the idea, "I'm only one; I won't be missed!" The Bible teaches that every person must bear his own burden. Our daily prayer should be, "Lord, help me always be in my place carrying my share of the load."

214 I Am Your Church

I am your church. Make of me what you will, I shall reflect you as clearly as a mirror. If outwardly my appearance is pleasing and inviting, it is because you made me so. If within my spiritual atmosphere is kindly, yet earnest; reverent, yet friendly; worshipful, yet sincere; sympathetic, yet strong; divine, yet humanly expressed; it is but the manifestation of the spirit of those who constitute my membership.

But if you should, by chance, find me a bit cold and dull, I beg of you not to condemn me, for I show forth the only kind of life I shall receive from you. I have no life or spirit apart from you.

Of this may you always be assured: I will respond instantly to your every wish practically expressed, for I am the reflected image of your own soul. Make of me what you will.

215 A Shining Light

In the Alps in Switzerland nestles an obscure village, with a castle and a church of rough, hewn stone, reached by worn steps up the mountainside. The peculiar thing about this church is that it has not a lighting system nor has ever had one.

A traveler there heard a church bell ringing and saw folks coming out of the narrow streets, each bearing a quaint little bronze lamp filled with oil and having a wick. She approached a worshiper and said, "Please, I am a stranger here, will you tell me why you carry a lamp to church?"

The woman replied, "Why, yes, I would be happy to. Years ago a duke lived in that castle. He built the church, endowed it, and asked that each worshiper bring his own lamp." The traveler replied, "I should think that would keep folks from attending the evening services."

"Oh, no, it works just the other way. It is called The Church of the

Lighted Lamps. Everybody that goes makes it a little brighter and when anybody is tempted to stay at home or go somewhere else, he just remembers that the dear old church needs everybody's lamp, and if your lamp isn't there, there is so much less light."

216 Not Good If Detached

Did you ever notice on a railroad ticket, or on many coupons of various nature, "Not good if detached?" The coupon was made of the same material as the rest of the ticket, was printed with the same ink, on the same press, and was kept in the same office and used by the same company. But it was not good if detached. Its usefulness, its ability to take you places, was dependent upon its relation to the rest of the ticket.

Of how much worth is a church member detached from the rest? How much fruit can a branch bear detached from the vine? How good is your hand when it is detached from your body? A Christian is one who stays with the rest of the church. He cannot serve apart from it. You may be a foot, a hand, or an eye of the body of Christ, but you are not worth much to yourself or to anyone else separated from the church, which is His body. Did you ever notice just how quickly a banana gets skinned after it leaves the bunch? So remember: "Forsaking not the assembling of yourselves together. . . ." (Heb. 10:25).

217 Gates and Gatekeepers

The strongest walls are useless if the gates are weak or if the gatekeepers are careless or disloyal. The Great Wall of China was penetrated by enemies at least three times, and each time the guards were bribed. The church desperately needs strong gates and loyal gatekeepers.

Commitment

218 Total Commitment

The difference in a contribution and total commitment is usually the difference in failure and success.

A chicken and a hog were walking past a church building one day when they noticed the Sunday morning sermon posted on the outside bulletin board, "Helping the Poor." They walked a ways when the chicken suddenly came across with a suggestion. "Say, Brother Hog, why don't we give all the poor people a nice breakfast of ham and eggs?" The hog thought a moment and replied, "That's all right for you to say because for you it is only a contribution, but for me, it's total commitment!"

Jesus succeeded in His mission because He was totally committed to the task before Him. He was willing to give up everything, even His life, for the cause He believed in. No one really succeeds in life until he reaches the point that he is willing to lay down his life. Jesus said, "Except a corn of wheat fall into the ground and die, it abideth alone." Disraeli said, "Nothing can resist a will that will stake even existence for its fulfillment!"

219 Leaving the Ground

There is no such thing as partial commitment. When the pilot of a giant airliner is speeding down the runway, there is a certain point where he cannot decide to remain on the ground. When he crosses that line, he is committed to the air, or the plane crashes disastrously. That pilot cannot change his mind when the plane is two-thirds of the way down the runway.

Unfortunately, our churches are filled with members who "have never left the ground." They have been sitting there for years and years gunning their engines.

220 True Revival

We hear much about revival these days, but the heart of revival is the Lordship of Christ. A mere emotional upheaval, a spurt of religious excitement, is not revival. When Christians become convicted of rebellion against the rule of Christ in their lives, confess their sins, renounce self, take the cross and let Jesus have the first and last word in everything, that is revival, by whatever name you call it.

221 Motivated by Conviction

Jonathan Edwards inaugurated the great spiritual awakening in colonial America because he was possessed by a conviction. "Resolved that all men should live to the glory of God," he wrote in his diary at the age of nineteen. Then he added, "Resolved, second, that whether others do this or not, I will." Jonathan Edwards was possessed by a great conviction.

William Booth's marvelous work with the Salvation Army was motivated by a conviction. He wrote in the autograph album of King Edward VII these words, "Some men's ambition is art, some men's ambition is fame, some men's ambition is gold. My ambition is the souls of men."

The same truth appears in the lives of men and women in every field. One of today's most prolific writers is W. Phillip Keller. His books on faith as seen through the eyes of nature have been phenomenally successful, particularly *A Shepherd Looks at Psalm 23*. In his autobiography, Keller describes the beginning of his writing career. His desire to write motivated him to use his space time to produce a book manuscript. He worked on it for hundreds of hours. He explained, "I would actually write and rewrite steadily for the next eleven years of my life before a single line was ever accepted for publication." Why did he do it? Because of a conviction that drove him.

Few have earned universal acclaim like Paderweski, whose name is synonymous with excellence on the piano. He would often play a bar of music forty or fifty times before a performance to get it right. After playing before Queen Victoria, he received this word of praise, "Mr. Paderewski, you are a genius." Paderewski responded, "That may be, but before I was a genius, I was a drudge." Why such discipline? Because of the conviction which controlled him. —*Brian L. Harbour*

222 Sure-Footed

As a young man in Europe, Donald Grey Barnhouse did considerable mountain climbing in the Swiss Alps and in the more dangerous and difficult French Alps. Roped together with other young men, he scaled many a peak; his snapshot book records moments of difficulty and peril that later made him wish to restrain others who might venture into similar places. The first time he went out with a young Frenchman, son of a pastor, and a young Swiss bank clerk, they gave him sound advice. "You have two hands and two feet," they said, "and that makes four. Always be sure that three out of the four are firmly on the rock. It is the only rule of safety."

This advice is also the rule of spiritual safety in our Christian life. In one of the Psalms, David told of slipping feet. He had been looking at men and their circumstances. He saw the righteous suffering and the wicked flourishing, and he could not understand; he was, in fact, dismayed. He had looked at men and their doings instead of looking at God. It is as dangerous to take your eyes from the Lord in spiritual things as it is to take your feet from the rock in mountain climbing.

223 The Souls of Men

David Brainerd had such an intense compassion for souls, and was so concerned for their salvation, that he said, "I cared not where or how I lived, or what hardships I went through, so that I could but gain souls for Christ. While I was asleep, I dreamed of these things, and when I awoke, the first thing I thought of was this great work. All my desire was for the conversion of the heathen, and all my hope was in God."

224 When Will Revival Start?

Gypsy Smith was once asked how to start a revival. He answered, "Go home, lock yourself in your room and kneel down in the middle of your floor. Draw a chalk mark all around yourself and ask God to start the revival inside that chalk mark. When he has answered your prayer, the revival will be on." Why not covenant with God to draw that private circle?

225 Baptism Identifies the Believer

Jesus says to identify new believers with God through baptism. Baptism in the Bible is used to mean identification (1 Cor. 10:1, 2; Rom. 6:3, 4). The relationship between water baptism and spiritual baptism is similar to the relationship of a wedding to a wedding ring. The ring doesn't marry you, but it clearly identifies the wearer as one who is married. The ring identifies one who has made a total, lifelong commitment to another person.

Baptism, then, identifies us with Christ's death on the cross and His resurrection into new life. This identification is not only with Christ but also in the name of the Father and Holy Spirit. This is significant because it shows that our lives are to be totally encompassed by the Triune God.

226 Just Drifting!

The Book of Hebrews declares that "we ought to give the more earnest heed to the things which we have heard, lest at any time we should let them slip" (Heb. 2:1). Another way of translating the final phrase of this verse is, "lest we drift away."

Nothing in the world is easier than drifting. No person drifts upstream, only downstream. It is so easy. All you do is sit back and relax and let the boat go. You are soon lulled into a lazy stupor, not caring where you go. You may not even be aware you are drifting until it is too late and the boat is on the rocks. Satan is very wise. He seldom urges a Christian to leave the church or to give up his faith in the Lord. Instead he causes us to relax, rest on the oars, and drift along in the Christian life.

All around us are Christians who have drifted into a state of coldness and indifference. They have stopped caring about others who need to hear the message of God's saving grace.

Are you drifting? Wake up now! Grab the oars and pull. Your active concern is needed as we seek to lead others to find Christ and His will for their lives.

227 Sacrifice

The story of Polycarp, Smyrna's bishop who studied under the Apostle John, comes to mind. Adamantly committed to the saving lordship of Jesus, which left no room for bowing to the empire, Polycarp was arrested and sentenced to death. Actually, he was given a chance to step out of the fire. The Roman proconsul gave Polycarp the choice of cursing the name of Jesus and worshiping Caesar to save his skin or continue embracing Jesus to his death. "Swear," said the proconsul, "and I will set you at liberty. Reproach Christ." Polycarp replied, "Eighty and six years have I served Him, and He has done me no wrong. How can I blaspheme my King who saved me?" After the proconsul threatened him again with the specter of burning at the stake, Polycarp added, "You threaten me with fire which awaits the wicked in judgment to come and in everlasting punishment. Why are you waiting? Come, do what you will." As they approached him and prepared to tie him to the stake to be burned, he shouted, "Leave me as I am, for He who gives me power to endure the fire, will grant me to remain in the flames unmoved even without the security you will give by the nails." Loosely bound, with flames flashing about him, Polycarp prayed, "O Lord God Almighty, Father of Thy beloved Child, Jesus Christ . . . I bless Thee that Thou has granted unto me this day and hour, that I may share, among the number of the martyrs, in the cup of Thy Christ, for the resurrection to eternal life." And so on February 23, A.D. 155, Polycarp paid the price. Then he went to heaven. The pay off is worth the price.

Then there was Patrick Hamilton who studied under Martin Luther in Wittenberg. He literally ignited the Reformation in Scotland. As he burned at the stake in 1527, he said, "As to my confession, I will not deny it for awe of your fire, for my confession and belief is in Jesus Christ . . . I will rather be content that my body burn in this fire for confession of my faith in Christ than have my soul burn in the fire of hell for denying the same."

228 Ending and Beginning

Revelation 1:8 reads, "I am the Alpha and the Omega, the beginning and the ending, saith the Lord."

Have you ever given thought to how many things about us are constantly ending and beginning? For example, today will end with the beginning of night and night will end with the beginning of tomorrow. Our Lord is both the beginning and ending of everything! Second Corinthians 5:17 speaks to us about some endings and beginnings within our own lives: "Therefore if any man be in Christ, he is a new creature, old things are passing away, and all things are becoming new."

For the believer, there is a constant change going on. Life is being re-shaped. It begins in a new-birth experience and as we grow in the Lord, this new life constantly changes, as we are reshaped into the image of Jesus Christ by the Holy Spirit dwelling within us.

229 Looking at the Goal

The snow covered the ground, and three young boys were playing in it. A man said to them, "Would you like to try to race, with the promise of a prize for the winner?"

The boys agreed, and the man told them that his race was to be different. "I will go to the other side of the field," he said, "and when I give you the signal, you will start to run. The one whose footsteps are the straightest in the snow will be the winner."

As the race commenced, the first boy began looking at his feet to see if his steps were straight. The second lad kept looking at his companions to see what they were doing; but the third boy just ran on with his eyes fixed on the man on the other side of the field.

The third boy was the winner, for his footsteps were straight in the snow. He had kept his eyes on the goal ahead of him.

A long time ago, another man using similar words taught the same principle. It was Paul who said, "Forgetting what is behind and straining toward what is ahead, I press on toward the goal to win the prize for which God has called me heavenward in Christ Jesus" (Phil. 3:13, 14).

230 Soaring Like Eagles

For thousands of years the eagle has been respected for its grandeur. When you observe its flight, its great wing span, and the power of its claws, it is inspiring, to say the least. In Proverbs 30:18, 19, Solomon says, "There be three things which are too wonderful for me, yea, four which I know not. The way of an eagle in the air; the way of a serpent upon a rock; the way of a ship in the mist of the sea; and the way of a man with a maid." The eagle does not travel in flocks nor do they conduct themselves irresponsibly. Strong of heart and solitary, they represent qualities we admire.

The eagle mates for life and returns each year to the same nest, making necessary repairs and additions. He takes his role to provide for his family and protect them from danger, and teaches the little eaglets to fly. With all this: responsibility, liberty, beauty, stability, and a lot more admirable traits of the eagle's makeup and such qualities, we agree with Solomon's view that it is nothing short of wonderful. The eagle is committed to that which he is destined to do, without concern for what is below him.

I would that we all were committed to our obligation of teaching and preaching the gospel as the eagle is committed to soaring in the heavens of God. If we could soar as the eagle without regards to the little petty issues of this life and do those things Jesus would have us to, we could have so much rest and contentment in doing those things that are required. We only have a few years to spend on this little planet, few are the ones who decide to ignore the average and fight against the pull of the mediocre magnet. Let's face it. It's tough! As the motto goes, "It's hard to soar like an eagle when I'm surrounded by so many turkeys." "Teach us to number our days and recognize how few they are; help us to spread them as we should" (Ps. 90:12).

231 Proof of Sacrifice

When I speak of sacrificial giving, I mean giving that is measured and motivated by the cross of Christ. It is nothing less than giving at its best.

Perhaps a story from the past will illustrate what I mean. Early in the nineteenth century the king of Prussia, Frederick William III, found himself in great trouble. He was carrying on an expensive war; he was endeavoring to strengthen his country and make a great nation of the Prussian people. But he did not have enough money to accomplish his plans. He could not disappoint his people, and to capitulate to the enemy would be unthinkable.

After careful reflection he decided to approach the women of Prussia and ask them to bring their gold and silver jewelry to be melted down and made into money for their country. He resolved, moreover, that for each gold or silver ornament he would give in exchange a bronze or iron decoration as a token of his gratitude. Each decoration would bear the inscription, "I gave gold for iron, 1813."

The response was overwhelming. And what was even more important was that these women prized their gifts from the king more highly than their former possessions. The reason, of course, is clear. The decorations were proof that they had sacrificed for their king. Indeed, it is a matter of history that it became unfashionable for women to wear jewelry. So the Order of the Iron Cross was established. Members of this order wore no ornaments, save a cross of iron for all to see.

The church today needs an army of people who are so committed to the King of Kings that sacrifice becomes a way of life! Such an army would do exploits for God. Such an army would hasten the coming and reign of "the King eternal, immortal, invisible (the) God Who alone is wise" (1 Tim. 1:17).

232 Living Proof

Can a young Marine, body shattered by the weaponry of modern warfare, rebound and turn personal defeat into personal victory?

Lt. Clebe McClary recounts his courageous story of rebuilding his devastated life. During his tour of duty in Vietnam he suffered the loss of one eye, his left arm, and subsequently underwent 33 operations to retain usage of the remainder of his body.

Today Clebe McClary is in the service of the Lord's Army, traveling the world over, attesting to personal faith in Jesus Christ. His life shows that he genuinely embodies a personal vow which he took upon entering the Marines: "Any mission assigned will be accomplished in a superior manner, no matter what the obstacles."

233 Singleness of Heart Required

It is always fascinating to read of wholehearted human endeavor—amazing stories of total dedication. For example, the U.S. Marines conduct a supersecret sniper program in Quantico, Virginia. The school admits 25 men for an eight-week course of 16-hour days. Very few pass. To graduate, each goes on a mock mission into a well-defined area where instructors search for the sniper. If they can find him, they can fail him.

To get in range of the target, a sniper may move forward at a rate of one inch per hour. He may sit for days absolutely still, despite cold, rain, insect bites, and fear. No one gets out without singleness of heart ("School for Snipers," *U.S. News and World Report,* 21 April 1986, p. 61). We expect that kind of intensity from Olympic champions, concert pianists, doctoral candidates, and everyone else at the highest levels of human achievements.

Likewise, God expects it when we come back to Him. God deserves singleness of heart because He is God! Most of us intend to come back to God—sometime. But we fail because our intention never becomes intense.

234 To Have and to Hold

Commitment. It is a word that we seem to be hearing a lot about lately. One automobile manufacturer says that they are "committed to excellence." Professional athletes, business persons, executives, etc., are all committed to their occupations.

Recently, I read a story of commitment that touched my heart and made me think of commitment in marriage. Most married people have affirmed a commitment to their spouse that goes something like this:

". . . To have and to hold from this day forward, for better for worse, for richer for poorer, in sickness and in health, to love and to cherish until death do us part. . . ."

Robertson McQuilkan's commitment in marriage was severely challenged when his wife, Muriel, contracted Alzheimers disease. Mr. McQuilkan was president of a Bible college and seminary when he was faced with a mountainous decision. He could not continue as president and take appropriate care of his wife who at this point could only speak in phrases and words and was prone to irrational behavior. She was afraid when she was not with her husband. Even his most trusted and godly friends advised him to put his wife in an institution for the sake of his ministry. After all, how could he retire when things were going so well and he was only 57 years old?

When the time came, McQuilkan's decision was firm. It took no great calculation. It was a matter of integrity. He commented, "Had I not promised, 42 years before 'in sickness and in health . . . till death do us part'?" Later he would go on to write of the joys and blessings he had received as a result of the special time spent with Muriel.

Commitment is a foundation for successful Christian living. The Lord is going to stand behind His promises—He is committed to what He has said and done. For the Christian there can be nothing less. Commitment is an absolute necessity.

A photographer tells of a young man who wanted duplicate copies of his girlfriend's picture. The photographer noticed the following inscription on the back of the portrait, "My dearest Tom, I love you with all my heart. I love you more and more each day. I will love you forever and ever. I am yours for all eternity." Signed, Dianne. "P.S. If we ever break up, I want this picture back."

We who have been saved have professed our love for Christ and for others. We belong to Christ. There can be no P.S. in our life given to God. We can never break up with Him. We are His. We belong to Him—forever.

235 What Is the Lord's Surname for You?

"He surnamed . . . he surnamed" (Mark 3:16, 17).

This is a very suggestive story. To three of His twelve Apostles He gave surnames. Perhaps He did the same for all. We do not know. The action in regard to these three is illustrative. Perhaps He even does the same for His own. If so, one wonders how He is surnaming us. The idea is purely speculative, but it is speculation on a profitable level, especially in the light of these revelations.

"Simon He surnamed Rock." This Simon was impulsive, restless, inconsistent, lacking cohesion. Yet He surnamed him Rock. The name was an indication of his unrealized natural capacities; and of the Lord's ability to realize them. The sons of Zebedee, James and John, He surnamed Sons of Thunder. They were men of gentle, filial nature, quiet men, content to abide at home in the service of their father. Yet He surnamed them Sons of Thunder; men of authority and power. The principle was the same. In James was the capacity to be so loyal to a Master and a cause as to die for them. In John was the mystic power which would make him a seer, and an interpreter of the great things of life. The Lord was able to bring these things to realization, and to employ them for His own glory in cooperation with His service.

And so again we wonder: what is He naming us? The consideration is for the hour of lonely communion with Him. In such an hour we shall discover that His surnaming is ever based upon two things; first, our capacities as the result of our first birth; and secondly, His power to realize those capacities. We shall find, moreover, that His power becomes operative when we are wholly yielded to Him.

236 A Hymn of Marriage

The question is asked, "Is there anything more beautiful in life than a boy and girl clasping clean hands and pure hearts in the path of marriage?" And the answer is given, "Yes—there is a more beautiful thing; it is the spectacle of an old man and an old woman finishing their journey together on that path. Their hands are gnarled but still clasped; their faces are seamed but still radiant; their hearts are tired and bowed down but still strong. They have proved the happiness of marriage and have vindicated it from the jeers of cynics."

237 Is This You?

Late one December, an elementary school principal said to his teachers: "Let's all write our New Year's Resolutions about how we can be better teachers, and I'll put them on the staff bulletin board. In that way, we can be mutually supportive in our efforts to keep those resolutions." The teachers agreed, and when the resolutions were posted, they all crowded around the bulletin board to read them. One of the young teachers in the group suddenly went into a fit of anger. She said, "He didn't put up my resolution. It was one of the first ones in. He doesn't care about me. That just shows what it's like around here." On and on she ranted and raved. The principal, who overheard this from his office was mortified. He hadn't meant to exclude her resolution. Quickly rummaging through the papers on his desk, he found it and immediately went to the bulletin board and tacked it up. The resolution read: "I resolve not to let little things upset me anymore." Resolution, but no commitment!

238 Steadfastness in View of Suffering

Jesus "steadfastly set his face to go to Jerusalem" (Luke 9:51, 53). He had a definite destination, and He knew what it held for Him. It meant Jerusalem with its sorrow, Gethsemane with its travail, the judgment hall with its injustice and shame, the cross with its anguish, and even the hiding of the Father's face. For Jesus there was no royal road to the throne of Israel. For Him the only path lay by Jerusalem and Calvary. It was a long and weary road, but Jesus took every step. He was tempted to turn aside from His goal, to be sure, and He was tempted in His sufferings. His friends wished to draw Him aside from His sufferings. Peter rebuked Him when He spoke of them. Satan tried to perplex Him, and His own soul trembled when the time for His crucifixion came. Yet, He knew that He had reached "the point of no return," and He proceeded in the midst of the storms of sin and doubt about Him to go toward the cross where He would be victor once and for all.

Those who have crossed the ocean have been impressed with the way the huge oceanliner keeps its bow to the sea, and, in spite of wind and wave, holds to its course. No sound is more reassuring than the steady throb of the huge engine. In looking at Christ's life, one thing that impresses us is His steadiness. He was never shifting, or even driven about. The throb of His life was constant and perfect.

239 Straddling the Fence

When I was in grade school, my family visited some friends who owned a farm in Kentucky. After we were there several days, I jumped at the chance to ride their horse, Prince. However, having never ridden a horse before, and realizing the horse was much larger than he looked from a distance, I proceeded cautiously.

Being an intelligent fourth grader, I decided to play it safe by climbing a wooden fence next to where the horse was standing and mount him from there. With one foot on the left side of the top fence rail, I threw the other leg over the horse who was on the right side. Immediately the horse began to sidle slowly away from the fence. Now I

hadn't planned on that, and I needed to make a hasty decision. You see, I wanted both to ride the horse and to hold on to the security of the fence. Needless to say, after my legs had stretched as far as they would go, I fell face down on the ground.

You would think such an experience would teach one a lesson. Yet in the years that followed, I would still find myself trying to "straddle the fence." And the results would always be the same as that first experience. Only the fence wasn't on the farm in Kentucky—it was the fence between commitment to Christ and the world. And believe me, the falls from this fence hurt a lot more. Save yourself a lot of pain—don't try to straddle the fence.

240 The Greatest Ability

There are great abilities that people acquire, cultivate and demonstrate. In the service of God there is one ability that is the greatest ability of all. What is it? Is it sociability, compatibility, accountability, adaptability, or reliability?

The greatest ability is *availability*. If we are not available to God, no matter what other kind of ability we have, it is no good. Ability without *availability* is a liability.

What does availability mean? It means to place one's self totally, absolutely, completely at God's disposal for Him to do anything and everything He wants to do in us, through us, with us, for us, when He chooses. Anything less than that is putting restrictions on God and writing fine print in your commitment contract to Jesus Christ.

241 Allegiance Confirmed

When Queen Victoria of England reigned as Empress of India, the Maharajah of Punjab was a little boy. To show his allegiance, he sent her a magnificent diamond. It became one of the crown jewels and was safely kept in the Tower of London. When he became a man, he went to London to pay his respects to the Queen. The young man asked the Queen if he could see the diamond. The precious jewel was brought in and presented before the Indian prince. Then, taking the diamond and kneeling before the Queen, he said with deep emotion, "Madam, I gave you this jewel when I was too young to know what I was doing. I want to give it again, in the fullness of my strength, with all my heart, and affection, and gratitude, now and forever, fully realizing all that I do."

242 Wanted . . . Men!

There is a story to the effect that a certain society in South Africa once wrote to David Livingston, "Have you found a good road to where you are? If so, we want to know how to send other men to join you."

Livingston replied, "If you have men who will come ONLY if they know there is a good road, *I don't want them*. I want men who will come even if there is *no* road at all."

243 The Go of the Great Commission

When our Lord said "go," He did not ask us to sit down and evaluate what the chances were that we would return. Two Coast Guardsmen were preparing to engage in a rescue attempt of two fishermen lost in a storm. Someone shouted out to them: "Don't go out there. You may never get back." One of the guardsmen replied, "We don't have to get back, but we have to go."

244 One-Legged Missionary

A one-legged school teacher from Scotland came to J. Hudson Taylor to offer himself for service in China.

"With only one leg, why do you think of going as a missionary?" asked Taylor.

"I do not see those with two legs going," replied George Scott.

He was accepted.

245 When Obstacles Confront Us

The successful man lengthens his stride when he discovers that the signpost has deceived him; the failure looks for a place to sit down. Thomas Edison did not sit down and give up when his first efforts to find an effective filament for the carbon incandescent lamp met with failure. He lengthened his stride! He sent men to China, Japan, South America, Asia, Jamaica, Ceylon, and Burma in search of fibers and grasses to be tested in his laboratory.

Luther Burbank, the plant wizard, did not quit when obstacles blocked his way. At one time he personally conducted more than 6,000 experiments before he found the solution.

George Westinghouse was treated as a mild lunatic by most railroad executives. "Stopping a train by wind! The man's crazy!" Yet he persevered, and finally sold the airbrake idea.

James Watt built model after model of his steam engine before he got one that worked efficiently.

Every man gets on the wrong road at times. He comes down hills, rough roads, and dangerous detours. What he does when he meets these obstacles determines his destiny. The world never hears from those who look for a place to sit down and quit.

246 Yes! You Can!

As we drove up the steep, winding road in the Cave of the Winds near Colorado Springs, we came suddenly to a narrow passageway between high rock walls through which it looked as if the car could not possibly go. But facing us was a sign which said: "Yes, you can! Millions of others have!" And so, driving carefully through, we soon came to a wider roadway.

So many times we face seemingly insoluble problems and impossible situations. But we can know that God is able to open ways before us which are now hidden from our view. We may hear God's message to us: "Yes, you can! Millions of others have gone this way. Be of good cheer. Trust in the Lord and go ahead!"

Heavenly Father, when we face difficult times, help us to trust in You to show us the way through. In Jesus' name. Amen.

247 Anybody for a Walk?

Paul Rogers of Centerville, Tennessee, has done some calculating of just how far the Apostle Paul walked in his efforts to spread the gospel. According to Acts, he took three missionary journeys. The second of these alone amounted to three thousand miles, two thousand of which would have been on foot. The average daily distance of a traveler of that time was about twenty miles, with a Roman Inn being located every 20 to 25 miles along the road. These inns were unbelievably filthy, immoral, and bug-infested. Paul traveled through snowy mountain passes and spring floods. He walked through areas famous for harboring robbers and criminals. He braved wild beasts which imperiled every traveler. The travel recorded in Acts 16 alone would have covered 740 miles. That of chapter 15 would be 500 miles. And to think he was walking not for his own health, but for the spiritual well-being of others!

Compassion

248 Silent Answers

Once a young couple lost their only child, a beautiful three-year-old daughter, as a result of a freak accident. Unable to justify this tragedy with their concept of a loving God, they went to their minister for help. "Why?" they asked. "It was God's will," the preacher told them.

The couple just couldn't accept that the passing of their little daughter could somehow serve God's will, and they sought out another preacher friend. He quoted yards of Scripture, trying to give them comfort, but his verses fell on deaf ears.

Finally, the young couple turned to a frail elderly woman in their church. Surely, she could give them a reason for the child's death, but the old woman didn't utter a single word. Instead, she tenderly wrapped her arms around the heartbroken couple's shoulders, and together they cried the hurt away.

Sometimes when theological answers are not easy to the complex misfortunes of life, perhaps we just need to hush our babblings. Sometimes when answers aren't easy, our best statement is silent caring.

249 Which Was Neighbor?

A certain woman went down from Washington to Richmond and ran over a spike which punctured her tire and left her stranded by the side of the road. After raising the hood of her car and tying a scarf to her radio antenna, she locked the door handles and sat in the car, praying for the Lord to send help!

By chance, there came a limousine that way with a bumper sticker that read, "Smile, God Loves You!" When the occupants saw the stranded woman, they passed by in the far lane—without smiling.

And likewise, there came a sports car with a CB radio and a bumper sticker saying, "Honk If You Love Jesus!" The man who was driving passed by in the far lane without honking and without using his CB to tell the Highway Patrol about the woman's dilemma.

But a certain working man, as he traveled to his job, came to the spot where the woman was and, when he saw her raised hood, white scarf, and flat tire, he had compassion on her. He stopped his old beat-up pickup—which had no bumper sticker—and crossed the four-lane highway, and offered to change the tire. The woman opened the door and gave him the key to the trunk.

The man took out the spare tire, jacked up the car, removed the flat tire, and replaced it with the spare.

When he had finished, the woman tried to pay him. He refused the money, saying, "If my wife were stranded on the highway with a flat tire, I'd want some Good Samaritan to stop and help her out."

He returned to his bumper-stickerless truck, smiled, honked at her, and went his way.

Which of these three was neighbor unto her who had a flat tire?

250 When Someone Is Needier Than You

In a leper colony clothes arrived for distribution among these outcasts of life.

One little leper boy was asked what he needed most. He replied, "My hands are still good so I can mend my clothes when they need it, but there are some lepers who have no fingers, and some whose hands are so crippled or sore that they cannot use them. When their clothes get holes in them, they cannot mend them but must see the holes get bigger and bigger. I am thankful for my good hands, so please give the clothes to those who cannot mend their own. They are more needy than I."

How we need such unselfishness. We should never complain when we know that there are others who are needier than we are.

251 Tell Peter I Am Alive

The angel said, "Tell His disciples and Peter," but why "and Peter?"

He was one of the disciples. Why single him out from among all the rest? Was he any better? No, he was, if anything, a little worse. He had denied his Lord—three times and with oaths. And he was feeling very bad about it. He was cast down, heartsick, almost overwhelmed. And Jesus knew it full well, and it was just like Him to send a special word of comfort to him. It must have cheered the Apostle beyond words to be told that Christ had mentioned him especially as one to be given the news of His resurrection.

252 Little Things That Help Others

A plainly dressed woman was noticed picking up something on a poor slum street where ragged barefooted little children were accustomed to play. The policeman on the beat noticed the woman's action, and watched her very suspiciously. Several times he saw her stoop, pick up something and hide it in her apron. Finally he went up to her, and with a gruff voice demanded, "What are you carrying off in your apron?" The timid woman did not answer at first, whereupon the policeman, thinking she must have found something valuable, threatened her with arrest if she did not show him what she had in her apron. The woman opened her apron and revealed a handful of broken glass. "What do you want with that stuff?" asked the policeman. The woman replied,

"I just thought I would pick it up so the glass would not hurt the children's feet."

253 Evangelism

A secretary on the job is engulfed in problems. Her husband left her; a son is in rebellion; she can barely make ends meet. She cries out for help. We don't hear.

A fellow employee is overwhelmed by the complexity of overcoming his chronic drinking problem. He longs for a friend. We're deaf to his cries.

The owner of the gas station where we've traded for years has just lost his wife. His eyes echo his loneliness. We don't see.

A wife would love to share with us the trauma and trivia of her day—just to have a listening ear. Our ears are closed.

And as the "perfect" ending to such a self-centered day, we hurry to the church building and get our weekly door-knocking assignment as we hasten to engage a cold prospect in an ambiguous process which we have labeled evangelism.

Does that approach make sense? It seems to me it is time we acknowledged the fact that a good translation of the Great Commission has it reading: "As you are going into all the world. . . ."

You see, we are in such a hurry to "go!" that we miss the very ones whom God brings into our path—"as we are going." May God awaken us to the realization that true evangelism is loving the world the way God loves it; allowing our hearts to be broken by the things that break God's heart; acknowledging that there is no dichotomy between "evangelism" and "benevolence"— that true evangelism begins with Matthew 10:42: "And if anyone gives a cup of cold water to one of these little ones because he is my disciple, I tell you, he will certainly not lose his reward."

254 Strange Fruit

Woman's Day magazine told of a strange happening on the campus of Green Acres Elementary School near Santa Cruz, California. One year a tree on that campus began to bear strange fruit, mostly sandwiches, but sometimes a cookie, a cupcake, an apple or an orange.

It came into being through the efforts of two teachers, Sophie Farrar and Sandra Enz, who were upset at the quantities of uneaten sandwiches discarded by the children. They suggested that the unwrapped sandwiches be placed under what the children began to call the free-food tree, for students who had come without a lunch or who had lost or forgotten their lunches. The idea was very popular among the children. Some youngsters asked their mothers to pack an extra sandwich so they would have one to put under the free-food tree.

255 How Long Has It Been Since You . . .

Took the time to go see someone who lives alone?

Wrote a letter to someone who crossed your mind?

Read the Bible to someone too ill to read for themselves?

Encouraged someone who was having a hard time being a Christian?

Prayed earnestly for someone who was faltering?

Tried to have a Bible study with someone you knew was lost?

Told a teenager that you were proud of his efforts to live for the Lord?

Spent more time on your knees praying than on the telephone talking?

EVERY CHRISTIAN CAN DO SOMETHING TO ENCOURAGE SOMEONE ELSE!

256 *Make Life a Little Sweeter*

O let me shed a little light
On someone's path I pray;
I'd like to be a messenger
Of happiness today!

It may be just a phone call,
A smile, or a prayer,
Or a long neglected letter
Would lift the edge of care.

I want to spread some happiness
In what I say or do,
Make life a little sweeter
For someone else! Don't you?

Complaining

257 A Chronic Grumbler

A lady who was an incurable grumbler complained about everything and everybody. But, finally, the minister thought he had found something about which she could make no complaint: the old lady's crop of potatoes was certainly the finest for miles around. "Ah, for once you must be pleased," he said with a beaming smile as he met her in the village street. "Everyone is saying how splendid your potatoes are this year." The old lady glared at him as she answered, "They are not so bad, but where are the rotten ones for the pigs?"

258 Honker or Helper

The story was once told of a woman driver whose car stalled in traffic and she was unable to get it restarted. The fellow who was behind her, and thus unable to move, thought it necessary to constantly show his impatience by honking his horn every few seconds. Finally, the woman walked back to his car and said, "If you will go try to start my car, I'll stay here and honk your horn for you."

So many times in the church this is the case. The one who is not doing anything to help is also the one who makes the most noise complaining that nothing is happening.

259 When You Carry Your Cross, You Will Have No Room for a Chip

Lord,
You said if I want to follow you, I will need to carry my cross every day. I want to follow, Lord.

But there are days when I'm dragging my cross, making a trail for everyone to see. There are days when I'm pushing my cross, making my own path miserable and dusty. There are days when I'm sitting on my cross, trying to get comfortable and going nowhere. There are days when I'm giving my cross to somebody else, who already has one of his own.

Help me, Lord, to carry my cross on my shoulder. When it's up there, it leaves no room for a chip!

260 Why Me, Lord?

My car broke down and it cost $400 to get it fixed . . . $400 that I did not have. Why me, Lord? After all, I've been as good as most people. In fact, I've been better than most. Why are you treating me this way? Why are you punishing me this way? Then the TV went on the blink, and so did the dishwasher, and the clothes dryer, and the lawn mower, and even the iron! Why me, Lord? Besides that, why, at my age, should I still be having financial problems? Why am I not "set" financially like some others I know? Why have you denied me opportunities for fame and fortune that you have given to others? Why me, Lord?

When I find myself starting to think like this, it sometimes helps for me to ask the same questions about other aspects of my life. Lord, what have I done that's so grand that you should have blessed me with a car, a TV set, a clothes dryer, a lawn mower, and an iron? Why did you give me all these things anyway? Why me, Lord?

Lord, why did you permit me to be born in America with all its plenty? I could have been born in poverty-stricken Bangladesh instead of in rich America. Why me, Lord? Lord, why did you give me the opportunity to have a job when so many, who are as deserving as I, are without work? Why me, Lord?

Lord, why did you give me good health? Others died at my age of heart attacks or are crippled by accidents or disease. Why should I escape ill health when other religious people do not? Why me, Lord? Lord, why have you spared me from the sorrows that strike so many other families? Others, wonderful people, have lost close relatives, but I haven't. Why me, Lord?

When I think of all the ways the Lord has blessed me, though I don't deserve it, I wonder how I could possibly complain about the relatively insignificant things that go wrong in my life from time to time. If I could only learn to count my blessings!

261 The Sympathetic Savior

Some years ago a man living in Wales had the misfortune of being involved in a mining accident which necessitated the amputation of his right leg. After a period in the hospital, he went to a prosthesis maker to be supplied with an artificial leg. When the appendage had been strapped to the stump, which was all that remained of the injured leg, the attendant requested that the patient get up and walk across the floor. Awkwardly, the man struggled to his feet and staggered across the room. Then, dragging himself painfully back to his chair, he slumped into it, utterly exhausted and discouraged.

"That's not how to do it," said the attendant. "Watch this!" Then he walked gracefully across the floor. "Ah," exclaimed the patient, "It's all very easy for you because you don't have any disability."

"Oh, haven't I?" replied the attendant. "Look." Pulling up the legs of his trousers, he disclosed that he was not wearing just one artificial limb, but TWO!

Too many times we doubt or we get depressed and discouraged and we are inclined to say, "Jesus, it was easy for you. You were God and could not sin. You never tasted the abundance of daily temptation, toil, and frustration. Yet the writer in Hebrews 4:15 tells us ". . . we do not have a high priest who is unable to sympathize with our weaknesses, but we have one who has been tempted in every way, just as we are—yet was without sin."

So the next time you find yourself doubting you can finish the race, look to Jesus, the author and perfector of our faith. The next time you're depressed about giving up things for God, look to Jesus who gave up even more. Or the next time you're discouraged, remember the ultimate sacrifice—Jesus bearing the sins of the world on the cross as God turned His back, to say "I LOVE YOU" to us.

Compromise

262 Choice—Conformed or Transformed

"And be not conformed to this world: but be ye transformed by the renewing of your mind, that ye may prove what is that good, and acceptable, and perfect will of God" (Rom. 12:2).

When an individual or a congregation has the attitude of compromise in regard to spiritual values and truths, dark days are ahead. All who strive to be Christians feel a certain amount of pressure from the world. Through the strength that Christ gives, we can overcome the world and its temptations.

A man starting a fish business put out his sign that read, "Fresh Fish For Sale Today" and invited all to visit his place of business on opening day. Many came and congratulated him on his new business, but one suggested that he change his sign. "Why the 'Today'? It is today." So he removed the "Today".

Someone else said, "Why, 'For Sale'? Everybody knows you have fish for sale—or else why the store?" The words "For Sale" came off the sign.

Another said, "Why the word 'Fresh'? You are a man of integrity, that guarantees your fish to be fresh." "Fresh" came off the sign.

Only one word was left, "Fish" and one complained about it. "I smelled your fish two blocks away."

The individual or congregation that tries to satisfy everybody ends up by pleasing nobody. If we start compromising, we will end up serving the devil. The man should have put up his sign and then stood by it. This is what we are to do in life. Accept God's will for our lives and stand on His promises.

263 The Uncertain Soldier

Paul Harvey tells the story of the uncertain soldier in our Civil War who, figuring to play it safe, dressed himself in a blue coat and gray pants and tiptoed out onto the field of battle. He got shot from both directions!

The Bible is full of examples of individuals who compromised in one form or another and their ensuing losses. Lot who separated from Abram and moved as far as Sodom (Gen. 13:12, 13; 19:1-29); Samson who compromised with Delilah (Jud. 16:1, 2); and Solomon who loved many foreign women (1 Kgs. 11:1-4) are but a few examples.

What about times when we are tempted to compromise our faith or beliefs? Will we stay strong or try and wear the blue and gray? Think about it!

"Finally, be strong in the Lord, and in the strength of His might" (Eph. 6:10).

264 Don't Negotiate With Satan

A hunter raised his rifle and took careful aim at a large bear. When about to pull the trigger, the bear spoke in a soft soothing voice, "Isn't it better to talk than to shoot? What do you want? Let's negotiate the matter." Lowering his rifle, the hunter replied, "I want a fur coat." "Good," said the bear, "that is a negotiable question. I only want a full stomach, so let us negotiate a compromise."

They sat down to negotiate and after a time the bear walked away alone. The negotiations had been successful. The bear had a full stomach, and the hunter had his fur coat!

Satan says to you, "Let us negotiate." But there are some things that cannot be negotiable. We cannot compromise the church with the world. Christ and His church deserve our very best and utmost loyalty.

Criticism

265 I Drew My Circle Again

When I first became a member of the church, my circle was very big . . . for it included all who, like myself, had believed. I was happy in the thought that my brethren were many. But, having a keen and observant mind, I soon learned that many of my brethren were erring. I could not tolerate any people within my circle but those who, like myself, were right on all points of doctrine and practice. Too, some made mistakes and sinned. What could I do? I had to do something! I drew my circle again . . . leaving the publicans and sinners outside, excluding the Pharisees in all their pride, with myself and the righteous and humble within. I heard ugly rumors about some brethren. I saw then that some of them were worldly-minded; their thoughts were constantly on things of a worldly nature. So duty bound, to save my reputation, I drew my circle again . . . leaving those reputable spiritually-minded within. I realized in time that only my family and myself remained in the circle. I had a good family, but to my surprise, my family finally disagreed with me. I was always right. A man must be steadfast. I have never been a factious man! So in strong determination, I drew my circle again . . . leaving me quite alone.

266 Are Your Shoes on the Wrong Feet?

One day a little boy complained that his new shoes were hurting his feet. I looked down at his feet. No wonder they hurt. His shoes were on the wrong feet! When I changed them he felt better and was soon the liveliest little fellow in the group.

Sometimes our lives seem all sour and stale. We find fault with everyone around us. We need to stop and take a good look at our feet. If we were wearing the same shoes the other fellow wears, would we be happy?

267 Broken Heart

I heard a story about a man who invited his neighbor to attend church with him. On the way home, the neighbor said, "I noticed you have a new preacher." "Yes," said his friend, "We fired the old one. He was always telling us unless we repented, we were going to hell." "But," the neighbor replied, "your new preacher said the very same thing this morning." "True," was the reply, "but our old preacher acted like he was happy about the situation. When our new preacher says this, it seems to break his heart."

268 What About Your Pocket?

A serviceman once wrote about a moment of comedy he had witnessed in the army. It happened during a company inspection at the Redstone Arsenal in Alabama.

The inspection was being conducted by a full colonel. Everything had gone smoothly until the officer came to a certain soldier, looked him up and down and snapped, "Button that pocket, trooper!"

The soldier, more than a little rattled, stammered, "Right now, sir?"

"Of course, right now!" was the reply.

Whereupon the soldier very carefully reached out and buttoned the flap on the colonel's shirt pocket. The officer had been quick to note the youngster's uniform problem, but hadn't noticed his own.

For some reason, we seem to be the same way. The faults of others stick out like a missing tooth, while our own are often hard to spot. Small specks in other people seem major, while the planks in our own eye seem excusable (Matt. 7:1-5).

Let's quit dwelling on the faults of others all the time. The church needs builders and workers—not a wrecking crew. Work on your own faults, then seek to help others in a spirit of gentleness.

269 That Anonymous Note

Dwight Moody was preaching when someone passed a note to him through the usher. It had only one word: "Fool." Moody looked at it and said, "I've often received notes that weren't signed. This is the first time I've received a note that someone forgot to write, but signed."

270 If You Are Mad at the Dog, Don't Kick the Cat!

A preacher asked a certain man why he had just ceased to attend the services of the church. The man replied, "They haven't treated me right over there." The preacher asked, "Then why don't you go home and beat your wife?" The startled backslider gave the preacher a look which questioned his sanity. "My wife hasn't done anything against me," he said.

"Well," the preacher said, "has the Lord Jesus done anything against you?" Being peeved at the brethren and forsaking the Lord is about as logical as being angry with the dog and kicking the cat. If you don't believe Christ is to judge your feeling for Him by the way you treat the church, then try Matthew 25:40.

271 Before You Criticize

When you are disposed to criticize a friend,
Just remember, the beginning's not the end;
When within this urge you find,
These three questions bring to mind:
Is it TRUE? Is it NEEDFUL? Is it KIND?

272 Don't Find Fault

Pray don't find fault with the man who limps

Or stumbles along the road,
Unless you have worn the shoes he wears
Or struggled beneath his load.

There may be tacks in his shoes that hurt,
Though hidden way from view,
Or the burden he bears, placed on your back,
Might cause you to stumble, too.

Don't sneer at the man who's down today,
Unless you have felt the blow
That caused his fall, or felt the same
That only the fallen can know.

You may be strong, but still the blows
That were his, if dealt to you
In the self-same way the self-same time,
Might cause you to stagger, too.

Don't be too harsh with the man who sins
Or pelt him with words or stones,
Unless you are sure, yea, doubly sure,
That you have no sins of your own.

For you know perhaps, if the tempter's voice
Could whisper as soft to you
As it did to him when he went astray,
T'would cause you to falter, too.

273 Watch Your Criticism

Be careful and cautious how you criticize. The man who had a good opinion of himself and his own virtues and thought he was so much better than anyone else, stopped in front of a taxidermist's window, in which there was an owl which had attracted quite a crowd of sightseers.

So sure he was far superior in his knowledge of birds, he remarked, "Well, if I couldn't stuff an owl better than that, I would quit the business. The head is not right; the pose of the body is awkward; the feathers are not right; and the feet are not under it right." Just then the owl turned its head and gave him a quick wink or two.

The crowd roared. They turned to comment to him; but he slunk away as fast as he could go.

Death

274 Death Frees the Soul

[A letter written to one's physical body.] 1 Corinthians 15:44.

"You and I have been together for a long time in a most intimate and valuable relationship. Now you have grown old. Your hearing and strength are failing. Your resistance to cold is diminishing. You cannot climb and run as you once did. In a word, you are running down. In a short time you will cease to breathe and your heart will stop beating. When you can go no further, you will be returned to the substance of which you were made, and I shall continue on in that life where you are not needed. A Power greater than you and I started us on this journey together. Now I recognize that you are aware of the fact that your journey is nearing its end, while my journey has scarcely begun. I know this to be true, for while you are feeble, I have never been more alive. Our separation, therefore, cannot be one of sadness, but will be one of joy. You are weary and want to stop. I am longing to alight from this slowing vehicle and go on without you. Death will mean that your desire to stop is granted, and my longing is satisfied."

275 Death for a Believer Is Sleep in Jesus' Arms

A farmer took his little son on a visit to a distant village. Along the way they came to a swift stream spanned by a rickety old bridge which frightened the little lad even though it was daylight. Returning at dusk, the boy recalled the stream and old bridge and became panicky. How would they cross that turbulent stream in the dark? Noting his anxiety, the father lifted the boy and carried him in his arms. Before they reached the bridge, he was fast asleep against his father's shoulder. As the next morning's sun streamed in his bedroom window, the boy awoke to discover he was safe at home. At death the believer falls asleep in the Savior's arms to awaken in His bright land of no night and no fear.

276 When Science Is Silent

Said Dr. Joseph A. Parker: "Some have found fault with me. They say I am old-fashioned and out of date; I am always quoting the Bible; why not turn to science this morning?

"There is a poor widow here who has lost her only son. She wants to know if she will see him again. Science shall give the answer, and I will put the Book away." So he took the Book and put it on the seat behind. "Will this woman see her son again? Where is he? Does death end all? What has science to say?" Here a long pause. "We are waiting for an answer, the woman is anxious." Another long pause. "The woman's heart is breaking. Science must speak. Nothing to say? Then we must take the Book," and here he reverently replaced it, and with great deliberation opened it and read: "I shall go to him, but he shall not return to me . . . The dead shall arise . . . for this corruptible must put on incorruption, and this mortal must put on immortality. O death, where is thy sting? . . . I saw the dead, small and great, stand before God."

Then, closing the Book, and patting it affectionately, he said, "We will stick to the Book!"

277 Death Is Not Necessarily Loss

A little girl whose baby brother had just died asked her mother where Baby had gone. "To be with Jesus," replied the mother. A few days later, talking to a friend, the mother said, "I am so grieved to have lost my baby." The little girl heard her, and remembering what her mother had told her, looked up into her face and asked, "Mother, is a thing lost when you know where it is?"

"No, of course not." "Well, then *how can Baby be lost when he has gone to be with Jesus?*" Her mother never forgot this. It was the truth.

278 If You Knew That Your Days Were Numbered

A man in Iowa discovered that he had terminal cancer. For weeks he moped around the house avoiding loved ones, inwardly cursing God and wondering why this tragedy had happened to him.

Then one day he made a decision: "I am not dead yet, and I am going to live each day to its fullest the rest of my life."

Sometime later, when he was interviewed, he said he had experienced a more abundant life in the weeks after that decision than during his prior 42 years—colors seemed more vivid, the laughter of his children more bright and precious.

One suggestion he gave to help others with terminal illness was, "Consider each day as a gift from God; enjoy it fully."

279 Called! Held! Kept!

Frances Havergal, the songwriter, lived and moved in the Word of God. His Word was her constant companion. On the last day of her life, she asked a friend to read to her the second chapter of Isaiah. When the friend read the sixth verse, "I the Lord have called thee in righteousness, and will hold thine hand, and will keep thee," Miss Havergal stopped her. She whispered, "Called—held—kept. I can go home on that!" And she did go home on that. She found His promises unfailing.

280 Sooner or Later Everyone Runs Out of Time

Much sooner than you can anticipate, you will be the silent guest at your own funeral. No doubt there will be relatives and friends present to mourn for you whom you haven't seen in years. After the preacher delivers a message in your memory, you will be taken to the graveyard, given a final farewell and buried.

The retirement that you spent your life working for will be gone forever. Remember the new car that you worried about scratching? Its new owner just wrecked it! The newlyweds bought your house and have redecorated the room that you had at last decorated to your liking. Your personal belongings have been sorted and some discarded. The dog is making a bed out of your favorite old coat. Other clothes of yours that no one could wear or did not want have been boxed and given to Goodwill. Your personal treasures that were valuable only to you—the carefully preserved flower, the lock of hair, the torn picture, the stained postcard—have been burned as trash.

You attended a number of funerals in your lifetime, but for some reason you just never expected to be lying in the casket yourself. Sure, someday, but not that particular day. "Maybe tomorrow," you always thought, "but not today." You remember telling the Lord each time you thought your time was close, "Not this time, Lord. Not today. Maybe tomorrow."

Sooner or later, **everyone** runs out of time. Paul states that everyone has an appointment with death and then the judgment (Heb. 9:27). The only time that you can decide whether or not your death will be a blessing is **today** while you are alive. Today is the day of salvation (2 Cor. 6:2). Today is the day to do the Lord's work. "Whatever your hand finds to do, do it with all of your might, for in the grave, where you are going, there is neither working, nor planning nor knowledge nor wisdom" (Eccl. 9:10).

Sooner or later, everyone runs out of **time** but no one runs out of **eternity**. Doesn't it make more sense to spend your time preparing for that which will not end, rather than squandering your time trying to hold on to that which will not last?

"Careless soul, O heed the warning,
For your life will soon be gone;
O how sad to face the judgment
Unprepared to meet thy God."

Will you be prepared on the day that you run out of time?

281 Known But to God

Shirley Pope Waite tells this moving story:

" 'You must visit the American cemetery,' our bed and breakfast hosts told us. We hadn't known about this cemetery three miles from Cambridge, site of one of England's most famous universities.

"Upon our arrival, we were surprised to see the American and British flags at half mast. Special

Memorial Day services were scheduled to honor the war's dead buried there.

"Established in 1943 on land donated by the University of Cambridge, it is the only permanent World War II military cemetery in the British Isles. The rolling grounds are framed by trees on two sides, and contain 3,811 headstones in seven curved grave plots.

"A large proportion of the servicemen and women buried there were crew members of British-based American aircraft. Others died in the invasion of North Africa and France, at sea, or in training areas within the United Kingdom.

"An impressive Wall of the Missing lies alongside a mall with a pool bordered by roses. The wall records names of 5,125 missing in action, lost, or buried at sea. Four huge statues represent a soldier, sailor, airman, and coast guardsman in uniform. A mosaic in the chapel of the memorial building stretches across the ceiling above the altar. It depicts the archangel trumpeting the resurrection and the last judgment.

"As we walked reverently around the beautiful grounds, we paused at the foot of a grave. It was one of 24 decorated with red and white carnations tied with a blue ribbon, and flanked by a tiny American and British flag. The words etched in the headstone read: "here rests in honored glory a comrade in arms known but to God."

"Tears came to my eyes as we stood in an attitude of worship. Unknown but to God, these service people were once known intimately by parents, siblings, friends, perhaps a spouse and children. Young men and women who fought for freedom and the dignity of humankind! Yet in death—known only to God!

"Relatives and friends may forsake us. We may feel alone in a world that offers many only poverty, cruelty, and apathy; but God knows each of us intimately. He is a husband to the widow: "for your Maker is your husband; the Lord of hosts is His name" (Is. 54:5). He is a father to the orphan: "Father of the fatherless . . . is God in His holy habitation" (Ps. 68:5). He is Father to us all!

"Unknown except to God! Isn't that the most important relationship of any? Thank God, we are known to Him not just in life, not just in death, but for eternity!"

282 The Shadow of Death

The first wife of Dr. Donald Grey Barnhouse, a well known minister in Philadelphia, died from cancer while still in her thirties. All three of his children were under 12. Dr. Barnhouse had such victory that he decided to preach the funeral sermon himself. En route to the funeral they were overtaken by a large truck which, as it passed them, cast a large shadow over their car. He asked one of his children, "Would you rather be run over by that truck or its shadow?" "By the shadow, of course!" replied the 12-year-old daughter. "A shadow can't hurt you." With that answer Dr. Barnhouse said to his three motherless children, "Your mother has been overrun not by death, but by the shadow of death." At the funeral he spoke on Psalm 23, "Even though I walk through the valley of the shadow of death, I will fear no evil, for You are with me."

283 Beyond Death

A sick man turned to his doctor, who was leaving the room after paying a visit, and said: "Doctor, I am afraid to die. Tell me what lies on the other side." Very quietly the doctor said, "I don't know." "You don't know? You, a Christian man, do not know what is on the other side?!"

The doctor was holding the handle of the door, on the other side of which came sounds of scratching and whining, and as he opened the door a dog sprang into the room and leaped on him with eager show of gladness. Turning to his patient, the doctor said, "Did you ever notice that dog? He has never been in this room before. He did not know what was inside. He knew nothing except that his master was here, and when the door opened he sprang in without fear. I know little of what is on the other side of death, but I do know one thing: I know my Master is there, and that is enough. And when the door opens, I shall pass through with no fear, but with gladness."

284 Praise Out of Tragedy

God can bring fresh praise out of both tragedy and glory, as illus-

trated by this story about a favorite hymn. Luther Bridgers began preaching at age 17 while he was a student at Asbury College in Kentucky. He was a young Methodist minister of unusual zeal and evangelism. In 1910 the future looked bright for the 26-year-old preacher, who by then had a young wife and three children. The Bridgers family was visiting Mrs. Bridger's parents at Harrodsburg, Kentucky. After the family retired for the night, a neighbor noticed flames coming from the house. He roused Mrs. Bridgers' parents and Luther, but the rest of the family members were beyond reach. The young pastor lost his wife and children.

In the awful days of sorrow that followed, Luther remembered that God offered songs of comfort in the night (Ps. 42:8), and would never forsake him. It was during this period that Luther wrote the words and music that we sing so many times: "There's within my heart a melody/Jesus whispers sweet and low/fear not, I am with thee, peace be still; in all of life's ebb and flow." In the fourth stanza he referred to his own experience: "Tho sometimes He leads through waters deep/trials fall across the way."

In the darkest night, in the depths of despair, God gave an inward song to Luther Bridgers that has blessed millions. Out of a pit of grief came a song of blessing.

285 Only the Cocoon

Arthur Brisbane once pictured a crowd of grieving caterpillars carrying the corpse of a cocoon to its final resting place. The poor, distressed caterpillars, clad in black raiment, were weeping, and all the while the beautiful butterfly fluttered happily above the muck and mire of earth, forever freed from its earthly shell. Needless to say, Brisbane had the average orthodox funeral in mind and sought to convey the idea that when our loved ones pass, it is foolish to remember only the cocoon and concentrate our attention on the remains, while forgetting the bright butterfly.

286 Crossing the River of Death

Christ crossed the river of death and the grave so that you and I as believers, whose sins have been forgiven, may not have to cross that river alone. The story is told of a shepherd who tried to induce his sheep to cross a swiftly flowing stream. Sheep are naturally afraid of rapidly running water, and he could not get them to cross. Then picking up a lamb and stepping with it into the river, he bore it carefully and tenderly to the opposite shore. When the mother saw her lamb had gone, she forgot her fear and stepped into the rushing current and was soon safely on the other side. All the rest of the flock followed her leadership. Thus we follow our leader, Christ, and those of our loved ones whom He has already carried safely over to the other shore.

287 The Clock

The clock of life is wound but once, and no man has the power to tell just when the hands will stop at late or early hour. To lose one's wealth is sad indeed. To lose one's health is more. To lose one's soul is such a loss that no man can restore.

Thirty-nine people died while you read these words. Every hour 5,417 go to meet their Maker. You could have been among them. Sooner or later you will be. Are you ready?

288 Image of Glory

"It is a peculiar thing," said an embalmer as he stood by a woman's casket, "but it isn't necessary to tell me she was a Christian. I always know as soon as I see a body; the glory leaves its stamp on the face."

289 The Glory of Death

George Truett once assured the wife of a Texas judge that when death came she should not be afraid. When the day finally arrived the nurse and doctor were there. She said, "Tell me frankly, doctor, is this death?" He said, "Yes, it is death." She turned to her husband and said: "Oh, dear husband, you know this is the hour for 30 years I have dreaded. This is the hour of all hours I have shrunk from." Yet later she said, "Husband, don't you see that face? Don't you hear that music? Christ is here. I have never known such rapture of light and peace and joy." In that glory she went to be with the Lord. She found that God's grace was sufficient. God's love was not limited.

290 Sin

There is said to be a church which is very attractive to tourists. The graveyard of the church is always kept locked, but on a gate is the following notice, "The key to the graveyard is to be found in the tavern."

A great army of men and women daily find in the taverns or lounges the key that opens the way for them into the graveyard.

291 How Do You Face Death?

An aged lady left Buffalo by boat for Cleveland to visit a daughter living there. Soon a dreadful storm arose and many of the passengers, fearing death, gathered for prayer. Only the aged lady seemed unconcerned about the tempest as she sat with her hands folded and prayed. After the storm had subsided, some of the passengers were eager to know the secret of her calmness. They gathered around her and asked her the reason. "Well, my dear friends," she replied, "it is like this. I have two daughters. One died and went home to heaven. The other lives in Cleveland. When the storm arose, I wondered which of them I might visit first, the one in Cleveland or the one in heaven, and I just left it to the Lord; for I would be glad to see either."

292 Unafraid of Death and Judgment?

A certain person was driving 70 miles an hour down one of those long, straight stretches of West Texas highway one hot afternoon. No other cars were in sight, but up ahead he saw the form of a large bird bending over and tearing flesh from a run over rabbit. As he got closer, a huge hawk straightened up defiantly and looked directly into the headlights.

Instead of taking flight as these birds normally do, the giant hawk spread his wings, almost blocking the road, and challenged the speeding car. Its body made a "whump" sound as the car hit it, and the proud bird was instantly dead. Neither the run over rabbit nor its pride were any good to it then.

On another occasion in East Texas, the same man was again driving 70 down a highway when he saw the small rounded form of a turtle making a slow journey across his path. He remembered the giant hawk, and thought of what a 4,000 pound car would do to an eight-ounce turtle.

The turtle looked up and saw the car coming. He didn't run; he didn't dodge out of the way, nor did he challenge the car. He stopped and pulled all four legs and his head into his shell. The car missed the motionless turtle that rested confidently in his shell.

The proud hawk and the deluded turtle are like two kinds of people ignoring the speeding advance of death and judgment: one is proud and defies the claims of Christ on his or her life; the other pulls into his or her own self-righteous shell.

293 "Shadow" Illustrated

Little boys sometimes do the strangest things for excitement. To break the monotony of their young lives, two small lads lay down by the railroad tracks to feel the track vibrations of the oncoming train, as well as to hear its thunderous sound. After it had passed and only the shadow of the train had passed over them, they were secure and no harm had been done to them, even in this seemingly precarious position.

Just so, when we pass through the "valley of the shadow," we only experience the "shadow."

Decisions

294 The Dividing Line

Lines are everywhere! There are lines in parking lots to designate the parking spaces. There are lines drawn at intersections so that pedestrians know where to cross the street. There are little, but important, lines drawn on rulers to show units of measure. There are lines drawn on baseball diamonds, basketball courts, and football fields to help the players and referees know if the balls, and players, are in or out.

Lines can be very important. They help us know where we stand. We are either on one side of the line or the other.

Exodus 32 tells us that Moses drew a line. Here's why: God's people had participated in a drunken party and had worshiped a golden calf. Drunken idolaters! Moses knew that God demands that people love, obey and worship only Him. In a very courageous move, Moses stepped in front of all those people and drew a line by saying, "Who is on the Lord's side? Let him come to me. . . ." (Ex. 32:26). That day, many crossed the line by standing with Moses and the Lord.

Jesus, too, drew a line when He called those from the multitude to follow Him. Jesus' words make a very clear line: either you are for Christ or you are against Him. That same line exists today. We must decide on which side of that line we will stand.

Many choose to stand on both sides of the line. And for those individuals Jesus replies, "I know thy works, that thou art neither cold nor hot; I would thou wert cold or hot. So then because thou art lukewarm, and neither cold nor hot, I will spue thee out of my mouth" (Rev. 3:15, 16). There is no middle ground with the Lord. In fact, for those who try, it makes Him sick to His stomach. Take a stand on God's side.

295 Dangers of Homogeneous Group Decisions

The more members of a group like and respect one another, the more probable it is they will make a poor decision. A well-known example of the dangers of this unhealthy group orientation took place during the John F. Kennedy administration. A faulty decision caused the defeat of American forces in the invasion of Cuba at the Bay of Pigs, embarrassing the President and the nation.

President Kennedy had surrounded himself with a committee

of some of the shrewdest advisors in the country. This group of experts didn't make a poor decision because of low IQs. They failed because they wanted to be liked by others in the group. They allowed friendship and loyalty to overwhelm their decision-making process.

Advisors who were tempted to speak up in opposition to the attack decided against it out of fear of being disliked, or because they didn't want to waste everyone's time. In a memorandum written before the committee assembled, Arthur Schlesinger, one of the members of the Kennedy inner circle, acknowledged that he considered the invasion of Cuba a mistake. But he kept silent when he participated in the discussion. Robert Kennedy, the President's brother and the U.S. attorney general, got Schlesinger in the corner after discovering that he opposed the invasion. Kennedy put it bluntly, "Arthur, you may be right or you may be wrong, but the president has made up his mind. Don't push any further." Schlesinger kept quiet. The environment wasn't right for voicing dissent.

296 Don't Ignore the Less Experienced

America's Supreme Court has an interesting custom. The newest member of the court speaks his or her mind on a decision first. Then the next newest speaks. This continues until all of the members have spoken, and then the Chief Justice speaks last. In that way, no one is held back by fear of differing with the opinion of a more experienced judge. This wouldn't be a bad idea for most of our churches or business committees to follow.

297 The Cost of Indecision

Former President Ronald Reagan says he learned the need for decision-making early in life. An aunt had taken him to a cobbler to have a pair of shoes made for him. The shoemaker asked young Ronald Reagan, "Do you want a square toe or a round toe?"

Reagan hemmed and hawed. So the cobbler said, "Come back in a day or two and let me know what you want."

A few days later the shoemaker saw Reagan on the street and asked what he had decided about the shoes. "I still haven't made up my mind," the boy answered. "Very well," said the cobbler.

When Reagan received the shoes, he was shocked to see that one shoe had a square toe and the other a round toe.

"Looking at those shoes every day taught me a lesson," said Reagan years later. "If you don't make your own decisions, somebody else will make them for you!"

The sovereign God has made us people, not puppets. We have His Word to guide us, His love to redeem us, and His assurance that we are capable of making choices.

Discernment

298 Which Direction?

Years ago my Father was searching for our family roots and had occasion to visit several cemeteries and read inscriptions. There was a tombstone on which was engraved,

"Pause now stranger as you pass by;

As you are now, so once was I.

As I am now, so soon you'll be.

Prepare yourself to follow me!"

Someone had placed a piece of wood next to the tombstone. On it was written,

"To follow you

I'm not content,

Until I know

Which way you went!"

(God says there are **two ways to go!**)

299 Man and the World

A small boy filled with all kinds of playful ideas anxiously awaited his father's return from work. An extra-long day at the office, however, had taken its toll, and his father longed for a few minutes of relaxation. Over and over again the boy tugged at his dad's leg with yet another suggestion of something they might do together. Well, finally in total frustration the father ripped from a magazine a picture of the world and tore it into a hundred pieces.

"Here," he said handing the child a roll of scotch tape, "go and put the world back together." Ah, peace at last, or so he thought. But, in just a few minutes, he was interrupted again, there before him stood his son—and in hands was a crudely fashioned picture of the world. "Son, that's incredible. How did you do it?" "It was easy," said the boy, "you see on the other side of the picture of the world was the picture of a man, and as soon as I got man straightened out the world came together."

What a profound answer from a child! How true! Get man fixed and the world will be okay.

300 If Men Had Chosen the Apostles

TO: Jesus, Son of Joseph
Woodcrafters Carpenter Shop
Nazareth 25922

FROM: Jordan Management
Consultants
Jerusalem 26544

Dear Sir:

Thank you for submitting the résumés of the twelve men you have picked for management positions in your new organization. All of them have not taken our battery of tests; and we have not only run the results through our computer, but also arranged personal interviews for each of them with our psychologist and vocational aptitude consultant.

The profiles of all tests are included, and you will want to study each of them carefully.

As part of our service and for your guidance, we make some general comments, much as an auditor will include some general statements. This is given as a result of staff consultation and comes without any additional fee.

It is the staff opinion that most of your nominees are lacking in background, education and vocational aptitude for the type of enterprise you are undertaking. They do not have team concept. We recommend that you continue your search for persons of experience in managerial ability and proven capability.

Simon Peter is emotionally unstable and given to fits of temper. Andrew has absolutely no qualities of leadership. The two brothers, James and John, the sons of Zebedee, place personal interest above company loyalty. Thomas demonstrates a questioning attitude that would tend to undermine morale. We feel that it is our duty to tell you that Matthew has been blacklisted by the Greater Jerusalem Better Business Bureau. James, the son of Alpheus, and Thaddaeus definitely have radical leanings, and they both registered a high score on the manic-depressive scale.

One of the candidates, however, shows great potential. He is a man of ability and resourcefulness, meets people well, has a keen business mind and has contacts in high places. He is highly motivated, ambitious and responsible. We recommend Judas Iscariot as your comptroller and right-hand man. All the other profiles are self-explanatory.

We wish you every success in your new venture.

Sincerely Yours,

Jordan Management Committee

"For the Lord seeth not as man seeth; for man looketh on the outward appearance, but the Lord looketh on the heart" (1 Sam. 16:7).

301 Watch Your "Cats"

The story is told of an old lady who rented a cottage for the summer. With the cottage was also a dog. The old lady liked a very comfortable armchair better than any other in the house. She always made for it the first thing. But, alas! she nearly always found the chair occupied by the dog. Being afraid of the dog, she never dared bid it harshly to get out of the chair, but instead she would go to the window and call "Cats!" Then the dog would rush to the window and bark, and the old lady would slip quietly into the vacant chair.

One day the dog entered the room and found the old lady in possession of the chair. He strolled over to the window, and looking out, appeared very much excited and set up a tremendous barking. The old lady arose and hastened to the window to see what was the matter, and the dog quietly climbed into the chair.

Deceits practiced on others will sooner or later be repaid against ourselves.

"Bread of a deceit is sweet to a man; but afterwards his mouth shall be filled with gravel" (Prov. 20:17).

302 A Child Is Born

In the early days of the nineteenth century, men were following with bated breath the march of Napoleon and waiting with feverish impatience for the latest news of the wars. And all the while, in their own homes, babies were being born.

Just think of some of those babies. In one year, lying midway between Trafalgar and Waterloo, there stole into the world a host of well-known men! During that year, 1809, Mr. Gladstone was born at Liverpool; Alfred Tennyson drew his first breath at the Somersby rectory; and Oliver Wendell Holmes made his initial appearance in Massachusetts. On the very self-same day of that self-same year, Abraham Lincoln made his debut in Old Kentucky. Music was enriched by the advent of Frederick Chopin at Warsaw and Felix Mendolssohn at Hamburg.

But, nobody thought of babies. Everybody was thinking of battles. Yet, viewing that age in the truer

perspective which the years enable us to command, we may well ask ourselves which of the battles of 1809 mattered more than the babies of 1809. When a wrong wants righting, or a work wants doing, or a truth wants preaching, or a continent wants opening, God sends a baby into the world to do it. This is why, long, long ago, a Babe was born at Bethlehem.

It was at a wayside inn that God began making the world all over again. Momentous things were set in motion at that inn at Bethlehem.

303 Who's Leading Whom?

Have you heard about the elderly woman on a busy street corner who was confused and hesitant to cross because of the heavy traffic? Finally a gentleman came up to her and asked if he could cross the street with her.

Gratefully she took his arm, but grew progressively more alarmed as he zigzagged randomly across the street, to the blare of horns and screech of locked brakes.

Finally on the opposite curb, she said angrily, "You almost got us killed! You walk like you're blind." "I am," he replied. "That's why I asked if I could cross with you."

Jesus said of the Pharisees of His day: "They be blind leaders of the blind. And if the blind lead the blind, both shall fall into the ditch" (Matt. 15:14). We need to be very careful not to entrust our souls to the guidance of someone who cannot see the clear teachings of our Lord, Jesus Christ. Our eternal destiny is too important to put at such risk.

304 Wrong Direction

The doubleheader train was bucking a heavy snowstorm as its engines pulled it west. A woman with a baby wanted to leave the train at one of the little stations along the route. She repeatedly called, "Don't forget me!" to the brakeman responsible to call out the stations they approached. Her husband was to meet her.

The train slowed to a stop, and a fellow traveler said, "Here's your station." She hopped from the train into the storm. The train moved on again. Forty-five minutes later, the brakeman came in. "Where's the woman?"

"She got off at the last stop," the traveler said.

"Then she got off to her death," the brakeman responded. "We stopped only because there was something the matter with the engine."

They called for volunteers to go back and search for the woman and child. When they found her, she was covered with ice and snow. The little boy was protected on her breast. She had followed the man's directions, but they were wrong—dead wrong.

Paul declares Christ is the one Mediator between man and God. Peter emphasizes there is no other name given under heaven whereby we must be saved. The Lord Jesus is our only Authority. His blood has made atonement for our sin. Only

He can tell us how to reach our final destination. Depend on the one who has experienced death and provided redemption for you, the One who will walk with you through the valley of the shadow of death.

305 A Gift for My Neighbor

If my neighbor needed a cup of sugar,
> I would give it to him;
> But what if he needed a friend?
> If my neighbor needed bread,
> I would share with him;
> But what if he needed love?
> If my neighbor needed shoes,
> I would provide them for him;
> But what if he needed compassion?
> If my neighbor needed water,
> I would dig him a well;
> But what if he needed God?
> *God grant me the wisdom*
> *To give my neighbor*
> *What he really needs.*

306 The Possessed Closet

Frantically a woman pulled her pastor down a dark hall towards a room in the rear of the house.

He understood well what Paul had meant about that "fear and trembling" as he stumbled along behind her. Not that he believed there was a demon in her closet, but he surely wondered *what* might be there! As they entered the dimly lit room, the pastor noticed a dark object protruding from between the garments hanging in her closet. "There it is!" she gasped. Upon closer examination, the pastor discovered a partially inflated dry-cleaning bag! Thereupon, he "exorcised" the possessed closet, removing the bag and showing it to the dear lady. He was, however, unable to convince the poor woman that she had not seen a demon.

As he looked around the room, he noticed on a night table nearby an open copy of that sordid book, *The Exorcist*. At the same time, he caught the faint odor of spirits— of the *liquid* variety, and he then knew the source of the problem. When superstition is combined with beverage alcohol, the outcome is predictably unpredictable! But such experiences are not uncommon for gospel preachers.

307 Ignoring Dangers

An airliner returned to the terminal because the pilot did not like the sound of the engines. As it taxied a second time for take-off, one nervous passenger inquired if the problem had been solved. "Yes, it has," smiled the stewardess. "We changed pilots."

When the *Titanic* went down, it was steaming full ahead. There had been a wide variety of warnings, but the danger signals were all ignored. The bands were playing, the passengers were dancing, and everyone was oblivious to disaster. Their collision course with destiny is much like our own. We are having too much fun to be disturbed, and a change of course seems out of the question. The stage and cast are set for distress of incredible proportions.

When the band on the *Titanic* changed its tune to "Nearer My God to Thee," it was already too late. God help us to strike up the band a bit sooner!

308 Three Voices

If we listen carefully to those around us, we will learn to distinguish three voices, or influences, which direct the thinking, attitudes and actions of us all. We can hear them at our work, in our homes, and in the quietness of our moments alone.

Fear (the first voice) disguises itself as "being safe," as "practical," "conservative," "cautious," or "reasonable." Look for the motive behind the disguise. **Fear** is a demanding master, never able to be satisfied. It disdains any voice but its own.

Fantasy (the second voice) disguises itself as "visionary," as "progressive," "imaginative," or "creative." Look for the motive behind the disguise. **Fantasy** is a demanding master, never able to be satisfied. It, too, disdains any voice but its own.

Both of these voices claim to be spiritual and wise. But both of these voices reveal an obsession with personal agendas. Both demand that all others see things from their perspective. Both deny that God may have a desirable goal beyond their view.

Faith is the third voice. **Faith** reminds us that this is God's world, that He is always with us, that He works with us and in spite of us, and that He will complete the wonderful work He began in spite of what it may look like to us today! **Faith** lives based on what God has done and said. And **Faith** lives in trust that God does break into our situations with power and resources and vision and peace beyond what we can presently imagine!

All three voices will call to you today. Only **Faith** offers life. May we govern our personal decisions and our decisions on behalf of the church through the voice of **Faith**.

309 Don't Treat Garbage as Treasure

It is easy for us to accumulate trash and then get so accustomed to it that we think it is treasure! Mother cleans out the basement while father is at work; but as soon as he arrives home, he moves "selected junk" back into the basement. In spite of flea markets and garage sales, we end up with more stuff than we started with.

Wise is the leader who knows rubbish when he sees it and who has the courage to cart it away. Like Israel at Passover, every ministry needs a regular housecleaning that will leave it purer and better. Perhaps we have collected organizational rubbish that is getting in the way of progress. Or it may be doctrinal rubbish that is grieving the Holy Spirit and hindering His power. Maybe the whole ministry needs trimming because we have too many people, too many committees, too many activities, and

we cannot find the foundation. Carting away the rubbish is not a popular job or an easy one, but it is an important one.

310 The Majority May Not Be Right

A danger exists in assuming that the majority is right. The majority, when against the Word of God, results in tragedy. Remember the people of Israel responding to the twelve spies. By far the vast majority sided with the ten spies. Only two from the entire nation sided with God. And only those two entered the land and received the blessings.

311 Beware Friendly Snakes

There is an old tale about a peasant who, while hoeing in his field during the spring thaw, came across a snake. He raised his hoe to kill it, but the snake begged for mercy. "I am too frozen to do you any harm," it cried. The farmer, full of compassion, picked up the half-dead serpent and put it into his tunic, against his chest. As he began to work, the snake got warmer and warmer. Suddenly, the snake bit the peasant. The peasant frantically reached into his tunic and pulled out the snake, throwing it to the ground.

"Why?" asked the man, "I befriended you. I trusted you."

"True!" hissed the snake as it slithered away, "but do not blame me. You knew I was a snake when you picked me up."

Many people today take sin into

their own bosoms and go about their business. Someday when these things have passed away and they are faced with eternity, they will cry out against sin and accuse it. But it will be too late for some! Sin will reply, "You knew I was sin! You knew that I was but for a season. Do not blame me!"

312 How Do You Make Decisions?

In Spain there is a very old proverb which says, "All laws go the way that kings desire." Behind this is an interesting story. About the beginning of the twelfth century there was a debate about whether the country's churches were to use Gothic or Roman prayer books in their services. The question eventually came before Alfonso VI, who was king at the time. Alfonso decided to leave the matter to chance, so he threw a copy of both prayer books into a fire declaring that the one that survived the ordeal should be chosen. However, when the Gothic missal survived the blaze, the king immediately threw it back into the fire and chose the Roman liturgies. Thus was the matter decided, and the proverb became popular throughout the country.

313 A Brother in Heaven

"How many brothers have you?" said someone to a little boy. The child stated the number, adding, "and one in heaven." "No, my son," interposed his mother. "You have no brother in heaven."

"Yes, I have," said the boy. "Didn't you tell me that God was my Father, and that Jesus Christ is the Son of God? Then He must be my Brother in heaven."

314 Learning How to Choose

A father who had three sons wanted to teach them a lesson in discretion. He gave each of them an apple that had some part of it rotten.

The first ate his apple, rotten and all. The second threw all of his away because some of it was rotten. The third picked out the rotten part and ate the good part.

No one is perfect in this world. Shall we reject all of them because they have some imperfection? The thing that we need the most is the spirit of discretion in choosing that which is good in everybody.

315 The Bones of the Missing Link

A number of years ago, a farmer in Louisiana plowed up some large bones. On reporting his find, a little "two by four" scientist drove out to the farm and pronounced the bones as that of the missing link. Scientists of all kinds began flocking in to that section of the state. Each declared that this undoubtedly linked man back to the lower animals. The newspapers carried this story far and wide.

A few days later an old countryman with a blade of alfalfa dropping out of one corner of his mouth stopped in at the office of the newspaper and said, "What's all this I hear about this prehistoric monster? About 30 years ago I owned that farm where those bones were found. Barnum & Bailey's big circus elephant died when they showed here in town and I permitted them to bury him on my land." And thus the missing link is still missing, the lower animals still produce lower animals, and all forms of life still beget life after their own kind, and we still believe that Jesus Christ is the Creator of this universe and all things therein.

316 The Right Perspective

A landscape artist does not always stand at an arm's length from his canvas. He must not limit his attention to the isolated details of what he is doing. Occasionally he steps back to view his work from a distance. He needs to see how his thousands of small brushstrokes fit together to produce an overall result.

Likewise, our perspective on life is much improved if sometime we can step back and see it whole. We can become so occupied with its daily brushstrokes that we have no real perception of the whole scene we are painting on the canvas of the ongoing years. Our attentions can be so consumed by the requirements of daily living that we have little awareness of the dimensions and directions of life itself.

Step back from the canvas a little, and try to see the picture whole. Look beyond the varied episodes of our daily doings and see the glory of it all. Look beyond the brushstrokes to see the art which the brushstrokes have made—and

are making.

"But we all . . . beholding as in a glass the glory of the Lord, are changed into the same image from glory to glory, even as by the Spirit of the Lord" (2 Cor. 3:18).

317 Correcting Faulty Lighting

Perhaps you have sometime visited the Lincoln Memorial in our nation's capital. In this white marble structure millions of people have stood and looked upon the overpowering statue of Lincoln by sculptor Daniel C. French. When the statue was unveiled in 1922, it was discovered that the facial features of Lincoln were grossly distorted by faulty lighting. Corrections were later made so that viewers may now see that face as it really is.

Lighting is so important in seeing a thing clearly. If we view life solely in the light of competition and conflict, we are not seeing all of it. If we look upon all other persons strictly in the light of some mean thing somebody once did to us, we are not seeing them as they are. Grotesque caricatures can be made when distortion lights are used. We can color what we see by the light in which we choose to see it.

We should seek to see all things in all the light there is—the illumination of the Spirit and the word of Scripture.

318 Creatures of Custom

As a boy in the Middle West, I used to amuse myself by holding a stick across a gateway that the sheep had to pass through. After the first few sheep had jumped over the stick, I took it away; but all the other sheep leaped through the gateway over an imaginary barrier. The only reason for their jumping was that those in front had jumped. The sheep is not the only animal with that tendency. Almost all of us are prone to do what others are doing, to believe what others are believing, to follow, without question, the testimony of prominent men.

319 The Circus or the Parade?

A little boy living in the country had never seen a traveling circus, and one was coming to his town on Saturday.

Saturday morning came. He asked his father for some money. His dad reached in his overalls and pulled out a dollar bill—the most money the boy had ever seen at one time.

Off the little wide-eyed fellow went. As he approached the town, he saw people lining the streets. Peering through the line at one point, he got his first glimpse of the parade. There were animals in cages and marching bands. Finally, a clown was seen bringing up the rear of the parade. The little boy was so excited that when the clown passed, he reached in his pocket and handed him the precious dollar bill. Thinking he had seen the circus when he had only seen the parade, the little boy turned around and went home.

The tragedy of most of our lives isn't that we aspire too high and fail. It's rather that we settle for too little. We could have a greater influence, and yet, because of fear or ignorance, shame, or inertia, we take the precious dollar of our lives and settle for the parade instead of the real thing.

320 To What Are You Listening?

A naturalist, walking with his friend through the busy streets of a great city, stopped suddenly and asked, "Do you hear a cricket?"

"Of course not," laughed his friend. "You could never hear a cricket with all this roar of traffic." "But I hear a cricket," persisted the naturalist, and turning over a stone, he uncovered the insect. "Did you actually hear the cricket chirping above the noise of the street?" asked his friend in astonishment.

"Certainly," said the naturalist. "I spend my time listening to nature, whether I am in the forest, the field, or the town. Everyone hears what he listens for." Taking a coin from his pocket, he dropped it on the pavement, and each passer-by put his hand in his pocket to see if he was the one who had dropped it. They were listening for coins.

What a lesson! If we are listening for the truth—for that which is stimulating, elevating, inspiring, we will hear it, even above the noise and bustle of this busy world, above the din of lies, tattling or gossip so commonly heard by many. And if our ears are attuned to scandal, backbiting and false reports, we will hear that, regardless of how loudly the principles of love, justice and truth may be proclaimed in our direction.

Disciples

Discipline

321 Cleaning Out

A certain man's garage is attached to his house. It's a wonderful convenience in inclement weather, but it's also a terrible temptation because all winter whenever he doe not know what to do with something, he puts it in the garage. Usually by March he is so ashamed of his garage that he doesn't want to open it up to the neighborhood.

By contrast, his neighbor keeps his garage spotlessly clean. He is one of those people who has a place for everything and keeps everything in its place. He has hangers for his shovel, his hammers, his screwdrivers, and his rakes. He paints his garage floor, and he actually vacuums his driveway. About mid-March the contrast finally gets to the first man, and he finally says, "This Saturday I'm going to tackle the garage." He gets up early in the morning, opens the door, tears into it, and by 4:00 in the afternoon, he has thrown half of it away. Then he gets all the rest organized, and feels absolutely fulfilled. In fact, he leaves his garage door open for three weeks so that everybody in the neighborhood can see how good it looks! But by that time, it's starting to look a little tacky again.

Biblical happiness is a life without the junk and clutter that a self-oriented life deposits in our spirits. It is a sense of well-being, cleanliness, and organization. It is to live an organized life so that there is the inner sense of well-being that harmony provides.

322 Freedom Restricted Becomes Power

No horse gets anyone anywhere until he's harnessed, no steam or gas drives anything until it is confined, no Niagara ever turns anything into light or power until it is tunneled, no life ever does great things it is until focused, dedicated, and disciplined.

323 The Power of Discipline

USA Today polled 238 players who participated in at least one of the NCAA Final Four Championship games from 1977 to 1986. The survey indicated that an amazing number of these athletes have been able to match their achievement on the basketball court with continued excellence in life.

What is their secret? The pollsters concluded that those who make it in school "seem able to channel the athletic lessons of discipline and self-sacrifice into their academic lives."

324 Today . . .

I did not come this far—nor to this place—alone, but in the presence and power of my God.

The circumstances of this moment are not greater than my God. He knows them better than I do, yet He permits them. And He will overcome them—within me if I will allow Him. Mine is not to fret as though He does not know, or care, or cannot overcome. Mine is to walk on knowing that He is here.

I am His by His creation, and His new birth. I am His to do with as He chooses—to bless or to use up, to serve or to simply endure. The day belongs to my Lord, and it is the only day I have to serve and glorify Him. And so I shall give all that I have and am that for this one day He shall be honored.

Discipling

325 Success Can Be Failure

A rehabilitation counselor took early retirement to spend the rest of his life preaching the gospel. Early in his career he found a young boy with several birth defects. He arranged financial and medical help. Skilled surgeons restored the child's facial appearance. Trained therapists taught him to speak and walk. By his teens, the boy was able to take part in all the activities of other young people.

"What do you think has become of this young man?" the counselor asked. One guessed he was a great athlete; another, a skilled surgeon. "No, none of these," the retired counselor said sadly. "The young man is a prisoner, serving a life sentence for murder. We were able to restore his physical features and his ability to walk and act, but we failed to teach him where to walk and how to act. I was successful in helping the boy physically, but I failed to help him spiritually."

326 Think About It

Watch your thoughts; they become words.

Watch your words; they become actions.

Watch your actions; they become habits.

Watch your habits; they become character.

Watch your character; it becomes your destiny.

327 A Generation of Mules

"The church today is raising a whole generation of mules. They know how to sweat and to work hard but they don't know how to reproduce themselves."

It's not known who said that, but it is a statement of incredible insight. Mules are hard workers. They have carried supplies, plowed fields, pulled wagons and transported people. The only problem is that they are almost always sterile and thus cannot reproduce. They are hard workers, but they are the end of the line. They do not produce more like themselves.

The church is full of hard workers. They teach classes, serve the physical needs of others, clean up and mow the grass, cook, move tables, organize social activities, visit and even write letters and cards, and do a host of other things. There is just one problem. They don't "reproduce." They don't teach the gospel to the lost so others can become hard workers. They are the end of the line.

The real job the Lord gave us is to go into the world and "reproduce ourselves" by making disciples of others (Matt. 28:18-20). It is a tough lesson to realize that you may have worked hard and yet still haven't gotten the job done. Let us say it plainly. If we are not evangelizing, we are not doing the job completely. If we are nothing more than a generation of mules, we are on the road to extinction. Hup, Mule! Gee-Haw!!!

328 Who Leads Whom?

A worldly kind of person came to the preacher, defending her practice of attending worldly entertainments. She said, "But, pastor, I can take Jesus Christ with me wherever I go." The pastor after a few moments of thought quietly replied, "Indeed, is that so? I didn't know that was the order of the Bible. Is it for you to lead Jesus to where you want to go or for Him to lead you where He wants you to be?"

Doctrine

329 Good Advice

There is a great line in one of Charles Schulz's *Peanuts* cartoons. It is raining "cats and dogs" outside the window when Lucy asks the most profound question of the day. "Boy, look at it rain. What if it floods the whole world?" Fully up to the occasion as usual, Linus, the resident theologian, answers that a worldwide flood is impossible since Genesis 9 promises that God will never again flood the earth. Obviously relieved, Lucy sighs, "You've taken a great load off my mind. . . ." Linus's final summation: "sound theology has a way of doing that!"

330 Profound Theology

The theological student was playing "Stump the Professor." He asked his instructor, a widely recognized scholar and author, to state in a few words his most profound theology.

The academician thought a moment, then replied, "Jesus loves me, this I know, for the Bible tells me so."

Centuries earlier a similar scene took place in Jerusalem. A theological "hot shot" approached a country preacher with the toughest question of the day: "Teacher, which is the greatest commandment in the Law?"

In this case the theologian was playing "Stump the Bumpkin." After all, how could a backwoods itinerant possibly answer the question

that the finest religious minds in the country couldn't?

That the preacher answered was a surprise; but what he answered was the real shocker. "'Love the Lord your God with all your heart, with all your soul and with all your mind.' This is the first and greatest commandment. . . .'"

The answer Jesus gave in Matthew 22:34-40 was not at all unlike the answer of the modern theologian. Just as children in Bible class today learn to sing "Jesus Loves Me" from the earliest age, children in first century Palestine learned to recite "Love the Lord your God" from infancy. In fact, that was what Deuteronomy 6:4-9 was all about—parents teaching their children to give God all the love they have.

The study of theology is fine if it is kept in perspective. But we must never allow our research to obscure God's revelation. The most profound theological truths are these: God loves me and I must love God.

331 Strength from Depth

The iceberg is steadied because the great mass of its bulk is beneath the surface.

So the life of the strong man must go deep. Underneath the surface lie the great principles that endure—truth and justice and rectitude and the things that make for wholesome life and character.

Failure

332 He Succeeded through Failure

Christopher Columbus was obsessed with the idea that he could get to the East by traveling west, but by sailing west he never did reach India. He failed, but changed the course of history by discovering America, a great achievement. If you set out to do something great enough, what you do incidentally may be of more significance than that which is accomplished on purpose by someone else.

333 Don't Give Up

An elderly lady was once asked by a young man who had grown weary in the fight, whether he ought to give up the struggle. "I am beaten every time," he said dolefully. "I feel I must give up." "Did you ever notice," she replied, smiling into the troubled face before her, "that when the Lord told the discouraged fishermen to cast their nets again, it was right in the same old spot where they had been fishing all night and had caught nothing?"

334 Belief That You Can Do It Does It!

When Rear Admiral Du Pont explained to his superior officer, Farragut, why he had failed to take his ships into Charleston Harbor, Farragut heard him through to the end and then said, "Admiral, there is one explanation which you haven't given."

"What is that?" asked Du Pont.

"This: you didn't believe that you could do it."

That lack of confidence has been the secret of failures not only in the field of war but also in this greater warfare of the soul.

335 Failure Not Final

Phillips Brooks became a teacher in Boston Latin School, a position for which he seemed preeminently qualified. He lasted only a few months. His headmaster commented that Phillips "had in him no single element of a successful school teacher" and set Phillips packing with the conclusion that he had never known a man who failed as a schoolmaster to succeed in any other occupation. He had failed at the age of 20. Phillips Brooks overcame that failure, however, to become one of the finest pulpiteers in all of American history. No failure need be final.

336 Motivation from Failure

Frank Laubach learned to live above his failure. At 45, missionary Frank Laubach was a theological seminary professor in the Philippines. He was next in line for president of the seminary. However, the board selected someone else. Laubach took off for the hills to sulk. He was angry about the unfairness of life and God's seeming lack of justice. He was a failure in his own eyes.

Was that the end of his story? Not on your life. Frank developed in his solitude a technique for teaching hundreds of millions of people throughout the world to read for the first time. He became the father of the modern literacy movement. A failure, Frank Laubach learned to live above that failure, and on that new level, he found how to achieve excellence.

337 Grace Before Greatness

A talented, young black girl made her debut at New York's Town Hall, but she was not ready for it. Consequently, the critics flailed her. She returned to Philadelphia in disgrace. Part of her early support had come from a special fund provided by members of her church. This "Fund for Marian Anderson's Future" had launched her career. Now she returned in failure.

Marian's embarrassment and depression lasted for more than a year. Through that time, her mother continued to encourage her. Finally, one of the motherly pep talks sank in. She told her daughter, "Marian, grace must come before greatness." Motivated by those words, Marian Anderson went on to a distinguished career during which she also helped many others discouraged by their first failures.

338 Don't Be Too Proud to Fail

Thomas A. Edison recorded 1,093 patents. Most of these inventions were impractical or unmarketable. They were failures. But a man who invented the phonograph, the mimeograph, and the electric light bulb could afford a lot of failures. He was so inept in business matters that he lost control of the profitable companies that he founded, and yet in the depths of the depression, he died with an estate of $2,000,000. Edison was a successful failure.

It is obvious that you learn as you fail. You also grow as you fail, but you must *dare* to fail. If you can fail enough, you will learn a lot; but if you are too proud to fail, then you will not enjoy success.

339 Stepping-Stones of Failure

Abraham Lincoln was considered by many Americans as a most successful president. It was strange that he was a man marked for failure, a man suffering from melancholia, who endured long periods of depression throughout his life. He could barely see out of one eye. He had frequent nervous attacks, severe headaches, indigestion and nausea. He had a couch placed near his desk in the White House so he could quickly lie down when one of his spells came over him. When Lincoln was 10 years old he was kicked in the head by a horse and experts now believe that the skull was severely fractured, leaving him with lifelong problems. When he came to deliver the now famous address at Gettysburg, he was coming down with smallpox.

Lincoln failed in business in 1831, was defeated for the legislature in 1832. The next year he suffered another business defeat and in 1836 had a nervous breakdown. He failed to be elected speaker in 1838, was defeated for elector in 1840, and for Congress in 1843, as well as in 1848. Lincoln failed to be elected to the Senate in 1855, and was defeated for the Vice Presidency in 1856 and for the Senate in 1858. However, being elected President in 1860, he could afford all those failures. Abraham Lincoln was truly a successful failure.

Some people are slow starters and may discover God's purpose late in life. Moses was 80 years old when he began his life's work. All that time God was preparing him to do *one* thing—lead the Hebrews out of Egypt. It could be that you are living to accomplish only one great task for God, and that all the rest of your life is merely preparation for that great heroic responsibility.

340 Paul—Successful Failure

Sometimes we are overwhelmed with failures because we are so aware of our own, but we fail to notice those of others. The athlete is not celebrated for the games he has lost; the photographer throws away his poor pictures; the potter reshapes his marred jars; and the painter displays only his best portraits.

Perhaps then, God has different measurements for failure and success than we do. Paul the Apostle was not acclaimed during his lifetime. He was rejected by Jews and held in suspicion by Gentiles. He was stoned, beaten, imprisoned, mocked by some, and ignored by others. He spent his life starting little churches that were soon overtaken with problems so big that the members needed revisiting and letters written to them to straighten out their difficulties. Paul taught the truth only to discover that some who received it on one day were turning the next day to some false doctrine. No glory crowned his life, nor was any success evident when, during his last days, his friends deserted him as he was held prisoner. In the end, he was shamefully executed.

Yet, looking back on the ministry of Paul, we see that he was indeed a successful failure. One-half of the books of the New Testament are from his pen, and he is now hailed as the greatest Christian missionary of all time!

341 Don't Quit After the First Failure

When the great Polish pianist, Ignace Paderewski, first chose to study the piano, his music teacher told him his hands were much too small to master the keyboard.

When the great Italian tenor, Enrico Caruso, first applied for instruction, the teacher told him his voice sounded like the wind whistling through the window.

When the great statesman of Victorian England, Benjamin Disraeli, attempted to speak in Parliament for the first time, members hissed him into silence and laughed when he said, "Though I sit down now, the time will come when you will hear of me."

Henry Ford forgot to put a reverse gear in his first car.

Albert Einstein failed his university entrance exams at his first attempt.

Thomas Edison spent $2,000,000 on an invention which proved to be of little value.

Very little comes out right the first time. Failures, repeated failures, are fingerprints on the road to achievement. Abraham Lincoln's life could demonstrate that the only time you do not fail is the last time you try something and it works. We can "fail forward" toward success.

342 Who Has Not Failed?

The Apostle Paul failed; Peter failed; every one of the twelve apostles failed.

David, Israel's greatest king, "a man after God's own heart," failed.

Moses, giant among the Israelites, giver of the law, deliverer of his people, failed.

Jacob, father of Israel, failed; Isaac, son of promise, failed.

Abraham, progenitor of Israel, father of the faithful, prototype of those who are righteous through faith, failed.

Even our first parents, in their human perfection, failed.

Who has not failed?

It is not failing that is the problem; it is what one does after he has failed.

To take failure as final is to be a failure. To see in failure the school of the Spirit is to let failure contribute to one's growth in Christ.

343 Defeat Does Not Mean Failure

Booker T. Washington said, "Success is to be measured not so much by the position that one has reached in life as by the obstacles which he has overcome while trying to succeed."

By taking two steps forward and one step back, we still continually move closer to the goal. A man who makes no mistakes is one who does nothing. Failure, disappointments, and setbacks are a part of life. We must learn not to identify with our failures.

There are many, many examples of people who overcame backward steps. Abraham Lincoln ran for political office seven times and was defeated each time. Bobby Kennedy failed third grade and could not even take care of his own paper route. Babe Ruth struck out more times than any other baseball player. Ed Gibson, one of the astronauts on the Skylab III mission, failed first and fourth grades.

Learn from your mistakes, but identify with your success. Press on, confident in your own ability to succeed, backed by the power of God. Never forget that people who accomplish great things believe they can do it.

344 When All Else Fails, Read the Instructions

We are so good at doing things our own way. Then, when they do not work out, we turn to God and say, "Help! Now what do I do?" We are so foolish, for if we had read His instructions in the first place, we wouldn't have had the problem in the second place. *"Thy Word have I hid in my heart that I might not sin against thee."* That's a powerful thought!

Faith

345 Attack of the Killer Rabbits

A counselor at church camp told of his experience with a nine-year-old boy who started to cry when they turned out the cabin lights the first night. "Was he afraid of the dark?" the counselor asked. "No," the boy replied; "he just didn't want to be attacked by the 'killer rabbits.'" Some older kids at home had told him that there were "killer rabbits" who would come out at night and attack the campers.

Jesus was constantly reassuring the disciples with the words, "Fear not." Their fears betrayed their lack of faith. When one traces these words and their usage throughout the Bible, it seems that one of man's constant needs is to be reassured of the presence and comfort of God almighty. Christians can draw on this presence to find comfort and destroy their fears.

Watch out for "killer rabbits!" They can destroy your peace of mind at camp and throughout life.

346 A Story of Faith

Pete had become lost in the desert and had been chasing mirages. He thought to himself, *I'll follow this last one.* It was a deserted town with a well in the very center. His mouth parched from the intense heat, he ran to the well with his last ounce of energy.

He vigorously pumped the handle only to find that no water came forth. Then, he looked up to a note nailed to the post. It instructed its readers to "look behind the rock where a five-gallon container of water will be found" and warned against drinking or using it for anything besides priming the pump. Every ounce was needed, and not even a drop could be spared, the note emphasized.

"After pouring the water down the pump, pump the handle vigorously and all the water you desire will come forth," the note said. One last instruction was to please fill the water can and place it behind the rock for the next weary soul who might happen to come along.

How hard it is for people to give up a "sure thing" for something they cannot see at the time. Pete had a sure thing in the bucket of water and yet was instructed to pour it "all" down the pump.

347 Faith and Works

An old boatman painted the word "faith" on one oar of his boat and "works" on the other. He was asked his reason for this. In answer, he

132

slipped the oar with "faith" into the water and rowed. The boat, of course, made a very tight circle. Returning to the dock, the boatman then said, "Now, let's try 'works' without 'faith' and see what happens." The oar marked "works" was put in place and the boatman began rowing with just the "works" oar. Again the boat went into a tight circle but in the opposite direction.

When the boatman again returned to the wharf, he interpreted his experiment in these strong and convincing words, "You see, to make a passage across the lake, one needs both oars working simultaneously in order to keep the boat in a straight and narrow way. If one does not have the use of both oars, he makes no progress either across the lake nor as a Christian.

348 Why Worry When You Are a Child of a Father Who Sustains the World?

Spurgeon speaks of an evening when he was riding home after a heavy day's work. He felt weary and depressed, when as suddenly as a lightning flash came this verse, "My grace is sufficient for thee." He said, "I should think it is, Lord," and he burst out laughing. It seemed to make unbelief so absurd.

"It was as if some little fish, being very thirsty, was troubled about drinking the river dry, and the river says, 'Drink away, little fish, my stream is sufficient for thee.'

"Or, it seemed like a little mouse in the granaries of Egypt after seven years of plenty fearing it might die of famine, and Joseph might say, 'Cheer up, little mouse, my granaries are sufficient for thee.'

"Again, I imagined a man away up on yonder mountain saying to himself, 'I fear I shall exhaust all the oxygen in the atmosphere.' But the earth might say, 'Breathe away, oh man, and fill thy lungs ever; my atmosphere is sufficient for thee.'"

Little faith will bring our souls to heaven, but great faith will bring heaven to us.

349 How Were People Saved in the Old Testament?

Dr. Harry Ironside, for 18 years pastor of the Moody Church in Chicago, told of visiting a Sunday School class while on vacation. The teacher asked, "How were people saved in Old Testament times?"

After a pause, one man replied, "By keeping the Law." "That's right," said the teacher.

But Dr. Ironside interrupted: "My Bible says that by the deeds of the Law shall no flesh be justified."

The teacher was a bit embarrassed, so he said, "Well, does somebody else have an idea?"

Another student replied, "They were saved by bringing sacrifice to God."

"Yes, that's right!" the teacher said and tried to go on with the lesson.

But Dr. Ironside interrupted, "My Bible says that the blood of bulls and goats cannot take away sin."

By this time the unprepared teacher was sure the visitor knew more about the Bible than he did, so he said, "Well, *you* tell us how people were saved in the Old Testament!"

And Dr. Ironside explained that they were saved by faith—the same way people are saved today! Twenty-one times in Hebrews 11 will you find the same words, "by faith."

350 What Does It Mean to Believe?

Many years ago now, when John G. Paton first went out as a pioneer missionary to the new Hebrides Islands, he found that the natives among whom he began to work had no way of writing their language. He began to learn it and in time began to work on a translation of the Bible for them. Soon he discovered that they had no word for "faith." This was serious, of course, for a person can hardly translate the Bible without it.

One day he went on a hunt with one of the natives. They shot a large deer in the course of the hunt, and tying its legs together and supporting it on a pole, laboriously trekked back down the mountain path to Paton's home near the seashore. As they reached the veranda both men threw the deer down, and the native immediately flopped into one of the deck chairs that stood on the porch exclaiming, "My, it is good to stretch yourself out here and rest." Paton immediately jumped to his feet and recorded the phrase. In his final translation of the New Testament

this was the word used to convey the idea of trust, faith, and belief.

"Stretch yourself out on the Lord Jesus Christ, and thou shalt be saved" (Acts 16:31).

351 Cancer Cannot—

Cripple love!
Corrode faith!
Eat away peace!
Kill friendship!
Silence courage!
Invade the soul!
Quench the spirit!
Destroy confidence!
Reduce eternal life!
Erase the promises of God!
Obliterate happy memories!
Shatter the hope of Heaven!
Lessen the power of the resurrection!
Keep the faithfully obedient from Heaven!

Cancer can only affect the physical body for a time. It may hasten death, but it is appointed unto man, once to die, anyway (Heb. 9:27). Therefore, if one is prepared through faith in Christ, and obedience to Christ's commands, we need not fear death! (John 12:48).

352 Faith, a Necessity

Faith is a daily necessity whether one is getting married, taking a job, struggling with an illness, or overcoming a handicap. And faith in God is the cornerstone of all other faiths. As one psychiatrist says, "When I learn a patient has no faith in God, I dismiss the case. There is nothing to build on."

353 Do Not Let Hurts Hurt You

"Though I say, 'I will forget my complaint, I will leave off my sad countenance and be cheerful' " (Job 9:27 NASV).

Rejections, defeats, and failures that all of us have experienced can create enough negative feelings to destroy us. Be careful! Often the most painful wounds are not the scars that are outwardly seen, but the hidden wounds deep in the heart. Being hidden, they are often the most dangerous.

Setbacks in our lives can take the joy out of living. Our faith is weakened and if we collect enough hurts it will stop us from wanting to press forward. Even success can make one the target of criticism. Don't let the hurts hurt you!

Look at Job. A man of the land of Uz, blameless, upright, one who feared God, and one who turned away from evil. Job had seven sons and three daughters, a beautiful family. He was considered "the greatest of all the men of the East." He lost it all in the twinkling of an eye. He lost his health, wealth and family. He hurt. His wife hurt. His friends hurt. He was knocked down but not out. He had lost some of the passionate power to grow and some of his enthusiasm had diminished but he checked his negative thinking and that of his wife and friends and stated, "I will forget my complaint, I will leave off my sad countenance and be cheerful." How could he do that after undergoing so much hurt?

Along the shoreline in California it is a common sight to see whales stopping alongside rocks to scrape off barnacles as they migrate from Alaska to Mexico. In our lifetime we also will pick up a collection of personal hurts that will attach themselves like parasites sapping the life out of us. They must be scraped off.

How did Job do it? The same way we can do it—through faith. Faith is the only thing that can heal the hurts. Job scraped the barnacles off. It was painful! It hurt! The scars would remain but his life was put back together. Strong belief in God was the medicine. His wife, his friends could not help him—only God could!

354 Fruitless Faucets

When Lawrence of Arabia was in Paris after World War I with some of his Arab friends, he showed them the sights of the city: the Arch of Triumph, the Louvre, Napoleon's tomb, the Champs Elysees, but none of these things impressed them. The thing that really interested them the most was the faucet in the bathtub of the hotel room. They spent much time in turning it on and off. They found it amazing that one could turn a handle and get all the water he wanted.

Later, when they were ready to leave Paris and return to the East, Lawrence found them in the bathroom with wrenches trying to disconnect the faucet. "You see," they said, "it is very dry in Arabia. What we need are faucets. If we have them, we will have all the water we want." Lawrence had to explain that the effectiveness of the faucets did not lie in themselves but in the immense reservoirs of water to which they were attached, and he had to point out that behind this lay the rain and snowfalls of the Alps.

What a tremendous application to our Christian lives. Like the faucet by itself, so as individual Christians by ourselves, without Christ we are useless (John 15:5), ". . . apart from me you can do nothing." The lives of many Christians are as dry as the Arabian desert. They have their faucets, but there is no connection to the Living Water. May we trust God by faith so that our lives may be abundantly fruitful. Don't be a fruitless faucet.

Faithfulness

355 Don't Give Up!!

Dag Hammarskjold once wrote: "When the morning's freshness has been replaced by the weariness of midday, when the leg muscles quiver under the strain, the climb seems endless, and suddenly nothing will go quite as you wish—it is then that you must not hesitate." He was unwilling to give up; he refused to quit!

The successful life prescribed by Christ requires faithfulness until death: a hand on the plow with no looking back, steadfast perseverance; racing hard for the tape, fighting the good fight of faith. The devil loves it when we simply relax our efforts. He has a good day if we become discouraged.

There are temptations to overcome, disappointments to handle, personal sins that beset us, burdens that depress us. And Satan is standing by urging that we quit trying. But wait; Christ is present. "Consider Him who has endured such hostility by sinners against Himself, so that you may not grow weary and lose heart" (Heb. 12:3).

Someone once asked James J. Corbett, at that time heavyweight champion of the world, what was the most important thing a man must do to become a champion. He replied, "Fight one more round." The Duke of Wellington said that the British soldiers at the Battle of Waterloo were not any braver than Napoleon's soldiers—but they were brave for five minutes longer.

That is about it for the Christian. A secret for success is: "fight just one more round. Be brave for five more minutes." It is the difference between defeat and victory.

356 Divine Spectacle

During an interview with Mr. Lincoln long after he had been inaugurated President, a friend asked him if he loved Jesus. The President buried his face in his handkerchief and wept and sobbed. He then said amid his tears, "When I left home to take the chair of the State I was not then a Christian. When my son died—the severest trial of my life—I was not a Christian. But when I went to Gettysburg, and looked upon the graves of our dead who had fallen in the defense of their country, I then and there committed myself to Christ. I do love Jesus. The spectacle of that crucified One which is before my eyes is more than sublime—it is Divine."

A gentleman having an appointment to meet President Lincoln at five o'clock in the morning went a quarter of an hour before the time appointed. While waiting for the appointed time he heard in the next room a voice as if in grave conversation, and asked an attendant standing by, "Who is talking in the next room? "It is the President, sir," replied the attendant. "Is anybody with him?" the gentleman inquired. "No; he is reading the Bible." "Is that his habit so early in the morning?" "Yes, sir, he spends every morning from four o'clock to five in reading the Scriptures and praying."

357 What Is Faithfulness?

A shepherd once came to the city of Edinburgh from the country. He had his small obedient dog with him. While there, the man died and was buried. That little dog lay upon its master's grave—not for a day, a week, or a month, but for 12 years. Every day at one o'clock a gun was fired in the castle of Edinburgh. When the gun was fired the dog would run to the local baker who gave it food and water. Then back to the grave it would go. This continued till the dog died 12 years later. That was faithfulness!

A man threw a goose, which had been run over and crushed by a car, into an oil drum. For seven years the gander, that goose's mate, never went more than ten feet away from that oil drum. That was faithfulness!

George Mueller prayed for 52 years for a certain man to come to Christ. A pastor visited an elderly man 21 times before being admitted, but then he befriended the man and led him to Christ. That was faithfulness!

A Welsh postman had the British Empire Medal conferred upon him by Queen Elizabeth; he had not missed a day's service in 43 years. Paul Dhrlick, the chemist, performed 605 unsuccessful experiments; the 606th was a success! Thomas Edison made 18,000 experiments before he perfected the arc light. After experiencing 50 failures on another project he said, "I have found 50 ways it cannot be done!" That was faithfulness!

During the Korean War a man buried himself in the muck and mud of a pig sty (except for his nose and mouth so he could breathe) for eight days and nights rather than betray his buddies and surrender to the enemy. That was faithfulness!

Are you not glad that Jesus was faithful in dying for us and that He now lives and is faithful to care for us? *God grant us grace to be faithful!*

Family

358 House or Home

A cute little girl was sitting on top of a pile of luggage in a hotel lobby. Her parents were at the desk registering for their room. A sympathetic lady asked the little girl if they were visiting relatives in the city. "Oh, no," the girl replied. "We're going to live at this hotel until we find a house. My Daddy has a new job and we had to sell our house and move." The lady said, "Oh, it's too bad you don't have a home." To which the girl replied, "Oh we have a *home*—it's just that we don't have a house to put it in."

359 Your Family Devotions Are Important

Twelve convincing reasons for having family devotions:

1. It unifies the family and sweetens home life.

2. It cultivates the Christian graces and relieves tension and misunderstanding that sometimes threaten the fellowship of the home.

3. It aids our boys and girls in becoming Christians, and helps them to develop ideals that guide them in vital Christian living.

4. It yields spiritual resources for daily tasks and assists us in cultivating dependence upon God.

5. It strengthens us in the face of adversities and disappointments and enables us to trust Christ implicitly in all of life's circumstances.

6. It makes us conscious during the day of the abiding presence of our Savior and Friend.

7. It bears a Christian witness to the guests in our home.

8. It undergirds the Christian teaching of the Sunday School and the ministry of the church.

9. It affords opportunity for the Christian family to pray for and to sharpen its concern for non-Christian families.

10. It helps us to give a right place to spiritual values and saves us from an undue concern for the temporal things of life.

11. It encourages us to put Christianity into practice in our homes.

12. It honors God and provides an excellent outlet for the expression of our gratitude for the abundance of daily mercies and blessings which come from Him.

Parents

360 Deficiency

A mother made an appointment with her young child's pediatrician. She said she had noticed that he had eaten dirt on several occasions.

To the doctor, she said, "I've always heard that if a child eats dirt, there is some deficiency. Do you think his dirt-eating indicates a lack of something?"

The doctor replied, "Yes—very definitely. A lack of supervision!"

361 Teach Your Child Integrity

In ancient China, the people desired security from the barbaric hordes to the north, so they built the great Chinese wall. It was so high they knew no one could climb over it and so thick that nothing could break it down. They settled back to enjoy their security. During the first 100 years of the wall's existence, China was invaded three times. Not once did the barbaric hordes break down the wall or climb over the top. Each time they bribed a gatekeeper and then marched right through the gates. The Chinese were so busy relying upon the walls of stone that they forgot to teach integrity to their children.

362 A Dollar for Your Child

"Bring them up in the training and instruction of the Lord" (Eph. 6:4).

His name was Rusty, and he was barely 11 years old. He still had the look of a little boy. He was homeless, not old enough to be hardened, but certainly old enough to be frightened. His mother lived in town, but she didn't want him. Rusty lived in the alley behind the shop of one of our church members. He slept in a cardboard box.

In an effort to get legal custody transferred to a Christian foster home, a little group met in an attorney's office: Rusty, Rusty's mother, the social worker, the attorney, and a pastor. They were severing all legal ties between Rusty and his mother . . . and she did not care. The attorney carefully explained to Rusty's mother what was happening. He wanted to make sure that she understood that, in effect, she was losing all rights to her boy. Everyone was on the verge of tears—all except Rusty's mom.

Then came the question. The attorney worded it carefully, "Mrs. Brown, do you understand that when you sign this form, you are signing over all legal custody to the designated children's home?" She nodded her head in the affirmative. "Mrs. Brown, do you have any questions?" She had only one. "Do I get any money for this?" she asked. Everyone seemed dazed by this sledgehammer query. There was a long pause. Finally, 11-year-old Rusty pulled out his pocket book, extracted a dollar he had earned sweeping floors, and gave it to his mother. And she took it!

In less obvious ways, all over America, there are parents who are trading their parental responsibilities for the almighty dollar. Kids shouldn't have to grow up by themselves. Let me paraphrase: "What does it profit a man if he gains the whole world . . . and loses his own children?"

363 What Do You Want Your Child To Be?

President Theodore Roosevelt had four sons. He was very proud when the first three sons announced their intention to join the military. But when his fourth son also decided to join the Army, the old Roughrider balked. "Not all my boys," he said to his wife. But she replied, "Ted, if you raised them as eagles you cannot expect them to fly like sparrows."

Every parent should have a dream for his or her children. Isaiah put it this way: "And all your sons will be taught of the Lord; and the well being of your sons will be great" (Is. 54:13). Three things to consider:

1. *You announce what you want your child to be by what you teach him.* It is not the church's responsibility to teach your children. It is yours as a mother and father. One man had been in a non-Sunday School congregation. When asked why, he said, "We did not object to classes. What we were afraid of was that parents would quit teaching at home." Was he right?

2. *You announce what you want your child to be by the example you set.* It is amazing how some parents put the ball games, camping trips, and fishing trips above attending worship, and then are amazed that their children leave the church. Someone wrote, "What you are thunders so loudly that I cannot hear what you say."

3. *You announce what you want your child to be by the plans you make for him.* Your children know if something is really important to you. Have you been saying from the time they started school, "Now make good grades so that someday you can go to college." They know how important that is to you. Have you encouraged them to be a preacher, a missionary, Bible school teacher, elder, etc.? By your plans, you have told them what you think is important.

364 Will Your Children Go to Heaven?

One congregation found that where both parents were faithful to the Lord, including active interest in the local congregation's programs, 93 percent of the kids remained faithful. On the other hand, if only one of the parents was faithful, that figure dropped to 73 percent. Where the parents were only what we would call reasonably active in the Lord's work, only 53 percent of the young people maintained their faith.

Now here comes the shocker: In those cases where both parents attended only infrequently, the percentage of their children who remained faithful to the Lord dropped to 6 percent. Want your children to go to heaven? Then make certain you are leading them.

365 Parents Blunder When . . .

1. They give a child everything he wants.

2. They laugh at a child when he does or says something wrong.

3. They avoid the words "no" and "wrong."

4. They pick up after their children instead of giving them the responsibility of doing it.

5. They take the side of their children against neighbors, teachers, and other responsible adults.

6. They make every decision for their children.

7. They bail them out of every situation instead of letting them face the consequences of their mistakes.

8. They are over-protective, and do not allow their children to do normal and healthy things.

9. They let their children talk back to them.

10. They criticize others openly in front of their children.

366 Parents Provoke Their Children When . . .

1. They are over-protective.

2. They show favoritism toward one of their children.

3. They compare the accomplishments or abilities of their children.

4. They push achievement, aims, and goals, and in so doing, put undue pressure on their children.

5. They do not reward or encourage their children.

6. They fail to allow childishness; that is, they do not understand that a child is a child, and not an adult.

7. They neglect their children's needs: spiritually, socially, intellectually and physically.

8. They nag their children.

9. They abuse them with hateful, ugly, and bitter words.

10. They punish them cruelly, or when the punishment is too harsh or severe for the mistake that was made.

367 Quality Time

I cringe every time I hear parents say that their schedules are really full, so they make a great effort to spend "quality time" with their children.

Think what this idea would look like if transferred to another area of life. What if a great basketball player decided, "I am pretty good now. I think I will just spend 15 minutes practicing my shooting today. It may not be very long, but it will be quality time." That approach would soon have him warming a bench. There is no quality time without investing a large quantity of time.

Father

368 What Kind of Father Are You?

Some people say any man can be a father; it is a job that takes little talent. However, the rate for failure in fatherhood is actually higher than in any other occupation. Fathers have a colossal full-time job that most people underestimate. It is the most important task a man can tackle.

Despite vast changes in America's social fabric in recent years, one thread of tradition shows no sign of unraveling: sons and daughters who follow in their father's footsteps.

A nationwide survey was taken recently to determine how much time fathers were spending with their children. The results were astounding. Fathers with children between the ages of 2 and 12 were spending 12 minutes a day with their children. Twelve-minute dads contribute greatly to 12-year-old delinquents.

But not all dads are 12-minute dads. A busload of dads and sons left a church parking lot for an overnight camping trip. The dads represented various vocations, but they all had one thing in common: they did not want to be 12-minute dads.

You cannot substitute a popsicle for Pop himself, though both may have their places. Whether it be a car or a candy bar, a fishing rod or a hot rod, you cannot substitute these "presents" for the "presence."

America is standing at a crossroads of history; our very survival as a nation may depend on the presence or absence of masculine leadership in millions of homes; leadership in the form of loving authority; leadership in the form of financial management; leadership in the form of spiritual training and leadership in maintaining good marital relationships.

369 Two Views of Fishing

Sometimes there are effects of our influence that we may never know. G. Brook Adams kept a diary from his boyhood. One special day

when he was eight years old, he wrote in his diary, "Went fishing with my father; the most glorious day of my life." Throughout the next 40 years of his life he never forgot that day he went fishing with his father, he made repeated references to it in his diary, commenting on the influence of that day on his life.

Brook's father was an important man; he was Charles Francis Adams, the U.S. ambassador to Great Britain under the Lincoln administration. Interestingly, he too made a note in his diary about the fishing trip. He wrote simply, "Went fishing with my son; a day wasted."

Of course the day was not wasted; its value may well have proved to make it one of the most well-spent days in his life. No one can measure the influence of a man on his children, and that is all the more reason to take the job and its responsibilities seriously.

Someone has written, "last night my little boy confessed to me some childish wrong; and kneeling at my knee, he prayed with tears, 'O Lord, make me a man like Daddy—wise and strong. I know you can.' Then while he slept, I knelt beside his bed, confessed my sins and prayed with low-bowed head, 'O God, make me a child like my child here; pure, guileless, trusting thee with faith sincere.' "

What kind of a father are you?

370 Too Many Orphanages

One family has opened its heart and its home to a number of Cambodian refugees, taking them right in with their natural sons and daughters and sharing all they have. It makes a crowded house, yet these orphans from a distant land are happy.

But there are many other orphans around these days. Some homes have become "orphanages," not because the father is dead, but because he is too busy pursuing his own dreams and providing physical and material needs. This group of "spiritual" orphans is growing by leaps and bounds.

No one wants children to grow up and follow a bad example. There is no greater tragedy than to lose the respect of one's own children. It will haunt one in a lonely old age. Good fathers are wanted—and needed.

371 Father's Day

Fathers and mothers have the greatest opportunity as teachers of anyone in the world. You see, that boy or girl in the home has the chance to see if Father and Mother really believe and practice what they teach.

A father who says he believes in Sunday school, and then does not go himself, is teaching by his actions that he really does not feel it very important. A father who teaches love and tolerance to all and yet maintains a critical attitude in the home toward his brothers and sisters in the church is doing a wrong to his children which never in this world can be undone. It is pure poison to the mind of the child, and will most certainly be a

stumbling block in the way of the child becoming a Christian.

A father who says he believes the Bible to be the greatest Book, to be God's Word to us, but leaves it on the shelf to gather dust while he spends hours with the newspaper, magazines, radio and television is in reality saying, "Children, the Bible is not too important. You should read it if you have any extra time."

Which one of you had not heard a little boy step proudly forward among his playmates and declare, "I KNOW that's so because my Daddy said so!" He has confidence in you, dear Dad, and the things which he sees you put first in your life are going to stand out as mighty important to him, too.

Is your prayer: "*Lord, fit me to be loved and imitated by my children*"?

372 A Preoccupied Father

One day a small boy was taking a walk with his father. When they passed an unusual looking truck, he said, "What is that, Daddy?"

"*I don't know,*" his father said.

Then they came to a large, old-fashioned warehouse, "What's in there, Daddy?" the little boy asked.

"*I don't know,*" his father replied.

After they had walked on a short way in silence, the little boy turned to his father and said, "Daddy, do you mind my asking you so many questions?"

"Of course not," commented his father proudly. "How else are you going to learn anything?"

373 God the Father, in Luke 15

In Luke 15 Christ related to the people one of the most poignant stories in all literature, that of the prodigal son. Nearly everyone can relate to one of the characters, the prodigal son, the elder brother, or the father. Each of the characters teaches important lessons for Christians to learn. In verses 20–24 we learn some things about the father that Christian fathers need to imitate as they try to raise their children in the nurture and admonition of the Lord.

1. *He was patient*—Although the son had been gone a long time (long enough for a famine to ravage the land), the father was still looking. He "saw him a great way off." His eyes never tired of looking for his wayward son. Fathers, how patient are you with your children when they falter on life's pathway?

2. *He was loving*—When he saw his son coming, he ran to him. He could not wait for his son to come to him. He immediately hugged and kissed his son. The father did not even ask for an explanation of where he had been or what he had been doing. He did not give him a lecture on "you should have known better," or "I hope you have learned your lesson." Fathers, how loving are you toward your children when they make mistakes?

3. *He was forgiving*—We know he was forgiving because his actions demonstrated it. So anxious was he to forgive his son that he did not let him finish his plea. (In vv.

18, 19 the son plans to ask his father to make him a servant. But the father cuts him off before he gets that far, vv. 21, 22). The father restored his wayward son to his original place and treated him with the highest honor. Fathers, how forgiving are you of your children when they do wrong?

4. *He had his priorities in the right place*—The most important thing was not that his son had sinned, not that he had taken advantage of his father, not that he had caused his father untold grief; the most important thing was that his son was alive and had come home.

374 The Relationship We Really Need

A little boy sat frustrated and near tears. He was trying to build a toy wagon, but he just could not get the wheels to go on. His dad came along, took the wagon and the four wheels and, in no time at all, had it rolling smoothly along. The boy was grateful for the loving and helpful touch his father added to his life. Though he is no longer a child, he still remembers his father's help that day.

It has been said that any man can be a father but that it takes a special kind of man to be a Dad! The ideal father does more than simply have a part in the procreation of the child, he helps to mold the child throughout his growing years through generous amounts of love, guidance, correction, forgiveness and praise. Fortunate are those who have had a father with whom they had such a personal relationship.

Whether or not this has been the case for you, this much is for certain: we can all experience the ultimate father-child relationship when we experience God as our heavenly Father.

375 Please, Daddy, Let's Go

A little boy with shiny eyes,
    His little face aglow.
Said, "It is time for Sunday School.
    Please, Daddy, let's go!"
"Oh no," said Daddy, "Not today.
    I have worked hard all week;
And I must have a day of rest,
    I am going to the creek.
For there I can relax and rest,
    And fishing's fine they say;
So run along, don't bother me,
    We will go to church some other day."
Months and years have passed away
    But Daddy hears that plea no more
"Please, let's go to Sunday School!"
    Those childhood days are o'er.
Now that daddy's growing old,
    When life is almost through,
He does find time to go to church,
    But, what does his son do?
He says, "Old Man, you're kidding!
    I have caroused around all night,
    A-popping pills, and smoking pot—
    You should have seen me fight!"

The daddy lifts a trembling hand
    To brush away the tears,
He seems to hear the pleading voice,
    Distinctly through the years.
He sees his small son's wistful face
    Upturned, with eyes aglow,
Saying, "It's time for Sunday School,
    Please, Daddy—won't you go?"

376 A Father's Prayer

Build me a son, O Lord, who will be strong enough to know when he is weak, and brave enough to face himself when he is afraid; one who will be proud and unbending in honest defeat, and humble and gentle in victory.

Build me a son whose wishbone will not be where his backbone should be; a son who will realize that to know Thee and know himself is the foundation stone of knowledge.

Lead him, I pray, not in the path of ease and comfort, but under the stress and spur of difficulties and challenges. Here let him learn to stand up in the storm; here let him learn compassion for those who fall.

Build me a son whose heart will be clear, whose goal will be high; a son who will master himself before he seeks to master other men; one who will learn to laugh, yet never forget how to weep; one who will reach into the future, yet never forget the past.

And after all these things are his, add, I pray, enough of a sense of humor, so that he may always be serious, yet never take himself too seriously. Give him humility, so that he may always remember the simplicity of true greatness, the open mind of true wisdom, the meekness of true strength.

Then, I, his father, will dare to whisper, "I have not lived in vain."

377 The Kind of Dad I Would Buy

If I went shopping for a man to be my dad, here is what I'd buy: one who would always stop to answer a little boy's "why?" One who would always speak kindly to a little girl or boy, one who would give a bit of sunshine and joy.

I would pick a dad who followed the Bible's Golden Rule, and one who went regularly to church and Bible school. I would buy the very finest Dad to place in our family tree—and then I'd try to live like him, so he would be proud of me.

378 Advice to Fathers About Their Children:

A Always trust them to God's care.
B Bring them to church.
C Challenge them to high goals.
D Delight in their achievements.
E Exalt the Lord in their presence.
F Frown on evil.
G Give them love.
H Hear their problems.
I Ignore not their childish fears.
J Joyfully accept their apologies.
K Keep their confidence.
L Live a good example before them.
M Make them your friends.
N Never ignore their endless questions.
O Open your home to their visits.
P Pray for them by name.
Q Quicken your interest in their spirituality.
R Remember their needs.
S Show them the way of salvation.
T Teach them to work.
U Understand they are still young.
V Verify your statements.
W Wean them from bad company.
X Expect them to obey.
Y Yearn for God's best for them.
Z Zealously guide them in biblical truth.

379 One Neat Dad

Did you ever notice in the TV family *The Waltons* how the father was always available; or in *Little House on The Prairie,* how Laura's dad was always there for the tight squeezes? Contrast these situations with the modern dad who is gone from morning to night. Things have certainly changed since the 1930s and the earlier house on the prairie days, maybe too much. Years ago, Dr. Charlie Shedd held a contest called "One Neat Dad." He asked contestants to send in letters recommending their dad for this great honor. Here's a list of the ten most appreciated qualities for "One Neat Dad."

1. He takes time for me.
2. He listens to me.
3. He plays with me.
4. He invites me to go places with him.
5. He lets me help him.
6. He treats my mother well.
7. He lets me say what I think.
8. He is nice to my friends.
9. He only punishes me when I deserve it.
10. He is not afraid to admit when he is wrong.

Qualities one to five are versions of the single word, "time!" Spell it—listen, spell it—play, spell it—help me, spell it—jump in the pickup . . . it all comes out in the same four letters, T-I-M-E. Time was the most appreciated trait of "One Neat Dad"!

380 Father's Lap

A prominent Philadelphia Christian businessman's wife felt he was not spending enough time with his six-year-old daughter. He decided to make up for that failing all at once.

He had his limousine driver take him to her school, where she was picked up and deposited next to him in the backseat. They took off for New York City where he had made reservations for dinner in an expensive French restaurant and had tickets to a Broadway show.

After an exhausting evening, they were driven home. In the morning, the little girl's mother could hardly wait to find out how the evening had gone. "How did you like it?"

The little girl thought a moment. "It was okay, I guess, but I would rather have eaten at McDonald's. And I did not really understand the show. But the best part was when we were riding home in that great big car and I put my head down on Daddy's lap and fell asleep."

381 In Daddy's Shoes

I watched him playing around my door,
My neighbor's little boy of four.
I wondered why a child would choose
To wear his dad's old worn-out shoes.

I saw him try with all his might
To make the laces snug and tight.
I smiled to see him walk, and then
He'd only step right out again.

I heard him say his voice so glad,
"I want to be just like my Dad."
I hope his Dad his steps would choose
Safe for his son to wear his shoes.

And then a shout and cry of joy,
A "Hello, Dad!" and a "Hi-yu, boy!"
They walked along in measured stride
Each face aglow with love and pride.

"What have you done today, my lad?"
"I tried to wear your old shoes, Dad,
They are big but when I am a man
I'll wear your shoes. I know I can."

They stopped and stood there hand in hand
He saw his son's tracks in the sand,
His words—a prayer—came back to me,
"Lord, let my steps lead him to Thee."

382 I'll Be Like You

To get his goodnight kiss he stood
Beside my chair one night
And raised an eager face to me,
A face with love alight.

And as I gathered in my arms
The son God gave to me,
I thanked the lad for being good,
And hoped he'd always be.

His little arms crept round my neck
And then I heard him say
Four simple words I can't forget
Four words that made me pray.

They turned a mirror in my soul,
On secrets no one knew.
They startled me; I hear them yet,
He said, "I'll be like you."

383 Let Your Children Know What You Value

A woman in Alabama told us about being with her husband at his father's deathbed. As the end approached, the father suddenly sat upright with a look of terror on his face. "What's happening to me, son?" he cried, grasping for the younger man, and then he sank back into the pillows.

The woman's husband was so visibly shaken, he staggered out into the hall. Joining him, the wife said softly, "This must be so terrible for you to have seen your Dad dying this way."

"That's not what got to me," her husband choked out, "It's that this is the first time in my life he ever called me 'son'."

Jesus didn't wait until the cross to let His disciples know how much He valued them. When He first met Nathaniel He said, "Behold an Israelite indeed, in whom there is no guile." And after a year or so with Simon, He said, "Blessed art thou, Simon, Bar-Jonah." The gospels radiate with His affirmations toward these and the rest of His disciples.

384 Daddy's Example

He couldn't see much reason
To go to Bible school;
And yet he didn't argue
With Daddy's Sunday rule.
But still he often wondered—
If Daddy's words were true,
Since Bible study's needed,
Why Dad did not go too?

One day when he was angry,
His Daddy overheard
Him say in tones emphatic,
A string of ugly words.
The boy was quickly summoned,
By an indignant shout;
And as the lad stood trembling,
His Daddy cursed him out.

And then a new adventure,
The boy embarked upon;
He tried a little smoking,
Which led to more than one.
His Daddy whipped and lectured:

'Twas quite a stern attack,
And then the son gave answer:
"I got them from *your* pack!"

We need no application,
The truth shines bright as day;
We teach much more by doing,
Much less by what we say.
Do naught but what you truly
Desire your child to do;
He may not always hear well,
But he is watching you!

385 The God-Image in Fathers

It has been said a child is not likely to find a Father in God unless he finds something of God in his father.

A Bible school teacher asked her class to draw a picture of God for her. A little boy finished first and said, "I drew a picture of my daddy because I don't know what God looks like, but I know what my dad looks like." (What a great responsibility we fathers have).

It is so important for us to be the kind of parents that will make our children want to honor their father and mother (Eph. 6:1-4).

386 Fathers Are Wonderful People!

I wish you could meet my Dad;
He's really quite a guy!
I wouldn't trade with anyone,
And here's the reason why:

Whenever I have problems,
Doubts, or questions, too,
We talk them all over, Dad and I,
And find what's best to do.

He helps me practice baseball,
And gives me useful tips;
And even lets me go along
When he takes fishing trips!

Then, too, my Dad's a Christian;
We often kneel and pray;
He helps me live as Jesus taught.
Yes, sir, my Dad's O.K.

387 Just Like His Dad

"Well, what are you going to be, my boy,
When you have reached manhood's years:
A doctor, a lawyer, or orator great,
Moving throngs to laughter and tears?"
But he shook his head, as he gave reply
In a serious way he had:
"I don't think I'd care to be any of them:
I Want to Be Like My Dad!"

He wants to be like his dad! You Men,
Did you ever think as you pause,
That the boy who watches your every move
Is building a set of laws?
He's molding a life you're the model for,
And whether it's good or bad
Depends on the kind of example set
To the boy who'd Be Like His Dad.

Would you have him go everywhere you go?
Have him do just the things you do?

And see everything that your eyes behold,
And woo all the gods you woo?
When you see the worship that smiles in the eyes
Of your lovable little lad
Could you rest content if he gets his wish
And grows to Be Like His Dad?

It's a joy that none but yourself can fill
It's a charge you must answer for;
It's a duty to show him the road to tread
Ere he reaches his manhood's door.
It's a debt you owe for the greatest joy
On this old earth to be had;
This pleasure of having a boy to raise
Who wants to Be Like His Dad!

388 People Are Important

Joseph M. Stowell gives this illustration:

"I thoroughly enjoy working in my yard. I've got my own system of fertilizing my lawn, cutting it, and caring for it. One year, when my son Joe was in his early teens, I spent all spring getting the yard to look just the way I wanted. We had a basketball hoop at the end of our driveway, and on several occasions Joe came along and said, 'Dad, let's play basketball.' My response was always, 'Joe, not right now. I'm busy working in the yard.' Or, 'I've got to trim this edge here.' Or, 'I've got to do the fertilizing now.'

Later that summer, I visited a hospital on several successive nights to comfort a family whose boy—about Joe's age—was dying. One evening as I drove home, it struck me that I had a boy just like that, that it was a great gift from God to have a healthy young son, and that I had permitted things—a *lawn*—to eclipse the value of time with him. I drove down our street and saw my beautiful, green, wonderfully manicured lawn. I drove into the driveway, saw the basketball hoop, and thought, *I don't care what I have to do tonight; one thing I'm going to do right now is play basketball with my son.*

So I threw open the door and yelled, 'Hey, Joe! Let's play basketball!' And he said, 'Not right now, Dad—I'm busy.' I was convicted, and I wondered, *How could I ever have let things eclipse the importance of my son*?

When you think about the truth about people, beware the treachery of the seduction of things."

Mother

389 Please, Mommy, Remember

Remember . . . that I am a gift from God, the richest of all blessings. Do not attempt to mold me in your image, my daddy's, my brother's, or our neighbor's. I am an individual and should be permitted to be myself.

Remember . . . not to crush my spirit when I fail. Don't compare me with others who outshine me.

Remember . . . that anger and hostility are natural emotions. Help me to find outlets for these normal feelings—in play or physical exercise—or else they may be turned inward and may become much deeper and much more serious.

Remember . . . to discipline me with firmness and reason. Do not let your anger throw you off balance. If I know you are fair, you will not lose my respect or my love.

Remember . . . that each child needs two parents. When you side with me against Daddy, I have feelings of guilt, confusion and insecurity.

Remember . . . not to hand me everything my little heart desires. Otherwise I will never know the thrill of earning, the joy of deserving.

Remember . . . not to make threats in anger, or impossible promises when you are in a generous mood. To me your word means everything. When I can't believe in you and Dad, I have difficulty believing in anything.

Remember . . . that there is dignity in hard work, whether it is performed with calloused hands that shovel coal or skilled fingers that manipulate surgical instruments. Let me know that a useful life is a blessed one, and that a life of ease and pleasure-seeking is empty and meaningless.

Remember . . . not to try to protect me from every small blow and disappointment. Adversity strengthens character and makes us compassionate. Trouble is the great equalizer; let me learn it.

Remember . . . to teach me to love God and our fellow men. And, Mommy, please don't *send* me to worship service and Bible school— *take* me there.

390 Mothers: Our Greatest Teachers

"Do not forsake the law of your mother" (Prov. 1:8).

The law of your mother—unwritten, but indelibly stamped upon your mind! It's the law of love, of kindness, of selflessness, of giving!

Motherhood—just think of its blessings, joys, sorrows, challenges and triumphs. There's no greater ecstasy than holding her newborn, and no greater anguish than the broken heart a child may cause. A mother's love is the nearest thing on earth to God's love.

The wisdom of God is exhibited in motherhood. We are not the by-product of some impersonal biological process. We were not made on an assembly line by the combination of chemicals. Our mothers nurtured us and formed an intimate relationship with us before we were born. She jeopardized her life for us. The greatest lessons we have ever learned have come from loving, caring, sacrificing mothers who were always available to us.

A woman's greatest, most fulfilling and far-reaching role is expressed in motherhood. LET US THANK GOD FOR CHRISTIAN MOTHERS! Let us be sensitive and grateful, not only on Mother's Day—but every-day for our mothers and the mother of our children.

391 My Child

I do not ask that you repay
The hours of toil and pain.
The sacrifice of youth and strength
Shall not have been in vain.
I do not ask for gratitude,
But only this, my child;
That you shall live your life so well,
My gifts be not defiled.

The nights I watched beside your crib;
The years of love and care will amply be repaid;
If once I see you standing there,
An upright and honest soul,
On whom success has smiled,
That I may say with humble pride,
That's my child!

392 Mother—A Definition

A little girl's definition of "mother": "A mother is a person who takes care of her kids and gets their meals and if she is not there when you get home from school you wouldn't know how to get your meals and you wouldn't feel like eating them anyhow."

393 Appreciation to Mother

One father was such an un-demonstrative man that the children used to worry, for he never seemed to show their mother proper appreciation for her gaiety and the many ways she made their

shabby old house a real home. But one afternoon she stopped at a neighbor's house to help with a sick child and delayed getting back. The father arrived home from work as usual and walked into the living room, which the eight children were filling with lively commotion.

The father stood in the doorway frowning, as he was surveying the scene. "Where is everybody?" he demanded.

Those children never again worried that their mother was not ap-preciated.

394 Now or ?

The man stopped at the flower shop to order some flowers to be wired to his mother who lived 200 miles away. As he got out of his car he noticed a girl sitting on the curb sobbing. He asked her what was wrong and she replied: "I wanted to buy a red rose for my mother, but I only have 75 cents and a rose costs $2.00.

The man smiled and said, "Come on in with me. I will buy you a rose for your mother." He placed his FTD order of flowers to his mother and bought a rose for the girl. As they were leaving he offered the girl a ride.

She responded, "Yes, please, if you could. Take me to my mother," and she directed him to a ceme-tery where she placed the rose on a freshly dug grave.

The man returned to the flower shop, canceled the wire order, picked up the flowers and drove the 200 miles to his mother's home.

395 Mothers Are Not Birds

My son found a bird's nest. It was empty. After just one season, the mother bird was finished with it. Next year she will build another. But I am glad human mothers are not like birds.

Did you know that if someone handles eggs in a wild bird's nest the bird may stop sitting on them? And, that if a mother bird has a defective chick she will shove it out of the nest and not allow it to grow up?

Thank God our mothers care for us, regardless of the many problems we have. They take care of us when we are hurt or sick. Like God, they love us even when we do wrong things.

A mother bird keeps busy feeding her young and protecting them. That is all she does, though. Think of how often our mothers have to be nurses, teachers, housekeepers, cooks, chauffeurs, counselors, and friends. With all we ask it is a wonder they don't push us out of the nest.

Baby birds are out of the nest in one season. The mother becomes free from caring for them. Our mothers are forever. They continue to do things for us even when we get older. They never stop caring for us. They pray for us. They become grandmothers and care for our children.

Mothers are a treasure. Take a moment to meditate on all that your mother has done for you. Be sure to honor and thank the mother God gave you.

396 A Mother's Beatitude

Blessed is the mother who understands her child, for she shall inherit a kingdom of memories.

Blessed is the mother who knows how to comfort, for she shall possess a child's devotion.

Blessed is the mother who guides by the path of righteousness, for she shall be proud of her offspring.

Blessed is the mother who is never shocked, for she shall receive confidences.

Blessed is the mother who teaches respect, for she shall be respected.

Blessed is the mother who emphasizes the good and minimizes the bad, for in like manner the child shall make evaluations.

Blessed is the mother who treats her child as she would be treated, for her home shall be filled with happiness.

Blessed is the mother who answers simply the startling questions, for she shall always be trusted.

Blessed is the mother who has character strong enough to withstand the thoughtless remarks and resentments of the growing child, for again, in due time, she shall be honored.

397 Staying With the Baggage

A few years ago a lovely Christian mother gave her pastor criticism he deserved. He had preached a strong sermon on personal evangelism pointing out every Christian's obligation to reach out and win others to the Lord. In the conclusion of the sermon he tried to obliterate every excuse that anyone might have for failure to lead others to Christ. The sermon needed to be preached, of course, as it still does. Only apparently he had been guilty of some unfair emphasis.

After the sermon he was invited home with a lovely Christian family. The husband was completing his resident work as a medical doctor, and had little spare time, but still he spent time in the church's personal work program. The wife beautifully cared for their three lovely children. All of them were very young—one still an infant in arms—and required a lot of time.

During the meal the wife asked the pastor if he remembered the Scripture, "For as his share is who goes down into battle, so shall his share be who stays by the baggage" (1 Sam. 30:24). He confessed his ignorance, and she gave the context of King David insisting that the home guard be rewarded equally with those who had the more obviously essential role of fighting in the front line.

And then she shared a wonderful truth which is so easily forgotten. She mentioned that she felt that taking care of children, patiently teaching them the ways of God and His great values, looking for moments of readiness to deflect them gently when they get on the wrong track was "staying with the baggage." She went on to point out that she often felt guilty for not doing more of the "church" work

than she did. But she felt her greatest ministry was being a dedicated Christian mother.

My friend, all you need to say after listening to a needed reprimand like that is one word—Amen.

398 What Mothers Ought To Teach Their Children

At a banquet, the mother of George Washington was sitting beside a distinguished French officer. Turning to Washington's mother, the officer asked, "How have you managed to rear such a splendid son?"

She replied, "I taught him to obey."

Too many people have a strong "will" and a weak "won't."

Children

399 She Took the Children

A little boy after reading Bunyan's "Pilgrim's Progress," asked his mother which of the characters she liked best.

She replied, "Christian, of course; he is the hero of the story."

The child responded, "Mother, I like Christiana best, because when Christian set out on his pilgrimage he went alone, but when Christiana started she took the children with her."

400 Hall of Fame

When he entered baseball's Hall of Fame, ex-slugger Harmon Killebrew recalled, "My father used to play with my brother and me in the yard. Mother would come out and say, 'You're tearing up the grass.'

" 'We're not raising grass,' Dad would reply, 'We're raising boys!' "

401 How Is Your Influence?

Max Jukes lived in New York. He did not believe in Christ or in Christian training. He refused to take his children to church, even when they asked to go. He has had 1,026 descendants—300 were sent to prison for an average term of 13 years each; 190 were public prostitutes; 680 were admitted alcoholics. His family thus far, has cost the state in excess of $420,000. They have made no contribution to society that is of any benefit.

Jonathan Edwards lived in the same state, at the same time as Jukes. He loved the Lord and saw that his children were in church every Sunday, as he served the Lord to the best of his ability. He has had 929 descendants—of these, 430 were ministers; 86 became university presidents; 75 authored good books; five were elected to the United States Congress and two to the Senate. One was Vice-President of this nation. His family never cost the state one cent but has contributed immeasurably to the life of plenty in this land today.

How is your influence and what legacy will you leave with your children, grandchildren, and great-grandchildren?

402 Early Childhood: An Enemy Stronghold

Is Satan actually interested in the childhood years? After all, children from birth to six could not be any real threat to him and his forces of darkness. Or could they?

Scripture tells us that Timothy, while still young enough to have to be fed, dressed and carried, *knew* the Holy Scriptures (2 Tim. 3:15). He had an experiential knowledge of them; they meant something to him. Samuel's heart was already submissive at weaning when taken to the temple to serve God (1 Sam. 1). John the Baptist leaped in the womb at the presence of Jesus in Mary's womb.

It has been said, "Give me a child the first six years of his life and you can do what you will with him thereafter." It is during that short period that the bulk of a child's personality, character, habits and intellectual makeup is established.

The battle lines in the warfare for our children's souls are clear. God says, "All your children shall be taught by the LORD, and great shall be the peace of your children" (Is. 54:13, NKJV). "By the year 2000 we will, I hope," says Women's Lib advocate and *Ms.* magazine editor Gloria Steinem, "raise our children to believe in human potential, not God."

Already born with an "I-want-what-I-want-when-I-want-it" nature, preschoolers are ripe to fall prey to a love for the world and all that is in it (1 John 2:15, 16).

Satan's snares are everywhere. The Saturday morning cartoon lineup is just one classic example. Constant scenes of violence and moral decadence purposefully desensitize impressionable minds. Hidden behind many of the seemingly cute and innocent cartoons are occult symbolisms. "Magic" lures them to eventually practice witchcraft. Youngsters, bombarded with appeals to materialism, plead, "Buy that for me, Daddy!" They can then vicariously "act out" cartoons and movies through similar toys.

Another please-meism snare are story books which convey that all of life is meant to be "fun, fun, fun." This attitude is further exemplified in shows like "Sesame Street" which teach that entertainment and education are inseparable. (Entertainment is Satan's counterfeit for joy.) Then there are Satan's whispers in parents' minds: "Play is a child's work. Let kids be kids! Their natures are innocent; they should be free to explore. Curriculum should be fun, according to the interests of each child and his experience."

Bit by bit, preschoolers can thus be taken captive because what they think upon, they will become (Prov. 23:7).

What can concerned parents do to prevent this from happening? We must stay alert to Satan's tactics and teach our children how to put on the whole armor of God to withstand his attacks (Eph. 6:10-12). This means actively, constantly and purposefully teaching them the love, discipline and understanding of God's Word. No time of day is exempt from this responsibility (Deut. 6:4-9). Therefore,

providing a God-centered, God-purposed education is also essential. In other words, every day should be consistent with Philippians 4:8. The ultimate objective should be to rear our children to view the world as a spiritual battleground—not a playground! For then they will be truly equipped for every good work, thinking and living as mature Christians (2 Tim. 3:17).

403 A Child's Ten Commandments to Parents

1. My hands are small; please don't expect perfection whenever I make a bed, draw a picture, or throw a ball. My legs are short; please slow down so that I can keep up with you.

2. My eyes have not seen the world as yours have; please let me explore safely: don't restrict me unnecessarily.

3. Housework will always be there. I'm only little for such a short time—please take this time to explain things to me about this wonderful world, and do so willingly.

4. My feelings are tender; please be sensitive to my needs; don't nag me all day long. (You wouldn't want to be nagged for your inquisitiveness.) Treat me as you would like to be treated.

5. I am a special gift from God; please treasure me as God intended you to do, holding me accountable for my actions, giving me guidelines to live by, and disciplining me in a loving manner.

6. I need your encouragement, but not your praise, to grow. Please go easy on the criticism; remember, you can criticize the things I do without criticizing me.

7. Please give me the freedom to make decisions concerning myself. Permit me to fail; so that I can learn from my mistakes. Then someday I'll be prepared to make the kind of decisions life requires of me.

8. Please don't do things over for me. Somehow that makes me feel that my efforts didn't quite measure up to your expectations. I know it's hard, but please don't try to compare me with my brother or my sister.

9. Please don't be afraid to leave for the weekend together. Kids need vacations from parents, just as parents need vacations from kids. Besides, it's a great way to show us kids that your marriage is very special.

10. Please take me to Sunday school and church regularly, setting a good example for me to follow. I enjoy learning more about God.

404 Let the Children Instruct Us!

Many of us come to worship expecting to be entertained. If the song leader is not great, if the preacher is not polished, and if the Scripture readers and prayer leaders are just common, they are disappointed, and often times seek a new congregation. As children participate in family devotionals, they always show great interest. The song leading is rarely great, but they are familiar with the songs so they sing with great enthusiasm. As they pray, and are led in prayer, it is with a keen interest in all that has happened that day, and with a Bible story, even if it is the twelfth time they have heard it. Why all this interest? Why are they not as "fickle" as those we mentioned above. The answer is obvious, RELATIONSHIP! Children are participating in a family event, therefore, they are interested. This is Mom and Dad stuff! Brothers and sisters are involved! This is who they are, therefore it is vital and important to them. They appreciate every little thing that is being done.

We need to let the children instruct us. We have allowed the thinking and philosophy of a spoiled world influence our thinking in the church, AND IT IS NOT GOOD! When we gather together, there is a lot of family stuff going on. Our Father is to be worshiped, our brothers are leading, our sisters are singing, there is a lot of our relationship going into that special time. What is wrong is that we have forgotten who we are, so the unique privilege is lost on us. We have come as one who expects to be entertained, not as a family member who expects to participate and appreciate. It is just that simple. If we will remember the relationship, we can better appreciate worship, even when it is not all that polished! Let the children speak!

405 Teenagers, the TV and the Garden

A teenager was lounging on the floor watching TV when the phone rang. "Hello, son," said the voice. "Where is your mother?" "She is out working in the garden." "What?" barked the father. "Your mother is not as young and strong as she used to be. Why are you not helping her?" "I can't," was the reply. "Grandma is using the other hoe."

406 Preparing Kids for Life

We want to send our children into the world with solid gold values that cannot be destroyed. A wise Dutch grandmother helped us think about it in this way: When our kids go off to camp, we don't just shove them empty-handed out the door with a cheery admonition to "have a great time!" We send them off prepared by packing a suitcase filled with all the things they'll need to survive and enjoy the experience. And if we're not sure what they'll need, we compare notes with other parents and check with the camp counselors. Since we won't be with them, we want to know they're leaving us with everything they need firmly in hand for the whole time they are away.

This defines parenting in a nutshell—but instead of Camp Muskeeta-bite-a as their destination, we're packing up our kids to head for *Life*. During the 18 or 20 years they'll live under our roofs, our task is to equip them with all they'll

need to go on as God's people through the rest of their lives, without us constantly at their side. That means without our dollars, our direction, our discipline, *or* our devotion to God.

In packing for Life, forgetting to instill an essential godly quality can have devastating consequences. Not knowing how to handle money can lead to financial ruin. Not being able to establish a loving relationship can bring them to divorce. Not discovering God for themselves can leave them spiritually empty and lost.

407 Overboard With Praise

It's possible. Dr. Ralph Minear, of the pediatrics department at Harvard Medical School, thinks we modern parents have gone overboard with most everything else. In his book *Kids Who Have Too Much,* he warns, "A social epidemic is endangering the physical and emotional health of our country's children. 'Affluenza,' the Rich Kids Syndrome, attacks not only the children of the wealthy but also those of middle-class and low-income families. Parents are pressuring their children into becoming over-achievers, while giving them excessive amounts of freedom, money, food, information and protection."

But is there a way to affirm our children without overdosing them on overblown accolades? Here are five "don'ts" to guide us:

1. Don't praise the kids for routinely taking care of the everyday necessities of life.

2. Don't praise the kids in extravagant terms for average achievements.

3. You don't have to provide opportunities for your kids to do everything.

4. Don't console the kids when what they need is challenge.

5. Don't take responsibility for things that aren't a parent's responsibility.

408 Turning Over Responsibilities

When our children are small, we carry enormous responsibility for them. But as they grow, we must turn over to them, one by one, responsibilities that are rightly theirs. They may not carry them as well as we did, and they may even fail sometimes. But if they are to be our heirs, they're going to inherit adult responsibilities as well as adult privileges.

How much more acceptable it is for them if we allow them to inherit those responsibilities a little at a time, not dumping them on them all at once when they are out of our house for good! And how comforting if we strengthen them to carry those responsibilities, cheering them on with encouragement that's based in reality.

409 Passing the Baton

A thought that strikes deeply is this: Many times a relay race is lost in passing the baton. We don't want to fail to pass the baton of hard work and money-sense to our children simply because our life circumstances aren't forcing us to do so.

Our children may well see a day when money doesn't come as easily as it does now. Their ability to sweat and scrimp may make the difference between surviving or sinking. And even if that doesn't happen, we believe knowing the joy of working hard and living simply will free them to live a happier and more God-honoring life.

Fear

410 Facing Fear

As a child it was fun to watch the movies about the swamp monster that ate an entire city, or the space alien that tried to conquer New York or Tokyo. These movies were fun because you could be afraid for an hour or so, and then it was all over. The monster was killed; the aliens were fought off.

It is not fun to be afraid in the "real" sense. Fear is that emotion that is so well known. It is produced by a sense of danger, impending calamity or some dire emergency, or even by walking into a dentist's office. It is a powerful emotion that can damage both the physical body and the personality. Fear can even block the thought processes.

John Madden, of CBS Sports crisscrosses the country many times each fall in a customized bus because he is afraid of flying. A few years ago, one first-round draft choice in the NBA quickly ended his career with an unconditional release by his team because of his paralyzing fear of flying.

Several years ago, a televised circus act with Bengal tigers was broadcast live. The tiger trainer went into the cage with several tigers to do a routine performance. The door was locked behind him. The spotlights highlighted the cage, the television cameras moved in close, and the audience watched in suspense as the trainer put the tigers through their act. However, in the middle of the performance, the lights went out! For 20 or 30 seconds the trainer was locked in a dark cage with Bengal tigers, a whip and a chair. The tigers could see the trainer, but he could not see them!

After the event was over, in an interview, the trainer was asked how he felt about his situation in the cage. He first admitted to the chilling fear of the situation, but he pointed out that the tigers did not know that he could not see them. He said, "I just kept cracking my whip and talking to them until the lights came on. They never knew I could not see them as well as they could see me."

This story says something about many fears. Face them and go on doing the best you can. As a child you may have had a fear of the dark. As an adult you may fear failure or rejection, the future, some potential health crisis, or of your death or the death of a loved one. The Bible has the answer for our fears.

John wrote: "There is no fear in love; but perfect love casts out fear. . . ." (1 John 4:18). Christ's love is the perfect defense against the physical and mental effects of fear. Paul said it this way; "I can do all things through Christ who strengthens me" (Phil. 4:13). The phrase "fear not" is found at least 365 times in various forms throughout the Bible. The Hebrews writer says, "that we may confidently say, 'The Lord is my helper, I will not be afraid. . . .' "

One writer said it this way: "The greatness of our fears shows us the littleness of our faith." We need to pray about our fears and our faith, and turn to the Lord for help to face our fears.

411 The Fear of Risk

Henry Fairlie of the *Washington Post,* writing in the *Tulsa World,* states that the "fear of risk is killing the American Spirit." He points out our over-reaction to Three Mile Island and the engine on one DC-10. He believes that the nation that won't build a dam because of a small snail darter, or that will delay a carriage to the stars because it might fall like Skylab is in deep trouble. He asked, "Was the Mayflower seaworthy?" He contends that a group of Americans today would not have the heart to cross the Rockies as our forefathers did years ago. It would be too risky!

There is a lesson here for the church of our Lord. Many good works go wanting for fear of the risk involved. Some Christians will not become soul winners because of the risk of being hurt. Others

have never given liberally to God because of fear of poverty. Elders refuse to become involved in domestic and world evangelism because they might not succeed. Another won't defend truth for the same reason. No doubt but what the "fear of risk" has killed many good programs in the church.

There is no "fear of risk" for Christ. He knew that He came into the world to die for all. He asked his followers to deny themselves daily and take up their crosses and walk! There will always be some perils, but think of the risk if we don't!

412 The Known or the Unknown

Several generations ago, during one of the most turbulent of the desert wars in the Middle East, a spy was captured and sentenced to death by a general of the Persian army. The general, a man of intelligence and compassion, had adopted a strange and unusual custom in such cases. He permitted the condemned person to make a choice. The prisoner could either face a firing squad or pass through the Black Door.

As the moment of the execution drew near, the general ordered the spy to be brought before him for a short, final interview, the primary purpose of which was to receive the answer of the doomed man to the query: "What shall it be—the firing squad or the Black Door?"

This was not an easy decision, and the prisoner hesitated, but soon made it known that he much preferred the firing squad to the unknown horrors that might await him behind the ominous and mysterious door. Not long thereafter, a volley of shots in the courtyard announced that the grim sentence had been fulfilled.

The general, staring at his boots, turned to his aide and said, "You see how it is with men; they will always prefer the known to the unknown. It is characteristic of people to be afraid of the undefined. Yet I gave him his choice."

"What lies beyond the Black Door?" asked the aide.

"Freedom," replied the general, "and I've known only a few brave enough to take it."

The story illustrates the situation many people face each day—a choice between the known and the unknown. Few have the courage to come alive, to stop being engulfed in a sea of mediocrity—humbled and dulled by failure to recognize their own potential. They lack the fortitude to stop living their lives in a mentally-chloroformed condition in that ignoble mass of humanity . . . the uncommitted. The choice is yours (Phil. 4:13). "By grace ye are saved through faith" (Eph. 4:28). "We live by faith, not by sight" (2 Cor. 5:7).

413 From Whom Are You Running?

Christian Clippings (Sept. 1993, pp. 14f) had this poignant example of a common human response:

"Sometime ago, newspapers carried the story of a young fellow named William, who was a fugitive from the police. The teenager had run away with his girlfriend because the parents had been trying to break them up. What William didn't know was that an ailment he had been seeing the doctor about was diagnosed, just after his disappearance, as cancer.

"Now, here was William, doing his best to elude the police, lest he lose his love, while they were doing their best to find him, lest he lose his life. He thought they were after him to punish him; they were really after him to save him. William is representative of every man, whose guilt tells him God is after him to straightjacket him in this life and torture him forever."

414 Headed Toward the Sun (Son)

Alexander the Great was regent of Macedonia at the age of 16, a victorious general at 18, king at 20—and then he died a drunkard before he was 33, having conquered the then-known world. His father was Philip of Macedon, also a military genius, who invented the famous "Greek phalanx."

While Alexander was still in his early teens, Philonicus the Thessalonian offered to sell Alexander's father, Philip, his horse, Bucephalus, a trained, but vicious horse. Philip took his son along to see the horse go through its paces, but the stallion proved so unmanageable that none of the men could even mount him. Alexander noticed that he seemed to be afraid of his own shadow, so he quieted the horse by turning his head toward the sun! Then Alexander mounted the horse, and let him run freely for a while. Soon, by keeping him headed toward the sun, he got him under control.

Millions today are "afraid of their own shadow," the "shadow" of their evil deeds, the haunting "shadow" of their own guilty conscience and the "shadow" of hundreds of fears and failures. But let some faithful Christian point them to Christ, and their shadows immediately fall behind them, for Christ is "the Light of the world" (John 8:12), and all who follow HIM "shall not walk in darkness, but shall have the light of life." The closer one walks to Him the more light he has; and the farther one gets from Christ, the deeper are the shadows. And he who is so foolish as to walk away from Christ, in unbelief, walks ever deeper into the shadows that will eventually plunge him into the eternal darkness.

Fellowship

415 Access

It is common for homeowners to have many locks in their houses, each with different keys, but to have one master key which opens all. So the Lord has many treasuries and secrets all shut up from carnal minds with locks which they cannot open; but he who walks in fellowship with Jesus possesses the master key which will admit him to all the blessings of the covenant; yea, to the very heart of God. Through the Well-beloved we have access to God, to heaven, to every secret of the Lord.

416 Bad Company

Have you ever heard anyone say, "Birds of a feather flock together"? Have you ever stopped and really asked yourself what it means? Let me tell you a story which will help you to understand.

One spring a great many crows began to pull up a farmer's young corn. The farmer loaded his shotgun and went out to frighten them away. Bang! The farmer fired at the crows, and hurried out into the field to see how many he had hit. To his surprise he found that, besides killing three crows, he had wounded Polly, his pet parrot!

You can imagine how excited his children were when he came home with Polly in his hands.

"O Daddy," they cried, "who was so cruel as to hurt poor Polly! Where was she?"

Before the farmer could explain, Polly began to say, "Bad Company! Bad Company!"

"That is certainly the truth, Polly!" laughed the man. Then he explained to his children that Polly had evidently seen the crows in the field and had left the house (she was allowed out of her cage a great deal of the time) and had gone to join the other birds. She had been among the crows when the farmer fired on them. "You see, Polly was keeping bad company, children," the man said. "And bad company is always dangerous. In the Bible we read, 'Enter not into the path of the wicked, and go not in the way of evil men' " (Prov. 4:13).

417 Seek God Daily

Ben Jochai was teaching a group of students about the miracle of the manna when Israel was on the way from Egypt to the Promised Land.

One of the students asked, "Why didn't the Lord God furnish enough manna for Israel at one time to last the entire year?"

The teacher said, "I will answer you with a parable. Once there was a rich man who had a son to whom he promised an annual allowance. Every year on the same day, he would give his son the entire amount. After a while, it happened that the only time the father saw his son was on the day of the year when he was to receive his allowance. So the father changed his plan and only gave the son enough for the day. Then the next day the son would return for the allowance for the day. From then on, the father saw his son every day."

This is the way God dealt with Israel. It is the way God deals with us.

418 Friendship

Friend! What a precious word. Most of us concur wholeheartedly with William Shakespeare who said:

Those friends thou hast, and their adoption tried,

Grapple them to thy soul with hoops of steel.

One of the privileges of friendship is being able to speak frankly. Little by little, and day by day, we become accustomed to saying what we think we ought to say instead of what we really think. How comfortable and how pleasant it is to speak freely without having to be on guard. As the Arabian says, "A friend is one to whom we may pour out the contents of our hearts, chaff and grain together, knowing that the gentlest of hands will sift it, keep what is worth keeping, and with a breath of kindness blow the rest away!"

Another privilege of friendship is that of being understood. Perhaps it was this quality which caused George Eliot to write: "Animals are such agreeable friends. They ask no questions; they pass no criticisms." Understanding is to be expected of friends. Total agreement and acceptance? Not necessarily! As one anonymous writer has said, "The strength and sweetness of friendship depends on sincerity tempered by sympathy."

A third privilege of friendship is the privilege of silence. If one is but a mere acquaintance we feel that we must talk. So we turn to such exciting subjects as the weather, our ailments, and our latest surgery. But what a joy it is to have a friend that will even understand your silence and not say, "My friend is not my friend anymore because he is not talking."

Friends have mutual interests. They enjoy doing the same kinds of things, and talking about their shared interests. That's why there is such great camaraderie between fishermen, woodworkers, gardeners, authors, etc.

Friends are mutually devoted to each other. When you are in trouble, it is not merely your friend's duty but his privilege to stand by. If he is in trouble, you count it a privilege to help.

Friendship is this . . . and a whole lot more. But it causes one to ask, "Are God and I friends?"

419 Does Anybody Ask About Your Arthritis?

Mamie made frequent trips to the branch post office. One day she confronted a long line of people who were waiting for service from the postal clerks. Mamie only needed stamps, so a helpful observer asked, "Why don't you use the stamp machine? You can get all the stamps you need and you won't have to wait in line." Mamie said, "I know, but the machine can't ask me about my arthritis."

We live in a world that has become extremely impersonal. You can take care of numerous business transactions without dealing directly with people. When you do talk with people, most of them aren't going to ask you about your arthritis. They want you to state

your business and get out of the way for the next customer.

We can get our lunch from a machine if we choose to. We can take our own blood pressure at the drug store. It's been a long time since many of us have had a conversation with a real, live telephone operator. When you live in that kind of context, it's hard to find anybody who is the least bit curious about your arthritis, your gout, your bad cough or anything else that ails you.

People still need human contact. Solitary confinement is still the most severe punishment that a prisoner can receive. As Christians we need to be sensitive to the need that people have to be touched and cared for. "For none of us lives to himself alone and none of us dies to himself alone" (Rom. 14:7).

Forgiveness

420 Reconciliation Seen from the Pulpit

In a large prayer meeting about seven years ago, the pastor was urging everyone present to put away every hindrance to an immediate personal transaction with God, by which the soul might find instant forgiveness.

He saw a man leave his pew in a hurried, excited state, and go into the inquiry room. Quietly, an usher called two or three others to follow the man. Shortly, the man, as well as the others returned quietly to their seats.

At the close of the service, the pastor inquired into the reasons for the commotion. He was told there had been a quarrel sometime before the service; the man, hearing God's Word, wanted to find peace with God; he realized he could not have it until he was first reconciled to his offending brethren. Consequently, he had sent for them to come into the inquiry room.

When the man asked them for forgiveness, they freely forgave and were as glad as he to have fellowship again.

421 The Forgiveness Flower

One day when Stan Mooneyham was walking along a trail in East Africa with some friends, he became aware of a delightful odor that filled the air. He looked up in the trees and around at the bushes in an effort to discover where it was coming from. Then his friends told him to look down at the small blue flower growing along the path. Each time they crushed the tiny blossoms under their feet, more of its sweet perfume was released into the air. Then his friends said, "We call it the forgiveness flower."

This forgiveness flower does not wait until we ask forgiveness for crushing it. It does not release its fragrance in measured doses or hold us to a reciprocal arrangement. It does not ask for an apology; it merely lives up to its name and forgives—freely, fully, richly. What a touching example of outrageous forgiveness!

422 The Buried Hatchet

Garth Brooks has a song which says "We buried the hatchet, but left the handle sticking out." One great obstacle of stumbling is non-forgiveness. The hatchet might seem to be buried, but people continue to grab hold of the handle when they want to use it against another. Jesus said if a brother repents, forgive him—that is, bury the hatchet *and* its handle. How

167

many times, you might ask? As often as the brother repents, we are to forgive.

Don't grab hold of buried hatchet handles, for they become stumbling blocks to forgiveness.

423 Forgiveness Needs Momentum

Corrie ten Boom likenened forgiveness to letting go of a bell rope. If you have ever seen a country church with a bell in the steeple, you will remember that to get the bell ringing you have to tug awhile. Once it has begun to ring, you merely maintain the momentum. As long as you keep pulling, the bell keeps ringing. Miss ten Boom said forgiveness is letting go of the rope. It is just that simple. But when you do so, the bell keeps ringing. Momentum is still at work. However, if you keep your hands off the rope, the bell will begin to slow and eventually stop.

It is like that with forgiveness. When you decided to forgive, the old feelings of unforgiveness may continue to assert themselves. After all, they have lots of momentum. But if you affirm your decision to forgive, that unforgiving spirit will begin to slow and will eventually be still. Forgiveness is not something you feel, it is something you do. It is letting go of the rope of retribution.

424 Soft on Enemies

One of President Abraham Lincoln's associates scolded him rather severely for being soft on his enemies. "Why do you insist on trying to make friends of them?" he chided. "You should be trying to destroy them."

To which Lincoln replied gently, "Am I not destroying my enemies when I make them my friends?" In speaking of those who were his enemies during the Civil War, Lincoln is reported to have said, "Insane as it may seem, I hold malice toward none of them. I have neither the time nor the energy in this life to hold that kind of resentment."

425 The Berry Spoon

"I'll never forgive him. I told him I would never forgive him." The attractive elderly lady spoke softly, but with resolve, to the night nurse. Her expression was troubled as she turned away, focusing her eyes on the drape closing in her nursing home bed. The conversation had traveled from the temporal to the eternal and now a deep hurt had surfaced.

She told of how her brother had approached her hospital bed, accusing her of taking more than her share of family heirlooms following their mother's death. He spoke of various items, ending with "the berry spoon." He said, "I want the berry spoon." For the 40 years since the parent's death he had hidden his feelings, and now they erupted. She was both hurt and angered by his accusation and vowed never to forgive him. "It's my spoon. It was given to me," she defended herself. "He's wrong and I won't forgive him."

A berry spoon. In the bed lay a woman given two months to live—60 days—and she would face eternity and never see her brother again in this life. Her mind and spirit were in anguish, and her only remaining family tie was broken over a spoon.

How many berry spoons are there in our lives? How many things, as insignificant as a spoon, in light of eternity, separate us from full communion with God? How much lack of forgiveness keeps us from fellowship with others?

"For if you forgive men when they sin against you, your heavenly Father will also forgive you. But if you do not forgive men their sins, your Father will not forgive your sins" (Matt. 6:14, 15).

426 There's Forgiveness

Don't struggle alone, in fear and distress
As if there's no hope, just your ugliness.
Our Lord offers grace, not judgment deserving,
He longs for your love and your soon returning.
THERE'S FORGIVENESS.

It's tough cutting through the darkness of sin
Striving for answers, His favor to win.
He stands with His arms outstretched and extended
To hold and restore you, just mercy intended.
THERE'S FORGIVENESS.

Why search other places your answers to find

To fill the vast void and touch the divine.
Lay down your excuses and learn to confess
Your sins and your shame to His holiness.
THERE'S FORGIVENESS.

There's healing and fellowship waiting for you
The moment you turn, His face to pursue.
You are the temple, His place for abiding,
The only thing missing is your mind deciding.
THERE'S FORGIVENESS.

Don't wait for a feeling or mystical lark,
Just bow down in quietness, open your heart.
Be honest, and tell Him no secret to keep
From there He restores you to fellowship sweet.
THERE'S FORGIVENESS.

His promise is certain, "I will forgive,"
Cleansing and freedom, it's yours to live.
From no other source full joy will you find.
He is your victory, your peace so sublime.
THERE'S FORGIVENESS.

To humble yourself, before Him in prayer,
Is your first step, in unloading your care.
There look Him squarely, straight in the face
And tell Him all of the ways you disgrace.
THERE'S FORGIVENESS.

Refreshment and fullness He will restore
The moment you sincerely open the door.
He is the life you thought you could win,
By going your way and living in sin.
THERE'S FORGIVENESS.

There's no one beyond the reach of His arm
To pick up and pardon, to rescue from harm.
Return to the Master of your faith's beginning.
Give Him your all, and you'll find yourself winning.
THERE'S FORGIVENESS.

What wonderful love eternity holds,
For those who are willing to be in the fold.
The Savior is waiting, Oh come to Him now,
At His nail-scarred feet, in humility bow.
THERE'S FORGIVENESS.

427 Our Sins Are Like the Clouds

You have seen a cloud drifting across the pure blue of the sky, and as you watch it, it breaks up and disappears forever. You will never see that cloud again.

So God deals with your sins. You believe in His Son as your Lord and Savior. Then He blots out your transgressions just as He sweeps the cloud from your sight forever.

The Bible abounds in these as-surances of utter removal of the penalty of sin from the child of God.

428 The Meaning of Forgiveness

"How sharper than a serpent's tooth it is to have a thankless child," says William Shakespeare's King Lear. Well, then, how about a thankless jailbird? If you want an answer to that one, ask District Judge Phillip Killien of Seattle.

Recently, a young man appeared before Judge Killien on charges of car theft. The judge saw no reason to keep him locked up while he awaited court action. He released him on his own recognizance.

A short time later, Killien's own car disappeared.

Police quickly found the stolen car, and the one who stole it. Then, Judge Killien was in court in a new role, not as a judge, but as a witness, against the same young man he had released, who stood accused of stealing the magistrate's wheels.

A Japanese proverb reminds us that forgiving the unrepentant is like drawing pictures on the water. Ignoring sin may gain the sinner's temporary gratitude, but makes no lasting impression. A forgiven car thief is still a car thief if no change of character takes place.

How about you? Do you seek to escape justice or to be justified by God's grace and Christ's mercy? God offers you liberty, not license, in the cleansing blood of Christ.

429 Do You Charge to Forgive?

A sign in a convenience store read, "Check Cashing Policy: To err is human. To forgive, $10." It's a funny way to recognize the fact that we make mistakes, but it's also evidence of the way many people think about forgiveness.

To forgive is to accept within yourself the consequences of the sins of others. It means to accept the pain, the problems and the burden that comes when someone sins against you. Forgiveness is neither an easy nor a frequent gift.

This is what God has done for us: ". . . knowing that you were not redeemed with corruptible things, like silver or gold, from your aimless conduct received by tradition from your fathers, but with the precious blood of Christ, as of a lamb without blemish and without spot" (1 Pet. 1:18, 19 NKJ). What did God give for your forgiveness? It wasn't money or anything of wealth or value in worldly terms. He gave His Son. Jesus took upon Himself the burden of our sins.

430 Distinctly Forgotten

Following the Civil War, Robert E. Lee was visiting in Kentucky where one lady showed him the remains of what had been an enormous, old tree. This tree stood directly in front of her house. She bitterly cried to General Lee of how its limbs and trunk had been shattered by Federal artillery fire. Having poured out her anguish she looked to the old soldier for a condemnation of the North. Following a brief silence, Lee responded, "Cut it down, my dear madam, and forget it."

It is better to forgive the injustices of the past than to allow them to take root and add bitterness to your future. Memory is a marvelous thing, particularly when it brings us wisdom or joy; however, forgetfulness is equally marvelous for it allows others to succeed where once failure reigned.

Forgiveness does not always mean that we trust the individual. In his weakness this does neither him nor you any favors. Forgiveness is the measure of putting yourself on his side, not seeking revenge but success. It is the opening of opportunity's doors, to say "try again, I will not shut you out." This requires setting aside or forgetting the emotions which might halt forgiveness.

Clara Barton, Red Cross founder, was asked if she remembered an especially cruel thing done to her years before. When she seemed not to recall it, a friend asked, "Don't you remember?" "No," said Miss Barton, "I distinctly remember forgetting it." God has forgiven us, is it now time that we forgive others so that we can get on to a bright future. Is some cruelty holding you back? Forgive and Live.

Gifts

431 Where Are God's Best Gifts?

Earthly thrones are generally built with steps up to them; the remarkable thing about the thrones of the eternal kingdom is that the steps are all down to them. We must descend if we would reign, stoop if we would rise.

Some think that God put His best gifts on a high shelf for them to reach up to them. It does not take long, however, for a Christian to realize that the best gifts are in the lower shelves, that the babes may get them also.

432 A Lesson from the Gulls

Some time ago in *Reader's Digest* there was a short article about a group of sea gulls that was starving to death in St. Augustine. They were not starving because of a food shortage but because they had forgotten how to fish. For years they had depended on the shrimp fleet operating out of the harbor to toss them scraps from the nets. When the shrimp fleet moved to Key West, they began to starve. They had lost their natural ability to fish because they had not been using it.

This is a rule of nature. If you do not use what you have, it will be taken from you. This is the lesson in the parable of the talents. The servant who did not use the one talent had it taken from him.

433 Different Gifts, Different Strengths

A concert violinist had a brother who was a bricklayer. One day a woman gushed to the bricklayer, "It must be wonderful to be in a family with such a famous violinist." Then, not wanting to insult the bricklayer, she said, "Of course we don't all have the same talents, and even in a family, some just seem to have more talent than others."

The bricklayer said, "You're telling me! That violinist brother of mine doesn't know a thing about laying bricks. And if he couldn't make some money playing that fiddle of his, he couldn't hire a guy with know-how like mine to build a house. If he had to build a house himself he'd be ruined."

If you want to build a house, you don't want a violinist. And if you're going to lead an orchestra, you don't want a bricklayer.

No two of us are exactly alike. None of us has every gift and ability. Our responsibility is to exercise the gifts we have, not the ones we wish we had.

And when it comes to making decisions about your own life and the direction it should take, focus on your strengths, not your weaknesses. Know yourself. Know what you do well, and then go with your strengths and shore up your weaknesses.

434 The Christmas Gift Is Too Much

In ancient history we are told that Caesar had a friend to whom he once gave a munificent present. But when he offered it, the friend said: "This is too much for me to receive." To which the emperor replied: "But it is not too much for me to give."

After all our sinfulness and rebellion, God's gift of pardon through Christ does seem too much for us to receive; but the riches of divine mercy are so great that it is not too much for Him to give. When God forgives, there is not one sin left unforgiven. Christmas was indeed too great a gift for man, but it was not so for God.

435 What If God Sent Us Bills?

The scene was a familiar one. The young couple were going over their monthly bills. In it were ones from the drug store, department store, oil company, etc. Trying to find something humorous to say in the situation, the man quipped, "Isn't it a good thing that God doesn't send bills?"

That is good, isn't it? But what if He just decided to bill us for this wonderful body He has given us?

The Psalmist said, "I will praise thee; for I am fearfully and wonderfully made" (Ps. 139:14). Shakespeare said, "What a piece of work is man!" Think about what God has made:

THE EARS: A piano has 88 keys, but each of your ears has a keyboard with 1500 keys. They are so finely tuned that you can hear the blood running through your vessels. The outside of your ear can catch up to 73,700 vibrations per second.

THE EYES: They are both microscopes and telescopes. They can gaze into the heavens and see a star millions of miles away, or inspect the smallest insect.

THE FEET: Did you know that each foot has 26 bones, none of which is wider than your thumb? But it is so "manufactured" (arched) with its ligaments, tendons, muscles and joints that a 300-pound man can put all his weight on these tiny bones.

THE HEART: Its size is about like your fist, but pumps (beats) 4,320 times an hour. In a year that would mean 40 million beats. A drop of blood can make a round trip in your circulatory system in only 22 seconds.

What if God sent you a bill for this marvelous body we live in? But God doesn't send us bills. He just loves us and takes care of us. Can we do any less than to return His love? We show Him our love by obedience to His Word and by faithful stewardship of that which He has entrusted to us.

Giving

436 Three Kicks in Every Dollar

William Allen White, a famous newspaper editor in Emporia, Kansas, once gave a 50 acre tract of land to the city for a park. At the dedication, he made the strange statement that there are "Three kicks in every dollar." He explained, "One kick is when you make it—and how I love to make a dollar! One is when you save it—and I have the Yankee lust for saving. The third kick is when you give it away—and the biggest kick of all is the last one."

It seems Mr. White discovered on his own what Jesus taught 20 centuries earlier: "It is more blessed to give than to receive" (Acts 20:35). Do you believe that? Want a big kick? Make a lot of money! Want an even bigger kick? Give your money to a worthy cause.

There is a "kick" in seeing needy people helped. There is a "kick" in seeing your money carry the good news everywhere. There is a "kick" in seeing your church touch the spiritual needs of the unsaved.

You, too, can get three "kicks" out of every dollar.

437 Let Me Give

I don't know how long I have to live

But while I do, Lord, let me give
Some comfort to someone in need
By smile or nod—kind word or deed.
And let me do what e'er I can
To ease things for my fellowman.
I only want to do my part,
To "lift" a tired and weary heart.
To change folks frowns to smiles again
So I will not have lived in vain.
I do not care how long I live
If I can give—and give—and give!

438 "And Then Some"

A successful businessman was once asked the secret of his success. His reply summed up success in three words: "and then some." He learned early in life that the difference between average people and the truly successful could be summed up in those three words. Top people did what was expected "and then some!"

Jesus taught the "and then some" principle. In the Sermon on the Mount he said: "And whoever compels you to go one mile, go with him two" (Matt. 5:41). "And if you greet your brethren only, what do you do more than others? Do not even the tax collectors do so?" (Matt. 5:47).

439 *Church Is Cheaper*

A woman took her two small boys and a daughter to see Peter Pan at the matinee one Saturday afternoon. The tickets were two dollars and fifty cents each. The young daughter watched as the mother pushed ten one dollar bills under the window and received four tickets.

The next day the same mother and daughter were at church. When the collection was taken the child saw her mother open her purse, take out a quarter, and put it in the plate as it passed them.

The little girl looked up at her mother and in a clear stage whisper which everyone around could hear said, "Mother, church is a lot cheaper than a movie, isn't it?"

440 *A Parable of Life*

Life is like another parable from another land. A blind Indian beggar sat beside a road, fingering the rice in his little bowl. Wearing only a loin cloth, he sat in poverty beside a road that stretched into nowhere both ways. The scarce travelers occasionally gave him a little rice. One day he heard the thunder of a chariot in the distance. It was the grand entourage of the maharajah. This was a moment that had never come before. Surely the great one would stop and give him baskets of rice.

Indeed, the golden chariot of the maharajah stopped before the poor beggar. The great one stepped down and the beggar fell before him. Then the sky seemed to fall in. "Give me your rice," said the great one. A fearful, hateful, scowl masked the face of the beggar. He reached into his bowl and thrust one grain of rice toward the maharajah. "Is that all?" said the great one. The beggar spat on the ground, cursed, and threw him one more grain of rice. The great one turned, entered his chariot, and was gone.

The beggar—angry, empty, and crushed—fingered the remaining rice he had hoarded in his bowl. He felt something hard, different from the rice. He pulled it out. It was one grain of gold. He poured out his rice, caring nothing for it now. He found one other grain of gold. Had he trusted the great one, he could have had a grain of gold for every grain of rice.

441 *Why Be a Volunteer?*

It's not for money, It's not for fame,
It's not for any personal gain.
It's just for love of fellowman.
It's just to lend a helping hand.
It's just to give a tithe of self.
That's something you can't buy with wealth.
It's not medals won with pride.
It's for that feeling deep inside.
It's that reward sown in your heart.
It's that feeling that you've been a part
Of helping others far and near
That makes you be a volunteer!

442 *I Am Glad I Am a Teacher*

How many times have I heard a fellow Christian say, "Oh, you mean you teach a class of little kids? Oh, you poor thing. You are a glutton for punishment." My mental reaction to such a statement is, "YOU poor thing. If you have never tried it, you don't know the wealth of blessing your are missing."

Poor thing, indeed! There are few moments so precious as seeing the dancing eyes of a little child as he sees the big fish (made up of a bleach bottle) literally swallow up Jonah (a puppet), and then to see relief come and his whole body relax and settle against his chair when he sees that "God took care of Jonah and He will take care of me, too, if I obey Him." Or, the excited voice of a little one tugging at Mother or Daddy to "come to see the 10 lepers that Jesus made well."

Me a poor thing? When I hear from three rows back the loud whisper, "Mommy, that's my teacher." Or when I receive the most moving, most enjoyable, most blessing-filled hour of the week, no, I wouldn't trade all that for a comfortable chair in a quiet adult classroom. Who knows, that Bible class I teach may lead someone to heaven who otherwise might not have known the way.

Sorry friend, that poor thing isn't me!

443 The Fate of a Poem— Saved by a Downdraft!

Frances Ridley Havergal wrote one of her most famous poems while she was in Dusseldorf, Germany. She had gone to Germany to do some specialized study. While there, she saw a copy of Sternburg's great painting: The *Crucifixion*. The title above the picture was, "All this I did for thee; what hast thou done for Me?"

Inspired by the probing question, she wrote her famous poem, "I Gave My Life for Thee." But she was not happy with the poem at the time, so she threw it into the fire. But there came a strong downdraft which blew the paper out of the fire and onto the hearth. Feeling that this might have been providential, Miss Havergal took the slightly scorched paper, folded it, and sent it to her father in England. He composed a tune to match the words and had it published. However, the tune we now use with this superb poem was written years later by P. P. Bliss, an associate of D. L. Moody. The tune he wrote is now the one we use with this great song: "I Gave My Life for Thee, What Hast Thou Done for Me?"

444 Influence

Drop a pebble in the water
And its ripples reach out far;
And the sunbeam dancing on them
May reflect them to a star.

Give a smile to someone passing
Thereby making his morning glad;
It may greet you in the evening
When your own heart may be sad.

Do a simple deed of kindness;
Though its end you may not see,

It may reach like widening ripples,

Down a long eternity.

445 Leftovers

When you invite special guests to your home, do you warm up the leftovers in the refrigerator and serve them on paper plates in front of the television? Of course not. Most of us prepare a special meal, use our best dishes and arrange our schedules so that we can spend quality time with our guests. In other words, we offer them our very best.

How many of us invite the Lord Jesus into our life and then serve Him "leftovers"? We give Him time "leftover" from our work, our families or our recreation. We give Him talents "leftover" from our social organizations, our sports activities or our hobbies. We give Him money "leftover" after we pay our bills and our taxes and put some money aside for our vacation.

"Out of all the gifts you receive you shall set aside the contributions to the Lord; and the gift which you hallow must be taken from the choicest of them" (Num. 18:29).

Have I given to the Lord who died for me the choicest, or have I given Him "leftovers"?

446 Do You Know What Sacrifice Means?

Two wealthy Christians, a lawyer and a merchant, joined a party that was going around the world. Before they started, their minister earnestly asked them to observe and remember any unusual and interesting things that they might see in the missionary countries through which the party was to travel. The men promised—carelessly, perhaps—to do so.

One day in Korea, they saw in a field by the side of the road a boy pulling a crude plow, while an old man held the handles and directed it. The lawyer was amused, and took a snapshot of the scene.

"That's a curious picture! I suppose they are very poor," he said to the missionary who was interpreter and guide to the party.

"Yes," was the quiet reply. "That is the family of Chi Noui. When the church was being built they were eager to give something to it, but they had no money so they sold their only ox and gave the money to the church. This spring they are pulling the plow themselves."

The lawyer and the businessman by his side were silent for some moments. Then the businessman said, "That must have been a real sacrifice."

"They did not call it that," said the missionary. "They thought it was fortunate they had an ox to sell."

447 Maintain Purpose in Life

Mr. Brown ran a sanatorium for rich women who had nothing much to do. They had been idle so long together that their nerves got the best of them. They fancied all sorts of things wrong with themselves as they grumbled about their aches and pains.

Brown and his wife were getting rich listening to them and babying them. Then one of the women made a few repairs on her old clothes which she gave to the needy. Another woman took notice then did the same. Soon most of them were repairing old clothes. Then one delivered her repaired clothes and came back excited about how the poor folk received them.

Then all the women repaired clothes and delivered them to the poor families. The result? Mr. Brown and his wife found their sanitorium empty. The women had found purpose in life. The sanatorium was no longer needed.

448 I Dare You to Do It Again

A little church was having a homecoming service to which ex-members, who had moved away, were invited. One of the former members had become a millionaire. When asked to speak, the wealthy man recounted his childhood experience. He had earned his first silver dollar which he had decided to keep forever. "But when a visiting missionary preached about the urgent need for funds in his mission work, and the offering basket was passed, a great struggle took place within me. As a result," the wealthy man said, "I put my treasured silver dollar in the basket. I am convinced that the reason God has blessed me richly is that when I was a boy I gave God everything I possessed."

The congregation was spellbound by the multi-millionaire's tremen-

dous statement until an elderly little man seated in the front row rose and said, "Brother, I dare you to do it again."

449 Tell Me Why

The movies say, "I'll entertain you, but you must buy a ticket first."

The restaurant asks, "Eat here but you have to pay the bill."

The insurance company offers to insure you, "But the premiums must be met."

The ball club says, "You'll see a good game, but you must have the price of admission."

The golf course says, "Play here but first pay the green fees."

The lake ranger says the fish are biting, "But you have to buy a license."

Then the Lord says, "In My church you will find spiritual food, fellowship, assurance of eternal life, consolation in time of trouble, spiritual blessings beyond measure and opportunities to do good to others and there is no specific charge. Pay as you are willing." And everybody tries to get by as cheaply as possible!

Can you tell me why?

450 A Tithing Testimony

Many years ago a lad of 16 was obliged to leave home because his father was too poor to support him any longer. So he trudged away with all worldly possessions in a bundle dangling from his hand, resolving as he journeyed to set up in business as a soapmaker in New York.

When the country boy arrived in the big city, he found it hard to get work. Remembering the last words of his mother and also the godly advice given him by the captain of a canal boat, the youth dedicated his life to God, determining to return to his Maker an honest tithe of every dollar he earned.

So, when his first dollar came in, the young man sacredly dedicated ten cents of it to the Lord. This he continued to do. And the dollars rolled in! Soon this young man became partner in a soap business; and when his partner died a few years later, he became sole owner of the concern.

The prosperous businessman now instructed his bookkeeper to open an account with the Lord and to credit to it one tenth of all his income. The business grew miraculously. The honest proprietor now dedicated two-tenths of his earnings; and then three-tenths, four-tenths; and finally, five-tenths. It seemed as if his sales increased in exact proportion to his generosity, so that soon his brand of soap became a household word throughout the world.

The late William Colgate was this man whom God so singly prospered in return for his faithfulness to his Maker.

451 It Is More Blessed to Give

One day, Mr. L., a businessman living in a southern city, knocked at the office door of the Salvation Army. The Army captain answered and was very surprised to receive a gift of $100 from Mr. L. That was big money at that time and was much appreciated by this charity organization.

As Mr. L. started to walk down the sidewalk, he heard steps behind him. It was the Army captain hastening to catch up with him.

"Our baby is sick," he said, "would it be all right to use some of this money to buy milk for it?"

"Go ahead and use all you need for your child," Mr. L. replied.

A number of years later, Mr. L. was running for a high government office and was to make a speech in the city where the Army captain worked. The large auditorium was filled to capacity with interested listeners, and the Army captain was one of them.

When Mr. L. finished his speech, the Army captain stood up and asked permission to speak. He told the incident how Mr. L. had given $100 and about his sick child receiving the needed milk.

There was a thundering applause from the audience—and a decided victory for Mr. L. in his campaigning!

"Cast thy bread upon the waters; for thou shalt find it after many days" (Eccl. 11:1).

452 What Is Tithing?

Mathematically it is a tenth. ". . . and of all that thou shalt give me I will surely give the tenth unto Thee" (Gen. 28:11).

Scripturally it is a law. "Thou shalt truly tithe all the increase" (Deut. 14:22).

Morally it is a debt. ". . . Wherein have we robbed thee? In tithes and offerings" (Mal. 3:8).

Economically it is an investment. "But lay up for yourselves treasures in heaven" (Matt. 6:20). "Give, and it shall be given unto you" (Luke 6:38).

Spiritually it is a blessing. "I will open the windows of heaven and pour you out a blessing that there shall not be room enough to receive it" (Mal. 3:10).

453 Inasmuch

In Edwin Markham's lovely poem, "The Shoes of Happiness," Conrad, the old cobbler, dreamed one night that the Master would come to be his guest. When the dawn was yet young, he arose and decorated his little shop with bright and gay flowers and waited. When the Master would come, he would wash the feet where the spikes had been and would kiss the hands that the nails had punctured.

But the Master did not come. A beggar came, and Conrad gave him a pair of shoes. An old woman came bent from the weight of a heavy burden. He lifted the load off her back and refreshed her with food. And finally, just before the day was about to fade away into darkness, a little child came. Her eyes were wet with tears, and in pity Conrad led her back to her mother. But the divine guest never came:

Then soft in the silence a voice he heard

"Lift up your heart, for I kept My word.

Three times I came to your friendly door;

Three times my shadow was on your floor.

I was the beggar with bruised feet,

I was the woman you gave to eat,

I was the child in the homeless street."

"Inasmuch as ye have done it unto one of the least of these My brethren, ye have done it unto Me" (Matt. 25:40).

454 Giving to God

Years ago it was the custom for the people to bring their gifts to the front of the church. A well-known preacher was making an appeal to the people to give for a good cause. Many came to present their offerings of love. Among them was a little crippled girl who hobbled along at the end of the line. Pulling a ring from her finger, she placed it on the table and made her way back up the aisle.

After the service an usher was sent to bring her to the preacher's study. The preacher said, "My dear, I saw what you did. It was beautiful. But the response of the people has been so generous that we have enough to take care of the need. We don't feel right about keeping your treasured ring, so we have decided to give it back to you."

To his surprise the little girl vigorously shook her head in refusal. "You don't understand," she said. "I didn't give my ring to you, I gave it to God!" Lovely.

"Each one must do as he has made up his mind, not reluctantly or under compulsion, for God loves a cheerful giver" (2 Cor. 9:7).

455 Success

Henry Ford once said, "Success is not rare. It is common. Very few miss a measure of it. It is not a matter of luck or of contesting, for certainly no success can come from preventing the success of another. It is a matter of adjusting one's efforts to overcome obstacles, and adjusting one's abilities to give the service needed by others. There is no other possible success. Most people think of it in terms of getting; success, however, begins in terms of giving."

456 Hard Work Appreciated!

A traveler had heard so much of the wonderful chimes of St. Nicholas in Amsterdam, that one day he went up into the tower of the church to hear them. There he found a man hard at work before an immense keyboard, thumping and pounding the keys.

The traveler was almost deafened by the harsh discordant clangor of the bells above his head, and hurried away wondering why people talked so much of the beautiful chimes of St. Nicholas.

The next day at the same hour he was in a distant part of the city sightseeing, when suddenly the air was filled with the mellow music of marvelously clear and full-toned bells.

"We hear the chimes of St. Nicholas," said the guide in answer to his question, and the man wondered no longer why travelers spoke enthusiastically of their melody. But he thought of the man in the tower, and wondered if he ever knew how beautiful his hard work became in the distance.

457 Unexpected Rewards

Three deer hunters from the city stopped at a humble farm dwelling and asked permission to stay there during deer season. The farmer and his wife graciously received them, and though crippled with arthritis, the farmer showed them some good deer haunts. Tired and hungry after an exciting day in the woods, they did justice to the piping hot meal that awaited them.

When each hunter had his deer, they made ready to leave. "Now, what do we owe you?" they asked. "Not a penny!" exclaimed the farm couple. Then they went on to say, "We have enjoyed your stay here. Come again!"

A few weeks later, two trucks drove into the farmyard. An electrician explained to them that he was sent to wire their buildings; the plumber in the other truck assured the surprised couple that they would soon have plenty of hot water in a sparkling bathroom and at the kitchen sink.

The three deer hunters had shown their appreciation this way for having had the privilege of staying there during the hunting season. The grateful recipients learned that their heavenly Father had a way to reward them for giving of their time and means. You can't outgive God!

458 Think of Another's Circumstance

"As we have therefore opportunity, let us do good unto all" (Gal. 6:10).

"Auntie, you are putting some of your choicest rose bushes away in the backyard!" "Yes," answered Auntie, "and I am going to put some geraniums and pinks and other lovely flowers which will bloom all summer out there, too. I know they seem to be out of sight, but there is a woman who sits and sews day after day, week in and week out, at the upstairs windows in the dingy house opposite, and I'm fixing that corner for her."

459 Heaven Notices a Penny

It was Christmas time, and the bell tinkled. Many people had passed by the Salvation Army kettle on the busy corner.

Then a small boy—six perhaps—looked into the kettle and asked, "Mister, what is that money for?" The tall man ringing the bell leaned over and quietly replied, "It is for girls and boys like you. But they are children that need food and clothing and toys for Christmas. The money will buy those things. Do you see?"

The tiny lad with face aglow plunged his hand deep into his pocket. Then, reenacting the Miracle of Christmas, he placed his gift—a penny—in the kettle with the rest.

"Only a penny?" you say. But it was a gift straight from a little boy's heart. If it did not go unnoticed on the busy street corner, surely it did not go unnoticed in heaven.

460 Rockefeller's Testimony

"Yes, I tithe," said John D. Rockefeller, Sr., "and I would like to tell you how it all came about. I had to begin work as a small boy to help support my mother. My first wages amounted to $1.50 per week. The first week after I went to work, I took the $1.50 home to my mother, and she held the money in her lap and explained to me that she would be happy if I would give a tenth to the Lord.

"I did, and from that week until this day I have tithed every dollar God has entrusted to me. And I want to say, if I had not tithed the first dollar I made I would not have tithed the first million dollars I made. Train the children to tithe, and they will grow up to be faithful stewards of the Lord."

461 He Gives Songs in the Night

C. H. Spurgeon once heard that in a certain part of England one could hear nightingales sing more beautifully than anywhere else. He journeyed there to hear for himself. He secured a room in the inn and was told, "As it begins to get dark, look out on the thorn bush. You will see the nightingale. You will hear his song."

But toward evening it turned cold and started to rain. Spurgeon despaired. Suddenly, he heard the beautiful, thrilling song of the nightingale, clear and sweet. He looked out the window. There perched in the thorn bush, with a cold rain pelting down, the little bird was lifting its voice in a truly beautiful song. He said, "It was so sweet and so beautiful that I do not expect to hear anything so thrilling until I hear the angels sing." Then he mused. "The God of the nightingale is the God whom I serve. In spite of darkness, cold, rain, or thorns—He can also give me songs in the night."

462 When Longing for Quiet, Think of Jesus

Five girls took advantage of their graduation and went together on a vacation. It was a lovely break from the constant crowds with whom they had to mix.

"I dearly love my work," said one of them, "but sometimes it seems to me I would give anything to get away from people awhile. I never have a quiet moment to myself. There is always someone who wants to see me. Do the rest of you ever feel that way?"

"Oh, yes," said one; and, "Yes," sighed another, "I feel as though I would like to go off to a desert island where I would not see a soul."

Then a girl by the name of Mary spoke. "I know just how you feel. I have felt the same way. But when it seems to me I cannot stand it any longer I think of how the throngs followed Jesus, yet He never turned away. He must have been very weary at times, but He was never impatient with the crowd. That thought has helped me so often."

463 A Better Kind of Indian Giver

An Indian one day asked Bishop Whipple to give him two one-dollar bills for a two-dollar note. When asked why, the Indian replied, "One dollar for me to give to Jesus, and one dollar for my wife to give." The Bishop asked him if it was all the money he had. He said, "Yes." The Bishop was about to tell him it was too much, when an Indian clergyman who was standing by whispered, "It might be too much for a white man to give, but not too much for an Indian who has this year heard for the first time of the love of Jesus."

464 Serious Commitment

A lovely story is told of the saintly Frances Ridley Havergal who wrote the lines we so often sing without due seriousness and commitment:

Take my silver and my gold,
Not a mite would I withhold.

It is a matter of record that this hymn was autobiographical. Frances Ridley Havergal did what she sang. In her writings is this personal testimony: "'Take my silver and my gold' now means shipping off all my ornaments—including a jewel cabinet which is really fit for a countess—to the Church Missionary Society. I don't think I need to tell you I never packed a box with such pleasure." This was giving with hilarity!

465 Timing Counts

Timing counts, too, so our obedience must be prompt. A businessman went to a missionary society with $280 toward sending a new recruit overseas. He was told that he was too late. They had just canceled her passage for lack of the money. In tears he then confessed, "God told me to give it some days ago, but I delayed."

466 Reward of Giving

When we stand before the judgment seat of Christ to render an account of our stewardship, we will fervently regret giving so little, since it is inescapably true that what we spend we lose; what we keep will be left to others; what we give away will remain forever ours.

467 Make a Better Day

Little things make a better day:

• Being grateful for another morning by being cheerful on the outside even though you might be in physical pain on the inside.

• Writing a little note of encouragement, congratulations, appreciation, sympathy or condolence to someone needing a little uplift.

• A visit to a sick friend—but don't stay too long.

• A telephone call to a lonesome friend.

• Give a gift to someone.

• Have a kind and warm greeting for a little child or an elderly person.

• Stop and enjoy the flowers.

• Get some little thing done that you have been putting off.

• Admit a mistake to yourself and resolve not to make it again.

• Show kindness to animals.

• Move close to your family.

• Explore the satisfaction of courtesy.

• Be able to go to sleep at the end of the day with the feeling that you have been a more considerate person today than you were yesterday.

All these add to the sweetness and smoothness of life. They bring us to pleasant communion with others, nurture friendships, and prevent the interference of those petty sophistications and elaborate etiquettes that keep us apart from others.

Though small, they create a beneficent radiation which enriches us and contributes to our own ennoblement. They enhance a tender inclination for the pleasantness that comes with the satisfaction of having done good. They strengthen the soul. They make a good day because they make us better persons.

468 A Love Thing

A Christmas candle is a love thing;
   It makes no noise at all,
   But softly gives itself away;
   While quite unselfish, it grows small.

469 More Than a Tithe

On his tenth birthday, a sensitive boy received 10 shiny silver dollars from a thoughtful uncle. The child was very appreciative. He immediately sat down on the floor and spread the coins before him. Then he began to plan how to use the money. He set aside the first dollar saying, "This one is for Jesus." He then went on to decide what to do with the second, and so on until he came to the last dollar. "This one is for Jesus," he said. The boy's mother interrupted, "But I thought you gave the first dollar to Jesus." "I did," the boy replied. "The first one really belongs to Him, but this one is a gift to Him from me."

470 Repaying

When we think of reciprocating, too many of us think in terms of repaying our benefactor. Perhaps recalling an occasion in the life of D. L. Moody will give us a different perspective.

Once, when Mr. Moody was in New York, he was helped tremendously by R. K. Remington. As he was leaving on the train, Mr. Moody grasped his friend by the hand and said, "If you ever come to Chicago, call on me and I will try to return your kindness." Mr. Remington replied, "Don't wait for me; do it to the first man that comes along."

471 God's Bigger Shovel

A farmer was known for his generous giving, but his friends could not understand how he could give so much away and yet remain so prosperous. One day a spokesman for his friends said, "We can't understand you. You give far more than the rest of us and yet you always seem to have more to give." "Oh, that is easy to explain," the farmer said. "I keep shoveling into God's bin and God keeps shoveling into mine, but God has the bigger shovel!" Here was a man whose ethics of giving were controlled by the power of an indwelling Lord.

472 Lincoln, a Boy and an Orange

"I was eight years old when my father took me with him to Washington," said a man who was later prominent in national life. "It was during the darkest hours of the Civil War.

"We were walking on the street when a tall, thin man with very long legs, loose clothes and a frowning, wrinkled face, came striding toward us. His eyes were fixed on the pavement. His lips were moving. I remember thinking how cross he looked and what long strides he took, making his coattails flop about his legs.

"But I was more interested in watching a ragged little urchin between us, standing on the curb, his big eyes fixed on a pile of oranges in a vendor's cart. The vendor's back was turned while he made change for a customer.

"The tall man passed the boy at the same time we did. He stopped suddenly, plunged a hand into his pocket, bought a big orange, gave it to the boy, and went on.

"The boy was grinning and had already set his teeth in the orange, much to my envy, when my father asked him whether he knew who gave it to him. He shook his head, his teeth going deeper into the orange.

"'That was President Lincoln, lad,' my father said, 'Hurry and thank him.'

"The boy ran, caught the flopping coat, and as the stern face turned sharply, he called, 'Thank you, Mr. President Lincoln!'

"Suddenly the face was transformed as I have never seen a face since then. A beautiful smile covered it, making it what has ever since seemed to me one of the handsomest faces I have ever seen. A voice which thrills me yet said: 'You're welcome, boy. You wanted to steal it while the man wasn't looking, didn't you? But you wouldn't because it wasn't honest. That's the right way. I wish some men I know were like you.' "

473 A Coat for Christ

"He that hath two coats, let him impart to him that hath none; and he that hath meat, let him do likewise."

It was a wild, wintry night. The temperature had dived to a polar position. Winds rose in shrieking crescendos and lashed the country with lethal blasts.

But the Czar's interests must be protected. A Russian soldier must patrol between two sentry boxes even on such a night. Poorly clad, the miserable man marched from one post to the other, shivering and chilled. Then it began to snow. Before long the hills which surrounded that frozen, forsaken place were covered with snow. The sentry was wrapped in the vicious embrace of a fierce, freezing blizzard.

Then a poor peasant happened to pass nearby on his way home. Answering the soldier's challenge, he identified himself and secured permission to proceed. But the peasant pitied the sentry. "You are cold and must patrol all night," he said kindly. "I am only a short distance from my cottage. Here, wear my coat tonight. You can return it to me in the morning."

The soldier gladly accepted the proffered wrap. But even the heavy borrowed coat could not keep out the cold which seeped through the sentry like poison. No wrap seemed warm enough on that night to fend off the icy fingers of death.

The next morning his comrades discovered the soldier frozen in the field. The peasant never recovered his coat. But he did see it again. A long time afterwards, when the peasant himself lay on his deathbed, he dreamed that Jesus appeared to him. "You are wearing my coat, Lord," the dying man said, recognizing the wrap he had loaned to the sentry.

"Yes," answered Jesus. "This is the coat you loaned to me that frightful night when I was on duty and you passed by."

"But Lord," objected the peasant, "You were not that soldier!"

"No," replied Jesus in the dream. "But inasmuch as ye have done it unto one of the least of these My brethren, ye have done it unto me. I was naked and ye clothed me!"

474 Thankfulness Comes From the Heart

A young girl sat at the counter of an ice cream store. "How much is an ice cream sundae?" she asked. "Fifty cents," the waitress said with hardly a glance at the child. The girl opened her fist and looked at her coins. She asked, "How much is a dish of just plain ice cream?" Annoyed, the waitress snapped, "Thirty-five cents!" The girl counted out 35 cents and handed it to the waitress. "I'll take the plain ice cream."

The waitress took the money without a word and brought the ice cream. After the small customer had eaten and left, the waitress, cleaning up, suddenly flushed with shame. There, placed neatly beside the dish were two nickels and five pennies—her tip.

God

475 Where Was God?

When a father received word that his son, a brilliant lad, had been killed in a railway accident, he turned to his pastor and cried in desperation, "Tell me, sir, where was God when my son was killed?" And in that tense and terrible moment guidance was given to the counseling pastor. "My friend," said he, "God was just where He was when His own Son was killed!"

476 How Can I Love God Whom I Have Not Seen?

Unseen, yet loved. A kind mother had one day been talking with her little girl about the duty of loving God. The child replied, "Mother, I have never seen God; how can I love Him?" The mother made no answer then.

A few days after, she received a package from a friend who lived a great way off; and in the package was a beautiful picture-book for the little girl. The child took the book and was for some time entirely engrossed in looking at the pictures, but soon she exclaimed, "Oh, mother! How I do love the good lady that sent me this book!" "But you never saw her, my dear," said the mother. "No," answered the child; "but I love her because she sent me this beautiful present." "My child," said the mother, "you told me the other day that you could not love God because you have never seen Him. And yet you love this kind lady whom you have never seen, because she has given you a present. Now you have all around you the presents which God has given you. Why can't you love Him for His presents?"

477 A Close-Up or an Overall View?

We are not able to comprehend the big beautiful picture that God is creating in our lives.

Reinhold Messner was a skilled mountain climber who was recognized as the best in the world. He was one of two men who first climbed Mount Everest without using bottled oxygen. Messner then decided that doing it with a partner was not good enough, so he went back and did it alone. He was asked, as most mountain climbers are, "Why do you do it?" He replied, "Because at the top all the lines converge."

Even though we may not always have the "view from the top," it is a great encouragement to know that God does! He is sovereign! He has said, "I am the Lord. I do not change!" (Mal. 3:6). Because He sees the "overall picture," He is worthy of our trust!

478 We Can't Do without Him

There comes a time in the lives of believers and unbelievers alike when God seems expendable. Noting that things are going along quite well, man, including Christian man, feels quite willing to go it alone.

Man, no matter how powerful, can be humbled by the weather—by the falling snow, as Napoleon discovered when he invaded Russia, or by the lack of rain or excess of it, or by an unusually bitter winter.

Whenever natural catastrophe struck, the spiritual leaders of our Pilgrim forebears used the pulpits of New England to remind the people that God was at work behind every catastrophe, and that He still spoke not only by the still, small voice but also by the thunder, the snow, the hail, the absence of rain, and if necessary even by death.

The Pharaoh was given sign after sign by God, and one after the other the signs were ignored. It was not until the tenth sign came that the Pharaoh let God's people go. Have we, too, hardened our hearts against God's message?

479 Watermelon Seed

William Jennings Bryan got more than refreshment from a piece of watermelon:

"I was eating a piece of watermelon some months ago when I was struck with its beauty. I took some of the seeds and dried them

and weighed them, and found that it would require some 5,000 seeds to weigh a pound; and then I applied mathematics to that 40-pound melon.

"One of these seeds, put into the ground, when warmed by the sun and moistened by the rain, takes off its coat and goes to work; it gathers from somewhere two hundred thousand times its own weight, and forcing this raw material through a tiny stem, constructs a watermelon. It ornaments the outside with a covering of green; inside the green it puts a layer of white, and within the white a core of red, and all through the red it scatters seeds, each one capable of continuing the work of reproduction.

"Who drew the plan by which that little seed works? Where does it get its tremendous strength? Where does it find its coloring matter? How does it collect its flavoring extract? How does it develop a watermelon?

"Until you can explain a watermelon, do not be too sure that you can set limits to the power of the Almighty and say just what He would do or how He would do it."

480 Amen!

The rabbis of the *Talmud* teach that "Amen" is an acrostic from the first letters of the three words, *El Melech Ne'eman*, meaning the Lord is trustworthy. "Amen" appears the first time in Numbers 5:22. The Lexicon states that it is an adverb of confirmation meaning truly, verily, certainly, and so be it.

481 The Name of God

The *Hashem* ("the Name"—referring to God) for the Jew is the epitome of Holiness. That is why the devout Jew, when writing, spells God as G-D or Lord as L-rd, and why he pronounces the name Jehovah by the word *Adonsi*, or by *Hashem* and adds the words, "blessed be He." That is why the *sefer* scribe, the one copying the *Torah* Scroll, will take a new quill pen to write the name of God, and a new mix of ink. Before he writes that name, he must say, "I intend to write the name of God." If he does not, the page of the scroll is unfit and must be discarded. Likewise, if he is interrupted while writing the name or if he makes a mistake, the page is unfit.

The very name of God in the Old Testament Scriptures is the revelation of God.

482 Incomprehensible

There is a great deal about God that we cannot understand. Who can understand the Trinity? John Wesley very appropriately said, "Bring me a worm that can comprehend a man, and then I will show you a man that can comprehend the Triune God!"

483 Cast and Carried

Henry Moorhouse, when engaged in a work that seemed to call upon him for a more than usual exercise of faith, received what seems like a most tender answer from God.

His little daughter, who was a paralytic, was sitting in her chair as he entered the house with a package in his hand for his wife. Going up to her and kissing her, he asked, "Where is Mother?" "Mother is upstairs." "Well, I have a package for her." "Let me carry the package to Mother." "Why, Minnie, dear, how can you carry the package? You cannot carry yourself." With a smile on her face, Minnie said, "Oh, no, Papa; but you give me the package, and I will carry the package, and you will carry me." Taking her up in his arms, he carried her upstairs—little Minnie and the package, too.

And then it came to him that this was just his position in the work in which he was engaged. He was carrying his burden, but was not God carrying him? "Cast" (Ps. 55:22). "Carry" (Is. 46:4).

484 Answer to Agnostics

Some people pride themselves on being agnostics. That is, they say that religious teachings are very well for those who care to be so stupid that they want to believe in God and heaven, something they cannot see. The agnostics, however, pride themselves on believing only those things which they can prove and understand. This reminds me of a story.

"I will not believe anything that I do not understand," said a man in a hotel one day. "Neither will I," said another. "Nor will I," said a third. "Gentlemen," said one who sat close by, "on my ride this morning I saw some geese in a field eating grass. Do you believe that?"

"Certainly," said one of the three listeners. "I saw the pigs eating grass. Do you believe that?" "Of course," said the three. "I also saw sheep and cows eating grass. Do you believe that?" "Of course," was again the reply.

"Well, the grass turned to feathers on the backs of the geese, to bristles on the backs of the swine, to white wool on the sheep, and to hair on the cow; do you believe that, gentlemen?" "Certainly," they replied.

"But do you understand it?"

485 He Raised His Son

Pliny the Elder was a Roman writer who lived during the same time period as Jesus. He told a story of the setting of an obelisk, which when erect would stand 99 feet tall.

Twenty-thousand workers were chosen to pull on the ropes and activate the hoisting apparatus. There was great responsibility and risk in the operation. Just one error could cause the obelisk to fall, ruining years of work.

The King demanded one act which insured the complete attention and best direction of the engineer. He ordered the engineer's own son to be strapped to the apex of the obelisk, so that his heart as well as his head would be given to the task.

One day on Calvary, God's only begotten Son was raised before a sinful, jeering crowd, as the Father watched intently from heaven. The heart and mind of God were directed toward Jesus on the day our Lord was raised. There, above the heads of mankind, Jesus hung in death so that we might know eternal life. Remember Jesus' words:

"I, when I am lifted up from the earth, will draw all men to Myself" (John 12:32). Jesus was raised for you and me!

486 He Removes Kings and Raises Up Kings

Daniel said it long ago. It is God who "removes kings and raises up kings." (Dan. 2:21). This was the way Daniel stated the truth that God is the One who controls and rules the world. Regarding Jesus, John said that He is now "King of kings and Lord of lords." Yet it still surprises us when faced with the reality of God's control. We don't like what we cannot easily explain. If we cannot say exactly how God does something, we are at a loss. It's time we accept the vantage point of many Bible writers when they could not explain, but they could declare the power of God.

November 9, 1989 stands as a testimony to the rule of God. That's the day the Berlin Wall fell. No one saw it coming; no political leader, no social scientist, no church leader saw what was happening. It shocked the world. No one can explain how it came about. Then nation after nation of Eastern Europe eliminated Communism as master. Is it answered prayer? Yes! Is it God's work? Yes! He now gives the church an open door. Do we believe He can get us through the door?

487 A Father's Love

Would you like to marry someone whom your parents chose for you? Dr. Joyce Hardin in her book, *Three Steps Behind,* recounts a conversation with a Korean young lady. Dr. Hardin expressed surprise at the custom of arranged marriages and questioned how a woman could ever marry a person whom her father picked out. The Korean replied that her father loved her and knew her better than she knew herself. She was convinced that her father would never do anything to harm her and would make only the best choice for her. Besides, she added, she had the right to reject his choice, but doubted that she would.

Are we willing to trust God as much as some trust their parents? If we are willing to completely surrender ourselves to Him we can believe that He will give us what is the very best for us (Rom. 8:28). What more comfort could we ask than to believe that even when we do not understand life's happenings, we can know that our Father loves us?

488 Which God Are You Banking On?

One day a brother was in a strange part of town and in somewhat of a rush. He needed to get some money from his bank, so he obtained directions to one of its branches—one he had never been to before.

The brother followed the advice, and sure enough there was a bank right across the street from the big store he was told to seek. He rushed in and handed over his book and other forms to the smiling teller.

"I'm sorry, sir. I can't accept this," she said. "Why not? I am sure it is all in order. I wrote it out very carefully," he countered.

"I am sure you did, but this is not our bank. The one you want is across the street." Shamefaced, he retreated to the other bank, the right one, which was also across the street from the big store, only on the other side.

In a similar way, how many people rush to a god, any god, seeking comfort, solace or salvation, only to find that it is not *the* God, our heavenly Father, His Son Jesus Christ, and the Holy Spirit?

One may rectify going to the wrong bank, but one cannot recover from banking on the wrong god.

489 When Life Caves In

John Newton signed on with a slave ship leaving from Africa with its "cargo." He was an experienced sailor and navigator, but his cursing and blaspheming turned hardened sailors' ears red. Soon the ship was caught in a horrible storm and was taking in water. The crew had to pump 24 hours a day to stay afloat. But the constant wind rocked the boat so dangerously that the sailors had to tie themselves to the deck to keep from being swept overboard. At one point, several of the crew tried to throw Newton overboard. They figured that God was punishing him like Jonah of the Old Testament. The captain declared that the only way the ship would make it in to safe harbor was by God's power. He commanded everyone—including Newton—to pray.

"God, if You're true," Newton prayed earnestly, "make good your Word. Cleanse my vile heart."

After four weeks of storms and constant brushes with death, the ship limped into an Irish port. John Newton, former "free thinker," former slave trader and atheist, declared his faith in Jesus. He became a well-known preacher and writer. In fact, we chiefly know him as the author of the hymn "Amazing Grace."

490 God Gave a Son

One time during World War II, a mother and her small son were walking down a street in the evening. The little boy noticed the little flags in the windows with stars on them and asked what they were. His mother explained that the people in those homes had given a son in the war. He saw two and even three in some windows. He suddenly noticed the first evening star and said, "Mommy, God must have given a son, too."

491 What the World Cannot Steal From the Christian

A missionary returned to the little village which had been destroyed by the enemies of the gospel. He found the people weeping over the ashes which were previously their thatched roofs. One of the natives said to him, "They even burned my Bible and my hymn book!" And then in the ruins he saw a little white paper not totally burned. He picked it up and read it. The only thing that remained was "Joy to the World, the Lord is come." He stopped for a moment and then he said, "That's enough for me."

Creator

492 Tracks of God

"Father," said Thomas, looking up from his studies. "How do you know there is a God?"

"Why do you ask that question? Do you doubt the existence of God?" asked the father.

"Well, I heard one of the professors say that we could not be sure that there is a God. Is there any way really to know?"

"Well, my boy. Do you remember the other day that you were laughing about Robinson Crusoe's dismay at discovering that there were other persons on the island beside himself? How did he discover them? Did he see them? No, he discovered one track of a bare foot in the sand, and he knew that it could not be his own. He knew that only a human being could have made it, and he knew that whoever made it could not be far off, for the tide had not yet reached it. All those things he knew to be true, although he had not seen a human being within miles of the island.

And the knowledge was all gained from a mark in the sand.

"If one print of a bare foot in the sand is absolute proof of the existence and presence of a human being, what are we to suppose when we see the prints of the Master's shoe, as Bunyan calls it, covering the whole wide world? We see on mountain and valley the print of the fingers of God. We see a million plants and flowers and trees that only God could make grow. We see all the rivers and the springs of the world fed from invisible specks of atmospheric moisture. What do all those things mean—those millions upon millions of footprints on the clay of the world? They mean God living, present, ruling, and loving! They mean God and nothing else!"

493 God's Existence

Imagine a family of mice who live all their lives in a large piano. To them in their piano-world came the music of the instrument, filling all the dark spaces with sound and harmony. At first the mice were impressed by it. They drew comfort and wonder from the thought that there was Someone who made the music—invisible to them—yet close to them. They loved to think of the Great Player whom they could not see.

Then one day a daring young mouse climbed up part of the piano and returned very thoughtful. He had found out how the music was made. Wires were the secret; tightly stretched wires of graduated lengths which trembled and vibrated. They must revise all their old beliefs: none but the most conservative could any longer believe in the Unseen Player. Later, another explorer carried the explanation further. Hammers were now the secret, numbers of hammers dancing and leaping on the wires. This was a more complicated theory, but it all went to show that they lived in a purely mechanical and mathematical world. The Unseen Player came to be thought of as a myth. But the Pianist continued to play.

494 Teaching Existence of God—Garden—Creator

A Scotch philosopher wanted to teach his five-year-old son about God. He went into his garden alone and with his finger traced out the lad's name. He planted cress and mustard seed in the outline.

About 10 days later the lad came running to his father crying, "My name is coming up in the garden."

His father said, "Nonsense! It can't be!"

They went to the garden, and his father said, "Oh, that must just have happened."

"No, no," said the boy, "somebody must have planted it."

So the lad learned his first lesson about the Creator.

495 Properly Equipped

An example from the animal world shows how God makes provision for stability in the most difficult circumstances. In bold defiance of gravity, the mountain goats that live from the Northwest United States through Canada into Alaska demonstrate incredible stability in the most difficult of terrains. They leap surefootedly from ledge to ledge and scamper around steep, rugged mountainsides with the utmost confidence. Unusually flexible, the two toes of the goat's hoof can spread apart wider than the hoof is long to distribute the animal's grip. Or they can draw together to grasp a knob of rock. The goat also has a rough, pliable traction pad on the bottom of each toe which makes them skid-resistant on ice. Dewclaws projecting from the rear of the ankles provide additional traction on steep, downhill routes.

Just as God makes provision in the animal world for creatures to stand with stability in the most difficult terrain, He will surely make provision for His redeemed children to stand in the most difficult spiritual circumstances. He can and will stabilize you in the midst of insuperable difficulty.

496 It Is All Part of a Plan

A medical student had a hard time accepting that the whole world and even Christ's birth was part of a plan.

One day this lady medical student said, "I was working on an arm and hand, studying the perfect mechanical arrangements of the muscles and tendons—how the sheaths of certain muscles are split to let tendons of certain muscles through,

so that the hand may be delicate and small and yet powerful. I was all alone in the laboratory when the overwhelming belief came. A thing like this is not just chance, but a part of a plan, a plan so big that only God could have conceived it.

"Religion had been to me a matter of form, a thing without conviction. Now everything was an evidence of God—the tendons of the hand, the patterns of the little butterfly's wings—all was part of a purpose."

The Psalmist wrote, "I am fearfully and wonderfully made: marvelous are thy works" (Ps. 139:14). But, has there ever been a better plan for the salvation of man than for Jesus coming into the world to save sinners? It was not a matter of chance, it was all planned and executed at the right time.

497 How Great Thou Art!

A few years ago, Joseph M. Stowell and his wife had the joy of teaching the Word of God in Hawaii. It was February, which happens to be when the humpback whales arrive. Humpback whales are about 40 feet long at maturity and weigh about one ton per foot. They carry a thousand pounds of barnacles, and when they jump, or "breach," they extend themselves totally in the air, and then free-fall back into the ocean. You can see the splash five miles away.

During the Stowell's stay, they went out on a whale-watching boat. As they watched the whales jump and play almost within reach, the guide told them that the whales come down from Alaska every year to calve in the warm Hawaiian waters. Year after year, each family comes back to the very same place around the island. When the calves are born (they weight about five tons), they are born breech—or tail first. If they were born head first, these air-breathing mammals would drown during the birth process. As a baby whale is born, another humpback whale comes alongside and pushes it up to the surface to help the baby take his first breath of air.

The guide also said that the humpback whale sings a "song" that can be heard more than 50 miles away under water. Every one of these whales sings the same song. Each year, the song changes slightly, and every humpback whale in the world will sing that year's song. Amazing! Incredible! What a display of the wonderful creative power of our God!

498 Design in Creation

The seal of the Designer is stamped upon all His created works, and it is a seal that cannot be obliterated. Design in creation is indelible like the watermark in paper. Scripture infers that the hand of the Designer is to be seen in all His works.

"He is the Rock, His work is perfect: for all His ways are judgment: a God of truth and without iniquity, just and right is He" (Deut. 32:4).

"Who hath measured the waters in the hollow of His hand, and meted out heaven with a span, and comprehended the dust of the earth in a measure, and weighed the mountains in scales, and the hills in a balance" (Is. 40:12)?

According to the latter verse, the waters, the heaven above, and the dust of the earth (matter, or the chemical elements) are measured. God has infinitely measured all the works of His hands. Number is the underlying principle of nature. There are no created works without the numbers inherent in them.

God has measured the waters. The Word of God was not given to teach science primarily, but some of its statements anticipate scientific discoveries, and wherever the Scripture statements touch upon science they are accurate. Every drop of water in the universe is a mathematical equation. Science tells us that water is the combination of two gases, hydrogen and oxygen. Two parts of hydrogen to one of oxygen meet to form water. It is measured. It is not an accident. It does not just happen so. Our universe is an orderly universe, and every drop of water reveals the hand of the Designer.

Faithful

499 Our Father Is Faithful to Deliver

Called by God to full-time Christian service, the man resigned a lucrative job, left a specialized career of 20 years, and took his family over 2,000 miles to a strange city to enter seminary.

He was able to obtain only part-time employment in his profession and his annual salary was barely one-third of what he had earned before God called him.

The costs of being in seminary and of keeping his two children in Christian elementary school became heavier and heavier. When things got too tight he stayed out a semester, but his children went to school. Finally, his wife, who had not worked since the first child was born, took a full-time job.

All the while the man's prayer was to share with God his heart's desire that he be given work in Christian service that would make ends meet while he went to school and served his Lord Jesus Christ.

Though he enjoyed many opportunities to preach and to minister without pay, full-time Christian work eluded him. He began to seek full-time employment at secular jobs, but he knew in his heart if he landed one that probably would be the end of seminary.

One day a series of unpredictable circumstances arose whereby in less than two weeks, without any effort on his part, the man was in a full-time job utilizing his specific talents, in full-time Christian service, and with an employer that insisted that he continue in seminary.

God faithfully prepares hearts in times of trial and temptation. And when His time is right, He delivers.

Father

500 When God Is Our Father

A missionary was teaching a Hindu woman the Lord's Prayer. When he got to the end of the first clause, "Our Father which art in heaven," she stopped him. "If God is our Father," she said, "that is enough. There is nothing now to fear."

All questioning about God ceases when He becomes our Father.

501 Father Is There

Many years ago a little boy lay on his small bed, having just retired for the night. Before going to sleep, he moved in the direction of the large bed on which his father lay, and said, "Father, are you there?" "Yes, my son," was the answer. The little boy turned over and went to sleep, without a thought of harm.

Tonight the little boy is an old man of seventy, and every night before going to sleep, he looks up into the face of the heavenly Father, and says, "Father, are you there?" And the answer comes back, clear and strong, "Yes, my son."

502 God's Correction of Us

"Happy is the man whom God correcteth" (Job 5:17).

Happy, because the correction is designed to bring him into paths of blessedness and peace.

Happy, because there is no unnecessary severity in it.

Happy, because the chastisement is not so much against us, as against our most cruel enemies—our sins.

Happy, because we have abundant words of consolation.

Happy, because whom the Lord loveth He chasteneth.

Happy, because our light affliction is but for a moment.

503 Why Dad Slept in the Attic

A minister's son was caught skipping school for three days. His father reprimanded him and prayed for him and though the boy wept and was truly contrite, he was still punished.

"Son, one of the facts of life is that where there is sin, there is suffering," the father said.

"You have been living a lie for three days, so for 72 hours I am banning you to the attic, with a bed and three meals a day, but you must stay up there and make amends," he charged.

The boy did as he was told. When supper was served, the minister prayed with his wife, but he was restless and could not eat. When it was time to go to bed he knew he would have no rest.

"Honey, I am going upstairs to sleep with our boy," he told his wife.

He found his son wide awake and he hugged him and lay down beside him. Each night, the father took the place of punishment with his child.

How like our own God, who despite our transgressions loves us enough to send His Son to be with us, and to die for us.

Loving

504 "Love Without End, Amen"

"For God so loved the world, that He gave His only begotten Son, that whoever believes in Him should not perish, but have eternal life" (John 3:16 NAS).

Country singer George Strait sings a song entitled, "Love without End, Amen." It tells the story of a young boy coming home from school after having a fight and expecting punishment from his dad. Fully expecting the wrath of his father, the son waited, expecting the worst. However, the father said, "Let me tell you a secret about a father's love . . . Daddies don't just love their children every now and then . . . it's a love without end. Amen."

The young lad grew up and passed this secret on to his children. One day he dreamed that he died and went to heaven. He was concerned, as he waited to go in, because he realized there must be some mistake for if they knew half the things he's done they would never let him in. It was then that he heard his father's words again, "Let me tell you a secret about a father's love . . . Daddies don't just love their children every now and then . . . it's a love without end. Amen."

Isn't it comforting to know that we have a Father like this? It is no secret, concerning our Father's love: God doesn't just love His children every now and then; indeed, it is a "love without end, Amen."

—Bill Thrasher

505 God Cares

Joel C. Gregory writes: "I've always been fascinated with hummingbirds, so fragile, tiny, and beautiful. There are actually 320 kinds of hummingbirds. The Encyclopedia Britannica tells us that the tiniest among them is the Bee Hummingbird. It is 2 1/8 inches long, and half of that is tail feathers and beak. It only weighs five grams, just about the same weight as several aspirins would be in your hand. And yet that bird can hover, it can go up and down, sideways, and in and out with the most amazing grace and flexibility. It flaps its wings ninety times a second. And that little bird somehow knows that when it begins to get cold, for its own health, it's best to leave far Northern Canada and migrate across the United States and the Gulf of Mexico, all the way to the Panama Canal Zone. And it knows when to turn around and go back. Just an accident? If you think so, you're the type who believes there could be an explosion in a printing plant and unabridged dictionaries would fall from the sky! Jesus points to the birds and says, 'Look at God's concern for that small creature—and learn.'

"God cares. Even for little hummingbirds. And that means He cares for us."

Merciful

506 God Knows What's Best!

In Greek mythology, Aurora, the goddess of the dawn, fell in love with Tithonus, a mortal youth. Zeus, the king of the gods, gave her the privilege of choosing a gift for her mortal lover. Aurora asked that Tithonus live forever; however, she forgot to ask that Tithonus remain forever *young;* consequently, Tithonus grew progressively older; in fact, he could never die. The gift became a curse.

The God of the Bible is not like a mythological god. He never forgets anything that is not considered before He answers our prayers. He does not grant us a request which ultimately will become a burden. He is never a deceiver. Therefore, we must accept His answers as the best for us.

507 God Makes No Mistakes

Oppressed by the noonday heat, a tired farmer sat under a walnut tree to rest. Relaxing, he looked at his pumpkin vines and said to himself, "How strange it is that God puts such big heavy pumpkins on a frail vine that has so little strength it has to trail on the ground!" And then looking up into the cool branches of the tree above him, he added, "How strange it is that God puts small walnuts on such a big tree with branches so strong they could hold a man!"

Just then a breeze dislodged a walnut from the tree. The tired farmer wondered no more, as he rubbed his head ruefully and said, "It is a good thing there wasn't a pumpkin up there instead of a walnut."

Hopefully, when the breezes of life blow, you will remember that

God, Who is great and wise, makes no mistakes. He deserves our praise under any circumstance.

Omnipotent

508 Omnipotence Questioned

A Bible class teacher was examining her pupils after a series of lessons on God's omnipotence. She asked, "Is there anything God cannot do?"

There was silence. Finally, one lad held up his hand. The teacher, disappointed that the lesson's point had been missed, asked resignedly, "Well, just what is it that God cannot do?"

"Well," replied the boy, "He can't please everybody."

509 Let the Fire Fall

Years ago, before we became conscious of ecology, tourists at Yosemite Park were treated to a nightly display that never failed to please the huge crowds that gathered to witness this demonstration. High over the valley floor, the park rangers would set a number of logs on fire and wait downstream near one of those marvelous precipitous waterfalls that grace that magnificent valley. When the hour of darkness had finally arrived, the sonorous voice of a park ranger would ring out from the valley floor: "Let the fire fall!"

Then the moment would come which all had waited so patiently to witness; a hail of sparks and flames would appear as the waters carried the burning logs over the brink of the falls and down the steep de-

scent of several hundred feet to the valley floor and the waiting stream. The crowd loved it. The fire fell along with the water. It appeared to happen as if it were solely at the command of one man with a booming and demanding voice—as if he had some special contact with heaven itself.

If that is how it appeared to these campers in Yosemite Park, how must if have appeared to those somewhat skeptical Israelite fence-sitters who refused to adopt wholeheartedly Yahweh or Baal as their God? For just as surely as the park ranger called, "Let the fire fall," so this rustic from the backwoods area of Israel called to the living God. He did not rig his demonstration—this was the real thing. It was so real it was terrifying. Anything that would eat up rocks, dust, water, animals, and all has got to be some sort of supernatural display.

Accordingly, God gives us three "demonstrations" of His power in 1 Kings 18. He demontrates His power through his messenger Elijah in verses 1-20; in His actions by sending fire to burn the sacrifice (verses 21-40); and in His answers to prayer when he relieves the drought in verses 41-46.

Omnipresent

510 Where God Ain't

He was just a little lad,
And on the week's first day,
Was wandering home from Sunday School,
And dawdling along the way.

He scuffed his shoes into the grass;
  He found a caterpillar;
  He found a fluffy milkweed pod,
  And flew out all the filler.

A bird's nest in a tree o'head
So wisely placed and high,
Was just another wonder
That caught his eager eye.

A neighbor watched his zigzag course,
  And hailed him from the lawn;
  Asked him where he'd been that day,
  And what was going on.

"Oh, I've been to Sunday School.
(He carefully turned a sod
And found a snail beneath it);
I've learned a lot about God."

"M'm'm, a very fine way," the neighbor said,
  "For a boy to spend his time;
  If you'll tell me where God is,
  I'll give you a brand new dime."

Quick as a flash his answer came!
Nor were his accents faint—
"I'll give you a dollar, Mister,
If you tell me where God ain't."

Omniscient

511 The Far-Seeing Eye

As the astronomer Mitchell was one day observing the setting sun through a large telescope and gradually lowering the instrument to keep in view the great body of light slowly sinking in the western sky, there came within his line of vision the top of a distant hill, upon which grew a number of apple trees.

In one of these trees were two boys, apparently stealing the apples. One was getting the fruit, while the other appeared to be keeping watch, to make sure that they were not seen. However, seven miles away, Professor Mitchell had his telescope trained on them and was watching their every movement as though he were on the hilltop.

"All things are naked and opened unto the eyes of Him with whom we have to do" (Heb. 4:13).

512 Where Are You Going?

We are on our way somewhere—and not just out to lunch after church or to a party next Thursday.

A small boy, with his father, was in an elevator going up in the Empire State Building in New York. As they flashed by the 66nd floor, the lad, in considerable anxiety, seized his father's hand, and in an awestruck whisper, said, "Does God know we are coming?"

This is an amusing story; but, the serious answer is: Yes, God knows we are coming!

Providence

513 Comforted by God's Promises

A preacher going to a country church one Sunday morning was

overtaken by a deacon who re-marked, "What a bitter cold morning, sir. I am sorry the weather is so wintry." "Oh," replied the minister, "I was just thanking God for keeping His Word." The man stared at him and asked, "What do you mean?" "Well, over 3,000 years ago God promised that cold and heat should not cease, so I am strengthened by this weather to emphasize the sureness of His promises."

514 A Fasting Father Takes a Meal

Siamese Bettas are called "fighting fish" because the males will fight each other to the death. Usually, if only one of the species is kept in a fish tank, it gets along well with the other fish. Yet in reproduction, it is the male that makes the nest. Using its saliva and air, the male builds a nest of tiny bubbles, each smaller than a BB-shot. When the nest is about the diameter of a coffee cup, the male mates with the female and the eggs fall. The male gathers the eggs and places each one in an air bubble.

After mating and during the gestation period, the male remains under the bubble nest, not eating. He carefully catches each developing egg when a bubble breaks and places it in a new bubble. He continues this effort around the clock under a forced fast for about two weeks. When the young hatch out, they usually are too small to be seen by the naked eye, but the male fighting fish cares for them until

they begin to leave the nest and adhere to the sides of the breeding tank looking like little shards of broken glass.

Suddenly the time of parenting is over. It is as though an alarm goes off inside the fish, as it turns from minister to marauder. If the breeder is not alert, he may lose all the young to the hungry father, who then eats up the very ones he so diligently cared for.

How fortunate is man that God has designed parents so that though the young may become independent and venture in life on their own, unlike these fish, ours are not short-term parents, but lifetime parents, even as God is our eternal parent.

515 Wonder of God's Providence

The year was 1772. One of those almost impenetrable fogs had settled down over the city of London.

In a dismal flat in the heart of the crowded East End, a man stood gazing into the fireplace. Then suddenly, overcome by emotions of discouragement, gripped by fears that he could not name, he threw his cloak about him and walked resolutely toward the door. He turned the key and walked out into the night.

Carefully he groped his way across the pavement and felt for the iron horse's head and the ring of the hitching post. Then, guided by the curbstone, he made his way to the nearest corner, where he knew a horse-drawn cab was always waiting.

He opened its door and ordered the driver, "To the Thames, sir!" For in his deep depression there seemed no way out but to jump from the bridge.

It should have taken 15 minutes, but after an hour and a half of negotiating the dark and foggy streets they realized they were hopelessly lost. In desperation, he decided to walk and paid the driver his fare.

But as he alighted, his arm struck a familiar object. It was the iron horse's head of the hitching post that to him was so familiar. After an hour and a half of fitful wandering he had alighted in front of his own home.

So impressed was he that he climbed the stairs to his flat, lighted the lamp, and knelt to ask God to forgive him for what he had thought to do. And then, there in that same room that had so lately overcome him with its gloom, he wrote these immortal words that were long a favorite hymn:

God moves in a mysterious way
His wonders to perform;
He plants His footsteps in the sea,
And rides upon the storm.

Ye fearful saints, fresh courage take;
The clouds ye so much dread
Are big with mercy, and shall break
In blessings on your head.
His purposes will ripen fast,

Unfolding every hour;
The bud may have a bitter taste,
But sweet will be the flower.

Blind unbelief is sure to err,
And scan His work in vain;
God is His own interpreter,
And He will make it plain.

Yes, it was William Cowper who learned that night something of the wonder of God's providence.

516 Lord of the Impossible

Research into the migratory habits of quail in the Middle East makes the miracle of the Lord's provision all the more exciting. Each autumn, the birds fly from central Europe to Turkey. There they prepare for a crossing of the Mediterranean. The flight across the ocean is done in a single flight at a very high speed. Any bird that falters falls into the sea. When the birds approach the land, they drop down in altitude but maintain their high speed. As soon as they are over the coastland they land exhausted and completely drained. They lie motionless for hours while they regain their strength. For years Bedouins who lived near the coast harvested the easy prey. Recently a law was passed and enforced which prohibited quail trapping.

The amazing thing about the biblical account of the provision of the quail is that the birds must have kept flying until they reached the wilderness of Sinai. How did the quail know to fly on farther after their already exhausting flight? Only the Lord who created them could have pressed them on.

517 *New Every Morning*

In the Philippines, there is a lovely flower, the hibiscus, whose blossoms range from white, yellow, orange to deep red. They seem to grow everywhere, throughout the days of the year. They color the countryside with great splashes of color and beauty. The blossoms have many shapes and textures.

One of the unique aspects of this flower is that it blooms every morning; however, the bloom lasts only one day. That means that a bouquet only lasts one day.

So it with God's steadfast love which comes with freshness to us every morning. Just as He provided fresh manna each morning for the children of Israel in their wilderness journey, so He provides for us, each day, renewed mercies and faithfulness. But, we must gather fresh manna each day.

518 *Heaven's Grocery Store*

As I was walking down life's highway a long time ago,
One day I saw a sign that read "Heaven's Grocery Store."
As I got a little closer, the door came open wide
And when I later found myself, I was standing there inside.
I saw a host of angels that were standing everywhere.
One handed me a basket and said, "My child, now shop with care."
Everything a Christian needed was in that grocery store;

And all you couldn't carry, you could come back next day for more.
First I got some PATIENCE, and LOVE was in the same row.
Further down was UNDERSTANDING, which you need wherever you go.
I got a box or two of WISDOM, and a bag or two of FAITH.
I just could not miss the HOLY GHOST 'cause it was all over the place.
I stopped to get some STRENGTH and COURAGE to help me run this race.
By then my basket was getting full, but I remembered I needed GRACE.
I did not forget SALVATION, for salvation there was free,
So I tried to get enough of that to save both you and me.
Then I started up to the counter, to pay my grocery bill.
For now I thought I had everything to do my Master's will.
At the end of the aisle I saw PRAYER and I just had to put that in,
For I knew when I stepped outside, I would run right into sin.
PEACE and JOY were plentiful. They were on the very last shelf.
SONGS and PRAISES were stacked nearby, so I just helped myself.
Then I said to the angel, "Now, how much do I owe?"
He just smiled and said to me, "Just take them wherever you go."
Again, I smiled at him and said, "How much do I really owe?"
He smiled again and said,
"My child, Jesus paid your bill a long time ago."

Growth

519 No Short-Cuts

When James A. Garfield was president of Hiram College, a man brought his son for entrance as a student, for whom he wished a shorter course than the regular. "The boy can never take all that in," said the father. "He wants to get through quicker. Can you arrange it for him?"

Mr. Garfield, a minister-educator said, "Oh, yes. He can take a short course; it all depends on what you want to make of him. When God wants to make an oak, He takes a hundred years, but he takes only two months to make a squash."

Many want instant spirituality—like instant coffee or potatoes! It doesn't come that way! There are no short courses! No short-cuts! No gimmicks! It takes time to grow! Growth is a sequence—an orderly arrangement! "For when for the time ye ought to be teachers, ye have need that one teach you again" was God's indictment of the Hebrew Christians (Heb. 5:12-14).

520 Perfection

If the world were controlled by perfectionists, there would be no place for those who can never quite measure up to their standards. On the other hand, if the world were under the domination of people who wake up in a new world every day, we would probably suffocate in the accumulation of our own garbage within a week.

Fortunately "practically perfect" people like Mary Poppins manage to get mixed up with the Dick Van Dykes of the world. A husband who is so organized that he can predict with a fair degree of accuracy when his next shoestring is going to break, inevitably gets paired with a wife who hasn't the foggiest notion what she's going to prepare for dinner at 3 o'clock in the afternoon. A wife, with such an obsession for cleanliness that she jumps out of bed at 1 o'clock in the morning because she suddenly remembers that she forgot to mop up a blob of spilled orange juice from the kitchen floor, marries a clod who comes in from a hunting trip and tracks mud all over the floor she just cleaned. So goes the struggle between perfection and the spirit of tolerance.

There is a certain amount of tension in every serious thinking Christian's mind concerning the biblical call to perfection. In one compartment of the brain, there's a tug to live up to all the standards of Christ, but then on the other hand, our attempts to measure up to those standards are always flawed.

The New Testament clearly articulates the need to "perfect holiness out of reverence for God" (2 Cor. 7:1). Perfection does not usually mean sinlessness in the Scripture. It usually means something like maturity or completeness. Even that can be illusive. Paul admitted that he had not "been made perfect" (Phil. 3:12). Yet he did not attempt to excuse himself from pursuing the goal of perfection. He said, "I press on to take hold of that for which Christ Jesus took hold of me." The person who excuses himself from serious effort because nobody's perfect, is just playing a game and he is not even playing according to the rules. While it is self-righteous and hypocritical to claim that one has already conquered the flesh at any point in this life, we play a deadly game of self-vindication when we ignore the pursuit of perfection.

521 How to See Growth in Christ

Dr. Bonar once said that he could tell when a Christian was growing. In proportion to his growth in grace he would elevate his Maker, talk less of what he himself was doing, and become smaller and smaller in his own esteem, until, like the morning star, he faded way before the rising sun.

522 A Christian Mandate

Do all the good you can
By all the means you can

In all the ways you can
In all the places you can
To all the people you can
As long as ever you can.

523 Are You Pushed or Pushing?

How long would you keep an automobile that had to be pushed everywhere it went? How much would it be worth to you? How much pleasure would you find in it? You might keep an automobile that just had to be pushed occasionally, but you would not have one for long that just could not be depended on, that would not go whenever you wanted it to go.

The Lord is no more pleased with one of His servants that continually has to be pushed than you would be with an automobile that continually has to be pushed.

God wants men of initiative and fervency of spirit. Paul taught us to be diligent, not slothful; fervent in spirit; serving the Lord (Rom. 12:11).

A man who has to be pushed continually in order to keep him in service and attending worship is not devoted to the cause. It is understandable that a newborn babe in Christ, a young convert, might need to be pushed or encouraged, but if one who has been a Christian for many years must still be pushed, he is not growing spiritually as he should. He is not spiritually mature.

Do you have to be pushed?

524 Manhood

Men and boys:
THE WORLD NEEDS MEN

. . . who cannot be bought;

. . . whose word is their bond;

. . . who put character above wealth;

. . . who are larger than their vocations;

. . . who do not hesitate to take chances;

. . . who will not lose their identity in a crowd;

. . . who will be as honest in small things as in great things;

. . . who will make no compromise with wrong;

. . . whose ambitions are not confined to their own selfish desires;

. . . who will not say they do it "because everybody else does it;"

. . . who are true to their friends through good report and evil report, in adversity as well as in prosperity;

. . . who do not believe that shrewdness and cunning are the best qualities for winning success;

. . . who are not ashamed to stand for the truth when it is unpopular;

. . . who can say "no" with emphasis, although the rest of the world says "yes."

God, make *me* this kind of man.

525 Longfellow's Prescription for a Long, Happy Life

The famous poet H. W. Longfellow was once asked how he managed a long and a happy life.

Pointing to an apple tree, the writer remarked: "The secret of the apple tree is that it grows a little new wood each year. That's what I try to do."

No matter what age you are, it is important to continue to grow spiritually each day, each month, each year. Such spiritual growth requires constant Bible study.

Why not start growing a little new wood now, by reading at least one chapter from the Bible each day? You will be blessed for it (Ps. 119).

526 Like an Eagle

The eagle is one of the largest and most powerful birds in the world. Some eagles weigh as much as 12 or 13 pounds and have a wingspan of about seven feet.

The nests of eagles are called eyries. They are built mainly of sticks and are often lined with fresh green leaves while they are being used. Once a year, the female lays one or two eggs, and they are carefully tended, sometimes even by the male eagle, until they hatch, in about 40 days. Both parents then guard the nest and take food to the young.

At about 11 or 12 weeks, a curious thing happens. If the eaglets have not ventured forth on their own, the parent eagle "stirs" or rocks the nest, tipping the eaglets out! The young eaglets flap about in panic, still novices at this flying business. The parent eagle hovers watchfully, waiting for the critical moment. With wings spread wide, the eagle then swoops down underneath those babies and delivers them back to the security of the eyrie.

Ours is a God of powerful gentleness. Ours is a God whose timing is perfect. Like the parent eagle, He is sensitive to our needs. He knows when the nest has become too comfortable and needs a little stirring. He, too, watches carefully, and, as with spread wings, catches us up, bringing us to Himself. But He wants us to learn from our fluttering and flopping. He wants us to leave behind our panic and to learn to wait on Him. Then, with our eyes on our parent eagle, we will begin to know what it means to soar on eagle's wings!

527 You Become What You Are

Max Beerbohm wrote a story entitled, "The Happy Hypocrite." The title sounds like a paradox, doesn't it? The story was about a character whose face personified evil. The man was faced with a dilemma: the woman he loved refused to marry him because he didn't look saintly. To solve the problem, the suitor put on a mask with a kind face. The young woman married him despite the face underneath the mask. Her husband proved to be an attentive, unselfish husband.

One day in a moment of rage, an enemy abruptly tore off her husband's mask before his wife's eyes. Instead of a cruel, grotesque face, the man had become what he had lived for many years. Kindness, not evil, radiated from his face!

The Bible urges us to "keep the faith" because someday we will look like Him in whom we believe (1 John 3:2).

528 Building Factories

An engineer who was responsible for building great factories said that all such construction is now planned with the machines that are to be housed in the factory in mind. The walls and floors of the buildings are constructed so that a machine can be built into the very foundation and structure of the building, rather than set in as an afterthought.

This is the way the Lord builds believers into Christ. We are built upon the foundation of the apostles and prophets, Jesus Christ Himself being the chief cornerstone, and in Him all the building is fitly framed together, so that it "groweth unto an holy temple in the Lord" (Eph. 2:20, 21). That is surpassing even the modern engineers. They can frame their building and foundation and machines together "fitly," but they cannot make the building "grow." The true believers are fused in Christ and grow in Him together with Him and together with one another.

529 Look Up

A house painter was at work atop a tall ladder that leaned against the second-story gable of a house. A small boy playing about the yard discovered the ladder, and as is natural for small boys, he began to climb it. His mother, checking on her child, was shocked to find that he was more than half way to the top of the ladder.

As the woman stifled a scream of panic, the man at the top looked down, saw the child, and instantly perceived the danger. Signaling the mother to be silent, he calmly said to the child, "Look up, sonny, look up here to me, and keep climbing." Rung by rung, he coaxed the child ever higher: "Come on now, keep looking up, keep coming." At last, the child safe in his arms, the painter carried him safely to the ground.

Well, each of us is somewhere on a ladder. If we look down, we may be terrified. God is saying, "Look up to me; keep looking up, and you will never be dismayed or undone by whatever is down there." So let's look up, up to where our safety lies; let's look up, and take heart, and keep climbing.

530 Soar on Wings Like Eagles

"Even youths grow tired and weary, and young men stumble and fall; but those who hope in the Lord will renew their strength. They will soar on wings like eagles; they will run and not grow weary, they will walk and not be faint" (Is. 40:30, 31 NIV).

An eagle knows when the storm is approaching long before it breaks. It will fly to some high spot and wait for the winds to come. When the storm hits, it sets its wings so that the wind will pick it up and lift it above the storm. While the storm rages below, it is soaring above it.

The eagle doesn't escape the storm, it simply uses the storm to lift it higher. It rides on the winds that bring the storm.

Isaiah compares people to eagles. He says, in the words of God, that we are blessed with that gift from God that enables us to ride the winds of the storm that bring sickness, tragedy, failure and disappointment in our lives. We can soar above the storm. Remember, it is not the burdens of life that weight us down, it is the way we handle them.

Heaven

531 Not Gone to Heaven

A little girl was walking in the cemetery with her aunt. She was examining the various gravestones when suddenly she cried out, "Oh, auntie, look here! Here is the tomb of some poor person who has not gone to heaven." "Not gone to heaven?" replied the astonished aunt, looking at the elaborate monument with weeping angels sculptured in marble. "Why, what do you mean?" "Well, auntie," said the child, "the lady or gentleman in the grave cannot have gone to heaven, or the angels would not be crying!"

532 Where Is Heaven?

One Sunday morning a faithful Sunday school teacher was teaching her class of boys about heaven. She asked the question, "Where is heaven?" And one happy boy replied, "It's in our home since my daddy became a Christian."

533 No Place Like Home

How can we forget some of the final lines in *The Wizard of Oz* when Dorothy keeps saying, "There's no place like home, there's no place like home." Most of us feel the same way. Man has always felt a fondness for that dwelling called home.

Adam and Eve were grieved when they were cast out of the garden of Eden—their home. Noah and his family listened as the waters covered their homeland. Moses left his homeland to follow the will of God for his life. Jesus found that a prophet was not without honor, except at home. The prodigal son knew that even as a servant, home was better than the pigpen.

We rejoice today as we round the corner to "our home." Whether it be a cardboard box in an alley, or a fine air-conditioned bastion of comfort in the stifling heat, we are glad to get home.

As temporary as the structures on earth are, our home in heaven will be permanent. God challenges us to live daily in preparation for that great eternal home that He is preparing for His children. It will be untouched by the elements of nature, unscarred by strife, pure, clean, and holy, and yes—IT WILL LAST FOR ETERNITY!

Do you feel as good about the home God is preparing for you as the one that may be gone tomorrow? If we anticipate that home with joy, how wonderfully we will live our lives today! May God bless us unto that end.

534 The Light

John Henry Jowett, prominent preacher of two or three generations ago, served as pastor of distinguished churches both in England and America. He used to tell of a stormy evening when he was entertained in the home of an English countryman. Sometime after nightfall, the hour came for him to leave, to catch his train back to the city. As he arose to go, his farmer host walked with him to the front gate. There the farmer gave him a lighted lantern, pointed to a light in the distance, and said, "Yonder light is Saddleworth Station; make for that. The lantern will keep you from falling into the ditch; but keep your eye on the glimmer in the distance."

In the daily walk of our life, sometimes in darkness or storm, we have to give a lot of attention to staying out of the ditch. We need to use the light, God's Word, to keep from falling in.

But there is something more. If we look carefully, in the distance we can see a glimmer. This is important; for the glimmer is the high goal, the object of the long quest, the Light that directs the course of our journey to heaven.

Friend, may you go from here today with a light for your next footsteps. But this alone is not enough: Never take your eyes off the glimmer that is in the distance.

535 Only One Way

A person may go to heaven—
without wealth

without beauty
without learning
without fame
without culture
without friends
But no one can go to heaven without Christ.

536 "I Know Where He Is Going"

Matthew Henry wrote a famous Bible Commentary. As a poor and unknown young man he wished to marry a girl whose father was wealthy and who did not approve of the marriage. The father argued that, although he was a good scholar and an excellent preacher, "they did not even know where he came from." The daughter had a ready answer. "But father," she said, "we know where he is going, and I want to go with him." The father acquiesced.

537 A Beautiful Christmas Evening

It was Christmas Eve. Six-year-old Mary Lou was walking down a dark city street with her father on their way to the children's service.

Her active little mind was filled with the wonders of the event she and her classmates were about to celebrate—the coming of the Christ Child from heaven to earth, to be born a tiny infant in a lowly stable.

Above them was the velvety blue-black canopy of heaven, Swiss-dotted (as it seemed to her) with an infinite variety of brilliant lights twinkling down to earth.

Her eyes were fixed on the shimmering tapestry above as she and her father walked, silently but thoughtfully, toward the lighted church at the end of the block.

Suddenly she looked up at her father and, with that rare insight peculiar to a six-year-old, observed: "Daddy, I was just thinking—if the wrong side of heaven is so beautiful, how wonderful the right side must be!"

538 Good Morning Up There

The late Harry Rimmer penned the following letter to Charles E. Fuller of the Old Fashioned Revival Hour, shortly before his death.

"Next Sunday you are to talk about heaven. I am interested in that land because I have held a clear title to a bit of property there for over 50 years. I did not buy it. It was given to me without money and without price; but the Donor purchased it for me at a tremendous sacrifice.

"I am not holding it for speculation. It is not a vacant lot. For more than half a century I have been sending materials, out of which the greatest Architect of the universe has been building a home for me, which will never need remodeling or repairs because it will suit me perfectly, individually, and will never grow old.

"Termites can never undermine its foundation for it rests upon the Rock of Ages. Fire cannot destroy it. Floods cannot wash it away. No lock or bolts will ever be placed upon the doors, for no vicious person can ever enter that land, where my dwelling stands, now almost completed and almost ready for me to enter in and abide in peace eternally, without fear of being rejected.

"There is a valley of deep shadow between this place where I live, and that to which I shall journey in a very short time. I cannot reach my home in that city without passing through that valley. But I am not afraid because the best Friend I ever had went through the same valley long, long ago and drove away all its gloom. He stuck with me through thick and thin since we first became acquainted 55 years ago, and I hold His promise in printed form, never to forsake me or leave me alone. He will be with me as I walk through the valley of the shadow of death, and I shall not lose my way because He is with me.

"I hope to hear your sermon on heaven next Sunday, but I have no assurance I shall be able to do so. My ticket to heaven has no date marked for the journey, no return coupon and no permit for baggage. Yes, I am ready to go, and I may not be here while you are talking next Sunday evening, but I will meet you *there* some day."

Holy Spirit

539 Guidance Available

, Along our highways, well placed at appropriate locations, are official signs which give us direction and warn us of danger. Most of these are the reflector type; that is, they are designed to reflect the light of auto headlamps. In darkness, they are invisible to anyone who travels without a light. But when our auto headlights are flashed upon these signs, they reflect back to us their message of guidance or caution. Their night-time aid to us depends upon the light we bring to them. They have no meaning for unlighted lamps.

God would like to guide us through the days and through the years of this life. His signs are out there—in all the appropriate places. But whether we see them will depend upon the light with which we approach them.

540 The Ungoofer

In *The Reader's Digest* sometime ago a lady reported a rather interesting experience. She telephoned her bank in an attempt to correct an error which the bank had made. Her call was transferred from one person to another, from office to office, and there was much talk, but no help.

At last, the eighth person proved to be calmly and sympathetically helpful. He was genuinely pleasant thoroughly efficient, even friendly. The business finished, the lady said, "You're great! What is your position in the bank?" He answered, "I'm the ungoofer."

The ungoofer! Most of us need one now and again. And we have one. That lady had a lot of trouble getting through to the bank's ungoofer; but, my friend, you and I have no difficulty at all in getting through to ours, if we really try. Keep in touch with the One who forgives, untangles, heals—ungoofs. If there are tangles and snarls, messes and mix-ups, tell Him about them—and trust Him.

541 The Strange Providences of God

The following incident is taken from an experience of Charles H. Spurgeon with an atheist.

There was an atheist in the vicinity of Mr. Spurgeon's home and he was very ugly to anyone who believed the Bible.

Mr. Spurgeon asked the Lord to direct him in what he should read for morning devotions. Then he seemed strongly impressed to read the book of Joel in its entirety.

When he came to Joel 3, he read the third verse: "And sold the girl for wine." Whereupon, Mr. Spurgeon checked his concordance to see how many times the word "girl" occurred in the Bible. To his great surprise, he found the word only occurred once.

A little later he thought he would take a walk. About a block and a half away he looked up and there was the atheist's house. He went up and knocked.

The atheist growled, "Well, what do you want?"

"I would like to read the Bible to you," Spurgeon replied.

"The atheist began his usual abuse, then suddenly stopped and said, "Will you tell me how often the word 'girl' is in the Bible?"

Mr. Spurgeon answered, "Once."

The atheist then said, "Tell me where it is found and I will let you in."

Spurgeon replied, "Joel 3:3."

The atheist then said, "Tell me before I let you in, how did you know it?"

Mr. Spurgeon answered, "I haven't known it two hours. In my morning devotions I read the book of Joel."

Then Mr. Spurgeon stepped in, and in half an hour the atheist was on his knees asking God to forgive his sins.

542 The Hand or the Glove?

I have a glove here in my hand. The glove cannot do anything by itself, but when my hand is in it, the glove can do many things. True, it is not the *glove, but my hand in the glove* that acts. The Christian is a glove. It is the Holy Spirit in us, the hand, who does the work. We have to make room for the hand so that every finger in the glove is filled.

Hope

543 Saved by Hope

A mother, the instant that she knows she is with child, lives her every moment in anticipation of her deliverance from the burden that is within her. After a time she cannot take a step, make a move, think a thought that is disassociated from the coming of her child.

In America, people are supposed to ignore the obvious fact that a woman is with child. In France the case is quite the contrary. If a man is introduced to a woman who is an expectant mother, it is the height of politeness for him to congratulate her. "*Je vous felicite de votre esperance.*" "I congratulate you on your hope," is a common phrase among the cultured.

Just as a woman becomes pregnant in anticipation of bearing a child, so a believer becomes saved in anticipation of being fully like the Lord Jesus Christ. It is unto this state of hope that we are saved.

544 Hearts Can Fool

The Wild West of yesteryear was full of illusions on distant horizons. One of George Custer's young officers was sure he saw a party of Indians a mile away. As the soldier charged, the Indians looked plainer each moment. But arriving at the point, there were no Indians at all—only some buffalo carcasses. Other travelers saw ships skimming across the desert sand in full sail, railroad tracks elevated on pilings, or water birds with brilliant plumage. All of these illusions occur when light rays pass through the atmosphere bent and distorted.

But no optical illusions in nature exceed the illusions that can be left by our own hearts. By diagnosis, the human spiritual heart is "beyond cure." Unaided by God, the response of each of us toward knowing his or her heart must be despair: "Who can know it?" (Jer. 17:9). No one can fathom the secrets or pierce the darkness of his or her own heart. This is especially true at the point of the question about whom we trust—here again, our hearts can fool.

But there is hope. It rests in this: God knows your heart (v. 10). He sifts, searches, explores, and probes the human heart. He tests and examines human emotions. This is our hope. When we get to know God, we get to know our own heart. You do not know your heart by looking into it yourself. You know your heart by getting to know God through our Lord Jesus Christ.

Humility

545 The Higher the Bamboo Grows, the Lower It Bends

A government official who came into President Lincoln's office was startled to find the chief executive shining his shoes. "Sir," he gasped, "surely you do not polish your own shoes!" "Of course," replied the humble President. "Whose do you polish?" The greatness of a man is evidenced by his humility. In the words of an old Filipino saying, "The higher the bamboo grows, the lower it bends."

All of this is illustrated in the life of Jesus. "Jesus did not come to be served but to serve, and to give His life a ransom for many" (Matt. 20:28). The highest title God ever allows in His church is "servant." Am I willing to serve people as Jesus did? I know, I cannot die for people to save them as Jesus did, but I can "die to self" to enable me to tell people that Jesus died for their sins, and thus serve them in the greatest way possible.

When I humble myself, then God will give me the grace to grow into maturity where, I like the tall bamboo, can lower myself to serve those of "low esteem." Notice, "Do not be proud, but be willing to associate with people of low position. Do not be conceited" (Rom. 12:16). How tall are you spiritually? Tall and flexible enough to serve people in all kinds of situations?

546 A Somebody with God

Joel C. Gregory writes:

"How many times have we had to reach the end of our own resources before we remembered to trust in God, the one steadfast resource of our lives? We're all in need of a spiritual exodus day by day. When our faith causes difficulties, our first response is to fall back on our familiar resources—people, things, self —and only when these do not help can we truly lean only upon God for our needs.

"I like what Dwight l. Moody said about Moses in this connection. Moody, not a very erudite man, had an unusual insight into Scripture. He said that Moses spent forty years in the king's palace thinking that he was somebody; then he lived forty years in the wilderness finding out that without God he was a nobody; finally he spent forty more years discovering how a nobody with God can be a somebody.

"And he was right. When Moses and the people found out they were nobodies without the resource of God, that's when the exodus began."

216

547 Brokenness

God uses broken things. It takes broken soil to produce a crop, broken clouds to produce rain, broken grain to give bread and broken bread to give strength. It is the broken alabaster box that gives forth perfume. It is the broken Peter, weeping bitterly, who returns to greater power than ever.

548 His Last Prayer

Nicolaus Copernicus was a famed astronomer born in Poland on February 19, 1473. He was a mathematician whose accomplishments changed men's ideas of the universe. Also he was a well-known writer. Although highly educated in astronomical science, he was much more—he was a child of God who had learned to know and trust his Savior, Jesus Christ. When he was critically ill with his final illness, his book, *On Resolutions of the Celestial Bodies,* just off the press, was laid in his arms.

At the close of his life, he did not think of himself as an astronomer or scientist, but as a sinner who needed the forgiveness of his Savior. He asked that the following epitaph be written on his gravestone:

"Lord, I do not ask the kindness Thou didst show to Peter. I do not dare ask the grace Thou didst grant to Paul; but, Lord, the mercy Thou didst show to the dying robber, that mercy show to me. That earnestly I pray."

549 Humility Never Parades

Some years ago I saw what is called a sensitive plant. I happened to breathe on it, and suddenly it drooped its head. I touched it, and it withered away. Humility is as sensitive as that—it cannot safely be brought out on exhibition.

A man who is flattering himself that he is humble and is walking close to the Master is self-deceived. Humility consists not in thinking merely of ourselves, but in not thinking of ourselves at all. Moses did not realize that his face shone. If humility speaks of itself, it is gone.

550 More Weight

The branch that bears the most fruit bows lowest to the ground while the branch with little or no fruit stands most upright. So it is with humility and conceit. Humility carries with it the weight of wisdom while conceit has the light-headedness of pride.

Hypocrisy

551 Thus Saith Our Lord

Ye call Me Master and obey Me not,
Ye call Me Light and see Me not,
Ye call Me Way and walk Me not,
Ye call Me Life and desire Me not,
Ye call Me wise and follow Me not,
Ye call Me fair and love Me not,
Ye call Me rich and ask Me not,
Ye call Me eternal and seek Me not,
Ye call Me gracious and trust Me not,
Ye call Me noble and serve Me not,
Ye call Me just and fear Me not,
If I condemn you, blame Me not.

552 We Are Social Hypocrites

The famous Robert Redford was walking one day through a hotel lobby. A woman saw him and followed him to the elevator. "Are you the real Robert Redford?" she asked him with great excitement. As the doors of the elevator closed, he replied, "Only when I am alone!"

553 Front Yard Christians

A small boy had a little wagon that was a new possession and the delight of his heart, but when he brought it out to the front walk one morning he was told that he must play with it at the back of the house. "This is Sunday," added the father by way of explanation. The boy obeyed, but he questioned wonderingly as he trudged away, "Isn't it Sunday in the backyard, too?"

554 A Soldier's Wish

By profession I am a soldier and take pride in that fact, but I am prouder to be a father. A soldier destroys in order to build; the father never destroys. The one has the potentialities of death; the other embodies creation and life. And, while the hordes of death are mighty, the battalions of life are mightier still. It is my hope that my son, when I am gone, will remember me not from the battle, but in the home, repeating with him our simple daily prayer, "Our Father Who art in Heaven. . . . "

—General Douglas MacArthur

555 Hypocritical Excuse

The man who says he is kept away from religion by hypocrites is not influenced by them anywhere else. Business is full of them, but if he sees a chance at making money he does not stop for that.

Society is crowded with them, and yet he never thinks of becoming a hermit.

Married life is full of them, but that does not make him remain a bachelor.

Hell is full of them, and yet he does not do a thing to keep himself from going there.

He wants to have you think that he is trying to avoid the society of hypocrites, and yet he takes not a single step toward heaven, the only place where no hypocrites can go!

556 Acting Saved

An interesting phenomenon is occurring in our society. There is a high interest in salvation but a low interest in Christian living.

Recent studies show that church attendance on any given Sunday morning across this great land is at an all time high. There are more men, women, and children filling church pews on Sundays than at any time in our history.

However, the same studies show that moral standards are at an all time low. Some of these same church-goers are divorcing mates, aborting babies, cheating on spouses, drinking liquor, gambling paychecks, and abusing children at an unbelievably high rate.

What's the problem here?

In a recent class, the teacher may have given us a good hint as to what is happening.

He stated, "More people today want to 'Get Saved,' than want to 'Act Saved.' " He referred to this conflict as "Justification versus Sanctification."

557 A Critical Eye

A certain hog farmer refused to have anything to do with the church because all he ever saw was a bunch of hypocrites who belonged to it. He always named two or three.

One day the pastor of the church came by to buy a hog from him. After looking over the farmer's entire swine herd, the pastor pointed to a scrawny, sickly, ugly little runt and said, "I want that one."

The farmer remonstrated vigorously, "Why, Preacher, you don't want that one. He's the scrawniest runt I ever saw. Look, here are some fine hogs over here." "That's all right," said the preacher, "I want that one."

After the purchase was completed, the pastor said, "Now I am going to haul this pig all over the country and tell everyone that this is the kind of hog you raise!"

"Hey, Preacher, that's not fair," the farmer protested. "I raise fine hogs. An occasional runt doesn't ruin my whole stock."

"I am only following your example of condemning a whole church because of the stunted spirituality of a few of its members," explained the pastor. The farmer got the point!

558 Deceptive Packaging

Through its laws, our country declares it a crime to lie about the contents in a box of cereal. These laws demand that the outside of the package tell the truth about what is on the inside. Deceptive packaging is illegal. "Truth in advertising" regulations are another way to protect the public. A good example of this is the warning on a pack of cigarettes: "Smoking causes lung cancer, heart disease, emphysema, and may complicate pregnancy."

Unfortunately, there are no such laws about people. We require no one to tell what really lies behind the packaging—the clothes, facial expressions, mannerisms, speech patterns, or affected behavior. No one is forced to tell you what he or she is really feeling, thinking, or planning to do.

Our deceptive packaging—the way we appear to others—is an accepted, even an expected part of our way of life. We have become experts in this type of trickery. Before we are going to get the help we need, we need to confess this sin of hypocrisy. Only then can we go on the path of discovering and knowing our real selves.

559 Strange People

People who talk about prayer but never pray.

People who say tithing is right but never tithe.

People who want to belong to the church but never attend.

People who say the Bible is God's Word to man but never read it.

560 Thou Art the Man

Some years ago in Chicago, after a traffic accident, a policeman awakened parents to report the death of their only daughter. He indicated that an empty bottle of liquor was found in the wrecked car. When the father heard this, he went into a rage and said, "When I find the man who sold liquor to these kids, I'll kill him." Later, upon seeking a bracer from his own liquor stocks he found a note in his daughter's handwriting which read, "Dad, we are taking along some of your good liquor. I know you won't mind." Compare this father's reaction to David's in 2 Samuel 12:1-7.

Judgment

561 What Kind of People Are in Your Town?

"Judge not, that ye be not judged" (Matt. 7:1). There was once a wise old man sitting at the gate of an ancient city. A young traveler stopped before entering the city and asked the old man, "What kind of people live in this town?" The wise man answered with a question, "What kind of people were in the town you just came from?"

"Oh, they were liars and cheats and thugs and drunks, terrible people," the young traveler replied. The old man shook his head, "The people in this town are the same way."

Later another stranger paused to ask the same question, and again the wise man questioned his questioner, "What kind of people did you just leave?"

The second traveler answered, "Oh, I left a fine town. The people were good and kind and honest and hardworking." The wise man smiled and said, "The people in this town are the same way."

People who are kind and forgiving toward others usually experience tolerance from others themselves; those who are harsh, censorious and critical toward others find that others exhibit much the same disposition toward them.

Of course, when our Lord warned, "Judge not," He was not talking about exposing the sins of the ungodly—we must do that. Neither was He talking about withdrawing from the immoral, or restoring erring Christians, or resolving civil disputes, or "knowing a tree by its fruits." He was forbidding illegitimate judgments that stem from a self-righteous, haughty, puffed-up, hypocritical spirit (Matt. 7:15; Luke 6:37, 38; Rom. 2:1-3). He was forbidding judgments based on inadequate information (John 7:21-24). He was forbidding judgments in which the person assumes the position of God, trying and sentencing brethren in regard to eternal salvation (Josh. 4:11, 12; Rom. 14:3, 4, 10, 13; 1 Cor. 4:5).

What kind of people live in your town?

562 Judging Others

A certain preacher had a method of dealing with those people who were critical of others. He kept a complaint book in his desk. When a church member would come to tell him of another's faults he would say, "Well, here is my complaint book. I'll write down what you say, and you can sign your name to it. Then I'll go and take it up with our brother."

221

Invariably the critic would stammer, backtrack, and insist that nothing be written or signed. In his 40-year ministry that preacher opened his complaint book hundreds of times—but never made a single entry.

How about it? Are you willing to write out and sign the ugly things you have said about others? If not, perhaps it would be best to leave judgment where it belongs—with God.

563 A New Window on the World

Ruth E. Knowlton tells this on herself: "Years ago I lived in an apartment building in a large city. The building next door was only a few feet away from mine, and I could look across the alley into the apartment on the same floor as mine. There was a woman who lived there, whom I had never met, yet I could see her as she sat by her window each afternoon, sewing or reading.

"After several months had gone by, I began to notice that her windows were dirty. Everything was indistinct through her smudged windows. I would say to myself, 'I wonder why that woman doesn't wash her windows? They look dreadful!'

"One bright morning I decided to do my spring housecleaning and thoroughly cleaned my apartment, including washing the windows on the inside.

"Late in the afternoon when I was finished, I sat down by the window with a cup of coffee for a rest. What a surprise! Across the way, the woman sitting by her window was clearly visible. Her windows were clean!

"Then it dawned on me. I have been criticizing her dirty windows, but all the time I was observing them through my own dirty ones!'"

564 Preparation for Judgment

Did you hear about the boy who failed all his college work? He wired his mother: "Failed everything; Prepare Papa." His mother wired back, "Papa prepared; Prepare yourself." This is the message a lot of us need in view of the coming judgment. God is prepared. We need to prepare ourselves!

565 The Other Man

Perhaps he sometimes slipped a bit—
Well, so have you.
Perhaps some things he ought to quit—
Well, so should you.
Perhaps he may have faltered—
Why, all men do, and so have I.
You must admit, unless you lie,
That so have you.
Perhaps if we would stop and think,
Both I and you,
When painting someone black as ink,
As some folks do;
Perhaps if we would recollect,
Perfection we would not expect,
But just a man halfway correct,
Like me and you.

566 Try the Side That Will Shine

There is a kind of crystal called Labrador Spar. At first sight, it is dull and without luster; but if it is turned round and round, it will suddenly come into a position where the light strikes it in a certain way, and it will sparkle with flashing beauty.

People are like that. They may seem to be unlovely, but that is because we do not know the whole person. Everyone has something good in him or her.

567 Old Ben Putnitoff

Ben Putnitoff was a member of the Lord's church. Morally, he was a good man. He did not lie, curse, drink, beat his wife, or smoke. He paid his income tax, came to Bible class and worship services, paid his bills and gave a "few bucks" to the Lord. He was never opposed to anything that was good.

One day old Ben Putnitoff died and stood before the Righteous Judge. The Judge said, "Ben, you are charged with trying to close the church. Are you guilty or not guilty?"

"Not guilty," pleaded Ben Putnitoff. "I didn't do a thing!"

"Guilty as charged," the Judge ruled. And then He continued, "Ben, you have confessed to the most effective way ever devised of closing the church. You 'did not do a thing.' You did not visit the sick. You did not encourage the weak. You did not feed the hungry. You did not reach out to the lost with the gospel."

"But, Judge," Ben pleaded, "I intended to do all of those things, but I was too busy making a living and enjoying myself. I have just been *putting it off*."

568 Jumping to Conclusions

A man sitting at his window one evening casually called to his wife, "There goes that woman Charlie Smith is so terribly in love with." His wife in the kitchen dropped the plate she was drying, ran through the door, knocking over a lamp, looked out the window. "Where, where?" she cried. "There," he said, "that woman in the gabardine suit on the corner." "You idiot," she hissed, "That is his wife." "Yes, of course," he replied.

569 Snap Judgment

When Gilbert Frankau was producing a play, he sent to a theatrical agency for a young man to play the leading part. After the screen test, Gilbert Frankau telephoned his agent. "This man," he said, "will never do. He cannot act, and he never will be able to act, and you had better advise him to look for some other profession before he starves. By the way, tell me his name again so that I can cross him off my list." The actor's name was Ronald Colman, who became one of the most famous actors the screen has ever known.

570 The Disliked Dislike

A psychologist asked a group of college students to jot down, in 30 seconds, the initials of the people they disliked. Some of the students taking the test could think of only one person. Others listed as many as 14. But the interesting fact that came out of the research was this: Those who disliked the largest number of people were themselves the most widely disliked.

571 Experience: A Good Teacher

There is an old story of a man in West Virginia who had a reputation for being wise and for giving sound advice. A young person went to him one day and asked, "Uncle Jed, how come you have such good judgment?" "Well, I have good judgment because I have had a lot of experience," he replied. And the boy said, "Yes, but how did you get all that experience?" "Well," the man mused, "I got it by making a lot of bad judgments."

If people have traveled the road before us and can tell us what that road looks like, then we are wise to listen to what they have to say.

Kindness

572 That Marcy Boy!

At 14 years of age, the "bad boy" of a little Massachusetts town, was so powerful in his influence for evil that no one was found able to teach the district school which he attended; it seemed "pretty poor soil." Everyone said the student in question was "bad clear through," "hopeless," and "bound to go to ruin."

One day a new teacher came who said he was not afraid to try. The school friends were quick to tell him all the stories of "the Marcy boy." All advised that he be forbidden to enter the school. However, he was allowed to enter. The teacher analyzed the "hopeless soil," and began at once to enrich it with kindness, justice, goodwill and confidence, and at the right time, dropped in seeds of ambition, hope and self-respect. The seed took root, developed, grew and began to bear fruit.

The promising young student dropped his bad habits, studied day and night, went to college, and graduated with honors. He studied law, answered the call for men in 1812, became associate justice of the Supreme Court, United States senator, governor of New York, and finally Secretary of State. His name was William L. Marcy. He served faithfully in every situation. All of this happened because a good teacher saw in a child the image of God!

573 A Lesson From a Terrapin

One brother said that during his childhood in the country, he once found a terrapin. When he started to examine it, the terrapin pulled in its head and closed its shell like a vice. This displeased the boy, and he picked up something and tried to pry it open. His uncle saw all this and said: "No, that is not the way! You may kill it, but you will not get it open."

The uncle took the terrapin into the house and set it on the hearth. It was not but a few minutes until it began to get warm. Then the terrapin pushed out its head, then its feet, and began crawling. "Terrapins are like that," the uncle said, "and people, too. You cannot force them into anything. But if you first warm them up with some real kindness, more than likely they will do what you want them to do."

574 Taking Risks

Norman L. Bales shares this lesson from life:

" 'Whoever claims to live in Him must walk as Jesus did' (1 John 1:6).

For Jesus, the walk with the Father sometimes meant encountering misunderstanding, criticism and danger.

"In Acts 16, Paul and Silas risked their safety by casting out an evil spirit. For their trouble they ended up in jail. But then the jailer risked his security by washing their wounds.

Discretion is sometimes the better part of valor, but discretion can be an excuse for cowardice. One day I walked down a Davenport street minding my own business when I saw two groups of angry girls emerge from a restaurant. Anger escalated into violence—hair pulling, slaps, blows. I did what the priest and Levite in Jesus' parable of the Good Samaritan did. I crossed the street and passed by on the other side. If I had to do it over, I still do not think I would have intervened, but at the very least I could have called the police.

"But then there is the case of Steve Palermo. Steve was an umpire in the American League. One particular day he called a Texas Rangers game and left to eat dinner at a local restaurant. Hoodlums attempted a robbery and assaulted some of the waitresses. Palermo and an SMU football player offered assistance, but the umpire caught a bullet in the back which traumatized his spinal cord, and even now he has to rely on leg braces and canes to walk. He may never umpire again. That is a high price to pay for an act of kindness, but compassionate people like Palermo run risks.

"Our contemporaries would like to live in a risk-free world. It does not exist. Followers of Jesus must learn to swim against the tide of 'risk phobia.' We walk in the footsteps of the One who said, 'I lay down My life for the sheep.' "

575 Never Too Busy to Be Kind

While Lincoln was a poor young lawyer in Springfield, he was going to his office one morning when he saw a little girl crying at the door of one of the houses. Lincoln stopped to see what was the matter. She sobbed out her story. She was going to visit a little friend of hers in another town. It was to be her first ride on the train, and the expressman had not come for the trunk.

Mr. Lincoln lifted the trunk onto his shoulders and started off, calling to the little girl to "come along." They just caught the train. No wonder the little girl never forgot him! A great, brave, noble man he was—never too busy to be kind.

Knowledge

576 Knowing God Holds the Future

The ancient Chinese had a unique mechanism for presenting their plays. They would present a play on a two-level stage. On the upper stage, the resolution of the drama was acted out as the story unfolded below. So as tension and mystery were building on the first level, the audience watching the resolution of the plot would yell to the people on the first level, "Hang in there! Don't give up! If you only knew!" What inspired that hope? It was the knowledge of what was happening on the second level.

Joseph M. Stowell recalls this special event:

"I will never forget the 1980 Olympics hockey match between the U.S. team—composed of small, young, amateur players—and the Soviets. During the final period, I was literally on the edge of my seat. I felt all the agony and anxiety of the contest as I watched it on television—and then suddenly we scored to go ahead late in the game! *Can we hang on?* I was tense, nervous, and traumatized. Our team went on to win, and at last I was ecstatic.

"Later that night, the network broadcast a replay of the game, so I invited some friends over to watch it. I watched the same game again, but was I on the edge of my seat? Of course not. I sat back, propped up my feet, had a bowl of popcorn, and leisurely sipped a cola. I was watching the very same game—but what I *knew* about the outcome made a radical difference in my attitude and actions."

577 Danger of a Little Learning

An astronomer who was on his way to give a lecture discovered that his seatmate on the airplane was a preacher. Early in the conversation he assured the clergyman that he knew everything about religion he needed to know. The preacher expressed delight and asked where the scientist had studied religion and how much he had read the Bible.

"Oh, no," the astronomer replied, "I've never studied theology, and I don't read the Bible, but I know the Golden Rule, and I figure that's enough religion for me."

"Well, on that basis," declared the preacher, "I guess I know all about astronomy."

The scientist scoffed and asked the pastor what he knew about the cosmos, to which the man of the cloth replied gravely, "Twinkle, twinkle little star; how I wonder what you are."

578 Stages of Life

The *twenties* are the molding years when the young person forms those habits that will direct his career. Then he finishes his school work, stands before the altar, establishes a home, and looks the world in the face.

The *thirties* are the years of discouragement. It is a hard and trying time. It is a time of battle without the dreams and poetry of youth.

The *forties* are the years of vision, when a man finds himself, finishes his castles in the air, and knows the value of his dreams.

In the *fifties* life comes to ripening. These should be the years of jubilee, and a man should do his best work then.

At *sixty*, a man has committed enough mistakes to make him wise beyond his years. He should live better and do better work than in any other decade in his life. No man has a right to retire in the sixties; the world has a need for his wisdom.

And in the *seventies,* some of the best work in the world has been done. It is the time when talent, experience, and insight combine to make a worthy and memorable life. Psalm 90:10 says, "The days of our years are threescore and ten; and if by reason of strength they be fourscore years, yet is there strength, labor and sorrow; for it is soon cut off, and we fly away."

Love

579 *He Did It Without Regret*

United States Senator Jake Garn of Utah did something most of us admire—and perhaps should consider doing ourselves. He donated one of his organs to save a life.

A recent survey says 73 percent of Americans approve organ donation. But only about 20 percent actually sign donor cards and make arrangements for our corneas, kidneys, or other organs to be used when we die.

In Senator Garn's case, however, he did not wait until his death to donate his left kidney. His 27-year-old daughter, Susan Garn Horne, suffered from progressive kidney failure due to diabetes. Her condition deteriorated, and doctors determined that she needed a kidney transplant immediately.

Jake Garn and his two sons were all found to be compatible donors. The senator insisted that he should be the one to give the kidney. "Her mother carried her for nine months," he said, "and I am honored to give her part of me."

So, on September 10, 1986, in a Washington, D.C. hospital, a six-hour surgical procedure was performed to remove one of his kidneys and to implant it into his daughter.

The radio news broadcast a story on Garns, and in it was a comment from the doctor who put the donated kidney into Susan's body. At a press briefing at Georgetown University Hospital, the doctor said, "The senator is awake, has a bit of a grin on his face. He seems very self-satisfied, and happy and peaceful."

The senator had to be in pain at that moment. The incision through which his kidney was removed goes from his back to his front ribs. There were tubes in him, needles yet to come, and several weeks of recuperation lying ahead. But he was smiling!

That grin on Jake Garn's face could have meant only one thing: no regrets. Love makes it possible for a person to do the most difficult and dreaded of things without looking back.

Think for a moment about what Jesus did to save you. He left the worship of angels to be born in a stable. He accepted the limitations of human form, suffered indignities of the greatest magnitude, and shed His lifeblood to purchase your redemption.

The most astounding thing about all He did is that there is not a word in the Bible which indicates that the Son of God regretted doing it. On the day of His ascension back to the Father, there may have been a bit of a grin on His face.

His only regret would come if you refused His gift of life.

580 Love and Actions

"I love Thee, I love Thee
and that Thou doest know;
But how much I love Thee,
my *actions* will show."

581 Puncture-Proof Heart

Some of these newfangled inventions are great—especially the puncture-proof tire. If you are driving along with ordinary tires and a nail goes through one of them, whis-s-s, you lose all the air. But a puncture-proof tire is different—if a nail goes through, there is some stuff inside that runs around and stops the hole and the air stays in.

The heart of a Christian is like that puncture-proof tire. An ordinary heart may be filled with love, but when someone does something to puncture that heart, all the love runs out and hatred and hard feelings take its place. But a puncture-proof heart is different. It is filled with the Spirit of Christ and when someone, through their words or deeds punctures that heart, immediately the hole is stopped up tight and the love stays in."

582 Love One Another

Joseph M. Stowell shares this memory:

"When my parents moved to southern Florida, they sorted through some of the family treasures and divided them among the children. My dad brought me a little box and said, 'Joe, I want you to have this.' When I opened the box and pulled back the cotton, there was an old pocket watch—one of those round ones that usually hangs from a fancy gold chain with a watch fob on it.

"I have a few antique clocks, so I was somewhat aware of the value of old timepieces. That watch did not have a famous maker's name on it, or a brass or gold or sterling case; it did not have a fancy gold chain or watch fob. In fact, it really was a common old watch with a leather thong tied to it. As a watch, it was not something of great worth.

"But my dad said, 'This was the first watch I ever owned. My dad gave me this watch.' I remembered that he and I used to fish the St. Joe River every summer, floating down the river and fly fishing in the evening. This was the watch he used to pull out every once in a while to see what time it was.

"You know, if my dad had taken that watch to an antique store, they would have told him it was worth little, if anything. But all the money in the world could not buy that watch from me. That watch is precious to my father, and since it is precious to him, it is precious to me.

"That is what people are like. That is why God in essence said, 'Love Me? Love people!' "

583 Service Over Showing Off

There is a story told about Sam Rayburn who was Speaker for the House of Representatives longer than any other man. One of his friends lost a teenage daughter and early the next morning Rayburn knocked on his door. "I just came by to see what I could do to help." The father replied that there was nothing to do. "Well," Rayburn said, "have you had your coffee this morning?" The man replied that they had not taken time for breakfast. While Rayburn was working in the kitchen, the man came in and said, "Mr. Speaker, I thought you were supposed to be having breakfast at the White House this morning." "Well, I was, but I called the President and told him I had a friend who was in trouble and I could not come."

What a different world this would be if we would learn to become more and more unselfish.

584 What Is Adoption?

A small girl recently gave her definition of the word "adoption." "It is when you love someone and you ask them to come and live with you." Simplicity is still the best way to say a thing, is it not? God loves us too, and He wants to adopt us as sons and daughters—how about it? Would you come and live with Him?

585 Love for People

Then there's the man who said, "Lord, maybe Charlie Brown is right when he says he loves mankind, but it is people he cannot stand. You see, I love people in general more than I do individually.

"Lord, it is like the joke about the father who yelled at his kids when they walked in the wet cement of his sidewalk; he can love them in the abstract, but never in the concrete.

"Maybe I need to see a little more of You in them. And maybe I need to see a little more of You in me."

586 Love Your Enemies

An Armenian nurse had been held captive along with her brother by the Turks. Her brother was slain by a Turkish soldier before her eyes. Somehow she escaped and later became a nurse in a military hospital.

One day she was stunned to find that the same man who had killed her brother had been captured and brought wounded to the hospital where she worked. Something within her cried out "Vengeance." But a stronger voice called for her to love. She nursed the man back to health.

Finally, the recuperating soldier asked her, "Why didn't you let me die?" Her answer was, "I am a follower of Him who said, 'Love your enemies, do good to them which hate you' " (Luke 6:27).

Impressed with her answer, the young soldier replied, "I never heard such words before. Tell me more. I want this kind of religion."

587 Orders to Go

When someone asked a missionary if he liked his work in Africa, he replied: "Do I like this work? No, my wife and I do not like dirt. We have reasonably refined sensibilities. We do not like crawling into huts through goats' refuse. We do not like association with ignorant, filthy, brutish people. *But is a man to do nothing for Christ he does not like?* If not, then God pity him. Liking or disliking has nothing to do with it. We have orders to 'go' and we go. Love constrains us" (2 Cor. 5:14).

588 Love Needed

Some years ago, Dr. Karl Menninger, noted doctor and psychologist, was seeking the cause of many of his patients' ills. One day he called in his clinical staff and proceeded to unfold a plan for developing, in his clinic, an atmosphere of creative love. All patients were to be given large quantities of love; no unloving attitudes were to be displayed in the presence of the patients, and all nurses and doctors were to go about their work in and out of the various rooms with a loving attitude.

At the end of six months, the time spent by patients in the institution was cut in half.

589 Lesson in Love

As a group of college students toured the slums of a city, one of the girls, seeing a little girl playing in the dirt, asked a guide, "Why doesn't her mother clean her up?"

"Madam," he replied, "that girl's mother probably loves her, but she doesn't hate dirt. You hate dirt, but you don't love her enough to go down there and clean her up. Until hate for dirt and love for that child are in the same person, that little girl is likely to remain as she is."

Until hate for sin and love for the sinner gets in a person, he will do little about the plight of the lost.

590 Love That Sacrifices

During World War II, an enemy submarine approached a fleet of ships in the North Atlantic. The captain of one vessel spotted the white mark of a torpedo coming directly at his ship. His transport was loaded with literally hundreds and hundreds of young soldiers on the way to the European front. He realized they would not have time to maneuver to avoid the torpedo. He grabbed the loudspeaker and cried out, "Boys, this is it!"

Nearby, though, a little escorting destroyer also observed the torpedo. The captain ordered, "Full speed ahead." His ship steamed into the path of the torpedo. The destroyer was blown up; it sank very quickly. Every man on it was lost. The captain of the troop transport ship sadly commented, "The skipper of that destroyer was my best friend." Now one verse in the Bible has an even deeper meaning for that captain: "Greater love hath no man than this, that a man lay down his life for his friend" (John 15:13).

591 A Good Teacher and a Great Teacher

"Teacher, I will follow you wherever you go" (Matt. 8:19).

A number of years ago a Johns Hopkins University professor asked his graduate students to locate 200 boys, ages 12–16 and research their family backgrounds. The assignment was then to predict their future. The students were sent to the slum area of the city to find the boys. The conclusion reached by the graduate students was that 90 percent of those researched would spend time in jail. The final chapter of this study would not completed until 25 years later.

When the 200 original students were sought after, some 25 years later, John Hopkins sent the researchers into the slum area again. Some of the group still remained in the slums, others had moved away, a few had died. In all they were able to locate 180 of the original 200. What they found amazed them. Only four had ever been to jail (remember the prediction had been 90 percent of 200)!

What caused this figure to be so low when all indications pointed to a larger number? When the researchers began to ask this question they found that they were getting the same answer, "Well, there was this teacher. . . ." Pressed further, the researchers found that the teacher in all cases was one and the same. The boys had all been influenced by the same teacher.

The graduate students traced down the teacher, now living in a retirement home, and inquired about her remarkable influence over a group of boys who were headed for a life of crime. She really could not think of any reason why she would have this kind of influence. She did mention that "I truly loved my students."

592 Pleasing Christ

A love desire to please Christ is not something extra for the Christian. It is basic to Christian sanctity. It is not a dessert, but the main course—not a sideshow, but the main tent. It is not a motive to which we can resort to when convenient; it is a controlling force to which we have committed our lives. We have abandoned everything else. In time, applause and pleas of the world have a hollow ring. We are marching to a different drumbeat. His smile is singularly our greatest delight! This is the lifestyle of love.

593 God Is Love

A certain farmer had an unusual weathervane on his barn. Inscribed on the arrow were these words: "God is love." A passerby turned in at the gate and asked the farmer, "What do you mean by that? Do you think God's love is changeable; that it veers about as that arrow turns in the winds?" "Oh, no," replied the farmer, "I mean that whichever way the wind blows, God is still love."

594 The Time to Trust

When nothing whereon to lean remains,

When strongholds crumble to dust;

When nothing is sure but that God still reigns,

That is just the time to trust.

595 He Never Stops Loving Us

The minister was retiring, and had delivered his last sermon from the pulpit where he had preached many years.

One of the faithful members stopped as she went out the door and asked, "Do you know what is the most important thing you said in all these years?"

"What was that?" the minister inquired, so he might learn of one way he had helped someone.

"You told us we cannot do anything to get God to stop loving us!" was the quiet reply.

The most important thing that you can learn in life is that God never stops loving you!

—*Peter* lied about being one of the disciples, but God loved him (Matt. 26:70).

—*The mothers and their small children* were a problem for the disciples, but God loved them (Matt. 19:14).

—*The woman* refused to give Jesus a drink of water from the well, but God loved her (John 4:9).

No matter what your life has been like, He still loves you! How much do you love God?

596 No Greater Love

From the days before ready access to vaccines comes this story:

The doctor looked down at the little girl in the hospital bed. He knew that her only hope was to receive blood from someone who had recovered from the same disease.

Quickly the doctor found the anxious family, and knelt beside a small boy. "Johnny," he said, "your sister needs your kind of blood to make her well. Would you be willing to give your blood so that she can live?"

Johnny's eyes grew big. The doctor watched them well with fear, but the little boy hesitated only long enough to swallow the lump in his throat.

"Sure, Doctor, I will do it," he replied.

After the needed amount of blood was taken from Johnny's small arm, he remained quiet for a few minutes as he had been instructed. Then he stood up, and asked softly: "Well, Doctor, when do I die?"

Only then did the doctor realize the extent of the child's sacrifice. Johnny had offered his life to save his sister, Jesus declared that there is no greater love.

Greater love than this no man has, that a man lay down his life for his friends (John 15:13).

Marriage

597 Those Sweet Short Years

There is no greater blessing on earth than a good marriage. A young couple was visiting with an older couple celebrating their 50th wedding anniversary. "Fifty years!" the young husband exclaimed, "That is a long time to be married to one person." The old gentleman looked over at his wife with love in his eyes and said, "It would have been a lot longer without her."

In Christian marriage, two people grow more and more one with every passing year. They are "fellow heirs of the grace of life" and they are more than happy to share. Each is helping the other on the way to eternity.

Someone asked, "Is there anything more beautiful than a boy and girl clasping clean hands and pure hearts in the path of marriage?" The answer is "Yes, there is a more beautiful thing: it is the spectacle of an old man and an old woman finishing their journey on that path. Their hands are gnarled, but still clasped; their faces are seamed but still radiant; their hearts are tired and bowed down but still strong. They have proved the happiness of marriage and vindicated it from the jeers of cynics."

598 How to Preserve a Husband

Be careful in your selection.

Once selected, give your entire thoughts to preparation for domestic use.

Some wives insist upon keeping them in a pickle, others are constantly getting them into hot water. This makes them sour, hard, and sometimes bitter. Even poor varieties may be made sweet, tender and good, by garnishing them with kisses, wrapping them in a blanket of love, keeping them warm with a steady fire of domestic devotion, and serving with peaches and cream.

Thus prepared they will keep for years!!

599 Tell Her So

Amid the cares of married life,
In spite of toil and business strife,
If you value your sweet wife,
Tell her so!

There was a time you thought it bliss
To get the favor of a kiss;
A dozen now won't come amiss—
Tell her so!

Do not act as if she has passed her prime,
As though to please her were a crime—

If e'er you loved her, now is the time;
Tell her so!

Never let her heart grow cold;
Richer beauties will unfold.
She is worth her weight in gold;
Tell her so!

600 Please Talk to Me

Pastor Charles Curtis stresses the importance of really communicating:

"My husband does not talk to me," is the complaint of 80 percent of American wives. It has been claimed that "One hundred percent of the people seeking professional help for their marriages have problems of communication." In our world, the power to send and receive messages reaches around the globe (even out into space), and this information is available in seconds! Yet, husbands and wives are unable to successfully communicate across the breakfast table. "Please talk to me" is the request and basic need in many homes.

Communication is a rich source of blessing. What a joy it is to talk and listen! Recently, I had a sore throat and was to preach that night. In order to save my throat, I wrote notes and did not speak for the entire day. It was maddening and frustrating. "A word spoken in season, how good is it" (Prov. 15:23)! "A word fitly spoken is like apples of gold in settings of silver" (Prov. 25:11).

The lack of communication multiplies our problems as it destroys bridges over which we need to travel. An old farmer had trouble guiding his mule, but said nothing. When asked why he didn't speak to the mule, he responded, "That old mule kicked me five years ago and I ain't spoke to him since." Marriage offers companionship, and this is impossible without communication. People can be lonely in a crowd or in a marriage. Lines of communication should be carefully built and maintained in the home. "People are lonely because they build walls instead of bridges" (Joseph E. Newton).

Communication is more than just speaking. How well do we listen? The Scripture admonished us: "Wherefore, my beloved brethren, let every man be swift to hear, slow to speak, slow to wrath" (James 1:19). While a senator, Lyndon Johnson had this sign in his office: "You ain't learning nothing when you're doing all the talking." Listening is essential to communication. Parents often fail to really hear what their children may be saying. Teenages run away from home "because it is the only way they know how to cope with a family that has forgotten how to listen" (Fred Gross). Listening has a way of saying—"To me, you are an important person. I appreciate you, I accept you, I love you, and I want to hear what you have to say." It is only by listening that we can correctly respond.

601 Nine Suggestions for an Ailing Marriage

1. Never consider divorce an option. It is not a solution to your problem. Divorce is not an acceptable alternative because God says it is not.

2. Do not compare your mate or your marriage to others. There is not another person on earth like you. Your mate is also unique. This means that your marriage is unique. Let God make it what He wants it to be. He will make it perfect!

3. Forgive your mate. You are to forgive as Christ has forgiven you. You are a sinner. He or she is a sinner. You are not perfect—so be willing to forgive one another. And do it right away before any bitterness can build up.

4. Stop all criticism. Love does not criticize and find fault. Therefore, if you are critical of your mate, you do not have a heart of love. Stop all criticism. Instead, try a little praise. It works like magic!

5. Start communicating with your mate. Communication is completely broken down in many homes and marriages. Start listening to what your mate is saying as well as to what he or she is *not* saying. Break down the barriers by being vulnerable. Try saying, "Honey, what is the biggest fault I have?" Then say, "Would you please help me, by the grace of God, to gain victory over that fault?"

6. Refuse any relationship outside your marriage in which affection is sought or given. This substitute could even be a relative, a friend, or a neighbor. Do not seek to make someone else a substitute for what you are not getting in your marriage. You will never solve your problem doing this.

7. Trust your mate. Trust your spouse, even if he or she is wrong —you are right in trusting. A marriage must be based on trust. It cannot survive without it.

8. Do something every day to please your mate—something that you know will bring your partner joy and happiness. This is not asking much—to do *one* thing—but it pays big dividends.

9. Thank God every day for the 25 best qualities in your mate. Write them down. Concentrate on them and the positive will soon outshine the negative.

602 Marital Turmoil

Some people think that courtship is when a man spoons, and marriage is when he must fork over. It is tragic to realize that in the church of Christ there are constant marital difficulties. Christian mates ought to be among the happiest of people on the face of the planet! Why should a man and woman who profess to be in love with the Lord continue in misery because of a rocky marital relationship?

The closer husbands and wives walk with Christ the easier their lives together will become. But show me a husband and wife who are unfaithful to the Bridegroom, Jesus, and I will show you a couple in deep trouble. Will a Christian wife nag and complain and bemoan everything or will she be a radiant help-meet for the man with whom she chose to live out her life? Will a husband come home and sequester himself behind the evening newspaper if he really wants to demonstrate Christian love?

Once a housewife asked her husband if he minded escorting her out to the garbage can. He asked why she would make such a silly request. She replied, "I just want to be able to tell the neighbors that we go out together once in a while." Marriage is a give-and-take proposition, and a wise couple soon realizes that each must give more than was thought during courtship.

Too many mates fritter their lives away and burden others by supposing they have insurmountable problems within their marriages. But Paul reminds us: "Wives, submit to you husbands, as is fitting in the Lord. Husbands, love your wives and do not be harsh with them" (Col. 3:18, 19). Unselfish love is the key to successful Christian marriages.

603 Divorce

Although one in every two married couples ends up divorced, certain categories of marriages have a much higher success rate. A national survey revealed that when two criteria are present—the couple attends church, and they pray together at home—there was only one divorce in one thousand marriages!

604 How Husbands Can Emotionally Meet Their Wives' Needs

When did you last tell your wife, "I love you?" When did she last hear those words that are music to her ears—"I really do need you"? Have you recently told her, "Honey, I think you are a really good mother for our children?"

The vast majority of wives are starving for verbal affirmation from their husbands. And most men are so thoughtless and insensitive that they will not give their wives what the wives desperately want and deserve.

We husbands gladly encourage our wives to buy food and grudgingly encourage them to buy clothes, but most who come to counseling just cannot dig deeply enough to give complimentary words. So, marriages are unfulfilling, wives feel unappreciated, and many marriages wither and die.

Husbands, speak up! God expects you, as the head, to do more than provide financially for your wife. He wants you to also provide for her emotional well-being.

Whisper it, write it, or shout it— just get those words of affirmation to the ears of your wife.

605 What Glues Husband and Wife Together?

Dr. Joseph Henry said that during the Second World War, two physics graduate students heard their professor say that someday a method would be devised for polishing glass that would replace steel as the flattest surface known to man. When this was done, he said, a revolution in technology would take place.

After graduation, these two young physicists formed a partnership and set out to prove their professor's theory. They established a laboratory and went to work. Several years later, after a very complicated process, they had a great breakthrough. They produced such a flat surface that it could be used to measure objects within two-millionths of an inch—a great improvement over anything previously developed.

When Dr. Henry visited their plant, one of the owners said to him, "See these two squares of glass? They have been put through this new process, and I want to

show you something." Then he simply placed the two pieces together, handed them to Dr. Henry, and said, "Now take them apart." After he pulled, pushed, twisted, turned and exerted all of his strength, Dr. Henry still could not budge them.

The young physicist explained, "Two surfaces are held together by a certain number of points of contact, but ordinarily there are so few they easily come apart. The points on these two pieces of glass, however, have been ground down until they are almost completely flat surfaces. They are held together by so many points of contact that it is almost impossible to get them apart."

If you let God rub down the rough edges in you and your spouse, nothing will be able to tear you apart.

Meekness

606 President Lincoln and the Dying Boy

During the hard days of the Civil War, President Lincoln made frequent visits to the hospitals that were always overcrowded with the suffering.

On one occasion he stopped to speak to one of the patients, a mere boy of 16, who had been mortally wounded and was nearing death.

President Lincoln, taking the thin, white hand, said, "My poor boy, what can I do for you?"

With a beseeching look the fellow turned his eyes to the homely, kindly face and asked, "Will you write to my mother for me?"

"That I will," answered the President, and calling for a pen, ink and paper, he seated himself and wrote a long letter. When it was finished, the President rose, saying, "I will mail this as soon as I get back to my office. Now is there anything else I can do for you?"

In some way the boy had come to know it was the President, and so, looking at him in the most appealing sort of way, he asked, "Will you stay with me till it is all over? I will not be long, and I want to hold onto your hand."

That was too much for the great-hearted President to resist. The tears came to his eyes, and he sat down by him and took hold of his hand. The fellow did not move or speak a word. This was some time before four o'clock, and it was long after six before the end came.

607 A Superior's Superior Attitude

Bruce Barton told of an incident in the life of Abraham Lincoln which illustrates a winning spirit. Lincoln, in search of firsthand information on the progress of the Civil War, sought out his general, George B. McClellan. McClellan was not at home when the President and a cabinet member arrived, so Lincoln waited an hour. At last the general returned, but instead of greeting Lincoln, he went upstairs and retired for the evening, sending a servant to explain that he was too tired to see the President.

Lincoln's companion exploded in rage, but the President laid his hand gently on the man's shoulder: "There, there, do not take it so hard. I will hold McClellan's horse if he will only bring us victories."

In his words we hear echoes of Paul's comment: ". . . I will not be enslaved to anything" (1 Cor. 6:12).

608 Learn from the Goats

Two goats met one another upon a narrow plank set up across a river, so that they could not pass by without one thrusting the other off. If they were human beings they would argue who had the right to survive. But the goats figured it all out, how one could help the other and, at the same time, help itself. One lay down, and let the other leap over it.

Obedience

609 Man's Great Power

When J. Wilbur Chapman was in London, he had an opportunity to meet General Booth, who at that time was past 80 years of age. Dr. Chapman listened reverently as the old general spoke of the trials and the conflicts and the victories he had experienced.

The American evangelist then asked the general if he would disclose his secret for success. "He hesitated a second," Dr. Chapman said, "and I saw the tears come into his eyes and steal down his cheeks," and then he said, "I will tell you the secret. God has had all there was of me. There have been men with greater brains than I, men with greater opportunities; but from the day I got the poor of London on my heart, and a vision of what Jesus Christ could do with the poor of London, I made up my mind that He would have all of William Booth there was. And if there is anything of power in the Salvation Army today, it is because God has all the adoration of my heart, all the power of my will, and all the influence of my life."

Dr. Chapman said he went away from that meeting with General Booth knowing "that the greatness of a man's power is the measure of his surrender."

610 A New Four-Letter Word

C. S. Johnson shares this family lesson:

"My son, Michael, was four years old the night I found him sobbing uncontrollably in the hallway. Concerned, I knelt next to him and drew him close.

" 'What's the matter, sweetheart? Are you hurt?' He shook his head and turned to me, but I was unprepared for his response.

" 'Daddy said a bad word to me!' he sobbed. I almost laughed out loud. I had known my husband 12 years and had rarely heard him raise his voice. But Michael had heard him say something, and I was curious enough to want to know what it was.

" 'Honey, what bad word did Daddy say?' And seeing a chance for sympathy, my sensitive four-year-old stopped crying and blurted out—'Obey!'

"I never think of that incident now without asking my Heavenly Father to keep me from believing, as my son did, that 'obey' is a bad word."

611 Do As You Are Told and Survive

More than 90 people conducted an all-night search for an eight-year-

242

old boy named Dominic. While on a skiing trip with his father, this little boy apparently had ridden a new lift and skied off the run without realizing it. They hoped to find Dominic somewhere on the snowy mountain slope before it was too late.

As each hour passed, the search party and the boy's family became more and more concerned. By dawn they still had found no trace of him. Two helicopters joined the search, and within fifteen minutes had spotted ski tracks. A ground team followed the tracks which changed to small footprints. The footprints lead to a tree where they found the boy at last.

"He's in super shape," the area search and rescue coordinator announced to the anxious family and press. "In fact, he's in better shape than we are right now." A hospital spokesman said the boy was in fine condition and was not even admitted.

The rescuer explained why the boy did so well despite spending a night in the freezing elements: His father had enough forethought to warn him what to do if he became lost, and his son had enough trust to do exactly what his father said.

Dominic protected himself from possible frostbite and hypothermia by snuggling up to a tree and covering himself with branches. As a young child, he never would have thought of doing this on his own. He was simply obeying his wise and loving father.

612 Legalism or Love?

Ancil Jenkins shares this illustration:

" 'Fasten your seat belt,' I said to my wife, Elaine, the other day. 'It is the law, you know.' As she fastened her seat belt, I thought, 'Dummy, that is not the reason you want her buckled up. You want her protected from the harm of any accident you might drive her into.' How shallow would be my concern if I was more in fear of paying a fine than in her being seriously hurt!

"How much this can describe our approach to our obedience to God! Almost all we do is from mixed motives. Yet which motive is overriding? Do we obey because we fear God's wrath and judgment? Do we feel He will break our leg or burn down our house if we disobey? Do we feel that Christianity is just a set of rules to be obeyed and our satisfaction comes from doing a good job of keeping rules?

"The result of such an attitude will only breed fear and guilt. Fear comes from any failure to obey, and there will be such failure. Guilt comes from many sources, such as finding there was a law you had been failing to obey. Any failure at perfect obedience can lead to regarding some laws as more important than others. All this can lead to a disregard of others who do not keep laws as well as we do (Luke 18:1). It can lead us to giving more attention to the minute details and neglecting the major virtues God desires us to have (Matt. 23:23).

We become ridiculous gnat strainers and camel swallowers (Matt. 23:24).

"We should obey God because we love Him. We obey because He has done so much for us and we have done so little for Him. We obey because love is never content to accept but must always give. Jesus said, 'If you love Me, you will do what I command' (John 14:15). We then come to realize that our disobedience not only breaks the laws of God, it also breaks the heart of God. How often they rebelled against Him in the wilderness and grieved Him in the desert! (Ps. 78:40).

"Such obedience is far fuller, richer, and freer than can ever come from a legal motivation. Imagine a woman who is a nurse and a mother. She may work at a hospital all day caring for the sick. When she has worked eight hours, she goes home. Upon arriving home, she finds her child is seriously ill. She will then give her child the same care she gives the hospital patients. However, when she has cared for her child for eight hours, she will not quit. She gives care no one can buy. The difference is the motivation.

"What is your major motivation? Seek to know God better, and you will find yourself obeying out of love. It will become 'richer, fuller, deeper' and will become 'sweeter as the years go by.' "

613 Full Obedience

Mary Murray tells this on herself:

"My dear mother must have chuckled at the little girl who obeyed 'halfway.' Mom loved to have her house just right. On Saturday, when she asked me to dust the furniture frames and the delicate glassware, I stared in awe at the task before me. I dusted as fast as I could, going 'around' the glassware; not picking them up and missing spots here and there on the furniture. Sometimes I would have to redust after 'inspection.' She was teaching me to 'obey right' the first time and to use self-discipline."

Pastors

614 A Different Viewpoint

A young pastor of a little church complained to the "Prince of Preachers," Charles H. Spurgeon, about the smallness of his church and its few members. Spurgeon asked him, "How many members do you have?" "Fifty," replied the young pastor. "Ah," exclaimed Spurgeon, "that is more than you will want to account for on the day of judgment."

615 Minister's Ulcers

Nearly every businessman complains of at least one ulcer. Think how many ulcers the poor businessman would have if he worked under the same circumstances as the average minister!

"Just suppose, Mr. Businessman, that you were the overseer of 100 workers. Suppose only about 50 percent of them ever showed up for work at a given time, and only 25 percent could be relied upon. Suppose that every time a simple flash of lightning appeared in the sky, large numbers of young workers pulled the covers over their heads and failed to report for duty.

"Suppose your workers only worked when they felt like it and yet you must be very sweet and never fire one of them. To get them back to work you must beg them, plead with them, pat them on the back, and use every means under the sun to persuade them without offending them. And suppose you were in competition with a notorious rascal, the devil, who had no scruples and is far more clever than you are and uses such attractive things as fishing rods, guns, soft pillows, televisions and a thousand other things to attract your customers.

"How many ulcers would you have?"

616 The Pastor as the Tool Man

You see them driving around most urban areas and even venturing out in small town USA. Their destinations are automotive garages and any other place of business that uses tools. Most of the vehicles are large vans or panel trucks and carry such logos as "Snap-On Tools," or "Matco."

What if it were the job of these drivers to rush from place to place tightening, untightening and doing all the actual mechanical repairing of the vehicles? Imagine the mechanics in these shops calling on the tool man every time they needed a bolt tightened or a screw

246 PASTORS

adjusted, sitting around waiting for them to arrive and do the work. It is a comical scene based on the ridiculous; hundreds of mechanics waiting for the help of few exhausted and distraught tool men.

The truth of the matter is, these tool men in their vans only provide the tools. It is the mechanics who do the work.

Sometimes we in the local church can actually get caught up in a similar comedy of errors. A church can look to their pastor as the one whom they hire to do their ministry for them. A pastor can also be at fault for allowing himself to be like the misguided tool man trying to do it all himself.

The truth of the matter is, in God's economy of work in the local church it is the individual people in the congregation who are called by God to do the bulk of the ministry. The pastor's job is to equip them for their ministry.

617 What Does a Preacher Do With His Time?

The preacher is a teacher, though he has to solicit his own class. He heals without pills or knife. He is a lawyer, a social worker, an editor, a philosopher, a salesman, a handy decorative piece for public functions, an entertainer, a chairman of the building fund and a first-class janitor.

People come to him and he goes to the people. He rejoices when they rejoice and weeps when they weep. He visits the sick, marries the young, buries the dead, prepares and delivers speeches to every organization under the sun, and tries to stay sweet when he is abused for not calling on certain people. He helps plan the program of the church and meets with every group he can, which may mean that some nights he must attend two and three meetings.

When he lies down at night, he is burdened and prays for certain "sheep," their weaknesses, their problems, and their absence from the service. And, oh yes, in his spare time, he prepares and delivers several sermons, Bible lessons, radio programs, class messages, etc. And when Monday comes and some chap roars, "What an easy job you preachers have!" he tries to smile and keep sweet.

Have you ever heard the above question asked? Or the remark made thoughtlessly, "What an easy task the pastor has! He speaks about 20 minutes twice on Sunday and once on Wednesday with the rest of the week all his own!"

However, with all these aggravations, many would rather be divinely called ministers of the gospel than be anything else.

618 Where His Sermons Went

Coming to the close of many years of faithful ministry, an aged pastor tied his sermon notes in a bundle and wrote on it: "Where has the influence of all the sermons I have preached gone?" One who had been under his ministry for years and who had grown in Christlikeness and in the knowledge of God's Word, gave the following heartfelt appraisal of his sermons: "Where are last year's sunrays? They have gone into fruits and grains and vegetables to feed mankind. Where are last year's raindrops? Forgotten, of course, but they did their gracious and refreshing work. Your sermons, preached over the years, have gone into my life and into the lives of others, to make me and them better, nobler, and more Christlike. They have deepened our love for God's Word, given us a vision of and love for unsaved ones, and have challenged us to go on in the Christian life!"

619 Preacher's Notes

Preachers fall into four categories:
1. Those who do not use any notes, so the audience has no idea how long they will speak.
2. Those who lay each page of their sermon down in front of them as they read it. These honest ones enable the audience to keep track of how much more is to come.
3. Those who cheat by putting each sheet of notes under the others in their hand.
4. And, worst of all, those who put down each sheet of notes as they read them and then horrify the audience by picking up the whole batch and reading off the other side.

620 Harvest Time

The youth minister was passing through the prison garment factory. "Sewing?" he said to a prisoner who was at work. "No, preacher," replied the prisoner gloomily, "reaping!"

621 You Asked for It

A preacher had been talking to a children's Bible class about kindness. He paused and asked, "If I should see a man beating a donkey and stopped him, what virtue would I be showing?"

A little voice responded with the unexpected answer, "Brotherly love."

622 Ezra: A Model For Preachers

"For Ezra had prepared his heart to seek the law of the Lord, and to do it, and to teach in Israel statutes and judgments" (Ezra 7:10).

Ezra sought the law of the Lord. Newer versions translate "study" instead of "seek," and study is, of course, the way we seek it. We do not go to the priest, or seer, or to the witch of Endor; nor do we inquire of the Urim and Thummin. God's will is not found by contemplating our navels or getting in touch with our inner impulses. "When they say to you, 'Seek them that have familiar spirits, and seek wizards that peep and mutter'; should not a people seek their God? Should they consult the dead on behalf of the living? To the law and to the testimony! If they speak not according to this word, it is because there is not light in them! (Is. 8:19, 20). The preacher must study. Study takes time. Euclid told Ptolemy, King of Egypt, "There is no royal road to geometry"; so there is no mystic shortcut to a knowledge of the will of God.

When we really know what God has revealed to man, we know something helpful and worthwhile to teach. When we teach what is helpful and valuable, people will come to hear and learn. They will not come again and again for empty platitudes or recycled outlines. Not even hogs will keep coming back to an empty trough. Study. Seek the Word of the Lord.

Ezra did the law of the Lord. Unlike the scribes of Jesus' day, who said but did not (Matt. 23:2), Ezra practiced what he studied. Studying the Bible is not just an academic exercise. We must not be forgetful hearers, but doers, in order to be blessed (James 1:23–25). We may pride ourselves on knowing the truth, but Jesus did not say "This know and thou shalt live." He said, "This do and thou shalt live" (Luke 10:28).

Ezra taught the Lord's statutes and judgment in Israel. So must we. "It is written in the prophets, 'And they shall all be taught of God.' Every man therefore that has heard, and has learned of the Father, comes to me" (John 6:45). What we have learned we are to teach to others, so that they can teach others also (2 Tim. 2:2). We are to teach to convert and then we are to teach the converted (Matt. 28:19, 20). A preacher is a teacher who pleads with his students to do what they have been taught.

Ezra set his heart to seek, to do, and to teach the law of the Lord. No one accidentally becomes a faithful servant of God. We will only be good students, faithful workers, and effective teachers to the extent we decide to be, and deliberately lay aside things that hinder us.

Let Ezra be our model. Let us be models like Ezra.

623 It Is Your Move

I gave you life; but cannot live it for you.
I can teach you things;
but I cannot make you learn.
I can give you directions;
but I cannot always be there to lead you.
I can take you to church;
but I cannot make you believe.
I can teach you right from wrong;
but I cannot always decide for you.
I can teach you to be a friend;
but I cannot make you one.
I can advise you about friends;
but I cannot choose them for you.
I can teach you about sex;
but I cannot keep you pure.
I can tell you the facts of life;
but I cannot build your reputation.
I can tell you about "strong drink"
but I cannot say no for you.
I can warn you about drugs;
but I cannot prevent you from using them.
I can tell you about lofty goals;
but I cannot achieve them for you.
I can warn you about sin;
but I cannot make your morals.
I can love you as a child;
but I cannot place you in God's family.

I can pray for you;

but I cannot make you walk with God.

I can teach you about Jesus;

but I cannot make Him your Savior.

I can teach you to obey;

but I cannot make Jesus your Lord.

I can tell you how to live;

but I cannot give you eternal life.

624 So Is the Devil

The early Methodist evangelist, George Whitefield, was one of America's most effective preachers, who won thousands to Christ. He was vigorously opposed by Charles Chauncy, pastor of Boston's famous First Church.

Rev. Chauncy objected to the idea of instantaneous conversions and to the emotional excitement caused by Whitefield's ministry.

In 1744, on Whitefield's second visit to Boston, the two met. Rev. Chauncy said, "So you have returned, have you?" "Yes," replied the evangelist, "in the service of the Lord." "I am sorry to hear it," Rev. Chauncy said bluntly. "So is the devil," retorted Whitefield.

The devil hates any preacher who fearlessly and effectively sounds the gospel trumpet.

625 Preacher's Predicament

A man had a heart attack and was rushed to the hospital. He could receive little company and was not to be excited. While in the hospital, a rich uncle died and left him a million dollars. His family wondered how to break the news to him with the least amount of excitement. It was decided to ask the preacher if he would go and break the news quietly to the man.

The preacher went, and gradually led up to the question. The preacher asked the patient what he would do if he inherited a million dollars. He said, "I think I would give half of it to the church."

The preacher dropped dead.

626 The Doc Prescribed, but the Patient Died

It was only a cold in her head when Mrs. Mosby came to Doc Bradley. The doctor poured out some medicine from his store and told her how often to take it. A few days later he was called to her home, for in those days doctors made housecalls. The cold had settled in her chest. More medicine was prescribed, but the woman died. She could have survived, and it hurt the doctor to know he had prescribed, but the patient did not survive.

A short time after the funeral, the doctor happened to meet Mrs. Mosby's sister and by accident learned that the sick woman had not taken a drop of his medicine, but instead poured it down the sink. The doctor then realized he was not responsible, for the patient had not followed orders.

Obviously the preacher is responsible to prescribe the right medicine. Too many in the church pews listen but do not take the gospel medicine. Only those who listen and follow what is prescribed can expect to find spiritual health.

627 *Five Ways to Get Rid of Your Pastor*

1. Sit up front, smile and say "amen" every time he says something good. He will preach himself to death.

2. Pat him on the back and tell him what good work he is doing in the church and community. He will work himself to death.

3. Increase your offering in the church. Then he will suffer from shock.

4. Tell him you have decided to join the visitation group and win souls for the Lord. He will probably suffer a heart attack.

5. Get the whole church to band together and pray for him. He will get so efficient that some other church will hear about him and give him a call. That will take him off your hands.

Prayer

628 Prayer Brings Revival

James Duncan, preaching with great unction and power, was asked what was the secret of such powerful preaching. "The secret," he said, was "thirteen hours of consecutive prayer."

When asked the secret of his spiritual power, Charles Spurgeon said: "Knee work! Knee work!"

Livingston of Shotts, on two different occasions, preached with such power that in each service 500 were converted. Both sermons were preceded by a night of prayer.

Charles Finney, after spending a day in the woods in prayer and fasting, preached that night to a phenomenally irreligious congregation. The sermon was accompanied by such divine power that the whole congregation, except one man, fell prostrate upon the floor, and voiced their agony under conviction of sin, in such loud outcries that the preacher was forced to stop.

Of "Uncle" John Vassar, the Tract Society colporteur, his pastor said: "He absolutely prayed day and night—prayed about everything, prayed for almost everything, prayed with almost everybody he met.

"He prayed when he went out and when he came in. He prayed before every religious service, and then prayed all the way through it. I have occupied the same room with him night after night and rarely went to sleep without hearing him in prayer, or awoke without finding him in prayer."

629 Prayer of a Husband and a Wife

Keep us, O Lord, from pettiness.

Let us be thoughtful in word and deed.

Help us to put away pretense and face each other in deep trust without fear or self-pity.

Help us to guard against faultfinding, and be quick to discover the best in each other and in every situation.

Guard us from ill temper and hasty judgment; encourage us to take time for all things, to grow calm, serene and gentle.

Help us to be generous with kind words and compliments.

Teach us never to ignore, never to hurt, never to take each other for granted.

Engrave charity and compassion on our hearts.

630 God Uses His People to Answer Our Prayers

During the World's Fair in Chicago many years ago, Mr. Dwight Moody was carrying on a campaign which cost a great many thousands of dollars. A little group met one day to plan and assist and pray with Mr. Moody about the work. As they sat down to eat, Mr. Moody said, "We need $7,000 today for the work. I have already received $1,000, but before we eat I propose that we pray and ask God for the other $6,000." So with simple childlike faith, Mr. Moody presented this problem to the Father.

About an hour later after the little group had finished their luncheon and completed their plans for the day, a boy came in with a telegram in his hand. Mr. Moody read it and handed it to Reuben Torrey to read aloud. This was what it said: "Mr. Moody, your friends in North Field had a feeling that you needed money in Chicago. We have just taken up a collection and there is $6,000 in the basket." North Field is nearly a thousand miles from Chicago. That morning, as a service was coming to a close in North Field, someone proposed that they take a collection for Mr. Moody's work in Chicago.

God lives! The believers know He is alive by their intimate experience of Him.

631 The Weariness of Prayer

"He . . . continued all night in prayer to God" (Luke 6:12).

We never read that Joshua's hand was weary with wielding the sword, but Moses' hand was weary with holding the rod. The more spiritual the duty, the more apt we are to tire of it. We could stand and preach all day; but we could not pray all day. We could go forth to seek the sick all day, but we could not be in our closets all day nearly as easily. To spend a night with God in prayer would be far more difficult than to spend a night with man in preaching. Oh! take care, take care, that thou dost not cease thy prayers!

632 How They Prayed for Missions

George Whitefield, the famous English evangelist, said, "O Lord, give me souls, or take my soul!"

Henry Martin, a missionary, cried as he knelt on India's coral strands, "Here let me burn out for God."

David Brainerd, missionary to the North American Indians in the early 18th century, prayed, "Lord, to Thee I dedicate myself, oh accept of me, and let me be Thine forever. Lord, I desire nothing else, I desire nothing more." The last words in his diary written several days before he died were, "Oh come, Lord Jesus, come quickly. Amen."

Thomas à Kempis, 1379–1471, said, "Give what Thou wilt, and how much Thou wilt, and when Thou wilt. Set me where Thou wilt and deal with me in all things as Thou wilt."

Dwight L. Moody implored, "Use me then, my Savior, for whatever purpose and in whatever way Thou mayest require. Here is my poor heart, an empty vessel, fill it with Thy grace."

Martin Luther prayed thus on the night preceding his appearance before the Diet of Worms: "Do Thou, my God, stand by me against all the world's wisdom and reason. Oh, do it, Thou must do it. Stand by me, Thou true, eternal God!"

"Praying Hyde," a missionary in India, pleaded, "Father, give me these souls, or I die."

Mrs. Comstock, a missionary in India, uttered this prayer of parting when she sent her children home: "Lord Jesus, I do this for Thee."

How do you pray for Missions?

633 Amen!

A layman who was widely known for his use of the term "amen," was asked on one occasion why he used it.

"Just what does 'amen' mean?" asked a friend.

The sincere brother replied, "In most cases it means just this to me: 'Yes, Lord, I am with it, and I will stand my share of the expenses.'"

"What do you mean when you say 'amen' at the end of your prayers?" he was asked.

"When I say 'amen' at the end of a prayer I mean just this: 'God, I am working with you that this may be true, but I am willing to receive any one of your three replies: yes, no, or wait.'"

634 How Much Does a Prayer Weigh?

There is a story of a man who tried to weigh a prayer. He owned a little grocery store. It was the week before Christmas, shortly after World War I.

A tired-looking woman came into the store and asked for enough food to make a Christmas dinner for the children. The grocer asked her how much she could spend.

"My husband did not come back; he was killed in the War. And I have nothing to offer but a little prayer," she answered.

The storekeeper was not very sentimental nor religious, so he said, half mockingly, "Write it on paper, and I will weigh it."

To his surprise, the woman took a piece of paper from her pocket and handed it to the man, saying, "I wrote it during the night while watching over my sick baby."

The grocer took the piece of paper before he could recover from his surprise and, because other customers were watching and had heard his remarks, he placed the unread prayer on the weight side of the old-fashioned scales. Then he began to pile food on the other side; but to his amazement, the scale would not go down.

He became angry and flustered and finally said, "Well, that's all the scale will hold. Here's a bag; you will have to put it in yourself, I am busy."

With trembling hands the woman filled the bag, and through moist eyes expressed her gratitude and departed.

After that the store was empty of customers, and the grocer examined the scales. Yes, they were broken and they had become broken just in time for God to answer the prayer of the woman. But as the years passed, the grocer often wondered about the incident. Why did the woman come at just the right time? Why had she already written the prayer in such a way as to confuse the grocer so that he did not examine the scales?

The grocer is an old man now, but the weight of the paper still lingers with him. He never saw the woman again, nor had he seen her before that day. Yet he remembers her more than any of his customers.

And he treasures the slip of paper upon which the woman's prayer had been written—simple words, but from a heart of faith, "Please, Lord, give us this day our daily bread."

635 Prayer for a New Year

Lord, I confess before You that:

I have had longings and nudges from You which I did not translate into action.

I have made decisions without consulting You, then have blamed You when things went wrong.

I have said that I trusted You, yet have not turned my affairs over to You.

I have been greedy for present delights and pleasures, unwilling to wait for those joys which time and discipline alone can give.

I have often sought the easy way and have consistently drawn back from the road that is hard.

I have been fond of giving myself to dreams of which I am going to do sometime, yet have been so slow in getting started to do them.

Forgive me for all the intentions that were born and somehow never lived.

And now I claim Your promise to change me. Do for me what I cannot do for myself. Lead me into a new tomorrow with a new spirit. Cleanse my heart; create within me new attitudes and new ideas, as only You can. Amen.

636 But for Those Prayers, We Should Have Failed

A clergyman from New York, during a call on President Lincoln at the White House said: "I have not come to ask any favors of you, Mr. President; I have only come to say that the loyal people of the North are sustaining you and will continue to do so. We are giving you all that we have, the lives of our sons as well as our confidence and our prayers. You must know that no boy's father or mother ever kneels in prayer these days without asking God to give you strength and wisdom."

His eyes brimming with tears, Mr. Lincoln replied:

"But for those prayers, I should have faltered and perhaps failed long ago. Tell every father and mother you know to keep on praying, and I will keep on fighting, for I know God is on our side."

As the clergyman started to leave the room, Mr. Lincoln held him by the hands and said: "I suppose I may consider this as sort of a pastoral call?" "Yes," replied the clergyman. "Out in our country," replied Lincoln, "when a parson makes a pastoral call, it was always the custom for the folks to ask him to lead in prayer, and I should like to ask you to pray with me today. Pray that I may have the strength and the wisdom."

The two men knelt side by side, and the clergyman offered the most fervent plea to Almighty God that ever fell from his lips. As they arose, the President clasped his visitor's hand and remarked in a satisfied sort of way: "I feel better."

637 *Replace Fretting with Trust*

Psalm 37:1 begins, "Do not fret," and those words are repeated later in the chapter. The dictionary defines "fret" as "to eat way, gnaw, gall, vex, worry, agitate, wear away."

Whenever H. Norman Wright hears this word, he is reminded of the scene he sees each year when he hikes along the Snake River in the Grand Teton National Park in Wyoming. Colonies of beavers live along the riverbanks, and often he sees trees that are at various stages of being gnawed to the ground by them. Some trees have slight rings around their trunks where the beavers have just started to chew on them. Other trees have several inches of bark eaten away, and some have already fallen to the ground because the beavers have gnawed through the trunks. Worry has the same effect on us. It will gradually eat away at us until it destroys us.

In addition to telling us not to fret, Psalm 37 gives us positive substitutes for worry. First, it says, "Trust [lean on, rely on, and be confident] in the Lord" (v. 3 AMP). Trust is a matter of not attempting to live an independent life or to cope with difficulties alone. It means going to a greater source for strength.

Second, verse four says, "Delight yourself also in the Lord" (AMP). To delight means to rejoice in God and what He has done for us. Let God supply the joy for your life.

Third, verse five says, "Commit your way to the Lord" (AMP). Commitment is a definite act of the will, and it involves releasing your worries and anxieties to the Lord.

And fourth, we are to "rest in the Lord; wait for Him" (v. 7 AMP). This means to submit in silence to what He ordains but to be ready and expectant for what He is going to do in your life.

Stop worrying and start praying (Phil. 4:6-9; Ps. 34:1-4). The passage in Philippians can be divided into three basic stages. We are given a *premise*: Stop worrying. We are given a *practice*: Start praying. And we are given a *promise*: Peace. The promise is there and available, but we must follow the first two steps in order for the third to occur. We must stop worrying and start praying if we are to begin receiving God's peace.

The results of prayer as a substitute for worry can be vividly seen in a crisis in David's life that prompted him to write Psalm 34. (See 1 Sam. 21:10; 22:2). David had escaped death at the hands of the Philistines by pretending to be insane. He then fled to the cave of Adullam along with four hundred men who were described as distressed, discontented, and in debt. In the midst of all this, David wrote a psalm of praise that begins, "I will bless the Lord at all times; His praise shall continually be in my mouth" (Ps. 34:1 RSV). He did not say he would praise the Lord *sometimes*, but at *all times*, even when his enemies were after him.

638 Amazing Prayer

God, Creator of all, invites us, mere creatures, to pray, and He assures us He will hear. He is holy, separate from sinners and undefiled, and we are rebellious and sinful, but as a Father, He invites us to ask favors and promises help. "Ask and it shall be given to you . . . for everyone that asketh receiveth . . . If you, then, being evil, know how to give good gifts to your children, how much more shall your Father who is in heaven give good things to them that ask him" (Matt. 7:7-11). Amazing!

Prayer changes things. The Bible says, "The effectual fervent prayer of a righteous man avails much" (James 5:16). Prayer for the sick is not a substitute for medicine, prayer for daily bread is not a substitute for work, and prayer for the lost is no substitute for the gospel, but those things are no substitute for

prayer either. Because Christians pray, some are well who would still be sick, some alive who would be dead (James 4:15), souls are saved that would be lost (Rom. 10:1), doors of opportunity are open that would still be closed (Col. 4:3), some are wiser than they were (James 1:5). "More things are wrought by prayer than this world dreams of." And many more things yet would be wrought by it, if we prayed more: "You have not, because you ask not" (James 4:2). How amazing!

God commands us to pray. "Pray without ceasing" (1 Thess. 5:17). "Continue in prayer, and watch in the same with thanksgiving (Col. 4:2). "Be anxious for nothing, but in everything by prayer and supplication with thanksgiving, let your requests be made known to God" (Phil. 4:6). The greatest of all privileges is not only allowed, but is even enjoined upon us. To let us pray would be marvelous, but He commands us. Amazing indeed!

God urges us to be persistent in prayer. If at first we do not get what we ask for, we are to keep asking. If God, who hears all things, appears deaf to our cries, we are to cry longer. Jesus told a parable about an unjust and uncaring judge, who finally ruled in favor of a poor widow simply because she wore him out with her persistent pleas. He told that parable, He said, to teach us that we "ought always to pray and not give up" (Luke 18:1). God is not unjust and uncaring, like that judge; but we are to be persistent, like that widow. God never wearies of our asking, even when it appears He is not hearing. Astoundingly amazing!

We are invited to pray and God has promised to hear. Great things happen because of prayer. We are commanded to pray by the One who loves us, and reminded that we show Him our love by keeping His commandments. We can "come boldly unto the throne of grace, that we may obtain mercy, and find grace to help in time of need" (Heb. 4:16). Yet, believing all of that, many of us pray so little! That is most amazing of all!

639 God Said "No" to David

The reign of David was the end of an era in Judah. David was 30 years of age when he became king and he reigned 40 years. His shoes were so big that none who came after him could ever fill them. As great as Solomon was, he never attained the stature of his father David, spiritually speaking. In Acts 13:36, Paul tells us that David served his own generation by the will of God.

David's dream was to build a house for the Lord. In 1 Samuel 7:1-3, David experienced a peaceful interlude, a calm, quiet period in his life, which for him was really unique. He was a courageous warrior, usually involved in battle with one or another of the surrounding nations.

At this point, while sitting quietly, he looked around at his own beautiful palace and compared it to the tent that housed the ark of God. The comparison sorrowed David. He wanted to build a beautiful, permanent home for the holy vessels of the Tabernacle. His motive was pure and admirable because he wanted it for God's glory, not his own. He expressed this desire to Nathan the prophet, who encouraged him.

But God had a different plan. The Lord spoke to Nathan and told him to tell David that it was not His will for David to build His house, but He promised to make David's dream come true through Solomon, his son.

God refused David's request, reminding him that he was a soldier, a man of war, but not a builder. How often we have wished for talents other than those God gave us. Many times, God's "NO" is just a redirection of His plan for us according to His will.

When we pray each day for divine guidance and direction, we need feel no guilt when our plans do not work out. We can have confidence that God's way is best and we can leave the results in His hand. When God says "NO," He has a better way, and our best reaction is submissive cooperation.

God has put each of us here for a purpose, however humble. Not many are called to fulfill such a great purpose as David, or to build temples. God's intended purpose for you may not be as great as your dreams, or it may be greater than you ever imagined. How sad that so many never become aware of that purpose which is the only way to true happiness and satisfaction.

640 Prayer: A Habit Worth Dying For

Nathan Hale, a great American patriot during the Revolutionary War, was captured and hung by British soldiers. His now famous final words were, "I only regret that I have but one life to lose for my country." He was willing to die for his nation and its freedom.

During the final days of World War II, it was apparent that the Japanese were fighting a losing battle. Yet many of their pilots, dubbed "kamikaze," willingly flew suicide missions. There was great honor in dying for a cause. The pilots were willing to die for glory.

Not long ago, a mother in Philadelphia went back into a burning building to rescue her children who were trapped inside. After saving two, she died in the flames trying to save the other two. The mother was willing to die for her children.

In the ancient empire of Persia, a law was passed making it a crime punishable by death to pray to anyone but the emperor. One aged government official refused to obey the edict. It was his habit to pray three times daily to the one true God. As a result, he was cast into a den of lions. Even though God saved Daniel, Daniel was still willing to die rather than give up his habit of prayer (Dan. 6:3-11).

How important is prayer to you? Is it a habit worth dying for? Or, would someone need to pass a law demanding daily prayer or a trip to the lions' den to get you into the habit of prayer? People are willing to die for that which is of great importance to them. Prayer should be that important! It is our link to God. Without the lifeline of prayer, we grow spiritually weak. Do not neglect the privilege that God has given to us as His children to pray.

641 Does Christianity Mean Easy Lives?

Do not pray for easy lives: pray to be stronger people! Do not pray for tasks equal to your powers; pray for powers equal to your task. Then the doing of your work shall be no miracle, but you shall be a miracle. Every day you shall wonder at yourself, the richness of life which has come to you by the grace of God.

642 Do Not Give Up

A lady in the church who invited her neighbor to go to services with her kept count of the times the neighbor refused. It came to 49. She pleasantly mentioned the count to her friend as she issued her fiftieth invitation at the time of a special meeting. At first the friend declined again but later called and said she would go. "If you are interested enough in me to ask me 50 times to go, I will go with you and see what it is like." She went out and liked what she saw. She returned and she was converted—all because someone did not give up too soon.

643 Not a Guest

A little girl of five was saying grace at the table. She prayed as she had heard others pray, "Come, Lord Jesus, be our Guest." Then turning suddenly to her mother, she said, "But, Mother, I do not want Jesus to be our Guest!"

"Why dear?" asked the horrified mother.

To which the little one replied, "Well, a guest is one who comes here sometimes. I want Jesus here all the time!"

644 Pray Believing

Little Johnnie was saying his bedtime prayers a week before his birthday. In a loud voice he listed all the things he wanted. "Do not pray so loudly," his mother instructed. "The Lord is not hard of hearing!"

"Maybe He isn't," admitted Johnnie, "but Grandma is."

A lot of our prayers may be like Johnnie's. We ask God, yet make other provisions. There is something good about the axiom, "Pray as if everything depended on God and work as if everything depended on you." But, in one sense, it reveals our spirit of independence. It conveys the notion: "I will have to do it all myself, anyway!"

We must admit the essentiality of dialogue with God. And our requests must come from righteous lips, for "he hears the prayer of the righteous" (Prov. 15:29). Prayers are like skyhooks—if we get enough fastened in up there we will have something to hang on to when the world is jerked out from under us.

Yes! Pray believing! Then God will answer your prayer. He may answer, "No!" He may answer, "Later!" He may answer, "Maybe!" Or he many answer, "Yes!" But let us understand one universal truth. The Father in heaven is eager to hear and answer in positive ways those of us who are his faithful children.

"Almighty Father, accept our prayers of faith as confessions of our utter dependence upon your love and generous mercy. In Jesus' name. Amen."

645 I Traveled on My Knees

Last night I took a journey
to a land across the sea,
I did not go by boat or plane,
I traveled on my knees.

I saw many people there in deep sin,
and I did not want to send my prayers in.
But Jesus said I should go and see,
how many I could win.

I said, "Jesus, I cannot go and work
with such as these."
He answered quickly, "Yes, you can by traveling on your knees."

He said, "You pray, I will meet the need.
You call and I will hear."
So I knelt in prayer and felt at ease
as I traveled on my knees.

I said, "Yes, Lord. I know I can do the job,
and my desire is to please.
I will heed Your call,"
and I traveled on my knees.

646 The Old Barn

An artist painted a picture of an old dilapidated barn. The barbed wire fence by the side of it was rusty and falling down. The door leaned drunkenly on hinges eroded by time and weather. It was a sad sight.

Some might call it "picturesque," but it was only a sad reminder of how temporary the things of life really are. Those who built it will not pass this way again. The things which were important to them are now only memories. The days of work and worry around this barn are long past. Life does not wait, and in its passing, "things" are left to rust and decay.

God has given us the means to correct this mistake of human weakness if we would only recognize it. He has given us "Sunday" in which to gather with those who share the dream of eternity with us; a time for reminding one another of things which do not ever swing on rusty hinges nor erode with time. He has offered us a constant audience with Him in prayer—a moment-by-moment opportunity to leave the temporary for the eternal.

Write out your prayers sometimes and see how much of the time you spend thanking God for and praying for the doors which hang on rusty hinges and how little time praising Him for the doors which open to things which "moth and rust" cannot corrupt.

647 How Moody Won the Children

Dwight L. Moody was passing along the streets of Chicago when he spied two little girls playing out in front of an underground saloon. His heart was instantly moved with compassion for the children, and he walked straightway into the cellar.

The barkeeper, thinking that he wanted a drink, said, "What will you have?" "Those children for my Sunday school," replied Moody. "Children for your Sunday school! Do you know where you are? An infidel club meets here every Thursday night."

But the tactful soul winner knew it was not a time for retreat, so, resting his elbows on the bar, he looked into the face of this father and pleaded with him earnestly in behalf of the little girls.

Finally, the man's heart was touched and he said, "I will tell you what I will do, parson. If you will come down here next Thursday night and meet the boys in a joint discussion, and you win, you shall have the children; but if not, it is all off." "Agreed," exclaimed Moody. "I will be here." Taking his departure, he looked up a little crippled newsboy whom he knew, who could pray effectually and said to him, "Tommy, I want you next Thursday night."

When the hour arrived, Tommy and the evangelist entered the saloon. It was full. The men were sitting on whiskey barrels, on beer kegs and on the counter, while others were at the windows in expectation of a debate.

Moody opened the meeting by saying: "Gentlemen, it is our custom to open our meetings with prayer. Tommy, jump on that barrel and pray," whereupon Tommy perched himself on the barrel, turned his little face up toward heaven, and how he did pray! As the tears stole down his cheeks, the more tenderhearted beat a retreat; and finally those more rocklike, subdued by the pathos and spiritual power of the occasion, slowly retired, until there were none left except the barkeeper, Moody and the praying boy.

"That will do, Tommy," exclaimed the evangelist. "I claim the children," said he, turning to the father. "They are yours according to contract," replied the father, "but it is a queer way to fight." "It is the way I win my battles," said Moody. He had instructed the little boy not to cease praying until he had prayed them all out. It was a piece of strategy full of tactfulness. The reality, the venturesomeness, and the tact of such a man is worth emulating.

648 Can You Wait?

Having to wait for someone or something is difficult. What we want, we want now. Our fast food must be just that—fast. Instant pudding, instant rice, and instant results are part of our way of life. One individual prayed for patience and told the Lord that he wanted it "Right away!"

However, we know so agonizingly well that the Lord does not work on our time table. Having to wait upon the Lord (Ps. 27:14; 37:34) can be painful at times! The principle of the Lord working as He wills requires faith. He is never late! His promises are sure.

May we have the faith and patience to wait! The Lord will work out His plan, His way and in His time.

649 Revelation

I knelt to pray when day was done,
    and prayed, "O Lord, bless everyone;
Lift from each saddened heart the pain,
    and let the sick be well again."
And then I awoke another day,
    and carelessly went on my way.
The whole day long I did not try
    to wipe the tear from any eye;
I did not try to share the load
    of anybody on the road;
I did not even go to see
    the sick man just next door to me.
But once again, when day was done,
    I prayed, "O Lord, bless everyone. . . ."
But as I prayed, into my ear
    there came a voice that whispered clear,
    "Pause just now, before you pray;
    Whom have you tried to bless today?

God's sweetest blessings always go

to hands that serve Him here below."

And then I hid my face and cried,
"Forgive me, God, for I have lied.
Let me but see another day,
and I will live the way I pray."

650 When Is It Time to Pray?

Have you ever had anyone come to you and say, "Tell me . . . how do you know when it is time to pray?"

I mean our stomachs growl when it is time to eat.

Our eyes start closing when it is time to sleep.

When our feelings get hurt, it is time for tears,

With a new birth it is time to care.

People will often tell us, quite so,

When it is time to come, or stay, or go.

But how do you know when it is time to pray?

Does an alarm go off next to your bed?

Or is there a clanging inside your head?

Do your eyes start blinking, a horn start blowing?

Or do you listen for a rooster crowing?

Just what is your way of knowing when it is time to pray?

With me . . .

I find it is time to pray

At the beginning and ending of each day.

And when I am sick and feeling bad,

Or scared, or lonely, or lost, or sad.

When the bills blow in like sand
I seek a touch of the Master's hand.

When I need patience, hope and peace

And an abiding love that will not cease.

When I am thankful for all there is

That now is mine, and yet is His.
Gladness, sadness, joy and grief
We share in prayer. And it is my belief

That whenever my heart has something to say

That is how I know when it's time to pray.

651 This New Year Everybody Can Do Something

A preacher asked a hard-working servant girl what she was doing for the Lord. She explained that she had very little time to be involved in "church work." "But," she added, "I always take the newspaper to my bedroom each night."

Surprised, the preacher asked what possible good that could do. "Well," she explained, "I turn to the column of births. I pray that each of the newborns will be led to the Savior at an early age and become a great blessing to the world. Next, I check the column of weddings and pray that the couples will always remain true to each other and build their homes on Christ. Then I go over the death notices and mention the bereaved families by name to God, asking that, in their sorrow they will turn to the Lord."

652 Success in Prayer

Prayer pulls the rope below and the great bell rings above in the ears of God. Some scarcely stir the bell, for they pray so languidly; others give but an occasional pluck at the rope; but he who wins with heaven is the man who grasps the rope boldly and pulls continuously, with all his might.

653 The Power of the Bended Knee

Have you ever watched how a bird sleeps on its perch and never falls off? How does it manage to do this?

The secret is the tendons of the bird's legs. They are so constructed that when the leg is bent at the knee, the claws contract and grip like a steel trap. The claws refuse to let go until the knees are unbent again. The bended knee gives the bird the ability to hold on to his perch so tightly.

Is this not also the secret of the holding power of the Christian? Daniel found this to be true. Surrounded by a pagan environment, tempted to compromise with evil, urged to weaken his grip on God, he refused to let go. He held firm when others faltered because he was a man of prayer. He knew the power of the bended knee.

From sleeping birds we can learn the secret of holding things which are most precious to us—honesty, purity, thoughtfulness, honor, character. That secret is the knee bent in prayer, seeking to get a firmer grip on those values which make life worth living. When we hold firmly to God in prayer, we can rest assured He will hold tightly to us.

654 Just Stopped by for a Visit

When I was a boy, we had a neighbor lady who frequently came to the back door of our home. She never wasted any time coming to the point. Her words were always the same: "I just want to borrow (something)." The problem was she never came at any other time. My mother graciously let her have what she wanted, then she would be gone.

I know my mother never appreciated her as much as the other neighbors, but she never complained.

I often think of this lady when I hear some people pray. Some people never call on God until they want something. God is loving, and He probably gives them what they ask of Him. But would not it be a lot better if they would call on God at other times?

We had another neighbor who came frequently, and never asked for anything. She always started her conversation by saying, "Just stopped by for a visit."

I think God would like us to do that, "Just stop by for a visit." The next time you pray, why not do it—just for a visit?

655 A Much Needed Prayer

Make deaf *my* ears to slander that is told:

Silence *my tongue* to aught that is unkind;

Let only *thoughts* that bless dwell in my mind.

Let me so kindly be, so full of cheer,

That all I meet may feel Thy presence here.

O clothe me in Thy beauty, this I pray,

Let me reveal Thee, Lord, through all the day.

656 The Lord Sent It

Years ago an old lady had no money to buy food. She prayed, "Dear Lord, please send me a side of bacon and a sack of corn meal." Over and over again she prayed the same prayer aloud. One of the town's unscrupulous citizens decided to play a trick on her. He dropped a side of bacon and a sack of corn meal down her chimney. It landed in front of her as she knelt in prayer.

Jumping to her feet, she exclaimed, "Oh Lord! You have answered my prayer!" Then she went all over town telling everyone the good news.

This was too much for the scoundrel who dropped the food down her chimney. He ridiculed her publicly and told her that God did not answer her prayer; he did.

The old lady replied, "Well, the *devil* may have *brought* it, but it was the *Lord* who *sent* it!"

God answers prayers in many ways.

657 Sometime—Somewhere

A young woman, a great lover of flowers, had set out a rare vine at the base of a stone wall. It grew vigorously, but it did not seem to bloom. Day after day she cultivated it and tried every possible way to coax it to bloom.

One morning, as she examined the vine disappointedly, her invalid neighbor called to her and said. "You cannot imagine how much I have been enjoying the blooms of that vine you planted." The owner followed her neighbor's gaze and on the other side of the wall was a mass of blooms. The vine had crept through the crevices and produced flowers on the other side.

How often we think our efforts are thrown away because we do not see fruit! We need to learn that in God's service our prayers, our toil, our crosses are never in vain. They will bear fruit and hearts will receive blessings and joy, sometimes, somewhere.

Preaching

658 Thanks for the Help

A preacher was suddenly called out of town and he asked the new youth minister to conduct services on Sunday. When he returned, he asked his wife how the young man had done. "Not so well," she reported. "It was the poorest sermon I had ever heard—nothing to it at all." Meeting the youth minister later, the preacher asked him how he had managed. "Pretty good, I guess," replied the young man. "As I did not have time to prepare anything myself, I just used one of your sermons."

659 Only a Boy

The old Scots minister climbed wearily into the pulpit. Bowed and dejected, he had just faced the harsh criticism of one of his deacons. "Sir, there is something radically wrong with your ministry. Only one person has been saved this year, and he is only a boy."

The words stung him, for he, too, felt heartbroken that so few had responded to the Gospel; yet still he trusted God for the results.

The service concluded, but the weary man of God lingered on in the church, wondering if there was any point continuing in the ministry. A young lad saw him and waited behind. Please, sir. . . ." "Yes, Robert?" "Do you think if I worked hard for my education that I could ever become a preacher?" "God bless you, my boy," replied the old man with tears in his eyes. "Yes, I think you will become a preacher!"

It was years later that an elderly missionary came back to London from Africa. He had pushed back the boundaries of geographical knowledge and brought savage chiefs under the influence of the Gospel of Peace, given tribes the Bible in their own tongues; but most of all, he had followed the Lord with all of his heart.

Robert Moffat—"only a boy," won to Christ by a tired old man—had become a soul winner!

On one visit to England, Robert told of the need of Africa. Among those who heard him that day was a young Scottish medical student who had given his life to God for missionary service. Robert Moffat's words pierced his heart: "There is a vast plain to the north where I have sometimes seen, in the morning sun, the smoke of a thousand villages where no missionary has ever been."

Filled with the vision of what God wanted him to do, the student asked Mr. Moffat, "Would I do for

Africa?" The direction of David Livingstone's life had been changed.

Who can tell what impact was made through the ministry of the first old Scotsman? "Only a boy" it seemed—yet far-off generations and tribes knew the effect of it!

You never know what God is doing and can do through your witness. Do not be discouraged. But trust and pray on!

660 Accentuate the Positive

In revival services, a young evangelist preached the severity of God's judgment on many of societies' ills. In the spirit of love, the older and wiser pastor approached him after a service and instead of showering compliments on him, said simply, "Young man, don't kick the darkness, turn on the light."

661 Simplicity Preaching

Some preachers have the instincts of aviators—they announce a text, taxi for a short distance, then take off from the earth and disappear into the clouds. After that, only the din of exploding gasoline is heard, signifying that they are flying high, very high, above the heads of their hearers. In other words, a sermon, rightly presented, should not be a meteor, but a sun. Its true test is "Can it make anything grow?"

George Fox, seeking spiritual guidance, walked seven miles to talk to a clergyman who had the reputation for being helpful. "But I found him but like an empty hollow cask," he reported sadly. The problem with our preaching is that too often people come seeking the Water of Life, only to find an empty cask. But sometimes they find water—when the preacher with simplicity and authority proclaims Jesus Christ.

Feed your people with the Bread of Life; cause them to drink deeply of the Water of Life. Be careful not to confuse simple, easy communication with superficial study and shallow preaching. You can dig deep, but you do not have to come up dry. Use your professional tools at home, but take the inspired Word alone into the pulpit. With God's help, your sermons can be profoundly simple and simply profound.

662 Empty Speaker

A minister visited a rural family for supper, and they ate just before church. The minister explained that he couldn't eat very much and preach a good message. After supper the wife asked the husband to go on to the service with the minister while she washed dishes.

When the husband returned, she asked him how the preaching was. "Oh, to tell the truth," was his reply, "he may as well et."

663 Cutting Hearts

Years ago in Atlanta, Georgia, some workmen were laying a sidewalk of stones. One Monday morning a preacher passed by. He watched these busy men with interest for a long time. How impressed he was that a workman could take a tool, strike a stone, and cut it as if it were warm butter.

The man cutting stones kept moving along on his knees cutting more stones and putting them in place.

Shortly the preacher interrupted: "Say, I wish I could cut the hearts of men with my sermons the way you are cutting those stones with that instrument."

The man laying the sidewalk looked up and said, "Did you ever try it like I am doing it—on your knees?"

664 Preaching That Transforms

There was a butcher who ran a little shop on the edge of London. He decided one Sunday that he would go into town and hear the great preacher, Charles Spurgeon. His wife chose not to go with him. So the butcher went to town, went to church, and returned home. That afternoon his wife began to question him about the service.

"What songs did they sing?" He said, "I do not remember." "Well, what was his text?" Again he said, "I do not remember." Somewhat exasperated, his wife wanted to know: "What good did it do for you to go to church this morning?"

The butcher was quiet for a moment. And then he said, "What good? I will tell you what good. You know those scales out in the shop that really weigh just 14 ounces to the pound? Well, before we open for business in the morning, I am going to correct those scales to where they weight a full 16 ounces to the pound."

665 We Cannot Leave the Cross Out

"I have a friend in Scotland," said James Denney, "who is a fishing-tackle maker and an enthusiastic fisherman. He told me once of losing his bait in a mysterious way without catching anything."

The explanation was that by some accident the barb had been broken from the hook. This is exactly what happens when people preach the love of God to men, but leave out of their gospel the essential truth that it is Christ on the cross in whom the love is revealed. In other words, the condemnation of our sins in Christ upon His cross is the barb on the hook.

666 How to Study and Preach

A visitor to the manse was visiting with an old man who lived there with the family after Robert McCheyne's death. "Tell me, how did McCheyne study and preach?" the visitor inquired.

The old man took the visitor into Mr. McCheyne's study and said: "Sit down. Now put your hands over your face, and let the tears fall; that is the way my master studied."

Then the old man asked the visitor to follow him into the church and up the platform to the pulpit. "Lean over; lean way over, and stretch your hands toward the congregation," continued the old friend of McCheyne's, "and now let the tears fall. That is the way my master preached!"

667 They Will Do It Every Time

The preacher had just concluded a hot and scathing sermon on the sin of swearing. He had stated several times that he knew that one of his hearers was guilty.

The service ended. The worshipers one by one filed out the door. The first to go was a woman never suspected of using foul language. With a red and angry face she exclaimed, "I will never darken this door again." Before the astonished preacher could recover from this blast, another said, "Well, brother, if I had known you were near last week, I would have been more careful of my language." A third said, "I think that you might at least have come to me privately about it, rather than telling it to the whole church." A fourth remarked angrily, "I was never so embarrassed in all of my life."

Then came the real culprit—the one at whom the preacher had aimed all his remarks. With a bland and innocent smile he grasped the hand of the preacher and said, "Brother, that was what I call a real sermon. You certainly did put it on them today!"

668 Coffee After the Sermon

A church that loved good fellowship always served coffee after the sermon. The pastor asked a little boy if he knew why they served the coffee. "I think," said the boy, "it is to get the people wide awake before they drive home."

Pride

669 We're Number 1?

When personalized license plates were introduced in Illinois, the Department of Motor Vehicles received over 1,000 requests for the number "1". The state official whose job it was to approve requests said, "I am not about to assign it to someone and disappoint a thousand people." What was his solution? He assigned the number to himself.

A little boy and a little girl were riding a mechanical horse in a shopping mall. The little boy, who was riding in front, turned to the little girl and said, "If one of us would get off, there would be more room for me."

Nowhere is man's creativity more apparent than in his ability to discover new and original ways to commit the original sin. It all began in the Garden of Eden when the devil convinced Adam and Eve that he had found a way for them to move God over and become "Number 1." And the beat goes on—and we keep looking for ways to succeed where Adam and Eve failed. We look for ways to be first on everyone else's priority list. We look for ways to be first in line. We look for ways to be first at the checkout counter. We look for ways to be the first ones getting out of the parking lot. We look for ways to win in the game of "first come, first served." But these are mere symptoms of the real transgression. In the case of Christians, our creativity as original sinners is revealed most clearly when we look for ways to be known as disciples of Christ without following His example.

"We are Number 1! We are Number 1!" All well and good, perhaps, to hear the chant ringing out from football fans, but when we hear it ringing out from our hearts, it is all pride and imagination. Remember, therefore, "He has scattered the proud in the imagination of their hearts" (Luke 1:51).

670 Legalism

The cross of Christ is the only real corrective for legalism. In Matthew 5, James rescues the law from the legalists. We human beings have discovered several ways to reject God's law. We can defy the law, taking the antinomian stance, "I am my own person, I do not need law." Or, like the scribes and the Pharisees, we can reduce the law to hundreds of rules we can keep.

For example, the rabbis "fenced" the Sabbath commandment with 39 categories of possible violation. Each category was then broken down into specific rules. They debated whether one could wear a wooden leg or a brooch on the Sabbath. Would this be "carrying objects" on the Sabbath? Legalism begins with reverence for God's law and ends in making the law trivial and absurd.

The legalist runs the risk of at least three sins. First, he loses sight of the Lawgiver in reducing the law to rules. Second, he reduces God's great claims upon us to manageable rules he can keep. He then loses sight of the holiness of God and the sinfulness of man. (An old African proverb asks, "How do you eat an elephant?" Answer: "One bite at a time.") Third, having lost sight of the holy God and his own sinfulness, the legalist becomes self-righteous and judgmental of others.

In Matthew 5, Jesus restates the law as the Word of the holy God. He is not fighting the liberals; he is taking the legalists to task for reducing the law to bite-sized chunks. "The holy law of the holy God cannot be watered down so easily as you think," he says. "Anyone who reduces the great claims of the law is least in the kingdom. For example, you do not kill. Do you hate? You are proud because you do not commit adultery? Do you lust? You give your wives a legal paper of divorce; what about your commitment to live with them until death do you part? You stay inside the law in your business dealings, but is your word your bond? You live by 'an eye for an eye,' but do you love your enemies and pray for them? You must not reduce God's great claims upon you to a list of rules you can keep."

In view of Jesus' teaching about the holiness of God and this law, what do we see in the cross of Christ? The cross was the sin of sins. But why? Because the Jews and Romans broke the law, "Thou shalt not kill?" Yes, but is that all? Was there not also a law which said that blasphemers must die (Lev. 24:16), and did not many in Israel sincerely see Jesus as a blasphemer? What happened that day outside the walls of Jerusalem was not only the breaking of God's law, it was also the rejection of the holy and loving God who gave the law, the prophets, and even His own Son. The sin was not just the breaking of the law, but the breaking of the Lawgiver's heart. Jesus was crucified by the most conscientious legalists in town.

As we stand before the cross we see a love so wide, so deep, so high that all human beings come within its reach. In the cross, God reaches out once again to those who refuse to acknowledge His law and to those legalists who trivialize His law and declare themselves righteous. All our human pride and pretension is shattered on the rock called Golgotha. The cross is the only real correction for legalism.

671 False Measurements

A little boy came running to his mother, shouting, "Mother, I am nine feet tall." His mother responded, "Don't talk such nonsense." "But," he said, "I really *am* nine feet tall. I measured myself." "Well, how did you measure yourself?" asked his mother. "I took off my shoe and measured myself with that. It is the same size as my foot, and I really am nine feet."

With a smile the mother replied, "Now I understand, my son, but I have to tell you that your measure was not the right one. We do not measure ourselves by the size of our own feet, but we must use a 12-inch ruler."

A lot of people are like the little boy. They are proud of something about which there is really no glory.

672 *Would You Hesitate to Ask?*

I heard the other day about a roomful of doctors eating together. One doctor got up from the table, left the room, and in minutes he was dead. A morsel of food had lodged in his windpipe, and so he choked to death.

The tragedy of this incident is heightened by the fact that probably any one of those doctors could have performed the Heimlich Maneuver or, if need be, a tracheotomy to restore his breathing. But they did not know anything was wrong—he did not tell them. He just got up and left. And so he died.

Have you been keeping a problem to yourself that is about to get you down? Why not share it with at least one of your fellow Christians? Do not let false pride keep you

from saying, "I need help." We all do.

673 *The Futility of Pride*

"When pride cometh, then cometh shame: But with the lowly is wisdom" (Prov. 11:2). "Only by pride cometh contentions" (Prov. 13:10). In the book of Proverbs, pride is used in two senses. (1) The good sense. In this sense, it is admirable and necessary. It is associated with self-respect and personal dignity. However, we must always avoid self-contempt. "I am a nobody" is not a way to gain respect from others. Acts 2:47 shows us that it is alright to have respect from other people. This kind of pride is acceptable. (2) The bad sense is associated with arrogance, self-esteem, self-importance, and all such similar vices. Webster defines it this way: The quality or state of being proud: as inordinate self-esteem: conceit. Let us keep pride as God wants it. The chin and head up, not our nose. The pride of life is a channel by which Satan tempts man to sin (1 John 2:15-17).

In John 13 we find the disciples would not wash one another's feet because it would show they were inferior and forfeit their position in the kingdom. Christ deflated their egos and pride by washing their feet, showing that He was the greatest of all and serves all. We see a lot of people in the church today fighting for the top, but very few reach for towels. There are many today that pride destroys. It kept Felix from obeying the gospel (Acts

24:25). It also cost Ananias and Sapphira their lives. Matthew 5:3 says, "Blessed are the poor in spirit, for theirs is the kingdom of heaven." We must be willing to assume the role of beggar to enter the kingdom of heaven. Pride will cause us not to admit wrong or have compassion on our fellow man. It will cause us to live beyond our means (Rom. 13:8). Pride leads to rebellion (Ps. 10:4); also apostasy (1 Tim. 3:6). "He who stands on a pedestal has no place but to step off"—a Chinese proverb.

674 Who Is King of the Jungle—the Lion or the Elephant?

A big, mean lion met a monkey in the jungle. The lion pounced on the poor monkey and said, "Who is king of the jungle?" The frightened monkey replied, "You are, O mighty lion." So the lion let him go. The next animal the lion met was a zebra. He pounced on it and roared, "Who is king of the jungle?" "You are, O mighty lion." So the lion let him go. The lion next met an elephant and asked the same question. The elephant grabbed the lion, twirled him around the threw him 50 feet. The lion picked himself up and huffed, "Just because you don't know the answer is no reason to get so rough."

675 Allow God to Play His Music in Your Life

He was an old organist of the celebrated Freiburg Cathedral, but now that his fingers had lost their skill, he was made custodian of the great organ.

One day a visitor came to the cathedral and asked to play the organ, but the custodian refused. "No one but myself and the present organist has ever touched the keys," the custodian objected.

But the visitor pleaded until he was given permission to play a few notes. He slipped into the seat and touched first one note and then another. Then, running his fingers over the keys, he filled the whole cathedral with such beautiful music that the organist was entranced. When the visitor finished, the old custodian came to him and asked his name. And the visitor replied, "My name is Felix Mendelssohn."

And until the end of his life, the old organist would exclaim over and over, "To think I almost missed hearing Mendelssohn play on my organ!"

How many souls have been the losers for not letting the Master touch their hearts with heavenly music!

676 No Errands, Please!

A beggar sat at the gate of the rich man's home from whose bountiful hand he had received constant gifts.

One day the rich man wanted to send a message as quickly as possible. Since his servants were all busy, he found the beggar and asked him to make the delivery for him. Lifting himself up with pride, the beggar answered his benefactor with these astonishing words, "I solicit alms, sir, but I do not run errands."

How many people treat their heavenly Father in this manner! If it were not for Him we would not have the many blessings which come from His hands. Then, when He wants us to go on an errand, or to carry a message of Jesus' love to wayward men, we say, "No, Lord; I solicit your blessings, but I do not run errands."

677 *Big Is Not So Important*

Napoleon Bonaparte was a very small man. While in training, he was often chided about his stature. One young officer especially delighted in "pulling rank" on the "Little Corporal," as he was called by the other men of his company. Said the arrogant one, "I am a bigger man than you any day." "Not bigger," replied Napoleon, "just taller." History was to prove how right he was!

678 *A Sucker or a Worker?*

One day a peasant drove his sturdy ox through the village on the way to work the fields.

A flea sat on the ox's nose. At the end of the day, the ox and peasant trudged back through the village, the fields now plowed, and the flea still perched on the ox's nose.

The peasant and the ox trudged by the villages in silence. The flea, however, bowed grandly to every side, proclaiming "We've been plowing."

679 *Alter Your Direction*

A newly commissioned Navy captain took great pride in his first assignment to be in command of a battleship. One stormy night the captain saw a light moving steadily in their direction. He ordered the signalman to send the following message: "Change your course ten degrees to the south." The reply came back: "Change your course ten degrees to the north."

The captain was determined not to give way to another vessel, and so he sent a counter message. "Alter your direction ten degrees. I am the captain." The answer flashed back promptly: "Alter your direction. I am the lighthouse."

There are times when all of us have to identify with the captain; times when we allow self-will to set us off on a collision course.

"I have my rights," we say, determined to have our own way. But God, whose Word is like a lighthouse with a penetrating and unchangeable beacon, reveals a rocky shore ahead and finally we do as the captain surely did. We obey.

Our prayer for ourselves, and for the church should be as Jesus prayed, "Not my will, but Thine be done."

Priorities

680 How Much of the Lord's Time Have You Stolen?

There was a story in a Rochester, Texas church bulletin about a young man who was working in a large department store, being told by his employer that he would be required to work on Sunday. It so happened that the hours assigned to him would have prevented his attending any of the worship services to which he had been accustomed to attending since childhood.

The young man informed his employer that he would not be able to continue his work under these conditions, and his employer told him he would have to go.

A few days later, the young man answered an ad in the paper from a bank which had advertised a vacancy for a teller. In checking the young man's previous employers, the bank president contacted the department store head and inquired as to the boy's record and whether he could recommend him. The store manager replied, "Why, yes, I will be glad to recommend him. He will make you a good man. I just fired him a few days ago."

"Fired him?" the bank president exclaimed. "Why would you recommend a man whom you just recently dismissed from your service?" The store manager explained the circumstances under which the boy was released, and remarked, "I know he will make you a good man for your bank, because if he will not steal the Lord's time, he will not steal your money."

681 Dearer Than Life

In the forests of Northern Europe lives the ermine, a small animal known best for its snow-white fur. Instinctively, this animal protects its glossy coat of fur with great care lest it become soiled.

Hunters often capitalize on this trait. Instead of setting a mechanical trap to catch the ermine, they find its home in a cleft of a rock or a hollow tree and daub the entrance and the interior with tar. Then their dogs start the chase, and the frightened ermine flees toward its home. But finding it covered with dirt, he spurns his place of safety. Rather than soil his white fur, he courageously faces the yelping dogs who hold him at bay until the hunters capture him. To the ermine, purity is dearer than life!

The Lord wants us to be a people who will keep ourselves "unspotted from the world."

682 Help! My Hair Is All Gone!

How do we get it all done? There are so many things to do. Housework, homework, away-from-home-

274

work, schoolwork and church work all demand our attention. We have got to bring home the bacon, put it on the table, get the kids to the ball-game, get everything done around the house, spend time together as a family and find time for the Lord all on the same day. This probably does not even begin to describe your busy schedule. In a world full of things that need to be done, where do we go to get some sense of what to do first? How do we determine our priorities? Most of us just jump right in and overload ourselves. As a result we begin to get very nervous. We say to ourselves, "Well, I will just have to try harder. After all, other people seem to be able to manage all this, so I should be able to do it too." The tension which results from this overload seems to correspond directly with the amount of hair on our heads. The more we overload ourselves, the more we pull out our hair in frustration. Finally we realize that we just cannot do it all. With this realization comes two choices: We can go crazy trying to keep up with the unhealthy pace we have set and be grouchy, mean, unsatisfied, unfulfilled and unhappy. Or, we can prioritize our lives to decide which activities are the most important and thus be happier, more fulfilled and much more satisfied with the direction we have taken.

Jesus told His disciples to be "wise as serpents" (Matt. 10:16). How can we become wise? How do we go about the process of or-ganizing and prioritizing our lives? Here are some suggestions that will help us get started.

1. Pray. This is the single most important thing that we do. We need guidance from the Lord, and He has promised to give it to us if we will only ask Him for it. We need to be as specific as we can, not for God's sake, but because it will help us to focus on exactly what we need to do and be asking for (James 1:5).

2. Seek wise counsel. Since we cannot know all that we need to know on every subject, we need to be searching for counsel from people we know who are wise.

3. Plan. Without an organized plan, even the noblest of ideas will fizzle out.

4. Prioritize. Once you have set your goals, decide which parts of your plan need your attention first. You may find that you need to streamline your objectives—maybe even cut something out (Matt. 6:33).

5. Act. Now that you have prayerfully and thoughtfully designed your plan, take action. Watch as some of your worries seem to disappear and your hair begins to grow back.

683 Follow Me—Now!

"And another also said, 'Lord, I will follow Thee; but let me first go bid them farewell which are at home at my house.' And Jesus said to him, 'No man, having put his hand to the plough, and looking back, is fit for the kingdom of God'" (Luke 9:61, 62).

• "I will follow You, Lord, but first let me see if my parents approve."

• "I will follow You, Lord, but first let me go to a few more parties. And as soon as I get that out of my system, I will settle down."

• "I will follow You, Lord, but first let me get married. As soon as I establish a home, I will follow you."

• "We will follow You, Lord, but first let us raise our children. They are so small now, and it is difficult to carry them along while following You."

• "We will follow You, Lord, but first let us get our children through high school. We have to work six days a week to pay the bills, and the children are so busy with school activities that there just is not time to follow You."

• "I would like to follow You now, Lord, but I must first see if my husband will come, too. I do not want to follow You alone."

• "I will follow You, Lord, but first let me retire. Then I will have time to follow you."

• "I would like to follow You, Lord, but it is too late now. I have not done it all these years, and You cannot teach an old dog new tricks."

Death comes at last, and the day of salvation is over. One is separated from God eternally because one put off following Christ until it was too late.

684 Too High a Cost

Dale Carnegie tells of a visit to Yellowstone Park in earlier days when tourists could watch the rangers feed the grizzly bears. One night the ranger brought garbage to attract the huge creatures, which, it is said, can whip any animal in the West except perhaps the buffalo and the Kodiak bear. But Carnegie noticed that while eating, the bears would growl and send other little animals scurrying, but they would allow one little creature to eat with them—the skunk! Though it was obvious that the grizzlies resented the skunk for its brazen impudence and would have loved to have their revenge, they didn't. And you can guess why. The cost of getting even was just too high!

685 Choice Between Sight or Memory

A man's sight left him. He sought the counsel of a trusted medical friend who prescribed a medicine for him. The man took the medicine regularly for four days, and his sight returned to him, but he could no longer remember anything. His friend suggested a remedy for that, too. After a few days his memory came back to him, but he went blind again. This continued for sometime. Eventually his friend said, "It looks like you have to decide which you want—your sight or your memory." The man thought for a moment and then said, "I believe I would prefer my sight. I would rather see where I am going than remember where I have been!" Where are you going?

686 Sir Walter Scott's Diary

The last words found in Sir Walter Scott's diary were: "Tomorrow we shall. . . ." But there was no tomorrow for him. He died with good intentions to accomplish a certain goal—a goal that was neither stated in his diary nor accomplished by him.

Every person has goals and dreams that he or she longs for, plans for, and even begins to reach for—yet there are many people who fall short of their goals simply because of limited time or opportunity. And that is why it is always important to get busy and do the right thing immediately. Never delay that which needs to be done today.

Settling accounts with the Lord should never be put on a back burner, neither for salvation, for commitment, nor for service.

687 Living in Constant Crises

Have you ever thought about an ambulance? An ambulance tears around town with its siren blaring. It is always going to a crisis or leaving a crisis. It is built for emergencies.

Many people live the same way. They run their lives with a siren going. Every day is desperate, and every moment is a crisis, or preparation for one. Such as harried existence leaves no room for smelling roses or enjoying sunsets. Even worse, it leaves no time for sharing friendships and building love.

Finally, what if some of the things you are tearing around to do did not get done? Suppose you substituted a quiet walk around the block or time off to call on a friend or time out to read a book? Suppose you wrote an encouraging note to someone who really needed it? Would your world fall apart? Or would it perhaps get back into perspective? So "Seek first his kingdom and his righteousness and all these things will be given to you as well" (Matt. 6:33).

688 Too Busy

Too busy to read the Bible, too busy to wait and pray
Too busy to speak out kindly to someone by the way!
To busy to care and struggle, to think of the life to come
Too busy building mansions, to plan for the heavenly home.
Too busy to help a brother who faces the winter blast.
Too busy to share his burden, when self in the balance is cast.
Too busy for all that is holy on earth beneath the sky;
Too busy to serve the Master, but not too busy to die.

689 Take Time

Take time to think—it is the source of power.
Take time to play—it is the secret of perpetual youth.
Take time to be friendly—it is the road to happiness.
Take time to love—it is a God-given privilege.
Take time to pray—it is the greatest power on earth.

Take time to give—life is too short to be selfish.

690 Feed Poor Boys, Sir!

"I am the bread of life" John 6:35. Terry Bell relates a memorable experience:

The year was 1969. It was my first "real" mission trip. I was in a little village in South India and terribly homesick. I was 20 years old and starving for a "good ole" American cheeseburger. I had not had one in 2 1/2 months.

The land around me was semi-jungle, semi-bush. Tarzan would have felt right at home, but I did not.

One boring afternoon I whiled away the hours by playing with the monkeys that forever enlivened our premises. Standing out on the balcony, I teased the little primate creeps by giving them doughballs made from a loaf of bread I was holding. A hairy hand (or is it a paw?) would reach over the edge of the roof, I would place a morsel in it, and like lightning, it was retracted to the squealing and grunting delight of his monkey-minded buddies. What a great game!

Suddenly I realized that on the street below my balcony a crowd had gathered. They were not nearly as entertained by this "monkeying around" as I was. One thin-faced, sickly looking boy looked up at me with bulging eyes. In broken English, he said, "Master, feed poor boys, not monkeys."

It was like a stab in the heart. In the street below were orphans, beggars, lepers . . . the off-scourings of humankind. Mothers and fathers who had starving children. Children who watched malnourished parents die. Parents who would watch their hungry children watching *them* die, knowing they left them to a miserable life on the streets. And there I was, playing games with the bread that for them was so precious. I was cut to the heart.

Every day this scene is reenacted in thousands of padded-pew churches, whose priorities are playing games with monkeys.

691 A Christian First

The mother watched as her four-year-old daughter played while taking her bath. The little girl sang songs that she had heard and the mother was fascinated by her ability to remember the words and the tunes of the songs. As she watched and listened to her daughter she began to think to herself, "I wonder what she will be when she grows up?" And as most of us as proud parents would do, she began to think about all the things that she could be. "She could be a singer, an actress, a teacher. . . ." After thinking about all the marvelous things her daughter might grow up to be she decided to ask her daughter what she wanted to be when she grew up. The little girl's response was, "A Christian first." The young mother said she was deeply humbled by the child's response. While she had been thinking in terms of a career, the little girl pointed out that first she wanted to be a Christian.

692 Charles Finney's Talk

Some years ago, a young graduate reported to a law office for training or apprenticeship. The senior lawyer who hired him quickly indoctrinated him in the office routine. Then the young lawyer sat at his desk and carried on this conversation with himself.

"What are you going to do when you finish your apprenticeship?"

"Hang out my shingle and practice law, of course!"

"What then?"

"Why, make a lot of money!"

"What then?"

"When I get rich I shall retire."

"What then?"

"Well, I will die."

"What then?"

His whole body trembling, Charles G. Finney rushed out of the office and ran to a park some few hundred yards distant. He remained there in prayer, vowing that he would not return to his office or to his room until he had settled his life's work. He saw himself as he was—selfish, ambitious, sinful. And he gave himself to the Lord for Him to use. Leaving the park, Finney stepped forth, in faith in God, to a life of usefulness rarely paralleled in the last two centuries.

693 What You Can and Cannot Control

You cannot control the length of you life—but you can control its width and depth.

You cannot control the contour of your face—but you can control its expression.

You cannot control the weather —but you can control the atmosphere of your mind.

Why worry about things you cannot control when you can keep yourself busy controlling the things that depend on you?

694 Christian, Think Before You Drink

Dr. Clarence McCartney told the following story:

A young man met with the church board and was received into membership; however, on his way out, he was asked what his business was. When the board understood that he was in the liquor business, the decision of the board was revoked, causing the young man to fly into a rage. The liquor business was that of his father and his grandfather as well. He wished hereafter to have nothing to do with any pastor or church. He had been "insulted."

Two months elapsed. The young man reappeared again with this explanation: "I followed your suggestion to visit the clients of my business. I followed our wagon to saloons, the rich man's clubs, the poor man's hovels, to destitute homes, and I saw the destruction that the liquor business I was engaged in caused. As a result, I have severed connections with my destructive business. I have confessed my sin to God, and I now desire to be received into membership in the church."

695 Palace on Earth—Shack in Heaven

A very rich lady dreamed she died and was taken to heaven. She was given an angel to escort her to her new home. She dreamed the angel took her past many exquisite mansions.

Passing one of the most elegant, the angel said, "And this is the mansion of your servant who died last year." Since this was a fine home, the lady became really excited about the anticipated size of her new home. Soon they rounded a turn and came upon a small shack.

"Here is your new home," the angel said.

"Is this all?" she said. "I was of a very wealthy family on earth," she said.

"Well," the angel explained, "this is all you sent up."

She awoke abruptly and resolved to make a drastic change in the priorities of her life.

696 How Much Time For God?

Said the preacher to the inactive member, "I am sorry to see that you have quit the church." Said the inactive member, indignantly, "But, I have not quit." The minister replied, "you do not attend worship or study. You do not give of your money. And you do not participate in fellowship or work. You do not offer to be of assistance in helping others. What is it you would do, if you quit, that you have not already done?

697 The Years of Our Lives

Someone has figured that in the average life span of 70 years, we will spend our time this way:

Eight years in amusements
Six years at the dinner table
Five years in transportation
Four years in conversation
Three years sick or convalescing
Less than one year for God—that is if a person attends a 90-minute service every Sunday and prays every day for 10 minutes.

698 The Law of Small Potatoes

Many years ago, Chinese farmers theorized that they could eat their big potatoes and keep the small potatoes for seed. Consequently, they ate the big potatoes and planted the small potatoes. As a result of this practice for many years, the Chinese farmers made the startling discovery: nature had reduced all their potatoes to the size of marbles.

A new understanding of the law of life came to these farmers. They learned through bitter experience that they could not have the best things of life for themselves and use the leftovers for seed. The law of life decreed that the harvest would reflect the planting.

In another sense, planting small potatoes is still a common practice. We take the big things of life for ourselves and plant the leftovers. We expect that by some crazy twist of spiritual laws, our selfishness will be rewarded with unselfishness.

But we cannot eat the big potatoes and have them, too!

What size potatoes have you been planting spiritually? "Be not deceived; God is not mocked; for whatever a man sows, that shall he also reap" (Gal. 6:7).

699 The Story of a Fool

One day there was a little task
God wanted me to do.
I said, "Lord, You'll have to wait,
I've got no time for You.

I have this little child to raise
And prices are so high;
Besides we've found a house and lot
We thought we'd like to buy."

So I took on some extra work,
No church—I was too tired.
But I got up on Monday morning,
I had to—or get fired!

And so I went along for years
With never a thought of God;
Until one day my little child
Was laid beneath the sod.

The lovely home we'd bought for her
Seemed empty now—so bare.
In anguish then I turned to God
And cried, "It isn't fair.

That you should take my little one
And cause my wife these tears;
When we have been so happy here
These few, short, busy years."

'Twas then I heard the voice of God
Come ringing in my ear—
"I called upon you once but then
My cry you would not hear.

Now in your grief you cry for Me,
'Why must this sad thing be?'
Your little child became your god,
She took the place of Me."

Oh my dear friend, find time for God
In everything you do
If not, you'll find that one day He
Shall have no time for you!

Problems

700 From Problem to Profit

About 100 years ago there was a candlestick maker who often stopped at a market and bought a fish for his evening meal. It was wrapped in ordinary paper which became soggy, and the passengers on the street car always complained about the odor.

One morning he dipped the paper in molten wax. That day he wrapped his fish in the treated paper. It did not become soggy, and there was no odor.

That is how waxed paper was born.

Got a problem? Do not curse it. Look for a cure.

701 Faith, Hope, Love

One of the most memorable sermons was preached by the late Emil Brunner at the Fraumunster Kirche in Zurich, Switzerland. It was based on the phrase, "faith, hope, and love." The points were these: Every man has a past, a present, and a future. Every man has a problem in his past, a problem in his present, and a problem in his future. The problem in our past is sin, but God has an answer to that problem. The answer is faith—faith in the death and resurrection of the Lord Jesus Christ. The problem in our future is death, but God has an answer to that problem also. The answer to that problem is hope—hope in Christ's return based on the fact of His historical resurrection and His promises. The problem in our present is hate, and God's answer to that problem is love. It is the love of Christ lived out in the lives of those who trust Him.

702 This Too Shall Pass

"What is your favorite Scripture?" someone once asked an elderly woman. "My favorite Scripture is, '. . . and it came to pass. . . .'" When asked why she chose this one she said, "Because it does not say, '. . . it came to stay. . . .'"

Everything is temporary. What will not be changed by the passing of time will be changed by the end of time. The biblical principle is that we are to look beyond any problem, suffering, and confusion of this time and look to the future reward. Paul said, "I consider that our present sufferings are not worth comparing with the glory that will be revealed in us" (Rom. 8:18).

We can live with present problems because of their temporal nature. Why bother to fuss, fume and stew over something that will be gone sooner or later? Instead, concentrate all your energy on what you can influence, and attempt to make a better life for yourself and those in your circle of influence.

703 Don't Let Hurts Hurt You

Rejections, defeats, and failures that all of us have experienced can create enough negative feelings to destroy us. Be careful! Often the most painful wounds are not the scars that are outwardly seen, but the hidden wounds deep in the heart. Being hidden, they are often the most dangerous.

Setbacks in our lives can take the joy out of living. Our faith is weakened, and if we collect enough hurts it will stop us from wanting to press forward. Even success can make one the target of criticism. Do not let the hurts hurt you!

Look at Job. A man of the land of Uz, blameless, upright, one who feared God, and one who turned away from evil. Job had seven sons and three daughters, a beautiful family. He was considered "the greatest of all the men of the east." He lost it all in the twinkling of an eye. He lost his health, wealth, and family. He hurt. His wife hurt. His friends hurt. He was knocked down but not out. He had lost some of the passionate power to grow and some of his enthusiasm had diminished, but he checked his negative thinking and that of his wife and friends and stated, "I will forget my complaint, I will leave off my sad countenance and be cheerful." How could he after undergoing so much hurt?

Along the shoreline in California it is a common sight to see whales stopping alongside rocks as they migrate from Alaska to Mexico to scrape off barnacles. In our lifetime we also will pick up a collection of personal barnacles that will attach themselves like parasites sapping the life out of us. They must be scraped off.

How did Job do it? The same way we can do it—through faith. Faith is the only thing that can heal the hurts. Job scraped the barnacles off. It was painful! The scars would remain but his life was put back together. Strong belief in God was the medicine. His wife and his friends could not do it—only God could!

Job said, "I know that you [God] can do all things; no plan of yours can be thwarted" (Job 42:2). Paul told the Corinthians, ". . . God will not let you be tempted beyond what you can bear . . . he will also provide a way out so that you can stand up under it" (1 Cor. 10:13).

The Lord blessed the latter days of Job (42:12) with great material blessings, and it was said of his new daughters that "in all the land no women were found so fair. . . ." Job lived 140 years after the hurts and saw sons, grandsons, great-grandsons, and great-great-grandsons. You can also forget your hurts, leave off your sad countenance, and be cheerful if you turn to God for your strength to do so.

704 I Am Not Discouraged!

A man stopped to watch a ball game between two young teams.

As he walked toward the bleachers, he asked one of the players, "What is the score?" The young fellow replied, "We are behind 18 to nothing."

"Well," said the man, "I must say you don't look discouraged."

"Discouraged?" the player said with a puzzled look. "Why should we be discouraged? We haven't had our turn to bat yet."

The army of Israel faced a giant, but a young man named David thought, "I have not had my turn," and he won!

The twelve disciples saw 5,000 hungry people and said, "Send the crowds away, so they can buy some food." But Jesus thought, "I have not had my turn yet!"

The angry mob had Pilate seal the tomb where Jesus was buried, but God knew, "I have not had my turn yet!"

The church is ready to "go to bat" and, like others, who have placed their trust in God, we will win!

Remember these words of Jesus: "I will build My church, and the gates of Hades will not overcome it" (Matt. 16:18).

705 When Our Blemishes Become Assets

The story is told of a friend by the name of Webb Young. Webb Young grew beautiful apples, and he advertised them to a very select clientele as "perfect." One year just before time to harvest his apples, a heavy hail storm came. It did not harm the apples, but it left unsightly brown spots on them. He felt hopelessly defeated. He could not afford to send his apples out with those brown spots on them.

A lesser man would have given up, but he kept thinking until he came up with a saving idea. He harvested the apples and packed them in boxes, as he normally did. Then in each box he placed a card which stated that these apples were grown in high altitude and that the chill of the mountain made the apples firm. He also explained that in these high altitudes they often have hail storms. Then he said that if one will look closely at the apples, hail marks upon them can be observed. It is a matter of record that the next year the overwhelming majority of his orders were for "hail-marked" apples.

For Webb Young and his apples— the blemishes became assets.

706 Trouble Tree

The carpenter I hired to help me restore an old farmhouse had just finished up a rough first day on the job. A flat tire had made him lose an hour of work, his electric saw quit, and now his ancient pickup refused to start.

While I drove him home, he sat in stony silence. On arriving, he invited me in to meet his family. As we walked toward the front door, he paused briefly at a small tree, touching the tips of the branches with both hands.

Then, opening the door, he underwent an amazing transformation. His tanned face was wreathed in smiles, and he hugged his two small children and gave his wife a kiss.

Afterwards he walked me to the car. We passed the tree and my curiosity got the best of me. I asked him about what I had seen him do earlier.

"Oh, that is my 'trouble tree,' " he replied. "I know I cannot help having troubles on the job, but one thing is for sure—troubles do not belong in the house with my wife and the children. So I just hang 'em on the tree every night when I come home; then in the morning, I pick them up again.

"Funny thing is," he said smilingly, "when I come out in the morning to pick them up, there are not as many as I remember hanging up the night before."

707 The Big and the Small Souls

The great soul prays, "Lord, make me as big as my problem." The little soul prays, "Lord, let me off easy."

The giant soul asks, "Lord, give me strength sufficient for a hard day," while the small soul begs, "Lord, let me have a lighter load."

The busy soul prays, "Lord, stand with me until I finish my task," while the weak soul says, "I got tired and quit."

708 Songs in the Night

Elihu, in the Book of Job, asked, "Where is God who giveth songs in the night?" David in the 42nd Psalm, answered, "In the night His songs shall be with me."

The strongest argument of the atheist has to do with the problem of human suffering. Epicurus, who lived 342-270 B.C., presented three concepts about God and human suffering: (1) If God wishes to prevent evil and cannot, He is not all powerful; (2) If God can prevent evil and will not, He is not good; (3) If God has the power and will to eliminate evil, why is there evil in the world? The fallacy is his belief that no good can be served by God's allowing evil or suffering.

Everyone will pass through dark valleys sooner or later. All will become ill. Some will become permanently ill. It is an illusion that this side of heaven all diseases will be wiped out. For all of us there will be periods of suffering, bereavement, discouragement, danger and difficulty.

There are those who give up their fidelity to God because they do not believe God is fair. They ask, "What have I done to deserve this?" "Why are children born retarded or born dead?" "Why is there cancer?" "Why me?"

How will we answer these and similar questions? How will we learn to sing songs at night? By having faith in the sovereignty of God. The world is not being ruled by a chance but by a God who is in control. Even a sparrow cannot fall without His notice. So, He cares about us. Nothing can happen that does not concern God.

Jesus sang in the darkest night of His life on earth. The Apostle John sang songs of joy and praise while in exile on the island of Patmos. At midnight, David arose to give thanks to God (Ps. 119:62). Paul said, "When I am weak, then I am strong" (2 Cor. 12:10).

Our lives will become stronger and our spirituality deeper when we learn to sing at midnight.

709 Why Not?

Why Not—give a friend a tract?

Why Not—help an older couple with their groceries?

Why Not—share with a neighbor in need?

Why Not—talk to a friend about his soul?

Why Not—help a friend with a personal problem?

Why Not—have a Bible study with a friend in your home?

Why Not—visit with the newcomer in your community?

Why Not—invite your children's friends to Bible study?

Why Not—show hospitality in your home?

Why Not—give encouragement to a new brother?

Why Not—give support to those who are having trouble in their marriage?

Why Not—encourage someone to take a Bible correspondence course?

Why Not—show concern to those who have lost a loved one?

Why Not—show to others that Christianity is worth sharing anytime, anywhere?

Why Not—invite the checkout person at the grocery to worship service?

Why Not—give a smile to someone today? Let them know that you are happy as a Christian?

Why Not—be nice to people even when you do not feel like it?

Why Not—let God work His purposes in your life?

Why Not—start loving your neighbors as yourself?

710 Mules, Wells, and Learning How to Live

There is a story about an old farmer whose mule fell into a well. After many unsuccessful attempts to haul the mule out of the hole, the farmer decided it was hopeless. With sadness, he instructed his boys to fill up several truckloads of dirt and just bury the old mule right in the well. Dutifully, the boys backed up the truck filled with dirt, and shovel by shovel, they began to fill the well and bury the mule. The mule didn't take kindly to this action. The first shovel of dirt hit him square on the head, got in his eyes and mouth, and made him sneeze.

Every shovel full after that hit him somewhere, causing the old mule to stomp around in the bottom of the well. Several truckloads of dirt later, the mule was still stomping and packing dirt firmly underneath his feet. Little by little, that mule was lifting itself out of the hole. Sure enough, about mid-afternoon that mule simply stepped out of the well and snorted at the whole business.

There are different ways people have of dealing with problems life throws at them. Some are constant complainers. They do not handle setbacks and upsets very well. Some of them cannot even handle normal events. Others are defeated at the slightest difficulty. Quite a few get confused, turned around and seem not to know what to do. Then there are a few who are unconquerable. They are like the mule. Problems can hit them square on the head, but they just stomp around enough until they actually use the problem to rise above it.

Look at the great heroes of the Bible. They were men and women who could match the occasion. Moses was that kind of man. Surely Joseph, who rose from the bottom of a pit to a leader of Egypt, was that kind of man. Could David have been anything other than the kind of man who rose above his faults and problems? Esther was surely the kind of woman who did not let problems paralyze her. On and on we could go, but you see the point.

How was all this done? The reason such people could rise out of the "wells" of life is because they all had a great faith in God. It is a childish attitude that says, "If God loved me, He would take away all these problems." Not so! The opposite is really true. If God loves you, He will reveal Himself to you through His Word and give you opportunity to let your faith lift you up. God wants us to learn how to do it. He wants us to work at it. When you realize that and accept it, it will give you a power to deal with living you never had before.

711 May We Always Have:

Enough happiness to keep us sweet;

Enough sorrow to keep us human;

Enough faith to give us courage;

Enough wealth to meet our needs;

Enough trials to keep us strong;

Enough failure to keep us humble;

Enough friends to give us comfort;

Enough determination to make each day a good one.

Repentance

712 First Step Toward New Life

Quite a few years ago, Governor Neff of the State of Texas received an invitation to speak at one of the penitentiaries in that state. He spoke to the assembled prisoners, and afterward said that he would be around for a while to listen to anything any of the convicts might wish to tell him. He would take as much time as they wanted, and anything they would tell him would be kept in confidence.

The convicts began to come, one at a time. One after another told him a story of how they had been unjustly sentenced, were innocent, and wished to get out. Finally one man came through who said to him, "Governor Neff, I do not want to take much of your time. I only want to say that I really did what they convicted me of. But I have been here a number of years. I believe I have paid my debt to society, and that, if I were to be released, I would be able to live an upright life and show myself worthy of your mercy."

This was the man whom Governor Neff pardoned.

713 The Power of Repentance

Christopher D. Green writes:

"You could say that it was part of the environment surrounding our house. It was an unwritten code held sacred to all in the family. From the time I can remember being able to remember things, I grew up understanding what it meant to say, 'I'm sorry.' From childhood, I recall my parents instilling in me and my sister that if we were truly sorry for something we had done, we could always ask for forgiveness and we would be forgiven. It was a mutual obligation both parties (the inflicter and the inflicted) had to accept. Through the realization we had wronged another member of the family, unity could be restored with those simple words, 'I'm sorry.'

"I remember a time when this worked amazingly well, until I abused the system. I still remember breaking my sister's baton over my knee when I was about eight years old. It was then I learned about the power of repentance. As I forced the midpoint of that lightweight baton over my knee, I remember thinking, 'Saying "I'm sorry" will fix this!' Repeated 'I'm sorry's' were declared in my defense, but Mom saw through the veil of charade. I had abused the right to say 'I'm sorry'! Finally, after a long discussion, I was forgiven. Not for breaking the baton as much as I was forgiven of abusing the ability to repent and say I was sorry.

"There are times now when I think of how I have abused the repentance God has provided through Christ. Have I taken advantage of our relationship?"

714 The Incurable Inebriate

A man named Henry Milans lay in a ward of Bellevue Hospital in New York. A group of students stood around his bed, while the instructing professor remarked: "We have discovered in this man all the marked indications of the incurable inebriate. Note the dancing eyes. Note the trembling of the hands and other members of his body. This man can never be cured. He must die as he has lived, a drunkard. Nothing can save him."

Not long after that, Ensign Hall of the Salvation Army describes what happened. "Amid the fervent 'Hallelujahs!' of Christians in the hall, Milans stumbled forward. The change that took place in him was remarkable. What science was unable to do, Christ accomplished in a moment."

Nineteen years after his conversion, he testified: "From that moment to the present I have never been tempted to take a drink of anything with alcohol in it. I should have to learn all over again to love the drink that was for 35 years the greatest love of my life."

715 A Tour and a Turn Around

A backslidden member of Dr. Philips Brooks' parish called at the study to request that his name be dropped from the roll. Dr. Brooks reminded him that the step he proposed was a serious one and appealed to him to reconsider. However, the man was insistent.

Just then a poorly dressed boy entered the study with a note scribbled in pencil on crumpled paper. After Dr. Brooks read it, he challenged his visitor: "My friend, this note is from a poor, sick woman who is requesting that I visit her. I must go to preach a funeral message in a few minutes. Would you be good enough to go along with this lad to his home and supply whatever his mother needs?"

"Certainly, Dr. Brooks, I shall gladly do that for you and for her," was the answer.

He followed the lad down the wide street into narrower streets and finally, into an alley. The boy stopped at a shanty whose half-open door, held by one hinge, led into an unlighted room. When the stranger stepped in, the half-blinded woman welcomed him, "Oh, Dr. Brooks, I knew you would come! You are God's man. You always come to the call of trouble. I am sick and hungry, but first I want you to pray for me. Please pray."

The backslider had not prayed in years. Should he tell her that he was not Dr. Brooks? While he was hesitating, she pleaded, "Oh, pray for me." His heart would not let him refuse the request. He dropped on his knees. Following his first sentence which was a petition for himself in his own backslidden condition, he prayed for her and closed the prayer. Then he explained, "My dear woman you have discovered by this time I am not Dr. Brooks. He is conducting a funeral and he sent me to help you. Oh, how you have helped me! What do you need?"

She told him anything would be appreciated. There was no food, fuel, or medicine. Accompanied by the son, they went to a store, filled a basket with fruit and goodies which the lad carried home. He then ordered and charged to himself, groceries, medicine, and coal to be delivered.

Hurrying back to the pastor's study, the man, no longer a backslider, found Dr. Brooks in his study. Renewed in spirit, the man extended his hand and said softy, "Oh, Dr. Brooks, I do not want to be dropped from the roll: I am all right now sir, I am all right."

716 Going Fishing Without Bait

A fisherman had planned a special fishing trip for several months. He made out a list of essentials and scratched each item off as he packed. He had his car checked and serviced. All of his appointments were under control. Everything was ready. He even made sure to leave his wife and family well stocked with whatever they might need. The long awaited time finally arrived, and he eagerly bid them goodbye, hopped in his car and left.

He arrived at his fishing cabin that evening, got things tidied up and his food in order, set the alarm for 4 AM, then went to sleep dreaming of the fish he would catch on the morrow.

He arose hurriedly at the first sound of the alarm, quickly ate eggs and bacon, almost gulping the food down in his anxiety to get out on the lake. Just as he was getting into his boat, he made a startling discovery: he had not brought along any bait—the bait box was empty!

Many people prepare to meet God in a similar way.

717 Defective Inside

A visitor to a sculptor's studio commented, "I saw some blocks of marble lying off in a corner. Out of one a hand emerged, out of another was a head, with face unfinished. Others had unfinished work. Why the abandoned pieces?

The artist answered: "All those pieces showed great promise on the outside, on the surface. But as I chiseled deeper, flaws and defects in the marble that were not visible on the surface showed up. They had to be abandoned."

The difference between marble defects and human defects is that the marble cannot repent and be cleansed, but the human can. The defective heart becomes the perfect heart at the touch of the Master.

Resurrection

718 It Matters Not How Long in the Grave

A closely sealed vase was found in a mummy pit in Egypt by the English traveler Wilkinson. In it were discovered a few peas, old, wrinkled, and hard as a stone. The peas were planted carefully under a glass, and at the end of 30 days, they sprang into life, after having lain sleeping in the dust of a tomb for almost 3,000 years—a faint illustration of the mortal body which shall put on immortality. "Because He lives, we shall live also."

719 A Solitary Grain

In April, the Sunday school teacher asked all eight children in her class to hide within an empty container a small object that represented life in the spring.

Not wanting to embarrass eight-year-old Stephen, whose mental retardation was becoming more manifest, the teacher suggested that the children all place their unlabeled containers on her desk. Since she feared that Stephen might not have caught on, she decided that she should open them.

The first had a tiny flower. "What a lovely sign of new life!" "I brought that one!" the donor exclaimed. Next came a rock. "That must be Stephen's," the teacher thought, since rocks do not symbolize new life. But Billy shouted that his rock had moss on it, and moss was new life. The teacher agreed.

A butterfly flew from the third container, and another child bragged that her choice was best of all.

The fourth container was empty. "That has to be Stephen's," thought the teacher, quickly reaching for the fifth.

"Please, don't skip mine!' Stephen interjected. "But it's empty." "That's right," said Stephen. "The tomb was empty, and that is new life for everyone."

Later that summer, Stephen's condition grew worse, and he died. On his casket at the funeral, mourners found eight containers. They were ALL EMPTY.

720 No Tomb to Visit

In one of the villages of Northern India a missionary was preaching in a bazaar. As he closed, a Muslim gentleman came up and said, "You must admit we have one thing you have not, and it is better than anything you have."

The missionary smiled and said, "I should be pleased to hear what it is."

The Muslim said, "You know when we go to Mecca we at least

find a coffin. But when you Christians go to Jerusalem, which is your Mecca, you find nothing but an empty grave."

But the missionary just smiled and said, "That is just the difference. Mohammed is dead; Mohammed is in the coffin. And false systems of religion and philosophy are in their coffins, but Jesus Christ, whose kingdom is to include all nations and kindreds and tribes, is not here; He is risen. And all power in heaven and on earth is given unto Him. That is our hope."

A living Christ! That is our hope. He is not dead, but alive forevermore.

721 The Disciples Made No Relic of Christ's Tomb

If ye seek Jesus, do not go to His grave. You will not find Him there. Is it not quite striking that after the disciples were convinced that He had risen they never again visited His tomb? At least there is no record of it. Why should they? It was only an incident, a temporary halting place in the experience of our Lord. They did not make pilgrimages to it. They did not esteem it above any other place. They did not bury it beneath tokens of affection. They did not break off pieces of the rock and keep them as relics for seeking souls to look at in the hope of meriting divine favor.

No, after that first Sunday evening, the disciples were done with the tomb. Why should they give their time to the veneration of places, when they had the living Savior with them? To us, Christ is all and in all. He is alive, and He has power to give life. Not by meat and drink, not by pilgrimages and fastings, but by looking unto Him do we enter into life that death cannot touch.

722 How Do I Know He Lives?

How do I know that Christ has risen?
What proof have I to give?
He touched my life one blessed day,
And I began to live.

How do I know he left the tomb
That morning long ago?
I met Him just this morning,
And my heart is still aglow.

How do I know that endless life
He gained for me that day?
His life within is proof enough
Of immortality.

How do I know that Christ still lives,
Rich blessings to impart?
He walks with me along the way
And lives within my heart.

723 You Cannot Stop a Real Resurrection

The chief priests and the Pharisees were determined that Jesus was going to stay in his grave. They used every resource and power available to see to that. They secured the tomb by placing a seal on the great stone that had been rolled in front of it to close the entrance (Matt. 27:66). They also posted guards at the entrance of the tomb. These were not the *spekoulatōr* who were bodyguards or executioners (Mark 6:27), nor the *phulax* who were keepers (Acts 5:23), but the elite *koustōdia* who were the Roman army's special forces.

In spite of all their human efforts, the Jewish leaders were unable to prevent Jesus from accomplishing what had already been determined and promised: "After three days I will rise again" (Matt. 27:63). These carnal-minded, religious leaders did not know that NOTHING in the physical realm has the ability to hinder the divine will from accomplishing its purpose. YOU CANNOT STOP A REAL RESURRECTION.

Paul states that all who are baptized into Christ are baptized into his death, and in the same manner that Christ was resurrected they are to be resurrected to a new life in Christ (Rom. 6:3-7). There are individuals who want others to believe that someone or something prevents their resurrection to a new life. Such a person remains the same individual that he was before his "conversion." At this point, you shoiuld again remember that YOU CANNOT STOP A REAL RESURRECTION in an individual's life. You can stop a fake, but not a genuine resurrection to a new life in Christ.

God's incomparably great power is available for those who believe. "That power is like the working of His mighty strength, which He exerted in Christ when He raised Him from the dead and seated Him at His right hand in the heavenly realms" (Eph. 1:19, 20). If you deliberately decide in your heart that you are going to bury your old self and be resurrected to a new life in Christ, you have God's promise that you cannot be stopped. However, if you are looking for an excuse for living the same old life day after day, you will find one. There are numerous people and things to blame. You can blame society, or your mate or your children, or your parents, or your neighbors or hypocrites in the church. You can blame bad breaks, the wrong side of the bed, circumstances, or your tough childhood. Excuses are endless, but if you want to be resurrected to a new life you will be. Nothing can stop you.

If you are a fake, you will always have an excuse why you cannot change. If you are genuine, you will not be stopped. YOU CANNOT STOP A REAL RESURRECTION!

Salvation

724 "Don't Put It Off, John!"

Speaking to his physician, John cried in great perplexity, "I might not live a week!"

"Of course you may not, John, but very likely you will, and the medicine will be in the house; it will keep; and if you find yourself getting worse, you could take some. I shall not charge anything for it. If you should feel worse tomorrow you might begin even then."

"Sir, I may be dead tomorrow!"

"When would you propose to begin your medicince then, John?"

"Well, sir, I hoped you would tell me to begin today."

"Begin today, by all means," consented the doctor, kindly. "I am glad to see you realize how foolish it is to put off taking this medicine." And then the physician, reflecting upon their past conversations about spiritual matters, inquired, "But are you not being just as foolish when you put off taking the medicine which the Great Physician has provided for your sin-sick soul? I plead with you, John; don't put it off!"

725 Considering Noah's Ark

Did you ever wonder . . .

Was the ark REALLY big enough for all those animals? On first glance, the figures can be frightening. At the time of this writing, science has classified one million different species of animals. With seven of every clean and two of every other kind, it would seem we need space for at least 2,500,000 animals on the ark. Can we just faith it? First, let us note the ark was no toy boat, but a gigantic barge with a volume of 1,396,000 cubic feet (assuming one cubit equals 17.5 inches). The ark had a carrying capacity equal to that of 522 standard stock cars.

(1) What about the multitude of animals, you may ask. Most of that list of a million are worms, insects, one-cell animals and sea creatures who would have no need to be on the ark. In fact, "there was need for no more than 35,000 individual vertebrate animals on the ark."

(2) Chipmunk to elephant, let us assume the average size of an animal on the ark to be a sheep. Currently the railroad can fit 120 sheep on a stock car. Doing some fast figuring, the ark needed only to carry 292 stock cars worth of animals. Plenty of room for Noah, his family and extra hay.

Today God provides room for all men to find salvation at the cross. Noah pleaded with men to, "Get on board the ark," and they did not understand until the flood came and took them away. So shall the coming of the Son of Man be (Matt. 24:39). Will there be spare room for those you know who could have made it? Are you doing your part?

726 No Half-Measures With Him

"Therefore, if anyone is in Christ, he is a new creation; the old has gone, the new has come" (2 Cor. 5:17). New status, new life, new creation—we must not separate these blessings. They belong together, and are given to all who are in Christ.

A simple illustration may help. If a vagrant comes to us in dire need, down and out, in rags and tatters, and sick, even starving, it will be good to give him a bath and a change of clothing, but not enough. For he is ill and undernourished. So, in addition, he needs food and hospital treatment. Similarly, we come to Christ down and out, in the rags and tatters of our sin, spiritually sick and starving. In Christ, we are at once made welcome and accepted, and given a bath and a change of clothes. God sees us as righteous in Christ. This is our new status. But it is only the beginning. The Good Physician knows we are sick. So he puts His Spirit within us to give us new life and health, and He feeds us with His Word until we grow strong and vigorous. There are no half-measures with Him.

727 What John 3:16 Did

Shortly after the Korean War, a hungry waif wandered the dark-ened streets trying to find shelter from the bitter cold of winter. A night watchman noticed his plight and said, "GoMa (child), go to yonder house and say to the one who answers the gate, 'John 3:16.' " "But I do not know what John 3:16 is," replied the lad.

Nevertheless, desperation took him to the gate and brought that strange expression to his lips. He did not understand, but he whispered, "John 3:16." The lady smiled and took him into her warm home. The lad was puzzled as he thought, "I do not know what this John 3:16 is, but it sure makes a cold Korean boy warm."

Seeing his gaunt cheeks, the lady soon had him seated before a steaming bowl of soup. As he ate, the lad thought again, "I do not know what this John 3:16 is, but it sure makes a hungry Korean boy full."

After a bath, he lay there on the warm bed with tears flowing down his cheeks, "I do not know what this John 3:16 is," he thought, "but it must be the most wonderful thing in the whole world. It makes a strange lady love a lonely Korean boy."

728 Imperfect Christians and the Perfect Christ

Two fellow travelers were seated together in a railway compartment engaged in earnest conversation of a religious nature. One of them, a skeptic, was evidently trying to excuse his unbelief by exposing the various evils which afflict Christendom, detailing with pleasure the hypocrisy and the craft, and the covetousness and divisions found in the professing church, and then he pointed to some of the leaders as the most markedly corrupt of all.

In front of them sat a Christian who was compelled to hear all this. He knew the accusations to be true—too true to be concealed from the most charitable mind—so all he could do was to bow his head and bear the deserved reproach. Soon, however, the accuser, anxious to extend the circle of his audience, addressed this fellow passenger in front of him.

"I see you are quick to detect evil," said the Christian, "and you read character pretty well. You have been uncovering the abominable things that have turned Christendom into a wreck, and are fast ripening it for the judgment of God. You have spared none, but given all a good measure. Now, I am a Christian and love the Lord Jesus and His people. Not a word shall I offer in defense, but I solemnly challenge you to speak the first word against the Lord Jesus Christ Himself."

The skeptic was surprised. He seemed almost frightened and sheepishly replied, "Well, no! I could not find fault with Him. He was perfect."

"Just so!" said the Christian. "Therefore was my heart attracted to Him, and the more I looked, the more I found I was not like Him at all, but only a poor, guilty, sinful man. All of the evil which professed followers of His may do cannot turn me away from Him. My salvation hangs on what He has done, and not on what they are doing."

729 Are You Refusing Your Inheritance?

While a student at Yale University, Eugene F. Suter, Jr.'s father died, leaving him an estate of $400,000. When Eugene refused the inheritance, the trustees of the estate insisted he take it, and even took him to court to force him to accept the money. In an unprecedented case held in New York City, Judge William T. Collins reluctantly ruled that the young man had a legal right to reject the $400,000. The order legally cut off the 22-year-old student from all future interest in the family fortune, leaving him without an income.

There are a lot of people in this world who are refusing a far greater inheritance than Suter did. God has offered us the opportunity to be joint-heirs with Christ and heirs of eternal life, and so many are refusing to profess belief in Christ and to be born again. Like Suter, they will be cut off from all future benefits from their Father's estate. Will *your* inheritance go unclaimed?

730 Grounded?

Some years ago in a little western town, a crowd of men gathered about a store window through which they saw a large American eagle. It was fastened by one of its feet to a chain which was secured at the other end by a ring in the floor. Held captive this way for some months, it had become seemingly indifferent to its condition. While the men were looking at the huge bird, a tall, young mountaineer pushed his way through the crowd and entered the store. He asked the proprietor what he would take for the eagle, and the owner said, "Two dollars."

When the young man took the money from his pocket and paid the price, the keeper of the store unfastened the chain and handed the eagle to his new owner. Followed by the crowd, he carried the great bird down the street until he came to a signboard, and on top of this, he placed the one-time child of the skies. But the great bird remained motionless and the crowd was disappointed. It had been bound so long to this earth that it did not seem to care to fly any longer.

Suddenly, high above the mountain, the sun struck its eyes, and the eagle seemed to remember that it was an eagle and that its home was up yonder among the crags and the cliffs. It lifted first one foot and then the other as if to make sure of its freedom and power; then it lifted first one wing and then the other. With a shriek and a bound, it flew away, and higher and higher it ascended until it was lost in the face of the sun. The crowd cheered.

731 Importance of Choice

A sailor and a miner lost control of the rowboat they were maneuvering above a waterfall. The swift water started hurling them to destruction. Someone from the shore flung a rope to the two as they were tossed from their boat into the pounding current. At that same instant, a floating log shot by. The sailor grabbed the rope and hung on, but the miner seized the log and wrapped himself around it, ignoring the rope. The man grasping the log was borne irresistibly along to his destruction. The other man was pulled safely to the shore.

The gospel message is that Christ is on the shore, throwing us a lifesaving rope. So many things seem to float by that are attractive, but life shows them to be fatal. Isaiah pled for Israel to grasp the hand of the Lord which is with His servants.

Cost

732 Christ's Intervention

In the sixteenth century, Oliver Cromwell ordered that an English soldier be shot for a cowardly crime. The execution was to take place at the evening bell. But at the appointed time no sound came from the belfry. Investigation revealed that the girl who was engaged to be married to the condemned man had climbed into the bell tower and clung to the clapper of the giant bell to prevent it from striking. They found her there with her hands bleeding and torn to shreds.

All of us are sinners under sentence of death. But Christ intervened in our behalf. Look at His bruised and bleeding nail-pierced hands on that cross.

733 Freedom

I will never forget the day I watched about 40 khaki-clad men get off an old rattletrap brown bus in Houston, Texas. Some had scars on their faces. I especially remember one man whose arm had been amputated. Some of them looked tough. I remember thinking I would not want to meet some of those guys in a dark alley. Others looked like clean-cut, all-American boys. They all had two things in common. Each man had served time in prison and each man had been freed. Freedom had been a long time in coming. They measured the time they had served by calendars.

As I talked with some of those men, it soon became apparent that adapting to freedom would require some adjustment. They were so used to forced regimentation that some of them really did not know they were free. They asked if I represented the Texas Department of Corrections.

As children of God, we sometimes do not quite comprehend the fact that we have been set free by our Savior. Some of us are imprisoned by the memories of a sinful past. Lloyd Ogilvie said, "The memory of past failure is like sand in the gears of our effectiveness." God did not put the handcuffs of past memories on you. They are self-imposed. He wiped out your sins in

order that you might have seasons of refreshing (Acts 3:19).

Other Christians are incarcerated by legalism. They read the Bible to learn of its rules. The legalist with a sensitive conscience knows he cannot keep God's laws perfectly. Maybe that is why the novelist John Updike said, "I agree with the Jews. One Testament is enough." If faith is solely a matter of lawkeeping, I would agree. The Psalmist was talking about the Old Testament when he said, "The law of the Lord is perfect, reviving the soul" (Ps. 19:7). There was no need for a new law code, but there was a need for freedom from the consequences of disobedience. Small wonder that legalists either live in a state of perpetual discouragement or self-righteous hypocrisy. The legalist does not understand that "everyone who believes in Him is freed from all things" (Acts 13:39 NASB).

If you are living in a prison of your own making, you can walk through the doors of freedom today. "It is for freedom that Christ has set us free" (Gal. 5:1).

734 The Beauty Remains

There was a conversation between the great artists Renoir and Matisse. At the time, Matisse was Renoir's young student. Renoir suffered from terrible arthritis. It was very painful for him to paint. He had to hold his brush between his thumb and index finger. And as he painted, students often heard him crying out in pain. On one such occasion, Matisse asked the old master, "Why do you go on if it hurts so much?" And Renoir answered, "The pain passes, but the beauty remains."

Explanation

735 Help From Above

An old Indian chief constantly spoke of the Lord Jesus and what He meant to him. "Why do you talk so much about Jesus?" asked a friend. The old chief did not reply, but slowly, deliberately gathered some sticks and bits of grass. He made a circle of them. In the circle he placed a caterpillar. Still silent, he struck a match and lit the sticks and grass. They watched the caterpillar. As the fire caught around the circle, the trapped caterpillar began to crawl around rapidly, seeking a way to escape.

As the fire advanced, the helpless caterpillar raised its head as high as it could. If the creature could have spoken, it would have said, "My help can only come from above."

Then the old chief stooped down. He extended his finger to the caterpillar which crawled up his finger to safety. "That," said the chief glowing, "was what the Lord Jesus did for me! I was lost in sin. My condition was hopeless. I was trapped. Then the Lord Jesus stooped down in love and mercy and He drew me out of the horrible pit of sin and shame. How can I help but love Him and talk of His wondrous love and care?"

736 His Name Was Jesus, the Savior

A visitor approached the preacher after listening to his sermons on the necessity of receiving Christ as Savior.

The man said he thought that Christianity should limit itself in presenting Christ as our example whom we should follow.

The preacher turned to the visitor and said, "If I were to preach Christ as our example, would you follow His example?"

"Why not?" was the flippant answer.

The preacher thought for a moment and said, "Okay, let us think then of some of the things that Jesus did and did not do. One of the things that is said of Him is that He did not sin. Can you take that step and follow His example in doing no sin?"

"No, I must be very honest about myself, I do sin."

The preacher then answered: "It is impossible then to follow Jesus unless you first make Him your Savior. It is He who must live in you so that you can say 'For me to live is Christ.' "

Jesus came into the world not to set an example for us, but to become our Savior. It is only as we receive Him that we are able to follow Him because He indwells us.

737 God's Transforming Power

A group of atheists were criticizing the Bible. One of them spoke about creation. He said, "What man with any common sense could believe that several thousand years ago, God stooped down and picked up a piece of mud, breathed on it, and changed it into a human being?" A Christian man standing by overheard the conversation and responded by saying: "I cannot answer all the questions about creation, but this I know: One night God stooped down and picked up the dirtiest piece of mud in this city, breathed upon it by His Holy Spirit, and changed a gambling, thieving, drinking wretch into a peace-loving man of God. I was that man."

738 He Swapped

A minister was speaking to fishermen on an English seashore. He was trying to make it plain to the men what Christ's work on the cross really was.

Presently, he said, "Now will one of you men tell me, in your own words, what the Lord Jesus did there on the cross?"

An old seaman looked up and, with tears on his weather-beaten face, said: "He swapped with me."

How gloriously true! "His own self bare *our sins* in His own body on the tree."

Invitation

739 Saved at the Bottom of the Sea

Off the Florida coast, Mike, a professional diver, was engaged in sal-

vaging parts of a ship which had sunk some months previously. He had just descended one morning and was making his way slowly toward the sunken hull when he noticed something white in the mouth of an oyster or shellfish of some sort.

Stooping, Mike picked up the small piece of white paper and turned his marine light on it. A gospel tract! He read its message slowly and carefully, and conviction struck home to his heart. If God's message of mercy in Christ had pursued him to the bottom of the sea, he could not hold out any longer.

Standing where he was that morning, Mike accepted Christ as his Savior. When he returned to the surface, he took with him the little tract which had followed him to the bottom of the ocean.

Requirement

740 Get on Board

A certain businessman arrived at the airport 30 minutes in advance of his flight. He went to the ticket window and received his boarding pass.

Next, he checked his suitcase in plenty of time to get it on the proper flight with him, then sat down with a magazine in the lobby waiting for time to board.

Since this was his first chance to relax all day, he closed his eyes for what he thought would be a ten minute "cat nap." He rested his eyes right through the first, second, and final boarding calls on his flight.

When he awoke, a quick glance at the clock on the wall snapped him back to reality. The flight had taken off without him. He had done everything right except one. He had not gotten on board.

Some people are going to miss the plane spiritually if they do not get on board. It is fine that we have faith and Christian parents and atmospheres in our homes. But we must accept Christ to get on board.

741 Do You Believe in Your Sins?

A pastor in New York urged an intellectual but dissipated man to become a Christian. The man replied, "I cannot believe in the inspiration of the Bible, in the deity of Christ, or in prayer." "Do you believe in your own sins?" asked the pastor. "Oh, yes," replied the honest soul; "there is no doubt about my being a sinner and sometimes I am in hell!" "Are you willing to bring your sins to Christ for forgiveness and let Him, whatever you think of Him, take your guilt?" "But," he said, "I cannot believe in the inspiration of the Bible, or in the deity of Christ, or in prayer." "Just now," persisted the wise pastor, "I am not asking you to believe these things. You know you are a sinner, and in sin there is a taste of hell. Now, I offer you Jesus Christ as your Savior from sin. Will you accept Him as such, and leave all questions that puzzle you for future solution?"

The man went to his home, and that night he accepted the Christ he knew as his Savior, and came to the meeting the next night to tell the people the joy of forgiveness that was in his soul. After several days of testimony which led others to Christ, the pastor gently asked, "What do you think now of the deity of Christ?" "Such a Savior," he said, with great emotion, "must be divine; if He were not divine He could not have done what He has done for me!"

742 Why the Doctor Arrived Too Late

It was almost one o'clock in the morning when the phone range in the Winters' home. Dr. Leon Winter, the highly acclaimed Chicago surgeon, was awakened with a start.

Tonight it was a young boy, they said, tragically mangled in a late night accident. Couldn't someone else handle it? Not this time. This time his hands were possibly the only ones in the city, or maybe in the whole region, which were skilled enough to save.

The quickest route happened to be through a rather rough area, but with time being a critical factor, it was worth the risk. He almost made it through the worst of the neighborhood. Almost. Then, at a stop light, his door was jerked open by a man in a gray hat and a dirty flannel shirt. "I've got to have your car!" the man screamed, pulling him from his seat. Winters tried explaining the gravity of his situation, but the man was not listening.

The doctor wandered for over 45 minutes looking for a phone. When the taxi finally got him to the hospital, over an hour had passed. He burst through the doors and into the nurses' station, but the nurse on duty only shook her head. Too late. The boy had just died about 30 minutes earlier. "His dad got here just before he died," the nurse told him. He is in the chapel. Go see him, would you? He is awfully confused. He could not understand why you never came."

Without explaining, Dr. Winters walked hurriedly down the hall and quietly entered the chapel. At the front knelt the huddled form of a weeping father, in a gray hat and a dirty flannel shirt. Tragically, he had pushed from his life the only one who could save.

How many today are pushing from their lives the only One who can save?

743 A New Man in the Suit

The program committee for a national barber's convention devised a graphic means of demonstrating the effectiveness of their profession. They found a social derelict on skid row with long, dirty hair. His face was unshaven and his clothes were ragged and filthy. His body reeked with odors of cheap liquor and filth.

The barbers cleaned him up. They gave him a bath, shampoo, shave, haircut and manicure. They liberally sprinkled talcum powder on him and added spicy cologne. He was dressed in a new suit and was presented before the convention as a changed man. He certainly looked the part. However, within a week the man was back on skid row, back in the gutter, back in his former pattern of living. The barbers altered his appearance, but their tonsorial services had not changed his inward nature.

Anyone who has the money to spend can put a man in a new suit, but only Christ can put a new man in the suit. "Therefore, if anyone is in Christ, he is a new creation; the old has gone, the new has come." Christ alters us from the inside out.

Result

744 A Christian Is a Butterfly in the State of a Caterpillar

Justification is instantaneous; sanctification is a long growth. Justification is the act of God whereby He takes a man who is dead in trespasses and sins and says, "I create within you the new life of Christ and now I look upon you and see you just as perfect as I see the Lord Jesus Christ."

Justification is the act of God whereby he declares an ungodly man to be perfect while he is still ungodly. It is as extraordinary a thing as if you were able to say that the caterpillar is really a beautiful butterfly. "Oh," you say, "but it isn't! It still looks like a caterpillar." Well, that is exactly what God does with us. He comes to us in our "caterpillar status" and declares us to be "butterflies."

In reality, that is what happens in nature, too; that caterpillar does become a butterfly. For God has given us this remarkable picture of metamorphosis—that which goes into the cocoon as a worm comes out as a butterfly, for it lives part of its life in one state and part in another. We call this process metamorphosis. It is very interesting to note the Greek word used in Romans 12:2: "Be not conformed to this world, but be ye transformed (metamorphosed) by the renewing of your mind."

745 The Human Tiger

A French explorer was crossing Africa from the Zambezi and came into the region of the Barotsi people. He had heard stories about the native king Lewanika, whose greatest delight had been to put to death, by newly invented tortures, those who offended him. He was also known as the "human tiger."

This French officer came to the station where Pastor Coillard was in charge, and the pastor himself, a Frenchman, entertained him kindly. Then came Sunday. The French officer was absolutely without God, but as a matter of politeness he went to church and sat through the service. When he came out he said, "Monsieur Coillard, who was that remarkable looking man sitting next to me, who listened so carefully?" That was King Lewanika, the 'human tiger.' " "Was it?" "Yes." "Then if that is what Christ can do, I mean to be His."

Satan

746 A Letter from Satan to His 'Friend'

Dear "Friend,"

I visited your Sunday school service and was overjoyed to see that many of your class members were absent. I was thrilled to see that those who came were late, or tired and sleepy during the Sunday School lesson and also the sermon.

I rejoiced in hearing some of the lessons that were not well-prepared, and that many of you just did not care. Of course, it is devilish to see some of you leave after Sunday school and not get your souls fed in the worship service.

Sunday is always one of my favorite days because that is the day I do some of my best work—getting Christians to stay home and watch television, or getting involved in sports and all sorts of "recreation."

I howl with laughter each time I see many of you fail to give much of your tithes and offerings; you make the board and minister squirm and fret over tight budgets and this takes away some of their effectiveness for the Enemy.

I hope you will miss services again this Sunday. Stay home where it is warm, and it will help you get used to the future climate. And one thing more—do not let them get you to become a "born again" Christian!

—Satan

747 Know Satan's Moves

If you have ever seen a wrestling match, you know it is not pretty. It is sweaty, sticky, dirty, and painful. When you wrestle, you get down and get dirty. There is no half-hearted involvement. You give it everything you've got, or you lose.

Anthony T. Evans wrote: "I know a bit about wrestling because my brother, Arthur, was the Maryland state wrestling champion in his weight class. At his championship match my brother weighed in at about 230 pounds and was going up against the three-time Maryland state champion who out-weighed him by 35 pounds. Before the match, a reporter asked, 'Who is the toughest wrestler in this room?'

"My brother, humble fellow that he is, said, 'You are looking at him!'

"The reporter looked at him and asked, 'What makes you think you are so tough? You are about to fight the man who has won the state championship three times in a row.'

"My brother replied with a very insightful comment, 'I know. He is bigger and perhaps stronger than I am, but I know his methods.'

"We are in a similar fight against Satan. Just as my brother needed to learn his opponent's moves, we need to understand Satan's moves. We need to know how he operates, so that we can prepare ourselves 'to resist in the evil day, and having done everything, to stand firm' (Eph. 6:13). No place in Scripture reveals Satan's schemes better than Genesis 3, which records Satan's initial contact with man. As the story unfolds, we clearly see Satan's strategy to ruin the human race."

748 Do Not Laugh at the Devil

Have you heard about the fellow who was seriously ill? A visitor asked him if he was willing to turn his life over to God and renounce the devil. "I am willing to give my life to God," he said, "But a man in my condition should not be making any enemies."

We may laugh, but we must not forget that the strength and influence of the devil is real. In fact, the number of his followers is increasing. Satan's church is growing and new groups are beginning. Satan's Bible is available in many bookstores. More and more signs of devil worship are now appearing in graffiti.

Never forget that the devil has one goal. He wants your soul. His desire is for all men to be in hell for eternity. He is the embodiment of evil. Twelve times the New Testament calls him "the evil one." He has the power to enter a person (Luke 22:3). With his craftiness, he can use even the best of people to achieve his ends (Matt. 16:23). He can trap man and take him captive (2 Tim. 2:26). He can fill the heart of man and lead him to death (Acts 5:3).

It is not old-fashioned or anti-intellectual to believe in a living, powerful person of evil. Perhaps we need to see more vividly the contest in which we are participants. "I am sending you to them to open their eyes and turn them from darkness to light, and from the power of Satan to God, so that they may receive forgiveness of sins and a place among those who are sanctified by faith in Me" (Acts 26:17b, 18).

Instead of joking about him, perhaps we need to restore a custom of the early church. Tertullian, (AD 155–222) recounted how converts not only confessed the Christ, but also said, "I renounce you Satan and all your service and all your works."

We may not be a member of Satan's church but we can still be his follower (1 Tim. 5:15). This is because we serve him by default. If we do not totally and wholeheartedly serve the Lord, we automatically become servants of Satan. "Do not you know that when you offer yourselves to someone to obey him as slaves, you are slaves to the one whom you obey—whether you are slaves to sin, which leads to death, or to obedience, which leads to righteousness? (Rom. 6:16).

The old dragon, the serpent, is not all-powerful. In fact, we can fight against him and win if we will seek divine assistance (Rom. 8:13, 26). We can resist him and flee his influence (James 4:7). Our weapons and strength are mighty, and we can fight against him and triumph (Eph. 6:13–18).

With such strength, we need not fear the devil. Yet we must constantly be alert to his schemes and devices. He wants us, he is powerful, but he can only win if we let him. "For we are not unaware of his schemes" (2 Cor. 2:11).

749 Do You Know the Devil?

That is a pretty unusual title for an article that is designed to uphold the Christian faith. Why would we ever want to know the devil? Because we will never overcome him unless we know something of his sinister purposes, his devious tactics and his universal influence.

George C. Scott portrayed George Patton in the film biography of the World War II general's career. There is a scene in which Scott as Patton reflects on the defeat of the German field Marshall, Erwin Rommel. He said something like, "Rommel, I read your book."

We have to read the book on our enemy, the devil. Among the things we need to know about him are the following:

1. He controls people. He has even been able to control people who walked in the physical presence of Jesus. Near the end of our Lord's earthly ministry, he predicted His own death. Peter resisted the thought that such a thing could

happen. Even with the passing of nearly 20 centuries, Jesus' reaction to Peter is a shock. "Out of my sight, Satan! You are a stumbling block to Me; you do not have in mind the things of God, but the things of men" (Matt. 16:23).

2. He lies. He is the father of lies (John 8:44) and he "masquerades as an angel of light" (2 Cor. 11:14). He can start with a premise or a practice that is clearly the opposite of what God wants and put a spin on it that makes it sound like you have God's backing for the most evil deeds imaginable.

3. He has universal influence. In Job 1, God asked Satan where he had been. In arrogance Satan shot back, "Ranging over the earth from end to end" (NEB). You cannot go anywhere on this planet where Satan does not go.

This is not said to make you paranoid about Satan, but so that you might be better prepared to resist the devil and force him to flee from you.

750 All These Things I Will Give You

Jesus had been in the desert for 40 days and 40 nights without food. He must have been extremely hungry when Satan approached Him! Always expect Satan to tempt you in your weakest moments. He said to Jesus, "If you are the Son of God, tell these stones to become bread" (Matt. 4:3). Jesus failed to respond to this temptation, so Satan attempted pride (v. 6). With another failure Satan "upped the ante" and offered Jesus greater THINGS than food; He offered the world. He said, "all these things will I give you, if you will fall down and worship me" (v. 9). With this statement, Satan finally arrived at the real issue: "Fall down and worship ME." All sin stripped of its glamour and laid bare is the dethroning of God to make some THING (living or non-living), a god.

Satan can offer you only THINGS; nothing more. Jesus offers you abundant life; life to its fullest (John 10:10). The life Jesus offers you has promises for both the present life and the life to come (1 Tim. 4:8).

People are foolish. They look for life and peace in THINGS, but Jesus says that you can have life and peace and joy with or without things (Matt. 5—7). Paul accepted what Jesus had to offer and said of himself, "I have learned the secret of being content in any and every situation, whether well-fed or hungry, whether living in plenty or in want. I can do everything through Him who gives me strength" (Phil. 4:12, 13).

THINGS cannot bring life and happiness because they are temporary. Only a foolish person spends his life acquiring THINGS to the neglecting of the life Jesus offers. Jesus once told of such a man (Luke 12:16-21). The man acquired so many THINGS that he had to tear down his barns and build bigger ones. With a sigh of relief, he said, "Soul, you have much goods laid up for many years; take it easy, eat, drink, and be merry" (v. 19). "But God said of you: then whose shall those THINGS be which you have provided?" (v. 20). THINGS have an end but ETERNAL LIFE is forever.

The THINGS Satan offers you are in no way certain because he is a liar. Jesus says, "There is no truth in him. When he lies, he speaks his native language, for he is a liar and the father of lies" (John 8:44). Satan cannot offer you anything without telling a lie. On the other hand, Jesus is TRUTH (John 14:6). Jesus cannot promise you anything that He will not or cannot fulfill.

Just as Satan offered Jesus ALL THESE THINGS, he offers them to you today. Are you accepting his offer? If your day-by-day life is consumed in acquiring THINGS, you have accepted. Satan is saying to you, "ALL THESE THINGS WILL I GIVE YOU" but I believe Jesus' estimation of Satan. You are being lied to!

751 Hostages in the Pew

Satan is not warring over those who are in the world, for he already has them in his grasp. His war is to conquer those who are sitting in the pew. Those who have been reconciled, he longs to take hostage once again. His strategy is deceptive, because he uses them to hinder the work of the church.

First, he deludes them with other goals in life which soon take priority over the work of the church and personal involvement. They become members of the body which become dysfunctional. Hands that will not work. Feet that will not travel to God's appointed place. A mouth that will not confess Jesus to others. Ears that soon fail to listen. A brain that refuses to think and dwell on things above. Lame, blind and deaf, the church struggles to fulfill its purpose.

Second, he lures them into complacency. Having become satisfied with less than God's desire for their lives, they settle for adolescence rather than maturing to adulthood, while at the same time believing they are adults. They fail to meditate upon God's Word, except while sitting in the pew. They give token gifts instead of a sacrifice. They listen to lessons with change or repentance far from mind. Maturity is not even in view, because their eyes have been blinded. Eventually, they find themselves attending but not involved.

Third, he tantalizes their sense with false teachings with the purpose of taking others off course. Having become numb, new sensations must fill the void. Having not understood God's purpose they change their attitude from not wanting to go beyond what is written to stretching the limits as far as they can. Deluded themselves, they delude others to a false sense of security. They now must seek bigger, greater sensational things to keep the momentum going so their individual spirits can feel fulfilled. The appearance of great things happening blinds their eyes to the fact they have been taken hostage, and

pride keeps them from being set free.

Fourth, he stalemates their vision with past accomplishments. Boasting in the glory of a successful past program they fail to launch out into new, more productive, fruitful efforts. They might even nurture a program long after its death. Individuals stop teaching and serving others after just a few victories. They fail to dream of God's use of their lives and God's vision for the church.

If the church and we as individual members are ever going to be what God desires, the hostages in the pews must be freed. The only thing that can set them free is the truth. No mystical, sensational experience, just reasonable, plain truth. Only the Bible can reveal if we are held hostage. Only the Bible can set and keep us free. Read it, study it, and make it yours, that you might heed the warnings and not be taken hostage.

752 On Being Deceived

A man is DECEIVED if he is a hearer and not a doer of the Word (James 1:22).

A man is DECEIVED if he says that he has no sin (1 John 1:8).

A man is DECEIVED when he thinks himself to be something when he is nothing (Gal. 6:3).

A man is DECEIVED when he thinks himself to be wise with worldly wisdom (1 Cor. 3:18).

A man is DECEIVED when he seems to be religious and does not bridle his tongue (James 1:26).

A man is DECEIVED when he thinks that he will not reap what he sows (Gal. 6:7).

A man is DECEIVED when he thinks that evil company will not corrupt good morals (1 Cor. 15:33).

A man is DECEIVED when he thinks that the unrighteous will inherit the kingdom of God (heaven) (1 Cor. 6:9).

Now Satan will try to DECEIVE you to not pay attention to the above. Will you let him?

Self

753 You Tell on Yourself

You tell what you are by the friends you seek,

By the very manner in which you speak,

By the way you employ your leisure time,

By the use you make of dollar and dime.

You tell what you are by the things you wear,

By the spirit in which you burdens bear,

By the kind of things at which you laugh,

By records you play on the phonograph.

You tell what you are by the way you walk,

By the things of which you delight to talk,

By the manner in which you bear defeat,

By so simple a thing as how you eat.

By the books you choose from the well-filled shelf,

In these ways and more, you tell on yourself,

So there is really no particle of sense

In an effort to keep up false pretense.

754 Tied to Old Habits

A drunken man entered his row boat one night to cross the river. He picked up the oars and pulled away—so he thought. He rowed all night but did not reach the destination. When daylight came, he was surprised to find that he was just where he started the night before. He had forgotten to untie his boat.

So it is with many of the Lord's followers. They are tied to their habits, desires, wills, or some cherished idol or idols of the heart. Consequently, their lives are fruitless. Shorebound Christians never flourish and are of little or no help to others.

Self-Centered

755 For His Glory

How oft have you sought some reward for a task you said was "for the Lord?" How oft have you felt a stinging slight and felt that you were not treated right? How oft have you said "I quit, I am through. Nobody says 'thanks' for the things I do."

How oft have you felt the precious thrill that comes from just being in His will? How oft did you count earth's glory dim compared to the joy of serving Him? What is it your heart has longed for? Does praise of men or His smile mean more?

756 Too Much and Too Little

Riches can be a handicap. A wealthy woman told her doctor she was frustrated by a restless desire for more and more things. He replied, "These are the usual symptoms of too much ease in the home and too little gratitude in the heart."

757 The Gospel According to the Little Red Hen

Remember the story of the Little Red Hen? Here is a church equivalent!

Once upon a time there was a church. One day the Lord found a lost and dying world, enslaved in sin and destined for hell.

"Who will share the gospel with those who know not the way of life eternal?" said He.

"Not I," said the elder.

"Not I," said the deacon.

"Not I," said the Sunday School worker.

"Not I," said the choir member.

"Not I," said the member.

"Very well, then," said the Lord. "I will find someone else." And He did!

After some time the gospel seed sprouted and grew. "Who will teach these young in faith the way of righteousness and truth?" asked the Lord.

"Not I," said the elder. "I have other things to do."

"Not I," said the deacon. "That is not my job."

"Not I," said the choir member. "I do not like the deacon."

"Not I," said the member. "Let the Sunday school worker do it."

"Very well, then," said the Lord. "I will find someone else to teach my Word." And He did!

"Now," said the Lord, "the church has children and teenagers. Who will shepherd and direct them in My ways?"

"Not I," said the elder. "That is not my job."

"Not I," said the deacon. "I do not like the choir member."

"Not I," said the Sunday school worker. "I have other things to do."

"Very well, then," said the Lord. "I will find another." And He did!

Again the Lord said, "The meeting house needs some work. Who will help clean it, mend its roof, paint its walls so that it may bring honor to my name and joy to those who gather there?"

"Not I," said the deacon. "I have other things to do."

"Not I," said the Sunday School worker. "That is not my job."

"Not I," said the member. "Let the deacon do it."

"Very well," said the Lord. "I will find someone else." And He did!

Later the Lord said, "Some of my children are in need. Who will share what is theirs so that others may have?"

"Not I," said the elder. "Let the deacon do it."

"Not I," said the deacon. "Let the Sunday school worker do it."

"Not I," said the Sunday school

worker. "Let the choir member do it."

"Not I," said the choir member. "Let the member do it."

"Not I," said the member. "Let the elder do it."

"Very well, then," said the Lord. "I will find someone else." And He did!

Eventually, after the gospel was preached, the weak taught, the young guided, the meeting house repaired, and those in need helped, the Lord said, "Who will share in the joys of Christian service? Who will come taste the blessings of faithfulness? Who will know the fruit of spiritual growth?"

"I will!" said the elder.

"I will!" said the deacon.

"I will!" said the Sunday school worker.

"I will!" said the choir member.

"I will!" said the member.

"No, you will not," replied the Lord. "My rewards will go to those who do My will, not their own."

758 The Snail in the Lobster Shell

A little snail that lived by the ocean noticed with envy the big and beautiful shell in which the lobster lived.

"Oh! How this little shell of mine pinches," whined the little snail. "What a grand palace the lobster carries on his back! I wish I lived in his place. Oh! Wouldn't my friends admire me in that shell! Think of a snail living in a mansion like that!"

In time a wonderful thing occurred. The watching, envious snail beheld the lobster work right out of his shell to grow up in another, larger one. When the empty, metallic green shell of the lobster lay neglected on the beach, the snail said, "Now I shall have my wish. Hurrah! The little snail is going to live in a lobster shell!"

In his pride he cried out to the birds overhead, "Ah, the little snail is going to live in a lobster shell."

He cried to the cattle in the field, "Oh, oh! Now you shall see. The little snail is going to live in a palace."

So the birds and the cattle in the field were curious and they watched the little snail. The snail pulled himself loose from his own little shell, and cried, "Well, I'm glad to say I'm through with you. Goodbye. You've pinched me and pressed me for the last time. I am going to live in the grand lobster shell."

The birds and the animals saw the little snail proudly crawl into the towering lobster shell and he huffed and puffed and blew and gasped in an effort to make himself fit. But with all his efforts he felt very small inside the grand lobster shell. He grew tired, too. That night he died because the great empty shell was so cold.

A wise old crow then said, "You see! That's what comes of envy. What you have is enough. Be yourself and save yourself from a lot of trouble. How much better to be a little snail in a comfortable shell than to be a little snail in a big shell and freeze to death!"

759 The First and Hardest Lesson

"All I Really Need to Know I Learned in Kindergarten," says Robert Fulgham's popular essay and book. In truth, one of life's most important and hardest lessons comes to us long before kindergarten.

This lesson is painful and upsetting to learn, and it goes against what we want to think is true. But it is vital that we learn it.

Many people never do.

The lesson is this: you are not the center of your universe.

You might as well face it.

Once, a long time ago, Nicolaus Copernicus studied the sky and declared, "If man is to know the truth, he must change his thinking! Despite what we have said for years, our earth is not the center of the cosmos—but just one celestial body among many. The sun does not move around us; we move around the sun."

That was a radical adjustment— a revolution in thought.

Years later, Jean Piaget studied children and declared, "Each child must experience his or her own 'Copernican revolution.' They must learn that they are not the center of their world."

This is a private, radical adjustment for every one. "After all," each infant thinks, "My wants have always been met. Let life continue that way!"

"Walls should move out of the way before I run into them. The floor should become soft just as I fall. Everyone should give me their toys if I want them. The rules of games should change so I can always win. And big things like cars should never drive where I might want to run or play."

Sooner or later, life does not cooperate and the child is shocked.

What about us adults? Have we learned the lesson?

Most of us learn it. But Satan urges us to put ourselves back in the center. And we often do, even when we know better.

Jesus Christ studied His audience and declared, "If you want to enter the kingdom of heaven, you must change your thinking! Despite what your sinful nature tells you, you are not the center of your world. To find life, you must know the truth. Accommodate yourself to that; it will set you free!"

That is the most radical adjustment of all. A hard lesson.

The illusion is easier. It justifies selfishness. And we all like being selfish.

Too bad that the selfish way is not true.

Too bad that it does not bring satisfaction or life.

A hard lesson. But an important one. Life goes much better once you have got it.

760 How Important Are You— to You?

Near Lincoln, Kansas, stands a group of gravestones that boggles the imagination. A farmer named

David, a self-made and determined man, managed to amass a considerable fortune, but had few friends and no relatives for whom he cared.

When his wife died, David erected an elaborate statue showing both her and himself sitting at the opposite ends of a loveseat. So pleased was he with this monument that he commissioned the sculptor to create another, this time showing him kneeling at her grave with a wreath in his hand. And that made such a fine impression upon him that he set out to erect still another tombstone depicting his wife kneeling at his future graveside with a wreath. He even put wings on her back as she now resided in another world. So, as time passed and one idea led to another, he eventually spent over a quarter of a million dollars on monuments to his wife and himself.

David had no interest in aiding his fellowmen or benefiting his nearby town. Nor did he become a blessing to the church, for he used all of his resources on shrines to self. He died at the age of 92, a resident of the poorhouse, and his cherished stones are slowly but surely sinking into the Kansas soil, victimized by vandalism and neglect, weathered by time.

761 Nine Great Ideas: All Mine!

1. My idea of visitation:
      everybody come to see me.
2. My idea of sympathy:
      everybody suffering with me.
3. My idea of a sinner:
      the man for whom I have a great dislike.
4. My idea of a meek man:
      the man who yields to me.
5. My idea of a contentious man:
      the man who takes issue with me.
6. My idea of a wise man:
      the man who listens to me.
7. My idea of unity:
      everybody agreeing with me.
8. My idea of cooperation:
      everybody working with me.
9. My idea of a good sermon:
      one that fits and hits everybody but me.

762 How to Be Miserable in 20 Easy Steps!

1. Use "I" as often as possible.
2. Always be sensitive to slights.
3. Be jealous and envious.
4. Think only about yourself.
5. Talk only about yourself.
6. Trust no one.
7. Never forget a criticism.
8. Always expect to be appreciated.
9. Be suspicious.
10. Listen greedily to what others say about you.
11. Look for faults in others.
12. Shirk your duties if you can.
13. Do as little as possible for others.
14. Never forget a service you may have rendered.
15. Sulk if people are not grateful for your favors.
16. Insist on consideration and respect.

17. Demand agreement with your own views on everything.
18. Always look for a good time.
19. Love yourself first.
20. Be selfish at all times!

763 Of Lice and Men

Human beings have a huge capacity for self-delusion. The Scottish poet, Robert Burns, wrote a famous poem about this entitled "To A Louse (On Seeing One On A Lady's Bonnet at Church)." In the poem he pictures a woman, strutting to church decked out in frills and finery, convinced that she is cutting a grand figure. But the sophisticated image she aims for is spoiled by a pesky louse crawling through the lace of her bonnet! The poem closes with some memorable lines (somewhat translated):

"O, that some Power the gift would give us

To see ourselves as others see us!"

What could we need more? The Bible urges: "Do not think of yourself more highly than you ought, but rather think of yourself with sober judgment" (Rom. 12:3 NIV).

In order to see ourselves realistically we must "In humility receive the implanted word. . . ." (James 1:21). Then we must use that word as a mirror in order to see our true spiritual condition and change what needs changing (James 1:23–25).

True Christianity means:

SERVE, even when we are not being served.

LOVE, even when we may not be loved.

HELP, even when we have not been helped.

GIVE, even when we have not received.

PLEASE, even if others do not please us.

Selfish

764 Touching in Church

What is all this touching in church? It used to be a person could come to church and sit in the pew and not be bothered by all this friendliness and certainly not by touching.

I used to come to church and leave untouched. Now I have to be nervous about what is expected of me. I have to worry about responding to the person sitting next to me.

Oh, I wish it could be the way it used to be; I could just ask the person next to me, "How are you?" And the person could answer, "Oh, just fine." And we would both go home . . . strangers who have known each other for 20 years.

But now the minister asks us to look at each other. I am worried about that hurt look I saw in that woman's eyes.

Now I am upset because the lady next to me cried and then apologized and said it was because I was so kind and that she needed a friend right now. Now I have to get involved. Now I have to suffer when this community suffers. Now I have to be more than a person coming to observe a service.

That man last week told me I had never known how much I had touched his life. All I did was smile and tell him I understood what it was to be lonely.

Lord, I am not big enough to touch and be touched. The stretching scares me. What if I disappoint somebody? What if I am too pushy? What if I cling too much? What if somebody ignores me?

O Lord, be here beside me. You touch me, Lord, so that I can touch and be touched. So that I can care and be cared for. So that I can share my life with all those others that belong to you. All this touching in church, Lord, it is changing me!

765 Life and Self

During a Peter, Paul and Mary concert, in the middle of a comic skit, Paul made an insightful and disturbing observation. In the 50s there was a magazine called *Life*. Then came *People* magazine. Now we have one called *Us*. What next? A magazine called *Me*? And now there actually is a magazine called *Self.* How indicative and indicting of a world infatuated and preoccupied with *self*. How contrary to the example and lifegiving principles of the Christ. He came to bring life. He revealed and demonstrated the principles of life. He clearly taught that life is not to be found in living for self, but rather in GIVING OF SELF in the service of God and others! He said in Luke 9:23–15:

"If anyone wishes to come after Me, let him deny himself, and take up his cross daily, and follow Me.

For whoever wishes to save his life shall lose it, but whoever loses his life for My sake, he is the one who will save it. For what is a man profited if he gains the whole world, and loses or forfeits himself?"

Happiness is not found in the pursuit of happiness. Life is not found in the pursuit of life. Both are found in a pursuit of God and His righteousness. As Jesus said, "Blessed are those who hunger and thirst for righteousness, for they shall be satisfied" (Matt. 5:6). The end of our current emphasis on SELF is not life, but disappointment and ultimately death! If we would discover TRUE LIFE, then we must pursue the things of God and the spirit! ". . . whatever is true, whatever is honorable, whatever is right, whatever is pure, whatever is lovely, whatever is of good repute, if there is any excellence and anything worthy of praise, let your mind dwell on these things" (Phil. 4:8).

766 Rivalry in God's Family

Jay E. Adams writes that under the roof in his back yard hangs a hummingbird feeder that he keeps filled with sugar water. There are four openings in it from which birds may suck the nectar. Yet, day after day, from early morning until after dusk, the feeder is the source of their own private version of star wars. One bird chases all the others away.

"As I said," Adams writes, "there is room for four birds at a time, and fully that number attempt to feed. But the top dog (excuse my use of this metaphor for a hummingbird!), who now 'owns' the feeder, will not let them. All day long he sits on the branch of a nearby apricot tree guarding 'his' feeder and defying others to transgress on what he has established as 'his' territory.

"This ongoing slice of life confronts us throughout the day as green and red Annas hummers streak across the yard, the king hummer in hot pursuit of an intruder. While the chase is on, others sneak a sip or two, only to be driven off when he returns.

"The whole business has become a sort of parable for our family. Here is an example of grace: I bought the feeder; I supply the sugar water. The birds do not earn it; they receive it all *gratis*. Yet, day after day, they fight over who may enjoy it.

"How like the people of God! All we have or are that is worthwhile is the gift of God's pure grace. And yet we are proud, self-centered, envious, and quarrelsome. Often we fight over God's good gifts rather than expressing our gratitude in humility and sharing what we have been given with others. Just as I am confronted daily with rivalry in my yard, even so God is confronted daily with rivalry in His."

767 *Taking and Receiving*

"It is more blessed to give than to receive" (Acts 20:35).

There is an old story that goes like this:

An unusual tree grew outside the gates of a desert city in the Middle East. It was an old tree, a landmark as a matter of fact. It seemed to have been touched by the finger of God, for it bore fruit perpetually. Despite its old age, its limbs were constantly laden with fruit. Hundreds of passersby refreshed themselves from the tree as it never failed to give freely.

But then a greedy merchant purchased the property on which the tree grew. He saw hundreds of travelers "robbing" his tree, and he built a high fence around it. Travelers pleaded, "Share with us." The merchant quoted in return, "It is my tree, my fruit, bought with my money." And a strange thing happened: the old tree died! What had happened? The law of giving, as predictable as the law of gravity, had expressed its immutable principle: when a tree stops giving, it stops bearing, and it dies.

Yes, this story illustrates well the law of give-and-receive. And when I think of how much I take from God's world, I bow in guilt at how little I give to His work. "But this I say, He that soweth sparingly shall reap also sparingly" (2 Cor. 9:6).

768 *The Bare Facts*

One night two friends were camping out in the deep woods on a warm summer's night. Suddenly, their sleep was abruptly interrupted by a large furry visitor. A huge black bear began to tear through their camp, crushing supplies, throwing backpacks, and scaring the two men half to death. Thinking quickly, one of the men began to lace up his sneakers for a quick getaway. "You will never outrun that bear!" his friend yelled. To this he replied, "I don't have to outrun the bear, I just have to outrun you!"

Jesus taught us to put others first. His very actions and dealings with the beggars, the lepers, and thieves showed that He had compassion for the lowly. So the next time you have trouble with your brother remember the following:

"The world measures a man's greatness by the number who serve him. Heaven's yardstick measures a man by the number who are served by him."

Self-Pity

769 What We Think

Our Thinking:
  "It's impossible."
  "I am too tired."
  "Nobody really loves me."
  "Nobody really cares for me."
  "I cannot go on."
  "I cannot figure things out."
  "I cannot do it."
  "I am not worth it."
  "I cannot forgive myself."
  "I cannot afford to."

His Thinking:
  "All things are possible" Luke 18:27.
  "I will give you rest" Matthew 11:20–30.
  "I love you" John 3:16.

"I care for you" 1 Peter 5:7.
"My grace is sufficient" 2 Corinthians 12:9.
"I will direct your steps" Proverbs 20:24; 3:6.
"You can do all things" Philippians 4:13.
"I am able" 2 Corinthians 9:8.
"It will be worth it" Romans 8:28.
"I forgive you" Psalm 103:12; 1 John 1:9.
"I will supply all your needs" Philippians 4:19.

770 "I Cannot Do Any More for These People!"

Have you ever said that as a pastor? You have done your very best and yet your very best has not found acceptance with the people you serve. You may be just like Moses.

The children of Israel were unreasonable. Having grown tired of manna everyday, they chided Moses for not giving them meat to eat.

Moses was angry. "I have had it with these rebels," he complained. "I have done my very best, and this is the thanks I get."

Was Moses feeling sorry for himself? Indeed! He did not think God was being fair. He felt sure he deserved better than he was getting (Num. 11:10–15).

The feeling that we deserve better than we are getting always seems to be the basis of self-pity.

Sin

771 A Worm in an Apple

How does a worm get inside an apple? Perhaps you think the worm burrows in from the outside. No, scientists have discovered that the worm comes from the inside. But, how does he get in there? Simple. An insect lays an egg in the apple blossom. Sometime later the worm hatches in the heart of the apple, then eats his way out.

Sin, like the worm, begins in the heart and works out through the person's thoughts, word and actions. For this reason, David once wrote, "Create in me a clean heart, O God."

772 On Being Side-Tracked

An old fable says that swift-footed Atlanta challenged her suitors to race with her, with herself as the prize or death as the penalty of losing. Many competed and lost their lives. Finally, a man named Hippomenes, secreting on his person three golden apples, entered the contest. As with the others, Atlanta swiftly passed him, but he threw an apple. She, startled, stopped to pick it up. He regained the lead, but soon Hippomenes again saw himself gradually slipping behind; and again he threw a golden apple. Atlanta, charmed by its glitter, de-layed to seize it, and fell behind. But once again, as they neared the goal, she was about to pass him, and Hippomenes threw his last golden apple. Atlanta, lured by its charm, stopped again—and lost the race.

Satan today throws along life's highway three golden apples that charm and destroy many a racer. They are: "the lust of the eyes, the lust of the flesh, and the pride of life" (1 John 2:16). Multitudes of Christians today are being turned aside from full obedience to the will and work of God by Satan's "three golden apples!"

773 Sin Separates

"But your iniquities have separated between you and your God" (Is. 59:2). The Bible says that sin separates; it comes between man and God.

Sin is like a giant canyon, with man on one side and God on the other. A canyon can never be removed; it will always be there. And it is useless to try to fill up a canyon. But when a bridge is put across a canyon, a man can cross it as if no canyon ever existed there. Forgiveness of our sin is like a bridge. A bridge allows us to have eternal life, even though there is sin which otherwise would separate us from God.

Sin is also like a cut or break in an electric wire. There must be a perfect connection from the source to the light bulb before there can be any light in the bulb. Sin separates our connection with God. Forgiveness is like a splice in a wire. It does not take a brand new wire to complete the circuit, but there must be a wire in which every single break has been repaired.

Sin separates man and God. There is only one way to get back to God; through Jesus Christ!

774 "He Pays Too Much for His Whistle"

"No temptation has overtaken you but such as is common to man; and God is faithful, who will not allow you to be tempted beyond what you are able, but with the temptation will provide the way of escape also, that you may be able to endure it" (1 Cor. 10:13 NAS).

Here is a quote from Thomas Fleming, in *The Man Who Dared The Lightning*. "When Benjamin Franklin was seven years old, a visitor gave him some small change. Later, seeing another boy playing with a whistle, young Benjamin gave the boy all his money for it. He played the whistle all over the house, enjoying it until he discovered that he had given four times as much as the whistle was worth. Instantly, the whistle lost its charm. As he grew older, Franklin generalized this principle. When he saw a man neglecting his family or business for political popularity, or a miser

giving up friendship for the sake of accumulating wealth, he would say, 'He pays too much for his whistle.'"

The above story has an excellent lesson in it: Too often we pay too great a price for something that looks so good and promises so much. Fish are hooked because they are attracted to something that looks like food and would make a good meal only to become food themselves. Do not be fooled, the world offers you whistles that are not worth the price.

775 Sheep Do Not Wallow

Children sometimes do not listen. They hear what they want to hear. We, as their parents, often strive to work in their lives and give them guidelines to follow for their own good and because we love them. We know and understand this, but many times our children do not. They become angry and resentful towards us because they believe we are robbing them of fully experiencing life, and we are taking away their opportunities for fun and happiness. We sometimes want to beat our heads against a wall in frustration.

I wonder if God feels that way also in regards to us, His children? Listen to this story:

There was once a lamb and its mother. It seems the lamb passed a pig pen each morning on the way to pasture with its mother. Watching the pigs wallow in the mud seemed like fun to the lamb, and on an especially hot day the lamb asked his mother if he could jump the fence and wallow in the cool mud. She replied, "No." Then the lamb asked the question, "Why?" The mother just said, "SHEEP DO NOT WALLOW."

This did not satisfy the lamb. He felt she had "put him down and exercised force she should not have," etc. So, as soon as the mother was out of sight, the lamb ran to the pig pen and jumped the fence. He was soon feeling the cool mud on his feet, his legs, and soon his stomach. After a few moments he decided he had better go back to his mother, but he could not. He was stuck! Mud and wool do not mix. His pleasure had become his prison. He cried out and was rescued by the kindly farmer. When cleaned and returned to the fold, the mother said, "Remember, sheep do not wallow."

776 Nine Out of Ten

A news documentary on TV claimed that 91 percent of the United States' students in colleges, universities and graduate schools cheat on exams and tests in order to graduate.

This is what happens when God is rejected and atheism is accepted. Atheism will bring down our civilization. Civilization is based on mutual trust.

Cheating is lying. It is stealing that which is not yours. What confidence do you have in your doctors when you realize that nine out of ten are not really qualified because they stole information they did not

know in order to graduate? How honest do you expect the billing to be when nine out of ten of them lied to get through college? If he cheated the college, how do you know he will not cheat you? How does society survive when you lose trust in 91 percent of college graduates?

The same is true of lawyers, politicians, and store keepers. Stores will post one price at the shelf and charge a higher price at the cash register. Customers seldom catch it because the little bars flash across the computer too fast. When it is caught, there is a quick apology, the figure is changed and it is blamed on "computer error." But the "computer error" is not corrected.

We remember when a man was as good as his word. A handshake over a deal was as dependable as a legal document. A man would rather die than lie or cheat. Neighbors who did not go to church, prided themselves in their own integrity. Christian standards formed the basis of society even among those who did not profess to be Christians.

777 Passing the Buck

Almost everyone is aware of the statement attributed to President Harry Truman that "The Buck Stops Here," but does it? There are people who will not accept responsibility for their actions. Included in this group are criminals and sociopaths. The war trials at Nuremberg brought out this idea. The Nazi war criminals claimed they were just following orders. "We really did not want to exterminate the Jews. Hitler made us do it." The criminal says, "I am a product of society. They are to blame, not me." The wife and child abuser says, "I was raised by abusive parents, so do not blame me; blame them." The denial of guilt does not remove or negate the responsibility of it.

In our society today we are just as sick as they were then. No one wants to accept responsibility for anything. Everything is relative, so do what you want to. It is O.K. Well, friends and neighbors, that is plain junk. It just ain't so. Of course, anyone can play the game of denial. It all started a long time ago. Genesis 3:1–19 tells us that Adam ate the forbidden fruit and God held him responsible. Adam said, "I am not responsible. You know the woman you gave me, remember her? She gave me fruit from the tree and I did eat. But do not blame me, you gave her to me so blame her, but not me." God then went and asked Eve, "What have you done?" Eve said, "The serpent deceived me and I ate." "The devil made me do it," was Flip Wilson's favorite line. God held them both responsible for their actions. He will hold us responsible for ours. The soul that sinneth shall die. When we sin, let us ask God to forgive us, and then we should take the consequence that goes with it.

778 Hidden Faults

At a U.S. arsenal a few years ago, a large cannon lay, marked "Con-demned." The attendant pointed out some indentations about the size of a pinhead which dotted the barrel in a dozen places. They did not appear to go deeper than a 32nd of an inch; and yet the weapon was condemned. There might be a weakness extending through the entire gun, so that in war the mighty engine capable of hurling half a ton of metal, a dozen miles and hitting a target with fine accuracy, might under the heat of battle and the strain of powder, burst into a thousand fragments. Some basic flaw may destroy our characters and ruin others, be we ever so perfect in other points.

779 The Force of Habit

How easy it is to tear a piece of paper along the line in which it has originally been folded! How easy it is for a second temptation to over-come when the first has been yielded to! A sin that has once gained the victory over our moral nature has put a fold, as it were, in that nature, and destroyed its straightness and smoothness, so that when the same temptation comes a second time, it seeks the weak point which it had formerly made, and along that line of least re-sistance we are turned from our righteous principles and strong res-olution.

780 Insensitivity to Sin

A little girl in London held up her broken wrist and said, "Look, Mommy, my hand is bent the wrong way!" There were no tears in her eyes. She felt no pain whatever. That was when she was four years old.

When she was six, her parents noticed that she was walking with a limp. A doctor discovered that the girl had a fractured thigh. Still she felt no pain.

The girl is now 14 years old. She is careful now, but occasionally looks at blisters and burns on her hands and wonders, "How did this happen?" She is insensitive to pain! Medical specialists are baffled by the case. It is called ganglineuropathy.

There is another insensitiveness which is deadlier and more dangerous—insensitiveness to sin! Paul said of people with this malady: they had "their consciences seared as with a hot iron" (1 Tim. 4:2).

781 Not Eatin', Just Holdin'

Johnny asked Mother, "Can I have some cookies, Mom?" Looking at the clock, she replied, "Not now! It is too close to dinner!"

About ten minutes later, Mother entered the kitchen. There was Johnny up on the counter with his arm in the cookie jar clear up to his elbow. "I thought I just told you, 'No cookies till dinner!' " Johnny's mother fumed. "Well, Mom, I'm not eaten' no cookies! I'm just holdin' some!"

Each of us has some point of vulnerability. It may be a problem with alcohol, or sensuous lusts, or a desire to gamble even to the point of cheating. We often compound our problems by putting ourselves into untenable positions and precipitous situations.

Johnny would have had a much easier time if he had avoided the cookie jar. We would not fail so often if we avoided places where we would be subject to temptations. We ought not go where alcohol is served; we ought to avoid the magazine rack where the flesh is enticed; we ought to abstain from those things which tempt us to be dishonest. Let us cease giving the flesh easy opportunities!

782 The Mark of Sin

"For the Word of God is living, and powerful, and sharper than any two-edged sword, piercing even to the dividing asunder of soul and spirit, and of the joints and marrow, and is a discerner of the thoughts and intents of the heart" (Heb. 4:12).

As the powerful chain saw cut its way through the oak tree, it uncovered an object foreign to a tree. There, embedded in the tree was a 22-bullet, once hidden from view, now made visible by the cutting asunder of the tree.

From the outside, the point of entry was no longer visible, but on the inside, the path of the bullet had clearly left its mark in the wood. Compared to the size of the tree, it was an extremely small mark, yet by its presence, had caused the area surrounding it to turn black with rot.

Had one been present when the bullet entered the tree, it would have been possible not only to see the mark, but to dig the bullet out. However, with the passing of time, the tree grew larger and stronger. The bark had grown thicker and the bullet remained hidden, a part of the tree.

Just as the bullet penetrated into the tree, so sin penetrates us. The point of entry may not be visible to anyone else, but the sin becomes embedded in our lives, and unless it is removed, causes a growing spot to rot.

783 Sin Scars

When Leonardo da Vinci was a young artist during the Renaissance in Italy, he is reported to have painted a beautiful portrait of a young child who appeared in the picture as an angel. The artist was so pleased with the work that he kept it in his studio where he could gaze upon it. Often, it is said, looking at that picture would comfort his soul in sorrow or tranquilize his heart in anger.

Much later in life, after many years had passed, he was doing another picture. For this canvas he needed the portrait of a man whose countenance would personify evil. Long and diligently he searched for a model and at last found one. The features had been so scarred by sin that the portrait was the exact opposite of that of the child.

Then an amazing thing happened. The model told the artist that he had been the child whose picture still hung in the studio. This crime-hardened man with dissipation written across his countenance had been the angelic-appearing child who had personified all that was good.

784 The Invasion of Evil

Over wide areas of the United States, carpenter bees begin swarming around the roofs and eaves of houses when spring arrives looking for edible wood in which to nest. The bees make a small hole in the wood and lay their eggs. Though the initial hole is small, over time more and more of the inner wood is eaten away. Even though the surface of the wood looks good, enough carpenter bees can eat away the strength of the supporting timbers of a home and eventually destroy it. The home owner must guard against such attacks.

Similarly, the Christian must guard against the attacks of sin which bore within, seeking a foothold in one's life. Just as the carpenter bees multiply and feed on the wood, sin multiplies and feeds on the soul. It is better to keep the sin out in the first place than to root it out after it invades.

785 The Cost of Compromise

Winter was coming on and a hunter went out into the forest to shoot a bear out of which he planned to make a warm coat.

By and by he saw a big bear coming toward him and raised his gun and took aim.

"Wait," said the bear, "why do you want to shoot me?"

"Because I am cold," said the hunter, "and I need a coat."

"But I am hungry," the bear replied, "so maybe if we just talk this over a little, we could come to a compromise."

So the hunter sat down beside the bear and began to talk over the pros and cons. In the end, the hunter was well enveloped with the bear's fur, and the bear had eaten his dinner.

We always lose out when we try to compromise with sin. It will consume us in the end.

786 *Licking the Blade*

Paul Harvey tells how an Eskimo kills a wolf. He coats his knife blade with blood and lets it freeze. Then he adds another coat of blood and then another. As each coat freezes he adds another smear of blood until the blade is hidden deep within a substantial thickness of frozen blood.

Then he buries the knife—blade up—in the frozen tundra. The wolf catches the scent of fresh blood and begins to lick it. He licks it more and more feverishly until the blade is bare. Then he keeps on licking harder and harder. Because of the cold he never notices the pain of the blade on his tongue. His craving for the taste of blood is so great that he does not realize his thirst is being satisfied by his own blood. He licks the blade till he bleeds to death, swallowing his own life.

That is the way the devil works on us. He gives us a taste of sin, knowing we will crave more. We go deeper and deeper in satisfying our desires. We never notice the blade inside till it is too late. Only when we are dying do we realize we have swallowed our own life in sin.

787 *Sin Against God*

A lady in a carpool took God's name in vain and immediately apologized to her companions. One of them quickly responded, "You do not owe us an apology. You did not use our names."

Sin does hurt people around us and requires a reconciliation with that person. But we must always remember, with David, "Against Thee, Thee only, I have sinned, and done what is evil in Thy sight" (Ps. 5:14 NASB).

788 *Our Concept of Righteousness*

There are Christians who, in effect, define righteousness by what they shun. They keep away from certain foods and drinks, from certain people, from certain places.

There certainly are occasions when Christians do well to keep their distance, but our Lord's emphasis was against that way of defining unrighteousness. He stressed one's internal attitude, regardless of the external surroundings: "What comes out of a man is what defiles a man. For from within, out of the heart of man, come evil thoughts, fornication, theft, murder, adultery, coveting, wickedness, deceit, licentiousness, envy, slander, pride, foolishness" (Mark 7:20–22).

It is convenient to focus on the sins of others; this keeps the spotlight away from oneself. And it is convenient to understand sin in terms of actions that can be physically avoided; one can thereby avoid disturbing thoughts about attitudes such as coveting, envy, and pride, which our Lord includes on his list of "evil things" right along with theft, murder, and adultery.

God everywhere shows a lot of concern about sin, and so should we. But it is the nature of sin to deceive us, even when we think we are being righteous. We must work at keeping our understandings and emphasis in line with what God has revealed.

789 A Fence or an Ambulance

A certain community was near a dangerous highway curve where several cars had misguided the curve and fallen over a cliff. Great discussion took place in the town over what to do about the situation. Some in the discussion group thought it a good idea to station an ambulance at the bottom of this cliff to give immediate aid to the victims. Wiser heads suggested it might be better to erect a fence around the curve on top of the cliff.

To us, such a discussion is ridiculous. We know it is much better to prevent accidents and deaths than to treat them after the fact. Let us not overlook the truth that this principle also has much spiritual merit.

We need not debate whether Christians sin. The New Testament speaks plainly. If we claim to be without sin, we deceive ourselves and the truth is not in us. If we claim we have not sinned, we make Him out to be a liar, and His Word has no place in our lives. The Apostle John immediately follows this truth with a powerful statement of assurance. "My dear children, I write this to you so that you will not sin. But if anybody does sin, we have One who speaks to the Father in our defense, Jesus Christ, the Righteous One" (1 John 2:1, 2).

Although forgiveness and grace are abundant, Jesus does not intend for us to just focus on these. He not only provides forgiveness, He also gives us the power to keep from sin. How much better that we focus on the "fence" at the top rather than on the "ambulance" at the bottom.

790 Intellectualism and Immoral Life

Josh McDowell relates how he was counseling a student who said she was fed up with Christianity because she did not think it was historically accurate nor that there was actually anything to it. She had convinced everyone in her circle that she had searched and found profound intellectual problems with Christianity as a result of her university studies.

One after another of her classmates tried to persuade her otherwise; but to no avail. Josh asked her several pointed questions. Within 30 minutes she admitted that she had fooled everyone including herself, and that she had developed her intellectual doubts in order to excuse her immoral life.

791 *Nip Sin in the Bud*

Sin is deceitful (Heb. 3:13). Sin's progression is one of its characteristics it seeks to conceal.

The "blessed man" of Psalm 1 (1) walketh not, (2) standeth not, and (3) sitteth not. Observe the progression. That Lot pitched his tent toward Sodom, and did not immediately move there, is illustrative of the progressiveness of sin.

Eve (1) heard the devil's lie, (2) believed the lie, and (3) obeyed it. Sin is progressive. The prodigal son gradually went to the far country, which illustrates sin's progression.

Peter (1) first deserted the Lord, (2) later fraternized with the enemy, (3) then, denied the Lord, (4) afterwards committed perjury, and (5) finally, he cursed and blasphemed. Sin was progressive in his case.

Be not deceived, for sin is still progressive. Social drinking can easily lead to alcoholism.

Dancing has been the first step in many cases leading to an ultimate destruction of one's virtue.

Missing the mid-week service can lead to missing the Sunday night service, then Sunday morning Bible school, then the Sunday morning worship service—yea, to complete apostasy.

Envy can grow into hatred, and hatred can grow into murder. Be not deceived. Sin is deceptive. It grows. It is progressive. Therefore, resist every temptation, choosing the way of escape always provided (1 Cor. 10:13). Give none occasion to sin. Abstain from every appearance of evil (1 Thess. 5:22).

Nip sin in the bud! Otherwise, it will grow! "Woe to the rebellious children, saith the Lord, that take counsel, but not of Me; and that cover with a covering, but not of My Spirit that they may add sin to sin" (Is. 30:1).

792 *Less Than Expected*

A fellow decided to rob a convenience store clerk. The robber had a neat plan to give the clerk a $10 bill, get her to open her cash drawer to make change, and then grab all the money. The plan worked! He got everything in her cash drawer—total $4.34—and left the clerk with his $10. He went in the hole to the tune of $5.66!

The undeniable truth is that sin never gives what it promises. It always returns less than the sinner invests in self-esteem, integrity, and spiritual security. Want proof?

—Adam and Eve were promised freedom, wisdom and life by Satan, only to be led to commit spiritual suicide.

—Sensuous Samson fell in love with a woman who did not love God, and he paid with his eyesight, freedom and life.

—Ananias and Sapphira were going to get credit for being generous and wound up being buried for being liars.

In each of these cases, sin promised something it could never deliver. The same thing is still happening in our world today.

—Adolescents are led to see God, their parents, and their teachers as enemies and wind up in rebellion's deep pit.

—People date and marry without taking into account that the spiritual element is the critical part of a relationship.

—Some church members hide behind masks and fool themselves and their friends, but not God.

Sin costs too much. You have to sell your soul to have whatever pretty trinkets it offers you for the moment. Then you have to face a time of bitter reckoning. You have to "pay the piper." Yet whatever had been promised to you as a reward has already gone up in a puff of smoke or has slipped through your fingers. And Judgment Day is coming! The basic lure of sin is the promise of quick gain, without regard to long-term consequences.

Truth and holiness work differently. With total honesty about the difficult demands at hand, the God who cannot lie promises to reward you down the line. Obedience, purity, integrity, repentance, denial— these are hard words and demanding deeds. But what lies at the end is invaluable!

Sin never delivers. Christ never fails. So don't get robbed while trying to pull a fast one on God.

793 Pain and Pills

You and I live in a world that is obsessed with the elimination of pain. Just take a stroll down the medicine aisle next time you are in the grocery store. You will see what I mean. When we have a headache, we take two aspirin, take a nap, and wake up feeling better. We forget the pain.

Face it, we do not like pain. But is that entirely healthy? Could it be that in some matter of my life, there is room for pain? Can it be at times I **should** feel some pain? The question pleads for affirmation.

Along with solutions to our physical pains, I am afraid we have mistakenly found a cure for our spiritual pain. Sadly, this is a deadly cure! To avoid the pain of sin, we have taken a deadly pill which diminishes the impact and consequence of sin in our lives. We have closed our eyes to the destruction of sin and swallowed a pill of deception. We do not feel the burdensome ache of sin.

For Israel, it was not enough for a prophet to forecast impending doom as a consequence of sin to get them to repent. More often than not, Israel had to face the consequence of sin to come to repentance; they had to feel pain. In Joel 2:12, 13, we see Israel's pain manifested: "Return to Me with all your heart, with fasting and weeping and mourning. Rend your heart and not your garments."

To rend something means to rip or tear in grief, anger, rage, etc. We must ask ourselves when we last felt the need to tear our hearts because of sin. Feel the injury of sin and avoid the problem of pain! Let us rend our hearts today and feel the pain. We must return to God.

Spiritual

794 Do We Really Love Heaven?

Field Marshall Viscount Montgomery, an Englishman who was not ashamed to assert his faith in God, was invited to speak at the opening of a hymn book publisher's new printing plant. He urged rewriting some of the hymns which he found dismally at odds with man's true nature.

Montgomery said, "We sing, 'O Paradise, O Paradise, How I long for Thee.' But we do not really long for that. We long to stay on here a bit longer."

Then he added, "I would like to see an author write 'O Paradise, O Paradise, I have a little shop, and just as long as profits last, here I mean to stop.'"

795 Ready To Perish

The man huddled on the cabin floor was slowly freezing to death. It was high in the Rockies in southwestern Alberta, and outside a blizzard raged. John Elliot had logged miles that day through the deep snows of the mountain passes. As he checked for avalanches, and as dusk and exhaustion overcame him, he had decided to "hole up." He made it wearily to his cabin but somewhat dazed with fatigue, he did not light a fire or remove his wet clothing.

As the blizzard blasted through the cracks in the old cabin walls, the sleeping forest ranger sank into oblivion, paralyzed by the pleasure of the storm's icy caress. Suddenly, however, his dog sprang into action, and with unrelenting whines, finally managed to rouse his near-comatose friend.

The dog was John's constant companion, a St. Bernard, one of a long line of dogs famous for their heroics in times of crisis. "If that dog had not been with me, I would be dead today," John Elliott says. "When you are freezing to death you actually feel warm all over, and do not wake up because it feels too good."

796 Political or Spiritual Liberty

On July 4, 1776, the Second Continental Congress declared the 13 American colonies free and independent from Great Britain. The Declaration of Independence is the only major national document of the United States that actually mentions the name of God. He is called "Nature's God," "The Creator," and "The Supreme Judge of the World." The fathers of our American freedom recognized that God's hand was at work in the affairs of the new nation. But far more important than the political liberty that we enjoy is the spiritual liberty we have in Christ. Jesus said, "And ye shall know the truth, and the truth shall make you free" (John 8:32).

Blindness

797 Tom Lincoln's Baby Boy

My favorite caricature about Abraham Lincoln shows two tired Kentucky pioneers with their skinny dogs. They meet on a bleak February morning. One asked, "What is new out here, neighbor?" The other replied, "Nuthin at all . . . nuthin' at all, 'cept for a new baby boy down to Tom Lincoln's. Nuthin' ever happens out here."

In the light of history we know that God was causing great things to happen on that cold February morning—things of which the despondent pioneers were not aware.

In the dark moments of discouragement, we, too, have felt like that pioneer: "Nuthin' ever happens out here." Then we realize that God is still working out His purpose in life. The fault lies in our own lack of awareness. We may miss what God is doing all around us. Could we but develop an awareness, our lives would be filled with light and joy. God's love envelops us, but we must respond to that love if we are to experience its real meaning.

798 The Calf Path

Edward Fudge tells this story:
One day through the primeval wood, a calf walked home as good calves should. But made a trail all bent askew, a crooked trail as all calves do.

Since then 300 years have fled, and I infer the calf is dead. But still he left behind his trail—and thereby hangs my moral tale.

The trail was taken up next day by a lone dog that passed that way. And then a wise bellwether sheep pursued the trail o'er vale and steep, and drew the flock behind him, too, as good bellwethers always do.

And from that day, o'er hill and glade, through those old woods a path was made. And many men wound in and out, and dodged and turned and bent about, and uttered words of righteous wrath because 'twas such a crooked path.

But still they followed the first migrations of that calf, who through this winding woodway stalked—because he wobbled when he walked.

This forest path became a lane, that bent and turned and turned again. This crooked lane became a road, where many a poor horse with his load toiled on beneath the burning sun, and traveled some three miles in one. And thus a century and a half they trod the footsteps of that calf.

The years passed on in swiftness fleet. The road became a village street; and this, before men were aware, a city's crowded thoroughfare. And soon the central street was this of a renowned metropolis.

And men two centuries and a half
trod in the footsteps of that calf.

Each day a hundred thousand
rout followed this zigzag calf about,
and over his crooked journey went
the traffic of a continent.

A hundred thousand men were
led by one calf, near three centuries
dead. They followed still his
crooked way, and lost 100 years a
day. For thus such reverence is lent
to well-established precedent.

A moral lesson this might teach
were I ordained and called to
preach. For men are prone to go it
blind along the calf paths of the
mind, and work away from sun to
sun to do what other men have
done.

They follow in the beaten track,
and out and in, and forth and back,
and still their dubious course pursue, to keep the path that others
do.

They keep the path a sacred
groove, along which all their lives
they move. But how the wise old
woods do laugh, who saw the first
primeval calf.

Ah, many thing this tale might
teach, but I am not ordained to
preach!

799 *Walking in Darkness*

Christopher D. Green writes:

"I cannot explain why I do it, but
I have always walked in the dark.
When I was a kid I used to do it
more as a challenge; an adventure.
Now as an adult, I suppose it is more
out of habit than anything else.

"If I get up in the middle of the
night, I refuse to turn on the lights.

Instead of simply flipping a switch
and lighting my way, I wander
around in the dark, relying on my
sixth sense to guide me. Usually, I
guess from all these years of practice, I can get to my intended destination without incident. However,
a few nights ago proved to be one of
exception and painful consequence.

"After being in bed for an hour or
so, I got up to get a drink of water.
With my mouth as dry as the inside
of a Kleenex box, I shuffled down
the hall half asleep but still awake
enough to enjoy the tickling feeling
the carpet made on my feet. As I
cleared the end of the hall, it felt
good to pause by the heater. Continuing on only a few shuffles more,
I met my doom. I think I actually
felt the pain before it happened.
With one fairly innocent shuffle, I
crashed my foot into the dining
room chair. The force was so great it
knocked the chair over, and left me
in a painful pile on the floor. The
scream was muffled only because I
had a mouth full of plush pile carpet.
If I had only turned on the light, I
would have avoided the pain!

"Too often Christians forget that
they should not spiritually walk
around in the dark. Not only should
they avoid the darkness, they
should also be a light that exposes
the evil that is found in darkness.

"Remember that if we 'walk in
the light as He is in the light, we
have fellowship with one another,
and the blood of Jesus, His Son, pu-
rifies us from every sin' (1 John
1:7)."

800 Thanks for What Is of Greater Value

There is a story of a young man who proposed marriage to a young woman. He gave her an expensive, beautiful diamond ring enclosed in an attractive blue velvet box. The following day after their engagement, the young woman said, "How can I ever thank you enough for the beautiful blue velvet box? I love it and will always cherish it!" How do you think her beloved felt?

A ludicrous story? Yes, except that it aptly illustrates the care and attention we humans give in this life to our body and physical well beings—which is like the blue velvet box. We spend about 99 percent of our resources and time on something that will return to dust. And we neglect the gift of the diamond, which is our living, eternal soul. We fail to thank God for such a priceless gift, purchased for us by the death of His Son, Jesus Christ.

Nourishment

801 Sermons—Not Remembered, But . . .

There was an article in a church paper entitled, "32,850 Sermons Later." It started off with a letter printed in the British Weekly from one of their English readers. The British letter went like this:

"Dear Sir,

'It seems ministers feel their sermons are very important and spend a great deal of time preparing them. I have been attending a church quite regularly for the past 30 years, and I have probably heard 3,000 of them. To my consternation, I discovered that I cannot remember a single sermon. I wonder if a minister's time might be more profitably spent on something else?

"Sincerely. . . ."

For weeks a real storm of editorial responses ensued. The uproar finally was ended by this letter:

"Dear Sir:

"I have been married for 30 years. During that time I have eaten 32,850 meals—mostly of my wife's cooking. Suddenly, I have discovered that I cannot remember the menu of a single meal. And yet, I have received nourishment from every single one of them. I have the distinct impression that without them. I would have starved to death long ago.

"Sincerely. . . ."

Sight

802 No Glass Between

The story is told of a little boy whose family was very poor. He never complained because he had no toys and received no gifts at Christmas time; but he wished for them. He spent his spare time looking in the store windows at the pretty things other little boys could have but that he could not.

One day he was run down by a car and taken to the hospital. When he started to feel better, one of the nurses bought him a toy. As he touched it he said, "There is not any glass between."

Some day we shall see Christ our Savior face to face, with no "glass" between.

803 Have Your Eyes Been Opened?

The Second Book of Kings and the sixth chapter tells us of an interesting event. Elisha, the prophet of God, was given knowledge of the planned activities of the Syrian King to destroy Israel. Elisha warned Israel, which angered the Syrian King, who then sought to kill Elisha. The servant of Elisha awoke one morning, looked out and saw the Syrian army surrounding the city. He became very frightened. But Elisha was not afraid because he could see the Lord's protection.

Then, in verse 17, Elisha prayed that the Lord would open the eyes of the servant that he, too, would see what Elisha saw. In this prayer, Elisha was not referring to physical sight. The servant had that, for he could see the army, but he had no spiritual sight to see the Lord's protection.

Now there are many people who have perfect vision in the natural eyes, but they are blind spiritually, just as this young servant of Elisha.

Only the Lord can give men spiritual eyes to see their lost and ruined condition. Only the Lord can show men the holy wrath of God against their sin. Only the Lord can reveal the glory of a beaten, scourged, and crucified Christ. Only the Lord can give men a revelation of the exalted, risen, Christ, ruling the universe and providing for, protecting, and caring for His redeemed. Without this revelation, no man will come to Christ in saving faith.

Have your eyes been opened to see the glorious person and work of the blessed Son of God? The young servant of Elisha could not see the mountains full of horses and chariots of fire around Elisha until the Lord opened his eyes. Neither can the sinner see the glory of Christ until the Lord opens his blind eyes.

"Lord, I pray Thee, open their eyes, that they may see."

804 John Milton's Example

John Milton (1608–1674) became totally blind at the age of 43, but he did not give up. During his childhood and early years he absorbed a vast knowledge and remembrance of the Scriptures. To this he added mastery of the Latin and Greek classics which he studied in their original languages. At the age of 47, while immersed in total darkness, he began writing his monumental epic, *Paradise Lost*, which he completed in 10 years, and which to this day is generally regarded as the most sublime and the greatest non-dramatic poem in the English language. As a writer, he ranks second only to Shakespeare.

The Holy Scriptures lifted him out of his perpetual darkness and thereby God "amply furnished my mind and conscience with eyes," as he stated to his friend, Philara, in Athens. He exulted in the Lord; his spirit was alive with unction from above: "While God so tenderly provides for me," he said, "while He so graciously leads me by the hand and conducts me on the way, I will, since it is His pleasure, rather rejoice than repine at being blind."

Stewardship

805 Where Is the Time?

Fred sat in his car, glaring angrily at the red traffic light—one minute, two minutes, three minutes! You would think for those little side roads they would have only a one-minute green light. There, only two cars went through all the time that he and the other motorists on the main road were waiting! How frustrating! Those lights always seem to turn red just as you drive up.

Behind Fred, in another car, sits Tom. But he does not mind the light a bit. It just gives him a chance to learn another Bible verse. He has a new one in a little stand on the dashboard, and he is saying it over and over. By the time the light changes, he will have another verse to use in witnessing!

It is estimated that the average motorist spends 26 hours a year waiting for traffic signals to change. And if Fred and Tom are average motorists, then Fred will spend 26 hours a year running his blood pressure up in angry frustration, and Tom will spend 26 hours a year memorizing God's Word so he will be a better servant of Jesus Christ.

806 It Is Finished

Apart from our Lord, it is hard to think of historical figures whose dying words were, "It is accomplished!" Alexander the Great conquered Persia, but broke down and wept because his troops were too exhausted to push on to India. Hugo Grotius, the father of modern international law, said at the last, "I have accomplished nothing worthwhile in my life." John Quincy Adams, sixth President of the United States—not a Lincoln, perhaps, but a decent leader—wrote in his diary: "My life has been spent in vain and idle aspirations, and in ceaseless rejected prayers that something would be the result of my existence beneficial to my species." Robert Louis Stevenson wrote words that continue to delight and enrich our lives, and yet what did he pen for his epitaph? "Here lies one who meant well, who tried a little, and failed much." Cecil Rhodes opened up Africa and established an empire, but what were his dying words? "So little done, so much to do."

807 Wealth of Time

If you had a bank that credited your account each morning with $86,400, that carried over no balance from day to day, and allowed you to keep no cash in your account, and every evening canceled whatever part of the amount you had failed to use during the day, what would you do? Draw out every cent, of course.

Well, you have such a bank, and its name is "Time." Every morning it credits you with 86,400 seconds. Every night it rules off, as lost, whatever of this you have failed to invest to good purpose. It carries over no balances. It allows no overdrafts. Each day it opens a new account with you. Each night it burns the records of the day. If you fail to use the day's deposits, the loss is yours. There is no going back. There is no drawing against tomorrow. You must live in the present—on today's deposits. Invest it so as to get from it the utmost in health, happiness and success!

Only one life
'Twill soon be past,
Only what is done for the Lord
Will last!

808 Tossed Salad

One day as a mother was scraping and peeling vegetables for a salad, her daughter came to ask her permission to go to an amusement center that had a bad reputation. On the defensive, the daughter admitted it was a questionable place, but "all the other girls were going."

As the teenage daughter pleaded to go, she suddenly saw her mother pick up a handful of discarded vegetable peelings and toss them into the salad. Startled, she cried, "Mother, you are putting garbage into the salad." "Yes," her mother replied, "I know' but I thought that if you did not mind garbage in your mind and heart, you certainly would not mind a little garbage in your stomach.

Thoughtfully, the girl removed the offending material from the salad, and with a brief, "Thank You" to her mother she went to tell her friends that she would not be going with them.

If you have spiritual indigestion and a poor testimony, maybe it is because you have tossed too much garbage in the salad.

809 Only One Life

With a shining quarter, a tiny little boy went into a candy store. With the utmost seriousness, studying each assortment with deep thoughtfulness, he wandered from case to case. Tired of waiting, his mother called, "Hurry, son, spend your quarter. We must be going." The child replied, "But Mama, I have got to spend it carefully; I only have one."

You, too, have only one life. How are you spending it?

810 Buried Talents

Talent is a strange word; it means a coin or one's capability or a gift.

So when we are given children and we neglect to tell them the stories of faith, we are burying our talents. When we are given friends and we neglect to significantly touch their lives, we are burying our talents. And when we are given a song to sing and we sing it not, we are burying our talents.

Whatever talent means—whatever it is we are burying—our

money, our faith, our love or a song, the meaning of the story is clear: burying talents means not using God's gifts.

811 Who Is Robbed in Unfaithfulness?

An interesting fable is told of a rich man who wanted to help a poor man. The rich man hired the poor man to build a house on the hillside and went away on a long journey. The carpenter said to himself, "My boss is away and I can use cheap materials for the parts of the house which will not show. The house will be weak and undesirable but nobody will know except me."

But when the rich man returned he said, "The house is not for me: it is for you!"

The carpenter accepted the key in astonishment. Instead of a first class home he now had a fourth-class home.

God gives us a job, a life to build. We have to live in the house we build. If we do a shoddy job, we cheat one person—ourself.

812 On Being Honest

Many stories are told of Paul Gerhardt whose hymns are still sung in Germany. John Wesley translated some of them into English.

Gerhardt's family was very poor. He was the shepherd boy who cared for the small flock of sheep and goats on the edge of the forest. One day a hunter came out from among the trees and asked the lad how far it was to the nearest village.

"Six miles, sire," he replied, "but the road is only a sheep track and can easily be missed."

"I have lost my way, and I am very tired," returned the hunter. "Leave your sheep and show me the way. I will pay you well."

"No, sire," said Gerhardt. "I cannot do that for they would stray into the forest and be stolen or eaten by the wolves."

"Never mind; your master would never miss one or two, and I would pay you more than the price of one or two sheep.

"But sire, my master trusts me with these sheep, and I have promised not to leave them."

"Well," said the hunter, "let me take care of the sheep while you fetch me food from the village and a guide."

"The sheep do not know your voice and would not obey you, sir."

"Can you not trust me? Do I not look like an honest man?" asked the hunter with a frown.

"Sir," said the boy slowly, "You tried to make me false to my trust, and break my word to my master. How do I know that you will keep your word to me?"

The hunter could not help laughing.

"I see you are an honest lad, and I will not forget you," said the hunter. "Which is the path? I must find my way for myself."

But Gerhardt would not let the man depart hungry, so he gave him the humble contents of his scrip. Just at that moment several men came hurrying through the forest uttering shouts of delight as they caught sight of the two of them. Gerhardt had been talking to the Grand Duke, and these were his attendants who had been much alarmed at his disappearance.

This was the beginning of Gerhardt's future career of honor and success. Pleased with the lad's honesty, the Duke had him well educated and thus gave him a good state in life.

Yes, God wants us to be honest in His sight, and to our fellowman. You will find throughout your life that it pays to be honest.

813 Mothball Christians

I once read that the United States Navy has 768 ships which comprise what they call the "mothball navy." These ships are anchored in various harbors around the country. They receive regular maintenance, being repainted periodically and receiving frequent electrical impulses to retard the process of rust and corrosion. Moisture content of the air in their inner compartments is kept at a proper level with giant humidifiers. While these ships can be readied for combat on very short notice, at the present time they just sit there doing absolutely nothing. The only purpose they presently serve is to provide jobs for those who provide the upkeep.

It set me thinking about "mothball Christians." How many do you suppose comprise that fleet? They are being preserved somewhat through the ministry of concerned friends.

They consume incredible amounts of time and energy in local churches. Periodically someone must go after them and try to reactivate them. Their talents and abilities are not being used for anything constructive. They are on the church roll and perhaps feel snugly harbored because of it. They receive a lot of attention and loving concern, but never give anything in return. They are served, not serving.

I can see a legitimate reason for maintaining our "mothball navy." National security is at stake. But there is no excuse for believers to remain inactive. The energy and manpower needed to win the world is sidetracked—used up on those who should be involved in helping reach the world. Every Christian is responsible for using his God-given abilities for the salvation of the world.

814 No Time for Time-Outs

In football when the team faces a tough decision, the coach often calls for a time-out. In basketball when the press is on, the captain can call for a time-out. In soccer when the team is bushed, they can gain a few minutes respite with a time-out.

But life does not work that way. There is no way that we can stop the clock to think about our problems. We cannot save, store, or stretch time. We may use or we may abuse time, but the clock keeps on ticking—inexorably. We can only plan how to spend the time given to us.

815 What Kind of Nail Are You?

Here is a parable of a nail that teaches a great lesson:

A new place of worship had just been completed. People came from near and far to see it. They admired the beauty of its windows, the walls, the carpet on the floors. Preachers were carried away with the handsome pulpit Bible.

On the roof a little two-penny nail held down a shingle. This little nail heard the people praise everything else, but none mentioned the shingle nail or seemed to be conscious of its existence. The little nail became very angry and said, "If I am that insignificant, nobody will miss me if I quit.' So, the little nail pulled out, raced down the steep roof and fell on the soft ground below. That night a big rain came and the shingle nail was buried in the mud. The difference between being buried in the mud and holding down the shingle is this: before the nail was obscure but useful. Furthermore, it was protected under the shingle. Now it will soon be eaten up by rust.

The worst of the story is yet to come. The shingle that the nail held down was now loose, and without the cooperation from the nail, it blew away, leaving a hole in the roof. The same big rain that buried the nail leaked in through the vacant spot where the shingle was, running into the beautiful auditorium. The water ran down the walls, leaving them all marred. It leaked upon the Bible and stained its pages. It leaked upon the carpet and the beautiful rug was stained. All because one little nail failed to do its job.

Paul says in Romans 12:4, 5 that we are "many members in one body, and all members do not have the same function, so we, who are many, are one body in Christ, and individually members of one another" (NAS). We have a world to win to the Savior and each of us has a responsibility to that task. What kind of nail are you? One that does his part and is essential to the glory of the Lord or one that fails to do what he is capable of and has the ability to do?

Every nail is important and essential.

Temptation

816 The Enemy's Ground Is Not Good Testing Ground

At an evangelistic meeting someone was converted. The next day one who was at the meeting saw the newly converted man put his hand into a chicken coop. "Say," called the older Christian, "I thought you were converted last night." Of course, it was evident that he was about to steal a chicken. His answer was, "I was converted sir, certainly I am, but I am just trying out the strength of my resolution." The wise reply of the older Christian was, "It is safer to fight Satan on your own ground than on his."

817 Seat Belts Save Lives

Temptation is a pretty common experience—and our batting average for resisting it is not always impressive.

Our experiences are a lot like the seat belts on cars a few years ago. If we did not fasten them, that infernal buzzer kept annoying us. We knew that the seat belts were not made to hurt us or unnecessarily restrict us. They were there to keep us safe, and the buzzer was our friend. But instead of doing what we knew was probably best for us, we would stick the belts behind us, fasten them and thus shut off the buzzer that was reminding us to do the safe thing.

We Christians know deep down inside what is right. We even know that the right thing is the best thing for us. And God coaches us from the inside with His "buzzer," the Holy Spirit, to help us resist temptation. But we often choose to ignore the buzzer and look for a way to shut it off. We ignore God's signal and follow our own, even though experience shows us that things get messed up when we do not listen to Him. We need to understand a little more about how Satan uses temptation and how we can win the battle. An understanding of the kinds of strategies Satan uses to defeat us can help us overcome temptation.

340

Tests and Trials

818 Shaped for Glory

During the Great Depression, a good man lost his job, exhausted his savings and forfeited his home. His grief was multiplied by the sudden death of his precious wife. The only thing he had left was his faith—and it was weakening.

One day he was combing the neighborhood looking for work. He stopped to watch some men who were doing the stonework on a church building. One of these men was skillfully chiseling a triangular piece of rock. Not seeing a spot where it would fit, he asked, "Where are you going to put that?" The man pointed toward the top of the building and said, "See that little opening up near the spire? That is where it goes. I am shaping it down here so it will fit in up there."

Some of you are going through terrible troublesome times. You may be experiencing some heartbreaking sorrow. Or perhaps you are enduring some painful physical illness. Or it may be something else—maybe even too excruciating to talk to anyone about. The blows of the hammer and chisel hurt.

But hold on to your faith. These difficulties will not get you down. They are only temporary. Glory is coming. It is the harsh blows to the outward man that often bring the greatest strength to the inner man.

Keep praying. Keep believing. The Master has to do some shaping of us down here so we will fit in up there.

819 The Great Divide of Life

High in the Canadian Rockies is a rushing stream called Divide Creek. At one point in its course, the waters reach a large boulder.

The water which travels to the left of the boulder rushes down into the Kicking Horse River and finally into the Pacific Ocean.

The water which travels to the right of the large rock makes it down into the Bow River which empties into two more rivers and then into the Atlantic Ocean.

Once the water divides at that boulder, its ultimate destiny is decided. Downstream from that great rock the course cannot be altered. The left side goes to the Pacific and the right side goes to the Atlantic.

Every person meets his divide point. It comes when one decides to accept Christ or to reject Him. This Great Divide determines one's eternal destination and whether that one can have abundant life here on earth.

"He who believes in the Son has eternal life; he who does not obey the Son shall not see life, but the wrath of God rests upon him" (John 3:36 RSV).

820 The Flood Releases the Fruit

Do you know how cranberries are harvested? When the fruit is ripe, the cranberry bog is flooded with water. As the water covers the bush, the ruby red berries separate from the bush and float to the surface where they are gathered and distributed to cranberry lovers around the country.

When the flood waters of trouble and trials sweep over your soul, what is the result? Is fruit "meet for the Master's use" released to bless and meet the needs of the hungry world around you?

821 Precious Lord, Take My Hand

Thomas Andrew Dorsey was a black jazz musician from Atlanta. In the twenties he gained a certain amount of notoriety as the composer of jazz tunes with suggestive lyrics, but he gave all that up in 1926 to concentrate exclusively on spiritual music. "Peace in the Valley" is one of his best known songs, but there is a story behind his most famous song that deserves to be told.

In 1932 the times were hard for Dorsey. Just trying to survive the depression years as a working musician meant tough sledding. On top of that, his music was not accepted by many people. Some said it was much too worldly—the devil's music, they called it. Many years later Dorsey could laugh about it. He said, "I got kicked out of some of the best churches in the land." But the real kick in the teeth came one night in St. Louis when he received a telegram informing him that his pregnant wife had died suddenly.

Dorsey was so filled with grief that his faith was shaken to the roots, but instead of wallowing in self-pity, he turned to the discipline he knew best—music. In the midst of agony he wrote the following lyrics:

Precious Lord, take my hand,
   Lead me on, let me stand.
I am tired, I am weak, I am worn.
   Through the storm, through the night,
Lead me on to the light;
   Take my hand precious Lord,
lead me home.

If you live long enough, you will experience heartache, disappointment, and sheer helplessness. The Lord is our most precious resource in those hours of trauma. "The Lord is a refuge for the oppressed, a stronghold in times of trouble (Ps. 9:9). Tom Dorsey understood that. His song was originally written as a way of coping with his personal pain, but even today it continues to bless thousands of others when they pass through times of hardship.

822 Songs Out of Sorrow

A piece of wood once bitterly complained because it was being cut and filled with rifts and holes. But he who held the wood and whose knife was cutting into it so remorselessly, did not listen to the sore complaining. He was making a flute out of the wood he held, and was too wise to desist for such an entreaty.

Instead, the flute carver said, "Oh, thou foolish piece of wood, without these rifts and holes thou wouldst be only a mere stick forever—a bit of hard black ebony with no power to make music or to be of any use. These rifts that I am making will change thee into a flute, and thy sweet music then shall charm the souls of men. My cutting is the making of thee, for then thou shalt be precious and valuable and a blessing to the world."

David could never have sung his sweetest songs had he not been sorely afflicted. His afflictions made his life an instrument on which God could breathe the music of His love to charm and soothe the hearts of men by such an entreaty through the ages.

823 Tunneling Through Obstacles

Nothing can stand in the way of a determined soul that obeys God. Helen Keller, deaf, dumb, and blind, joyously welcomed those who tunneled into her imprisoned soul by means of the single nerve of sensation in the palm of her hand, allowing her to conquer vast fields of knowledge. At 14 years of age, she received $250 for a magazine arti-cle. How this ought to shame some of us who lie down lazily in front of obstacles, which a little pluck and self-denying exertion would carve into a stairway for higher achievement.

824 The Value of Afflictions

There is a legend about a grandfather clock that stood in a corner for three generations, faithfully ticking off the minutes, hours and days—its means of operation was a heavy weight suspended by a double chain. One of its new owners, believing that an old clock should not bear such a load, released the weight. Immediately the ticking stopped. According to the legend, the clock asked, "Why did you do that?" The owner replied, "I wanted to lighten your burden." "Please put my weight back," replied the clock. "That is what keeps me going."

825 Genuine Faith

Joel C. Gregory writes:

"The testing we go through demonstrates the genuineness of our faith. In the phrase 'the testing of your faith,' the word 'testing' is an almost untranslatable word. The Williams version explains it as showing what is "genuine in your faith." The idea refers to iron ore that has gone through the refining fire and comes out the other side clean and pure and genuine. This is the word Job used when he said, 'When he has tried me in the fire, I will come out like gold.'

"Actually, there may be something suspect about a faith that has never been tested. An army going through basic training is not ready for battle. Not until soldiers have faced the battle and been under fire, do they consider themselves proven, hardened, worthy. A ship cannot prove that it's been sturdily built as long as it stays in dry dock. Its hull must get wet; it must face a storm to demonstrate genuine seaworthiness. The same is true of our faith. When we hold fast to belief in Christ in spite of life's storms and crushing criticism, that's when we demonstrate the genuineness of our faith."

826 This Thing Is from Me

"How can a God of love, who has everything in His control, let such a thing happen to me?" So asked a young woman who had received severe injuries through a fall from a horse. "Crippled for life," she overheard the doctor say.

The pastor was silent for a moment. "Did you suffer much pain when they put you in the cast?"

"The pain was terrible," she replied.

"Where was your father then?"

"He stood right by me," she replied.

"Did your father allow the doctor to hurt you that way?"

"Yes, but that was necessary."

"Did your father allow the doctor to hurt you even though he loved you, or because he loved you?"

"You mean to suggest that because God loves me, He also allowed me to be hurt?"

The pastor answered with a nod. " 'This thing is from Me.' Let these five words comfort you. They will

furnish a silver lining to the cloud. Yours is not a case of 'hard luck.' This trial was planned by God."

If you are His child, He is preparing you for better service. Shakespeare said: "In sickness, let me not so much say, 'Am I getting better of my pain; but am I getting better for it.' "

Let us not say, "When will I be getting out of this?" but, "What will I be getting out of this?" He will draw you closer to Him through this trial.

827 Praise for Pressure

A young man was fascinated by a moth and performed a little experiment to see what would happen when it was released from its cocoon without a struggle. Using his pocketknife, he slit the enclosure, allowing the insect to emerge freely. However, it had none of the expected color, it could not fly, and it soon died. As he thought about this, he concluded that the pressure exerted on an emerging moth is essential to its proper development—yes, to its very existence. He later learned that through the moth's struggle to free itself, its body fluids are stimulated, and the luster is developed on its wings. So too for the Christian, life's pressures can produce positive results.

828 Borrowed Burdens

A man found himself staggering alone under a load that was heavy enough to crush half a dozen strong men. Out of sheer exhaustion, he put it down and had a good look at it. He found that it was all borrowed!

Part of it belonged to the following day; part of it belonged to the following week; and here he was borrowing it that it might crush him now! It was a very stupid but a very ancient (and also modern) blunder.

829 The Value of Adversity

If Abraham Lincoln was a young man today, the traveling library would supply him with books; a county caseworker would see that he had enough light to read by; the government would see that his parents got a monthly welfare check, housing assistance and food stamps. Abe could apply for an educational loan and some social service clubs would see that he went to camp each summer.

End result: There would be no Abe Lincoln such as the one we remember and love who overcame poverty and adversity to become one of the greatest Presidents of all time.

830 No Cross, No Crown

A grapevine says, in the early spring, "How glad I am to get through the winter! I shall have no more trouble now! Summer weather will come, and the garden will be very beautiful!" But the gardener comes, and cuts the vine here and there with his knife. The twigs begin to fall, and the grapevine calls out, "Murder! What are you cutting me for?" "Ah," says the gardener, "I do not mean to kill

you. If I did not do this, you would be the laughingstock of all the other vines before the season is over." Months go on and one day the gardener comes under the trellis, where the great clusters of grapes hang, and the grapevine says, "Thank you, sire, you could not have done anything so kind as to cut me with that knife." No pruning, no grapes; no grinding mill, no flour; no battle, no victory; no cross, no crown.

831 Unchangeable Truth

Do not let your troubles get you down. Genghis Khan, the 13th century Mongol conqueror, asked his philosophers to come up with a truth that would always be unchangeable. Thinking about it for awhile, they came to their leaders with this quote: "It too shall pass." This reminds me of a dear black lady who was asked by her pastor what her favorite verse of Scripture was and she said: "And it came to pass." God in His mercy never gives us more than we can bear.

832 I Shall Meet Tomorrow Bravely

I shall meet tomorrow bravely,
I am stronger now,
The disappointments that befell me
Strengthened me somehow.

The dawn shall find my face uplifted,
Serene, in the sun,
And with Him my problems sifted,
One by one.

833 Testing

A blacksmith known for his strong faith, had a great deal of illness. He was challenged by an unbeliever to explain why his God would let him suffer.

He explained, "I take a piece of iron, put it into the fire to bring it to a white heat, then I strike it once or twice to see if it will take temper. I plunge it into water to change the temperature, put it into the fire again, then I put it on the anvil and make a useful article out of it.

"If it will not take temper when I first strike it on the anvil, I throw it into the scrap heap and sell it for a half-penny per pound. I believe God has been testing me to see if I will take temper. I have tried to bear it as patiently as I could, and my daily prayer has been, 'Lord, put me into the fire if you will; put me into the water if you think I need it; do anything you please, O Lord, only do not throw me on the scrap heap.' "

834 Toughened by Storms

When solid timber is needed, we pass by the things grown in the hot house. We seek the oak grown on the storm swept hills. The great in God's Kingdom have been taught by the hills and vales of temptation. Yielding creates littleness, overcoming creates greatness.

835 The Example of the Pine

One day a boy and his father went into the mountains. They took shelter from a storm in the lee of some great gray boulders that lay like sleeping giants close to the crest of a lonely ridge. As the two looked upward, they saw the wind lay its grim hands on a mountain pine that towered from the summit of the ridge. It was a sentinel that could escape no danger, an outpost to receive the first shock of the enemy's attack. Savagely the wind tore at it, shook it violently, and howled through the branches.

To the boy, the tree, strong though it was, seemed about to be torn to pieces. "Look, Father!" he said, pining upward, "what the wind is doing to that pine!" The full fury of the blast just then made the pine shudder and sway. It heaved desperately against the black sky.

"Storms are an old story to that tree," said the father. "A tree like that lives in a struggle from the time it is high enough to catch the first breath of air. Tennyson says a tree is 'storm-strengthened on a windy site.' The strongest trees are always those that have weathered the greatest number of gales. Besides, the question is not what is happening to the tree, but what is happening in the tree."

"The pine does not really seem to mind fighting the storm, does it?" the boy asked.

"No, because it is able to withstand the strongest wind," the father answered. "It is the same with us. It really does not matter what happens to us, but it matters a great deal what happens in us."

836 *Joy in Times of Trial*

James in his customary forthright way tells us to "Count it all joy, my brethren, when you meet various trials, for you know that the testing of your faith produces steadfastness" (James 1:2, 3). In case we are inclined to modify these words as the utopian command of one who had not really experienced sorrow, let us remember that James was one of the principal leaders of the Christians in Jerusalem who continually faced persecution from those outside the Church (culminating in his own martyrdom in his sixties), as well as internal dissension associated with a Judaizing element. James surely knew what it meant to "meet various trials!"

But James had also learned that difficulties can produce steadfastness or patience, though the natural reaction is annoyance or bitterness. He never tells us to pretend that a trial is nonexistent. Instead he wants us to recognize and rejoice that any problem can be the occasion for God to work in and through us in a way that He otherwise would not.

This is indeed a "testing of our faith"; it calls upon us to believe in the goodness of God, and to trust that He is not only willing but able to accomplish His purposes, no matter what befalls us. Any difficulty, whether great or small, is an occasion for joy, but only when we remind ourselves of the nature of the God who loves us and wills only the best for us.

837 *Greatness of a Different Form*

What do you do when faced by a closed door in life? A young boy from Missouri named Harry had to answer that question. He gave evidence of brilliance on the piano even as a child. In addition to being gifted, Harry had such discipline that at the age of seven he was at the keyboard by five each morning. He practiced faithfully for hours each day. Under the tutelage of Mrs. E. C. White, he produced each day stronger hope that he would eventually reach greatness.

When Harry was 15, Mrs. White brought news to her star pupil. Paderewski, the greatest pianist of the day was coming to town. The young boy was thrilled as he listened to Paderewski play. Mrs. White took her pupil backstage after the concert to meet Paderewski. With trembling voice, the young boy told the world-renowned pianist that he played his minuet. "There is a part of it," young Harry explained, "that I do not know how to execute." Paderewski walked back with the boy to the empty stage and to the piano. The boy sat at the same piano where Paderewski had played only a few minutes before. As the student played, Paderewski gave a smile of approval to the boy's teacher. A bright future seemed to loom before him.

Then ensued the closed door. The next year Harry's father lost everything in the Kansas City grain market. Harry had to go to work, and his dreams of the concert stage were shattered.

Did the boy give up on life? Did he let this closed door stop him?

Not at all, for this young, gifted, promising pianist would become world famous before his life was over, as President of the United States. His name was Harry S. Truman.

838 Does Anything Ever Turn Out Right?

Picture with me, if you will, a man running through the wilderness being chased by a lion. He knows that if he is fast enough and dodges through enough thickets, that he could possibly elude the lion. Luckily, he does manage to elude the lion, only to be confronted by a bear. Again, he runs with all his speed and strength, realizing now that his only hope is to reach the safety of his house. Once again, he is successful and manages to elude the beast by reaching his house. He runs inside, slamming the door behind him and feeling pretty good about having overcome the obstacles of life. But, as he leans against the wall with his hand to catch his breath, he is bitten by a snake.

This was an actual illustration that God used in Amos 5:19 to show Israel the hopelessness of their situation.

We all have days and weeks like that, do we not? But are we like the woman who said that she had quit praying for patience because God might give her more? But God, being the wise and all-knowing Father that He is, will often give us what we need to grow healthy and spiritually strong, even though we do not ask for it—though He would like to hear us ask now and then. Children almost never ask for a bath, but we give it to them anyway, because we know that it will help them.

839 Beautiful Music Out of Deep Tragedy

He wrote some of the most beautiful music in the history of humanity. Yet his life could not be called beautiful; it was full of tragedy. By the age of ten, both parents had died. He was raised begrudgingly by an older brother who resented another mouth to feed. Even as an adult, his life was difficult. His first wife died after 13 years of marriage. Of 20 children from two marriages, ten died in infancy, one died in his twenties, and one was mentally retarded. Eventually he went blind and then was paralyzed from a stroke. Yet he wrote great music—music of profound praise, thunderous thanksgiving, and awe-filling adoration.

Who is this victim of so much tragedy? Johann Sebastian Bach—a Lutheran and perhaps the world's greatest composer of church music. Perhaps it was because Bach knew the depths of tragedy that he also knew the heights of faith and praise.

So when we seem to be in the depths of despair, look up, for the Lord is going to bless us and others.

840 The Sand in Our Shoe

A man who had hitchhiked from coast to coast and had walked many miles in the process was asked what he had found the most difficult to endure. To the surprise of his questioner it was not the steep mountains or the dazzling sun or the scorching desert heat that had troubled him, but, in the words of the traveler, "it was the sand in my shoe."

Frequently the little things in life make the practice of the Christian faith most difficult. Somehow the great trials of life—moments of crisis, of serious illness, of death and bereavement—have a way of raising us and bringing us closer to the only source of spiritual strength, our Savior, Jesus Christ.

But those smaller trials, how they plague us! How they succeed again and again in causing us to fail and stumble. Those little irritations in the home, those endless vexations at the shop or office, those little rubs with the neighbors, those petty quarrels at church—those are the "sand in our shoe," which wear our Christianity thin.

Thankfulness

841 Two Little Words

A doctor wrote a letter of thanks to a schoolteacher for having given him so much encouragement when he had been in her class 30 years before. He later received this reply: "I want you to know what your note meant to me. I am an old lady in my eighties, living alone in a small room, cooking my own meals, lonely, and seeming like the last leaf on the tree. You will be interested to know that I taught school for 50 years, and yours is the first letter of appreciation I have ever received. It came on a cold, blue morning and cheered my lonely old heart as nothing has cheered me in many years."

842 Do Not Delay Expressing Appreciation

A young man was an organist in a large church in Texas. He was a fine musician, but, being blind, was unable to read in the faces of his audience the great pleasure his music was giving. His caressing touch on the keyboard sent out through its great pipes the songs of his soul. People would talk to each other about the beauty and the uplifting influence of his music. Often his music sent tears down furrowed cheeks. But no one ever thought to tell the organist, who was longing to hear a word of response.

One morning it was announced that he would not play after that service. His decision was final; another organist must be secured. After the service a woman who had enjoyed his music thoroughly went up to him, and said, very earnestly, "I am sorry you will not play for us any longer. I have enjoyed your music so much. It helped me greatly; it soothed and comforted me when I sorrowed. I have thought many times I would tell you what an inspiration I have received through your music. I thank you for it."

The young man's voice faltered and tears rushed to his sightless eyes as he whispered, "Oh, why didn't you tell me sooner? I needed comfort and inspiration, too."

843 Think of Those Who Have Less Than You

A mother and her two little children were destitute. In the depth of winter they were nearly frozen, and the mother took the cellar door off the hinges and set it up in front of the corner where they crouched down to sleep so that some of the draft and cold might be kept from them. One of the children whispered to her, "Mother, what do those poor children do who have no cellar door to put up in front of them?"

844 Finding the Blessings with a Thankful Heart

If one should give me a dish of sand, and tell me there were particles of iron in it, I might look for them with my clumsy fingers, and be unable to detect them; but let me take a magnet, and sweep through it, and it would draw to itself the most invisible particles. The unthankful heart, like my finger in the sand, discovers no mercies; but let the thankful heart sweep through the day, and as the magnet finds the iron, so it will find some heavenly blessings.

845 Go Ahead and Embarrass Thankless People

A mother took her three children to a restaurant to eat breakfast one morning. The smallest of the three children sat at the very end of the row. She saw other people being served and eating right away without stopping to say thanks. It surprised her. When the food was served to her, she shouted out to her mother: "Mommy, don't people ask the blessing in this place?" You can well imagine the embarrassment of those present. Her mother tried to hush her. But, the waitress said to little Mary, "Yes, we do, sister! You give thanks!"

Amazingly, at that very moment everybody else also bowed their heads and offered thanks.

Embarrass them and maybe you will bring them to their senses to say "Thank you, God."

846 If You Think, You Must Thank

Sir Moses Montefiore, the Jewish philanthropist, had as the motto of his family, "Think and Thank." In the old Anglo-Saxon, thankfulness means "thinkfulness." Thinking of all God's goodness draws forth gratitude.

847 How Rich Are You?

They huddled inside the storm door—two children in ragged, outgrown coats.

"Any old papers, Lady?" they asked a passerby.

She was very busy; she wanted to say no, until she looked down at their feet wrapped only in thin little sandals, sopped with sleet. "Come on in and I will make you a cup of cocoa," she said. There was no conversation. Their soggy sandals left marks on the clean hearthstone.

Cocoa and cake would fortify against the chill outside. After serving them, she went back to the kitchen and started on her household budget as they sat enjoying the warmth.

After a few minutes, the silence in the front room struck through to her. She looked in.

The girl held her empty cup in her hands, looking at it. The boy asked in a flat voice, "Lady, are you rich?"

"Am I rich? Mercy no!" She looked at her shabby slipcovers.

The girl put her cup back in its saucer carefully. "Your cups match your saucers." Her voice was old with a hunger that was not of the stomach.

They left then, holding their bundles of papers against the wind. They had not said thank you. They did not need to. They had done more than that. Plain blue pottery cups and saucers—but they matched. She tested the potatoes and stirred the gravy. "Potatoes and brown gravy, a roof over our heads, my husband with a good, steady job—these things matched, too," she mused.

She moved the chairs back from the fire and tidied the living room. The muddy prints of small sandals were still set upon the hearth, and she let them be. "I want them there in case I ever forget how very rich I am," she told herself.

848 Harvest of the Heart at Thanksgiving

Thanksgiving is the harvest of the heart
After the fruit and grain are stored away.
The quiet season of remembering,
The moment when we pause to praise and pray.

849 "In All Things"

"Gratitude is what always spoils life when it is left out." A thankful spirit enables one to praise God even when circumstances are difficult.

Alexander Whyte, the Scottish preacher, always began his prayers with an expression of gratitude. One cold, miserable day his people wondered what he would say. He prayed, "We thank Thee, O Lord, that it is not always like this."

850 Observing Thanksgiving

"Count it all joy" (James 1:2).
Count your blessings instead of your crosses;
Count your gains instead of your losses.
Count your joys instead of your woes;
Count your friends instead of your foes.
Count your smiles instead of your tears;
Count your courage instead of your fears.
Count your full years instead of your lean;
Count your kind deeds instead of your mean.
Count your health instead of your wealth;
Count on God instead of yourself.

851 I Give Thee Humble Thanks

"Giving thanks for all things . . ." (Eph. 5:20).
For all the gifts that Thou dost send,
For every kind and loyal friend,
For prompt supply of all my need,
For all that is good in word or deed,
For gift of health along life's way,
For strength to work from day to day—
I give Thee humble thanks.

For ready hands to help and cheer,
For listening ears Thy voice to hear,
For yielded tongue Thy love to talk,
For willing feet, Thy paths to walk,
For open eyes Thy Word to read,
For loving heart, Thy will to heed—
I give Thee humble thanks.

For Christ who came from heaven above,
For the cross and His redeeming love,
For His mighty power to seek and save,
For His glorious triumph o'er the grave.
For the lovely mansions in the sky,
For His blessed coming bye and bye—
I give Thee humble thanks.

852 Those Who Do Not Give Thanks

A godly farmer was asked to dine with a well-known gentleman. While there, he asked a blessing at the table as he was accustomed to do at home. His host said jeeringly, "That is old fashioned; it is not customary nowadays for well-educated people to pray before they eat." The farmer answered that with him it was customary, but that some of those on his farm never prayed over their food. "Ah, then," said the gentleman, "they are sensible and en-

lightened. Who are they?" "My pigs," the farmer answered.

853 Two Hundred Miles of Thanks

If you are grateful, say so! Thanksgiving is only half said until you have done something to show your thankfulness.

A missionary to India was traveling through a city and stopped to speak to a man beside the road. He talked with the man for a time about Jesus. Then, having to travel on, he gave him a few pages of the Bible in the man's language. The Indian read them and was thrilled to learn of Jesus.

To show his gratitude, the man measured the footprints left by the missionary, and made a pair of moccasins. He then traveled 200 miles to give them to the missionary as an expression of thanks.

The missionary's life was enriched by the gift, but the Indian man was much more enriched because he had expressed his thanks.

Have you ever tried to give 200 miles of thanks?

Try it—you will be a better person because of it.

854 Spiritual Maturity

One day, Johann Tauler of Strosbourg met a peasant.

"God give you a good day, my friend," he greeted him. The peasant answered briskly, "I thank God I never have a bad day."

Tauler, astonished, kept silent for a moment. Tauler then added, "God give you a happy life, my friend."

The peasant replied composedly, "I thank God I am never unhappy."

"Never unhappy!" cried Tauler bewildered, "What do you mean?"

"Well," came the reply, "when it is sunshine—I thank God, when it rains—I thank God, when I have plenty—I thank God, when I am hungry—I thank God; and since God's will is my will, and whatever pleases God pleases me, why should I say that I am unhappy when I am not?"

Tauler looked upon him with awe. "Who are you," he asked. "I am a king," said the peasant.

"A king?" Tauler asked, "Where is your kingdom?" The peasant smiled and whispered softly, "In my heart."

855 Their Money Is Worth

Rudyard Kipling at one time was so popular that his writings were getting ten shillings per word. A few college students, however, did not appreciate Kipling's writings; they facetiously sent him a letter and enclosed ten shillings. It read, "Please, send us your best word." They got back a letter from Kipling that said, "Thanks."

856 The Art of Thanksgiving

The art of thanksgiving is thanksliving. It is gratitude in action.

It is thanking God for the gift of life by living it triumphantly.

It is thanking God for your talents and abilities by accepting them as obligations to be invested for the common good.

It is thanking God for all that men and women have done for you by doing things for others.

It is thanking God for happiness by striving to make others happy.

It is thanking God for beauty by helping to make the world more beautiful.

It is thanking God for inspiration by trying to be an inspiration to others.

It is thanking God for health and strength by the care and respect you show your body.

857 The Best Thanksgiving Day

As we gather 'round our firesides
On this new Thanksgiving Day,
Time would fail to count the blessings
That have followed all our way;
Grace sufficient, help and heal-ing,
Prayer oft answered at our call;
And the best of all our blessings,
Christ Himself, our all in all.

While we love to "count the bless-ings,"
Grateful for the year that's gone,
Faith would sweep a wider vi-sion,
Hope would gaze yet further on.
For the signals all around us
Seem with one accord to say,
"Christ is coming soon to bring us
Earth's last, best Thanksgiving Day!"

858 Why Only One Day for Thanksgiving?

Charles Dickens said that we are somewhat mixed up here in America. He told an audience that instead of having one Thanksgiving Day each year we should have 364. "Use that one day just for complaining and griping," he said. "Use the other 364 days to thank God each day for the many blessings He has showered upon you."

859 Why Be Thankful?

(Psalm 100:4b)

"I do not have to thank anyone for anything I have," an old miser grumbled. "Everything I have I got the *hard* way—by the sweat of my own brow."

"But who gave you the sweat?" asked his neighbor.

The old miser hung his head in guilty silence. He could not ignore the fact that God had given the "sweat," the strength to work hard and gain material wealth.

Yes, everything that we are or that we possess is because of God's lovingkindness. Therefore, it is good for us all to pause at least once a year and say, "Thank You, God." Actually, everyday should be one of thanksgiving. Why? *Because of spiritual and material blessings.*

Mrs. Green thanked Tom, the grocery boy, for delivering a loaf of bread.

"Do not thank me. Thank Grocer Jones," Tom smiled. "He gave me the loaf to deliver."

But when she thanked the grocer, he said, "I get the bread from Baker Brown. He makes it, so he deserves the thanks."

So Mrs. Green thanked the baker. But he told her that Miller Milligan should be given the gratitude. "Without Miller Milligan's flour, I could not make bread," Brown replied.

The miller told her to thank Farmer Foster because he made the flour from Foster's wheat. But the farmer also protested, "Don't thank me; thank God," Foster said. "If He did not give my farm sunshine and rain, I could not grow wheat."

Yes, even a common loaf of bread can be traced back to God, the Giver of "every good and perfect gift" (Josh. 1:17).

Tongue

860 A Tongue's Soliloquy

I am your tongue! I am an important fellow. The Bible mentions me about 215 times (Prov. 18:21; 21:23, etc.). When I speak kind, thoughtful and true words, there is *happiness;* when I speak mean, untrue, angry or complaining words, there is *trouble.*

861 Rumors

There is nothing as effective as a bunch of facts to spoil a good rumor.

There is a new magazine on the market named *Rumor* because it spreads so quickly and easily.

It is easier to float a rumor than to sink one.

A lot of people seem to have "rumortism."

All rumors should be fitted with girdles to keep them from spreading.

Whenever we fan the flames of a rumor, we are likely to get burned ourselves.

A groundless rumor often covers a lot of ground.

We still cannot understand how rumors without a leg to stand on get around so fast.

862 Most Potent Venom

A scientist has found out that poison from the skin of a tiny South American tree frog is far more toxic than any other known venom. Rain forest Indians use the venom from the skin of the kokoi frog to poison their blowgun arrows.

There is a poison even more deadly—the poison from an evil tongue. "The tongue is a fire, a word of iniquity." "With their tongues they have used deceit; the poison of asps is under their lips: whose mouth is full of cursing and bitterness" (James 3:6 and context; Rom. 3:13, 14).

Are you a Christian, able to control your tongue? If so, you are a mature Christian. "For in many things we offend all. If any man offend not in word, the same is a perfect man, and able also to bridle the whole body" (James 3:2).

863 Squeezing Toothpaste

Have you ever squeezed too much toothpaste onto your toothbrush? And then have you ever tried squeezing toothpaste back into the tube? That calls to mind the old proverb, "Three things once released will not return again: an opportunity neglected, and arrow released from its bows, and a word spoken in haste." May we add a fourth—toothpaste squeezed from a tube. We could spend the next six months drawing lessons from this familiar proverb. An opportunity neglected, an arrow released, a word spoken in haste.

Sometimes in our efforts to say exactly the right thing at the right time, we speak words in haste. Usually we immediately wish we could recall those words. Words spoken in haste are all those words we speak without weighing how each could be understood by the hearer(s), all those words we utter in jest, and everything we say without thinking.

Perhaps the preacher was right when he quipped, "God gave us two ears and one mouth—that ought to tell us something."

864 "Foot-in-Mouth" Disease

How many times have you said something you wish you had not? Oh, the pain! But after it is said, it is next to impossible to recall the bumbling rhetoric. Once an attorney was pleading the case of his farmer client who had lost a shipment of 24 pigs. He was prosecuting the trucking company that had lost the animals. The lawyer wanted to impress the jury with the magnitude of the loss so he said very innocently, "Twenty-four pigs, gentlemen! Twenty-four! Twice the number in the jury box!" Oops! Too late! The damage was done. It was all over but the verdict.

865 Misplaced Values

An English nobleman once visited Josiah Wedgwood to see how he made his legendary china and pottery. A young apprentice was instructed to give the nobleman a tour of the factory. The nobleman did not believe in God and was sacrilegious, foul-mouthed, and consistently ridiculed the Bible during the tour. At first the young apprentice was shocked but after a while he began to laugh when the man made his cynical remarks. Josiah Wedgwood was greatly disturbed by this, especially when he saw how his young apprentice was being influenced by this wealthy nobleman. Later the atheist asked if he could purchase a particularly expensive vase. As he handed it to the nobleman, Wedgwood deliberately let it crash to the floor. With a vile oath the nobleman angrily said, "That is the one I really wanted and now it is shattered by your carelessness." Josiah Wedgwood replied, "Sir, there are things more precious than any vase—things that can never be restored once they are ruined. I can make another vase, but you can never give back to my helper the pure heart you have defiled by your vile language and sacrilegious talk!"

Treasure

866 Values That Last

Certs, Breath Savers, chewing gum are all big sellers. Americans are conscious about "bad breath," and they spend millions of dollars to hide or change it. The problem is that the remedies do not last long.

There is a bizarre new breath mint on the market now which lasts for two hours. It is a time released pill that sits between your upper gum and cheek and slowly puts out a minty taste for hours. You do not have to chew it, or even suck on it.

The price for a bottle of 200 mints is $30. It seems high, but the selling point is that it is really more economical.

Everybody is interested in things that last. Our cars wear out, so do clothes, shoes, and everything about us. The faces on Mount Rushmore have to be continually repaired. Jesus tells us in Matthew 6:19 that all earthly treasures are beset by risks and finally end in total loss.

The real treasure of wealth is to be found in heaven. We can store truth, love, and faith. Our emphasis must always be on the values that last.

"Heaven and earth shall pass away; but my word;" says Jesus, "shall not pass away" (Mark 13:31).

867 Life Was Good, Until . . .

Several years ago a farmer increased his farm holding from 300 acres to 9,000 acres. Everyone was proud of him and glad to see him prosper. He had a lovely family—two boys and a girl, and one of the sweetest wives in the world. He was a leader in the church and the family was very faithful. Needless to say, he became very wealthy. Life was good. As the responsibilities of the farm increased, his involvement with the church decreased. Over time the entire family became so involved with the farm and the wealth that they all became unfaithful and placed the church on low priority in their lives. The father died and the children fought over the land, lost it, and spent all the inheritance. Today, they have very little to do with each other and have gone through several difficult personal problems. Their mother died in poverty and loneliness.

What good does it to do gain the whole world and yet lose your soul and those of your loved ones? What can the world give in place of the soul?

868 The Christian's Riches

In CHRIST we have—
A LOVE that can never be fathomed;

A LIFE that can never die;

A RIGHTEOUSNESS that can never be tarnished;

A PEACE that can never be understood;

A REST that can never be disturbed;

A JOY that can never be diminished;

A HOPE that can never be disappointed;

A GLORY that can never be clouded;

A HAPPINESS that can never be interrupted;

A LIGHT that can never be darkened;

A STRENGTH that can never be enfeebled;

A BEAUTY that can never be marred;

A PURITY that can never be defiled;

A WISDOM that can never be baffled;

RESOURCES that can never be exhausted.

869 Worthless Treasures

Hidden treasures today are rare. In the ancient biblical lands, however, they were common. Palestine, which was a land bridge between Egypt and the great empires, was repeatedly invaded, ravaged, and captured. Multitudes buried gold. There were no banks. The government, nobility, clergy, and Arab invaders all robbed the common people often and without warning. Because of this, the people quickly buried treasure in the ground, in walls, in tree trunks, or wherever

they could. Earthquakes could cover up entire cities and bury gold with them. All kinds of people quickly buried what they had in the face of invasion or political change. They left, they died, they were captured, and no one knew where the treasure was hidden.

W.M. Thompson was a missionary in Syria and Palestine for 30 years. He told of workmen digging up a garden in Sidon. They found several copper pots of gold. They did exactly like the man in the parable—concealed their find with care. But then, wild with joy, they could not keep their mouths shut. The governor of the city caught them, and recovered two of the pots, and it was found that they contained 8,000 pure gold coins of Alexander and his father Philip. Thompson saw hundreds of persons all over the country spending their last pennies looking for such treasure.

870 He Thought Nothing of Money

He paid $70,000 for a house to live in for a few years upon this earth.

He thought nothing of money.

He paid $10,500 for a car.
He thought nothing of money.

He paid $800 for a television set.
He thought nothing of money.

He paid $300 for fishing gear.
He thought nothing of money.

He paid $400 for a deer hunt.
He thought nothing of money.

He paid $20 one evening watching the Dallas Cowboys play.

He thought nothing of money.

He paid $10 per week for tobacco.

He thought nothing of money.

He gave $5 whenever he went to church.

He thought nothing of money!

871 Money in the Bank

A man gave several thousand dollars to help build a church. Then came the 1929 Stock Market crash. He lost everything. Someone said, "If you had that money you gave to start the church, you would have had enough to set yourself up in business again." He replied, "I would have lost that money, too, in the crash. As it is, it is the only money I saved. It is now in the bank of heaven, yielding interest which will accumulate until eternity." Hundreds have come to Christ through the church he helped build.

872 Gratitude as an Asset

Men reckon up their goods—so much in bonds, so much in stocks, so much in notes, so much in personal property, so much in real estate. In taking account of their possessions, do men ever take into consideration the asset of a thankful heart? Probably not. And yet there is no greater wealth in itself, and no greater producing agent of wealth than the faculty of gratitude.

Contentment is a personal feast. The richest man in the world can use no more than enough for his de-

sires. If you have the same, you are as rich as he.

873 A Cablegram From Heaven

A merchant was asked to contribute to a certain piece of church work. He gladly wrote a $250 check and gave it to the solicitor. At that moment, a cablegram was brought in. The merchant read it and looked troubled. "This cablegram," he said, "tells me that one of my ships has been wrecked and the cargo lost. That makes a difference in my business. I will have to write you another check."

The solicitor thought he understood and handed back the check for $250, and the merchant wrote out another and gave it to him. When the solicitor read it, he was utterly amazed; it was for $1,000. "Have you not made a mistake?" he asked. "No," said the merchant, "I have not made a mistake." Then he added, "To me, that cablegram was a message from my Father in Heaven. It reads, 'Lay not up for yourselves treasure upon earth . . . but lay up for yourselves treasures in heaven where neither moth nor rust doth corrupt, and where thieves do not break through nor steal' (Matt. 6:19, 20)."

874 The Value of Redemption

In the world in which we live we always think of the price of things.

We look at a car, and we admire its features, but the price stands in the way of having it as our own.

We look at a new home, and we would love to live in it, but again, it is beyond our reach if the price is too high. We go into a jewelry store and see the exhibited diamonds and we would like an expensive one to show our love to a special person, but again, the price stands in the way.

The amazing thing about God is that He places the greatest fulfillment of our need at no price at all. However, we are likely to not appreciate the greatness of the gift, just because it is free.

875 Not Possible in our Own Strength

A ship was plowing through a stormy sea when part of the mast broke off. The captain ordered a lad to climb up and repair the damage. The boy started up, but he slid back down and ran into his cabin for a moment. He then came back, climbed back to the top of the ship and made the necessary repairs. When he was on the deck again, the captain said to him, "Why did you run down into your cabin for a minute before you climbed aloft?" "Why, sir," he said, "I went down to offer a word of prayer and to place this New Testament in my pocket. My mother told me before I left home that if I would pray and carry the Word of God with me, I would be well protected from any storm."

"For in that He Himself hath suffered being tempted, He is able to succor them that are tempted" (Heb. 2:18).

876 Going Deeper

A small company in the early days of gold mining in South Africa sank shaft after shaft in different locations, finding only a small amount of gold in each shaft. Ultimately, the prospectors discovered that all they needed to have done was to go deeper in the first shaft for, as they did so, they found gold in abundance.

Roy Hession writes that he has found this to be true in the spiritual life also.

"I testify that although I have tried all sorts of different shafts, hoping for greater results in my life, Christ has now become the end of all my searching. Revival for me has meant coming back to the place where I first began, and I intend to stay there. Tell me not of any other way. I need to go deeper at His cross—much deeper."

877 Contentment

"But godliness with contentment is great gain. For we brought nothing into the world, and we can take nothing out of it. But if we have food and clothing, we will be content with that" (1 Tim. 6:6-8).

Our generation wants it all. Many people who are 30 and under have always had it all. The lack of material things during the Great Depression has affected the attitudes of many older people. So many, both young and old, are concerned with driving the right car, wearing clothes with the right label and vacationing at the "in" places. Yet, having all these only leads to a desire for more.

How we accumulate! The man who has everything needs a place to put it. Our closets are running over. We buy houses with two car garages and then leave our cars outside. The garage is full of things. Mini-warehouses and storage facilities are a growth industry. Is this accumulation perhaps one reason vans and pickup trucks are so popular? We need bigger vehicles to carry what we have.

But has a richer life produced a better life? The most popular prescription drugs relieve anxiety and hypertension. The most popular over-the-counter drugs are aspirin and related pain killers. Also, if abundance brings happiness, we would assume that the people who have the most possessions have the greatest happiness. Yet even the most casual observer can see this is not true.

In his accumulation of things, is not man searching for contentment? The bottom line, according to Paul is not how much you have. The bottom line on personal profit and loss is finding godliness with contentment.

What do we need to be content? Paul's statement is almost heretical to our materialistic ears. All that is necessary is food and clothing. These should be the limit of our earthly desires. Matthew Henry well said, "The necessities of life are the bounds of a true Christian's desires. Truly, the secret of contentment is

not having much but wanting little. This is not to say we cannot have more than food and clothing. It means that having more than these presents a temptation (1 Tim. 6:9). May we, as God's children, refuse to let the world squeeze us into its mold, and refuse to imitate it as it seeks everything to live with and nothing to live for.

878 Hold My Mule!

The old man could not carry a tune in a syrup bucket, but he loved to sing, even if it was off-key! Besides, he was bad about "amen-ing" the preacher. Services had degenerated into an "undignified" assembly because of the old man. He simply got too involved in the "goings on" and forgot himself.

Four of the more well-to-do members decided that this old fellow was just too crude for the congregation. They appointed themselves as the ones to go and talk to the old man.

When they arrived at the old fellow's house, he was in the field plowing with his old mule. Though it was beneath their dignity, they finally walked out through the dusty ground which soiled their fine clothes to talk to the old timer. "Brother Jones," they began, "we want to talk to you about your singing. Not meaning any offense, but you just cannot sing. We wish you would try not to sing so loud because frankly, your singing ruins our services!"

"I am sorry," the old fellow replied, "but it is just that when I look at these old clothes that I wear and then I think of them robes that God has for me, I just cannot help singing. And when I see that old shack over yonder that I live in and realize that it is liable to fall any time, and then I think about the beautiful palace that God has for me, I just have to sing praises to my Lord. You fellers see this old hat I got on? Well, when I see that crown in my mind that God has for me, I just have to yell that wonderful name of Jesus at the top of my lungs!"

"As a matter of fact," he said, "would one of you fellers mind holding my mule? I feel like singing now."

They left him right there, singing away in the field! And as these four men left the old fellow out there singing they viewed him in a different light. One said to the rest, "You know, his singing is not really all that bad." Another said, "I never really realized how sweet his voice really is." The third said, "I just hope that God will allow me to sing in the same group that he sings in."

Now there are several lessons in this story. Possibly the reason these men had never really seen things in their true light before was that the world was just too much with them. I wonder if the reason that we have difficulty sometimes appreciating the things that God has reserved for us in heaven is that the world is just too much with us, too. (Amen!)

Trust

879 Learning to Trust

"Dear God, what am I supposed to do?" asked missionary Marge Elam. "I am so worried for my little girl. I am not able to hover over her to protect her."

"The night was warm and quite dark. I could hear several alligators not far from the house calling back and forth in their strange creaky way. Nightbirds, frogs and other night creatures added their sounds as a background to my prayer. I soundlessly left my bed and felt my way to the hammock where my eight-year-old slept.

" 'Lord, she has to ride her bicycle alone two miles through the jungle to go to school. There are many wild things out there, and always snakes.'

"While looking down at the faint outline of my sleeping child with her small white face pillowed on her bent arm, a memory went across my mind. It was the other day: her eyes were large with excitement, her voice almost squeaked, 'Mom, it was the biggest, fattest snake. Its body stretched all the way across the road. I did not know what to do, so I just pulled up my legs and rode my bike over it.' "

"I could actually hear the thump of my own heart in the darkness.

Then, I heard a voice. It almost seemed to come out of the darkness, but I knew it was inside of me. He said, 'I was able to take care of your daughter in the United States, and I am able to take care of her here as well.' After that, I was able to sleep the night through and every night since for 17 years. I knew that if He was able to take care of one eight-year-old girl, He was able to take care of everything else."

880 Feeling Sorry for Yourself

So you think you have problems. Who doesn't? That is no reason for you to quit the church or abandon the Faith. "You have heard of the perseverance of Job and seen the end intended by the Lord—that the Lord is very compassionate and merciful" (James 5:11).

Put yourself in the shoes of Job for a moment:

1. HE LOST HIS WEALTH. In rapid succession three messengers came telling Job of the destruction of his property and servants by bands of robbers and by lightning.

2. HE LOST HIS FAMILY. A fourth messenger came telling of the death of all of Job's children. Seven sons and three daughters were crushed in a moment when the house fell.

3. HE LOST HIS HEALTH. Job was smitten from head to foot with most loathsome ulcers. He was constrained to sit down among the ashes and scrape himself with a potsherd.

4. HE LOST HIS FRIENDS. His servants turned their backs on him. The children in the streets despised Job and mocked him. His friends told him that his sufferings were because of his wickedness. And his wife nagged him to curse God and die.

If you take any of these trials separately they would be great, but view them collectively and one is almost overwhelmed. But in the midst of calamity, "Job arose and tore his robe and shaved his head, and he fell to the ground and worshiped" (Job 1:20).

And you know what? Job learned that the Lord is very "compassionate and merciful."

881 Message of the Robin

Martin Luther said, "I have one preacher that I love better than any other on earth. It is my little tame robin which preaches to me daily. I put his crumbs on the window sill. He hops on the sill and takes as much as he needs. From there he always flies to a little tree close by, lifts up his voice to God, sings his song of praise and gratitude, tucks his head under his wing and goes to sleep, leaving tomorrow to look after itself. He is the best preacher I have on earth."

882 Ours to Obey, His to Make Way

A pilot was having trouble bringing his plane down to land. From the control tower, he was given instructions. "But there is a pole there," he objected. The answer came back, "You take care of the instructions; we will take care of the obstructions."

So with the child of God. In the Word, he or she has God's instructions. God will take care of the obstructions. It is ours to obey the instructions from God's Word.

883 Learning to Fly

When an eagle wants to teach its little ones to fly from the nest high upon a cliff, hundreds of feet up in the air, it prods one of the little eaglets and with its beak noses it out of the nest. The eaglet starts to fall, and the great eagle flies underneath, puts its wing out, catches the little one on its back and flies a mile into the air. When you can hardly see the eagle as a point in the sky, it turns sideways, and down falls the little eaglet, fluttering maybe a thousand feet. Meanwhile, the eagle circles around and underneath the eaglet; the eagle catches the eaglet on its wings and carries the eaglet up in the air again. After dishing the young one out again and letting it go, the eaglet comes down farther and farther—sometimes within a hundred feet of the ground. Again the great eagle catches the little one on its back and they go up another mile. The little eagle is at perfect rest, and little by little it will learn to fly. The eagle knows when the eaglet is tired; it spoons the eaglet into the nest, noses out the next one and starts off again.

God says, "That is the way I take care of you." But you may say, "I do not like to have my nest stirred up. I like everything cozy and tidy, and I just like to stay in my baby ways where I am." But God loves you. That is why He will not let you stay as a baby; He wants you to learn to fly. Sometimes you have to be carried aloft, and you may have a horror of having to go by yourself, but it must come if you are to grow.

884 *Abraham Lincoln's Testimony*

Abraham Lincoln, 16th President of the United States, was born in 1809. A well-known writer says: "The worldwide interest in President Lincoln, from the time he left his home in Springfield, Illinois to take the presidential chair at Washington in 1861, and the universal and real sorrow for his untimely death on the 15th of April, 1865, are very pronounced. Even to this present day there exists among the different nationalities of the earth a great interest in this wise and benevolent ruler. President Lincoln had endeared himself to the hearts of millions by his human sympathy, great wisdom, and kindly acts toward friend and foe alike in the most critical and difficult periods of the history of the United States, and

after his death this was more fully realized and appreciated by all."

When Lincoln left Springfield, in 1861, on his way to Washington to take the Presidency of the United States to which he was elected, he made the following farewell address: "My friends, no one not in my position can appreciate the sadness I feel at this parting. Here I have lived for a quarter of a century, here my children were born, and here one of them lies buried. A duty devolves upon me which is greater perhaps than that which has devolved upon any other man since the days of Washington. He never would have succeeded except for the aid of Divine providence, upon which he at all times relied. I feel that I cannot succeed without the same Divine aid which sustained him, and on the same Almighty Being I place my reliance for support. Again I bid you all an affectionate farewell." These simple words, addressed to his friends and neighbors, plainly show a reliance upon God, and indicate a work of God in his soul at that time.

885 *Trustworthiness*

A Louisville Kentucky woman, very active in church work, had walked over to the edge of the swimming pool to watch the youngsters at play. She was thoroughly enjoying their fun when a 13-year-old boy ran up to her and asked, "Say, lady, do you go to Sunday school?"

"Why, yes I do," she replied, a bit surprised.

"Then," he said, "please hold this quarter for me while I go into the pool."

886 When the Best Defense Is Fleeting

A beautiful lesson comes to us from Proverbs 30:26. "The conies are a feeble folk, yet they make their houses in the rocks."

The cony is a weak, timid little animal like our rabbit or hare. He has no means of defense in himself, so when his foes, the vulture or the eagle, come in sight the cony does not turn at bay and do all he can to defend himself before he flees. If he did he would be torn to pieces in an instant by his fierce enemies of the air. Nay, the cony has learned a wiser course than this. He knows he is a "feeble folk," so he rushes straight to the rocks. He lets the rocks defend him without attempting any defense whatever in his own strength, which is but weakness.

Likewise it is with us. Our only course is to learn the cony lesson, to fly straight to our Rock, Christ Jesus, in prayer, and trust the Rock to keep us.

887 Bless Me, God

Do we really understand when we say "Bless me, God?"

The word for bless in the Greek New Testament is *eulogéō*, which means to speak well of.

We are really quite daring when we ask God to speak well of us. When we bless God we are eulogizing or speaking well of Him, and He indeed is worthy of being well spoken of. But how dare we ask Him to speak well of us? In the Bible, God's words are God's actions. The Lord created the world with His word. So when we ask God to speak well of us, it is the same as asking Him to act in our lives.

So many of us have the wrong idea about the blessing of God. We have a tendency to believe that God should hold a rubber stamp and automatically approve our plans.

"How can you look so pleasant tonight?" a man asked his friend. "You have had a score of interruptions this afternoon, when you had plans to accomplish so much." "That is all right," was the answer. "Every morning I give my day to Christ. I take what He sends. These interruptions came in the way of duty. Why should I complain about the service He has appointed?"

Would you really ask God to bless you if you knew that He might interrupt your planning?

888 God Is My Refuge

Do you have that kind of inner resource? When life is under attack, do you have a fortress with inner provision that can withstand the siege? Between the two World Wars, the French built an 87-mile-long defensive wall called the Maginot Line—the great wall of France that defended its border with Germany. Three lines of defense were incorporated into the wall. The first were strong houses, small fortified barracks designed to sound the alarm. The second line of defense was deep, reinforced bunkers to delay enemy attack. But the third line of defense was called *ouvrage*, deeply buried multi-storied forts every four to six miles. Below the barracks, at the deepest level, were the storehouses of ammunition, food, and above all else, a constant supply of water from deep wells.

When the Germans did move against France, they did not even try to attack these final forts. Not a single one of the *ouvrage* was ever overcome or taken by the Germans. Why? The Germans knew the soldiers in these bunkers could survive and resist almost indefinitely because of the deep, endless supply of water.

All of us need fortifications for life. But every line of defense is inadequate unless deep within us there is a resource hidden, abundant, untouchable. When the assault of life's enemy comes, we need not fear if that Source is within us. Absolute trust in God means that Source of life can never be taken, despite rejection, poverty, loss of vocation, misunderstanding. Jeremiah himself experienced all of that and more. Yet what was true for him can be true for you. Jesus said it best: from within, streams of living water.

889 *"For the Lord Your God Will Be With You Wherever You Go"*

"Have I not commanded you? Be strong and courageous. Do not be terrified; do not be discouraged, for the Lord your God will be with you wherever you go" (Josh. 1:19 NIV).

It was Palm Sunday, 1987, when a dear woman was waiting for service to conclude and looking forward to an afternoon when the entire family would enjoy a rare day together. As the final song was beginning to flow from the congregation, she knew something was wrong. Pushing past the other family members, she made it as far as the outside steps. It was Tuesday when she awoke and found herself in the hospital surrounded by her family and physician. A visit to a neurologist was suggested.

The neurologist found an aneurysm in the major artery of the brain. No symptoms: no headaches, no blurred vision, no motor problems—never been in better health. Still young in years, still eating correctly, still exercising—yet within a touch of death. She had two choices: 1) live with the knowledge of the aneurysm and hope for the best; or 2) have brain surgery.

How does someone handle news like this? How would you handle it? How did our friend handle it? Where is God at a time like this?

The tears came first, then the resolve to stay busy. So she went back to work and did not tell anyone about it. She discussed it only with family and a trusted physician. Her decision—surgery. She began to review life and wonder why, and at the same time, be thankful for what God had already provided.

Then the panic attack came. Would the surgery leave her paralyzed, blind, or even dead? All were possible. There were long talks with her husband far into the night—there was inability to sleep—it was real—it was happening and it was happening to her!

On one of those sleepless nights she walked downstairs, picked up her Bible, looked at a red ribbon imprinted with suggested topics: sorrow, worry, loneliness, courage —and picked courage. The passage was Joshua 1:9, and the words jumped out at her: "Be strong and courageous. Do not be terrified; do not be discouraged, for the Lord Your God will be with you wherever you go." Tearing a piece of paper from a note pad, she copied the verse and clasped it in her hand. The sense of panic then drained away.

The piece of paper remained with her during the days leading up to the day of the surgery. Surgery day found her with no fear of the surgery or the future. The piece of paper remained in her right hand as she was moved into the operating room. The final exam by the attending nurses revealed the paper.

The piece of paper with the verse had served its purpose. She told the nurse to throw it away. But in her beautiful wisdom, the nurse responded, "I have to take it now; but when you wake up, you will find it taped to your palm."

Twenty-six hours later two smiling nurses appeared. "Did you find your verse?" Slowly she opened her fist. The tattered scrap was secured with surgical tape. Reading it would not be possible for a long time, but the words are etched forever in her memory: ". . . for the Lord your God will be with you wherever you go."

Only He can give us the courage to face life and death. May we be moved to call upon His power and promises daily.

890 Pedal

At first, I saw God as my Observer, my Judge—keeping track of things I did to know whether I merited heaven or hell. He was out there—sort of like a President. I recognized His picture but I did not know Him.

Later on, when I met Christ, life became a bike ride. It was a tandem bike, and Christ was in the back helping me pedal. I do not know just when He suggested we change places, but life has not been the same since. Christ makes life exciting.

When I had the control, I knew the way. It was rather boring, but predictable. It was the shortest distance between two points. When He led, He knew delightful long cuts—up mountains and through rocky places—and at breakneck speeds. It was all I could do to hang on! Even though it looked like madness, He said "Pedal!" I worried and was anxious and asked, "Where are you taking me?" He laughed and did not answer, and I started to trust.

I forgot my boring life and entered into the adventure. And when I would say, "I am scared," He would lean back and touch my hand. He took me to people who gave me gifts of healing, acceptance, joy and peace for our journey. He said, "Give the gifts away." So I did to people we met. And I found that in giving I received, and our burden was light.

I did not trust Him at first to control my life. I thought He would wreck it. But He knows how to make bikes bend to take sharp corners, jump to clear high rocks, fly to shorten scary passages.

I am learning to be quiet and pedal in the strangest places. I am beginning to enjoy the view and the cool breeze on my face. And when I am sure I just cannot do any more—He just smiles and says, "Pedal!"

891 How Do We Hallow the Name Of God?

In the Lord's prayer, Jesus taught His disciples to pray, "Our Father in heaven, hallowed be your name" (Matt. 6:9). To hallow the name of God is to regard it as holy, to treat it differently from all other names.

One of the ten commandments warned, "You shall not misuse the name of the Lord your God, for the Lord will not hold anyone guiltless who misuses His name" (Ex. 20:7). Those who hallow the name of God take special care to avoid light, meaningless and profane reference to God in their daily speech.

We must realize, however, that hallowing the name of God is not just a matter of vocabulary. Many people fail to hallow God's name, who would never think of using His name in a vulgar or obscene context. They simply do not take God seriously in the way they live. Every day is consumed with activity that does not take God into consideration. Problem solving becomes a matter of relying on human resources. God is nowhere to be found in the picture. Which is the more serious breech of God's command? To speak God's name profanely? Or to give lip service to Him in church and then ignore Him in everyday life?

Several years ago, J. B. Phillips wrote an interesting book which he titled, *Your God Is Too Small*. In the book he wrote about some inadequate concepts of God, and Mike Cope suggests that our God is "too middle-sized." We affirm a lot of things about God. He is omnipotent, omniscient and omnipresent. He is majestic and glorious. He is the God to Whom we must give account. We are invited to draw near to Him. Our *doctrine* of God is right on target.

But when it comes to practical living, then we are not sure God is capable of doing all those things He has promised. Cope suggests we do not believe what we know. You can talk about Him in Bible class, but when you are struggling with the mortgage payments or a sick child or the loss of a job, Bible-class talk about God tends to sound rather hollow. That is because we believe in a middle-sized God. He is big enough to judge us in eternity, but not big enough to help with the job problem. To hallow the name of God means to treat His name with respect, not only in the way we talk, but also in the way we trust.

892 The Painting of My Life

Brian J. Waldrop relates this slice of life:

"Flipping through the channels of my TV the other morning, I stopped to watch a painter skillfully painting a desert landscape. As the man proceeded to color the canvas in deep browns, reds, and yellows, the picture really started to look good. I felt that the painter ought to stop. To me, the picture looked complete.

"As I was thinking those very words, I cringed to see the artist add a dark blackish color of paint to the canvas. As I had feared, the dark blob looked awkward and out of place. But as the man continued to add texture and other colors to the blob it began to take shape. When the painter was finished, the part of the picture that I thought was ruined looked great! It was exactly what the painting needed to make it beautiful and complete.

"As I sat there watching the program that day, I was really surprised to find myself cringing at many of the moves the artist made with his brush. I got to thinking how typical this is of my Christian life. Many times in my life, after much struggling and hardship, I have come to a place where I am comfortable. As I am basking in the goodness of the Lord, God has chosen to institute a change I neither expected nor wanted. During this time I cry out, 'No, Lord, You are ruining the picture!' But often, as I allowed God to continue His work on the canvas of my life, to my surprise the picture would begin to look pretty good. Finally, I would thank Him for the addition or subtraction to my life.

"There have been times, however, that the change never looked good to me and perhaps never will. During these times I must remember that God is still painting. The picture has not been completed yet. I must travel on in faith knowing that when I see Him face to face, my painting will be beautiful.

"In the meantime, I can take comfort knowing that every situation, though it may be ugly and bad, is paint that the Master Craftsman can use for good.

"Paul stated it this way, 'And we know that in all things God works for the good of those who love Him, who have been called according to His purpose' (Rom. 8:28 NIV).

"Lord Jesus, take my life and create a masterpiece!"

893 Never Moved a Mountain

Our thanks to an unknown author for the following lyric testimony to God's providence:

Lord, I have never moved a mountain and I guess I never will. All the faith that I could muster would not move a small ant hill. Yet, I will tell you, Lord, I am grateful for the joy of knowing Thee, and for all the mountain moving, down through life you have done for me.

When I needed some help You lifted me from the depths of great despair. And when burdens, pain and sorrow have been more than I can bear, you have always been my courage to restore life's troubled sea, and to move these little mountains that have looked so big to me.

Many times when I have had problems and when bills I have had to pay, and the worries and the heartaches just kept mounting every day, Lord, I do not know how you did it. I cannot explain the wheres or whys. All I know is that I have seen these mountains turn to blessings in disguise.

No, I have never moved a mountain, for my faith is far too small. Yet, I thank you, Lord of Heaven, you have always heard my call. And as long as there are mountains in my life, I will have no fear, for the mountain-moving Jesus is my strength and always near.

Truth

894 Say What They Need to Hear, Even If It Kills You

John the Baptist's message from the wilderness was not, "Smile, God loves you." It was "O generation of vipers, who hath warned you to flee from the wrath to come." Jeremiah was not put into a miry pit for preaching, "I'm OK, you're OK." It was for crying against the adultery, idolatry and other wickedness of his nation. Noah's message from the steps of the ark was not, "Something *good* is going to happen to you." He condemned the world and was a preacher of righteousness. Jesus Christ was not crucified for saying, "Consider the lilies, how they grow," but for saying, "Woe unto you scribes and Pharisees, hypocrites . . . children of hell . . . fools and blind guides . . . whited sepulchers . . . generation of vipers."

895 A Psychiatrist's Confession

I am a psychiatrist, but I can attest to the fact that all truth—including psychological truth—is already written in the Bible. All of the "findings" of the social scientists and psychologists have their basis first of all in the Bible. A person could visit three different psychiatrists and get three different approaches to his problem! He could visit them again a few years later and discover they have shifted their views even more. Those of us who believe the Bible have an unchanging foundation on which to build.

896 Tell the Truth Every Time

A small boy was on the witness stand in an important lawsuit. The prosecuting attorney cross-examined him, then delivered, he thought, a crushing blow to the testimony. "Your father has been telling you how to testify, has he not?" "Yes," the lad replied and did not hesitate with the answer. "Now," said the lawyer triumphantly, "just tell us how your father told you to testify." "Well," the boy said modestly, "Father told me the lawyers would try to tangle me in my testimony, but if I would just be careful to tell the truth, I could repeat the same thing every time."

Unbelief

897 What Is the Difference . . .

—Between the atheist who would not dream of financially supporting the church and the Christian who will not financially support the Lord's church?

—Between the skeptic who does not believe the Bible and the negligent Christian who never reads it?

—Between those who do not believe in Bible classes and those who choose never to attend a class?

—Between the atheist who does nothing to build up the Lord's church and the Christian who finds fault with others but does nothing himself?

—Between a man of the world and a person in the church who lives like a man in the world?

—Between a man of the world who lives for self, and a person in the church building who lives for self, not God?

These are tough questions for Christians who live in a tough world. The fact is that Christians make no difference until they are different.

Again, what's the difference?

898 Play It Safe

A Georgia farmer, ragged and barefooted, was standing on the steps of his tumbledown shack. A stranger stopped for a drink of water. "How is your cotton coming along?" he asked. "Ain't got none," replied the farmer. "Did you plant any?" asked the stranger. "Nope," was the reply, "afraid of bollweevils."

"Well," continued the stranger, "how is your corn?" "Didn't plant none," came the answer, " 'fraid there weren't gonna to be no rain."

The visitor persevered: "Well, how are your potatoes?" "Ain't got none. Scairt of potato bugs."

"Really, what did you plant?" pressed the stranger. "Nothin'," was the calm reply, "I jest played safe."

899 It Just Happened

Once, an unbeliever visited Isaac Newton, the great English scientist and Christian. Newton had a mechanical model of the solar system in his study.

The unbeliever asked, "Who made this?"

"Nobody," Mr. Newton replied promptly.

"You must think I am a fool!" the unbeliever said, "It would take a genius to make this."

Newton said, "This is only a puny imitation of a much grander system. I cannot convince you that

374

this mere toy is without a designer, yet you profess to believe that the great original from which this design is taken has come into being without a Designer or a Maker."

900 Transformed Lives!

As Dr. Harry A. Ironside preached one day, he noticed a man in the crowd writing on a card, which he presently handed to the speaker. The man was Arthur Lewis, an agnostic lecturer, and he proposed a challenge to the speaker to debate the subject, "Agnosticism versus Christianity," and offered to pay all expenses involved.

Dr. Ironside read the card aloud to his audience and then said: "I accept on these conditions:

"First, that you promise to bring with you on the platform one man who was once an outcast, a slave to sinful habits, but who heard you or some other infidel lecture on agnosticism, was helped by it and cast away his sins and became a new man and is today a respected member of society, all because of your unbelief.

"Second, that you agree to bring with you one woman who was once lost to all purity and goodness, but who can now testify that agnosticism came to her while deep in sin and implanted in her poor heart a hatred of impurity and a love of holiness, causing her to become chaste and upright, all through a disbelief in the Bible."

"Now, sir," he continued, "if you will agree, I promise to be there with one hundred such men and women, once just such lost souls, who heard the gospel of the grace of God, believed it and have found new life and joy in Jesus Christ our Savior. Will you accept my terms?"

As might be expected, the atheist could only walk away silently.

Unity

901 Bear One Another's Burdens

One hot day, Herman Trueblood, all clean and cooled off by a nice swim in the ocean, saw a sweating man and his two sons trying on a hot day to push his disabled car up an incline. Two voices started yelling at each other inside him. One said, "There is an opportunity for service; you ought to help them push." The other voice protested, "Now that is none of your business. You will get yourself all hot and dirty. Let them handle their own affair." He finally yielded to his better impulse. He put his shoulder to the task. The car moved and kept moving.

A simple thing then happened which Trueblood never forgot. The father stuck out his dirty hand, and Trueblood stuck out his dirty hand. The father said, "I am very glad that you came along. You had just enough strength, added to ours, to make the thing go."

"Years have passed since that hot day, but I can still hear that man saying, 'You had just enough strength, added to ours, to make the thing go,' " Trueblood reflected more recently. "There are many thousands of people struggling to get some heavy load over the hill, and I probably have 'just enough strength, added to theirs, to make the thing go.' "

902 Strength in Union

One of Aesop's fables tells of four oxen who were such great friends that they always kept together when feeding. A lion watched them for many days with longing eyes, but never being able to find one apart from the rest, was afraid to attack them. Whenever he came near they turned their tails to one another so that whichever way he approached them he was met by horns. At length he succeeded in awakening jealousy among them, which grew into a mutual aversion, and they strayed a considerable distance from each other. The lion then fell upon them singly and killed them all.

The moral is, "United we stand, divided we fall."

903 Each His Part

"I did," said the sticks. "I did," said the paper. "I did," said the boy. "No, I did," said the wind. But they all flew the kite together. If the sticks had broken, the tail caught in a tree, the paper torn or the wind was lulled, the kite would have come down. Each had a part to play.

The application is inescapable. We each have a work to do. If the work of the Lord is to be a success, then every member of the church must play his part. We have the work of visiting, giving, preaching, and countless other jobs to do to make the church and its work successful. We must all work together and each do what he can to help. It is a matter of teamwork (1 Cor. 3:6-9).

904 Togetherness Can Build Up a Church

A clergyman once remarked to Sir John Barbirolli how he wished he could fill his church building the way Sir John and the Halle Orchestra filled every seat of a large concert hall. The conductor replied, "You could, if you had a hundred members who worked together as well as the members of this orchestra."

The white cuffs of the violinists stood out against a black background and made a bold horizontal line across the left side of the stage. As they played, those white cuffs remained an almost perfectly straight line which often moved up and down very quickly. It was a splendid demonstration of how the members of a great orchestra will not only play the right notes, but will play them together.

A great church is somewhat like a great orchestra. The members will not only make the right moves, but will make them together. They must learn to decide upon a task and execute it with perfect harmony. A musician who always wants to play his favorite piece (which may be exceptionally beautiful) and refuses to play—or else plays very halfheartedly or slowly—when another composition is chosen, not only will not help the cause but will be a detriment to the whole orchestra and may destroy its appeal. And a church member who is out of step with others, and who approaches his tasks carelessly or reluctantly, may generate more sour music than the sweet notes all the rest can draw out.

905 The Church As a Team

The story is told of a horse-pull in Canada. One horse pulled 9,000 pounds, another 8,000. Together you would expect them to pull 18,000 pounds. Not so! When teamed together, they pulled 30,000 pounds.

The principle is called synergism. By definition, the simultaneous action of separate agents working together has a greater total effect than the sum of their individual efforts. More can be done in a team effort than can be accomplished solo. In order for the principle of synergism to work like it should, there has to be teamwork.

Everything we do takes teamwork and trust. Every person in the local church is valuable and needed. The church is a team, and together we can build for the Lord.

906 Laborers Together

An old legend tells of a noisy carpenter's shop in which the tools of the trade were arguing among themselves. Brother Hammer was told by his fellow tools that he would have to leave because he was too noisy. To which he replied, "If I am to leave this carpenter's shop, Brother Gimlet must go too; he is so insignificant that he makes very little impression."

Little Brother Gimlet arose and said, "All right, but Brother Screw must go also; you have to turn him around and around again and again to get him anywhere."

Brother Screw said, "If you wish, I will go. But Brother Plane must leave also; all his work is on the surface, there is no depth to it."

To this Brother Plane replied, "Well, Brother Rule will have to withdraw if I do, for he is always measuring others as though he were the only one who is right."

Brother Rule then complained against Brother Sandpaper and said, "I just do not care, he is rougher than he ought to be and he is always rubbing people the wrong way."

In the midst of the discussion, the Carpenter of Nazareth walked in. He had come to perform His day's work. He put on His apron, and went to the bench to make a pulpit. He employed the screw, the gimlet, the sandpaper, the saw, the hammer and the plane and all the other tools. After the day's work was over and the pulpit was finished, Brother Saw arose and said, "Brethren, I perceive that all of us are laborers together with God."

Is it not wonderful how God uses all of us and our unique gifts in the building of His pulpit!

Will

907 The Will to Do It

The late Dr. Wernher Von Braun once was asked what it would take for man to reach the moon, and he replied, "The will to do it." This answer holds good in nearly every field of human endeavor. In medicine, determination and persistence have paid off in spectacular break-throughs in conquering diseases. In transportation the dream of traveling around the world in a matter of hours has become a reality because the will to do so was strong. "The will to do it!" How vitally important this attitude is in Christianity! If you really want to do God's will, you can, but you must will to do it. This is true in so many areas of our lives.

908 Where the Storm May Carry You

There is a beautiful figure in one of Wordsworth's poems about a bird swept from the rough and rocky country habitat by the strong winds of a storm. The bird battled desperately, trying to get back to its familiar home, but all in vain. At last, it yielded to the wind, thinking that the storm would carry it to its death, but the gale carried it across the waves and brought it to a sunny land with green meadows and forest glades.

How many of us have been like that little voyager, fretting and fighting against the will of God? We think life can never be the same again when we are carried seaward by the storm, until at last, we cease our struggling and yield to the wind, only to find that we have been carried to a place far better. God's Word encourages us to praise the Lord in the midst of raging waves and the strong winds of the storm. We can be assured that in God's own time and way, He will bring us to a better haven He has prepared for us. Remember: none lives so pleasantly as he who lives by faith.

909 God's Will

Here is an illustration of how to find God's will that has been useful to many: There was a certain harbor that was treacherous and danger-ous. In order for the captain to guide his ship safely into this harbor, he had to be very attentive to the three lights that were used to guide him. When all three lights lined up as one, he knew it was safe to pro-ceed. Then, and only then, would he be able to bring his ship safely to port.

As we seek guidance, we, too, have to be attentive to three lights that are used to guide us into the harbor of His will: the Word of God, outward circumstances, and inner conviction. When all three of these lights line up, we can proceed with assurance that we will be led safely into the harbor.

910 Respect God's Will

A good pilot must have a healthy fear of gravity. This respect is not in the conscious mind of most pilots, but it forms the foundation of everything they do. When a headstrong pilot comes up against gravity, gravity will win—no matter how strongly the pilot opposes it. A pilot who does not respect gravity is not around to tell us about it. In a sense, this healthy respect of gravity is similar to our living in submission to God's sovereign will. Ultimately, whether or not we choose to accept it, God's will wins out.

911 How to Find God's Will

A young man went into a church and started praying. He was so anxious to find God's will for his life that he took a piece of paper and wrote down all the things that he was going to do for God. Then he started to pray that God might reveal to him whether these promises were acceptable to Him.

"This is not the way I want you to find My will. All I want of you is for you to sign your name and leave the paper blank for Me to fill."

Wisdom

912 Integrity and Wisdom

"My boy," said the store owner to his new employee, "wisdom and integrity are essential to the retail business. By 'integrity' I mean if you promise a customer something, you have got to keep that promise—even if it means we lose money."

"And what," asked the teenager, "is wisdom?"

"That," answered the boss, "is not making any stupid promises."

913 Ten Rules for Happier Living

1. Give something away (no strings attached).
2. Do a kindness (and forget it).
3. Spend a few minutes with the aged (their experience can be priceless guidance).
4. Look intently into the face of a baby (and marvel).
5. Laugh often (it is life's lubricant).
6. Give thanks (a thousand times a day is not enough).
7. Pray (or you will lose the way).
8. Work (with vim and vigor).
9. Plan as though you will live forever (because you will).
10. Live as though you will die tomorrow (because you will die on some tomorrow).

914 Lessons From Teardrops

Two little teardrops were floating down the river of life. One said to the other, "Who are you?" It replied, "I am a teardrop from a girl who loved a man and lost him. Who are you?" The first responded, "Well, I am a teardrop from the girl who got him!"

Life is like that. We cry over things we cannot have. If we only knew it, we would probably cry more if we had received them. Paul had the right idea when he said, "I have learned in whatsoever state I am, therewith to be content" (Phil. 4:11).

915 Wise Advice from Abraham Lincoln

Abraham Lincoln once said, "You cannot bring about prosperity by discouraging thrift. You cannot strengthen the weak by weakening the strong. You cannot help the wage earner by pulling down the wage payer. You cannot further the brotherhood of man by encouraging class hatred. You cannot keep out of trouble by spending more than you earn. You cannot build character and courage by taking away man's initiative and independence. You cannot help men permanently by doing for them what they could and should do for themselves.

916 Seek Counsel from More Than One

Here is a caution about seeking experienced counsel: It's dangerous to go on just one person's experience. Mark Twain told about a cat who sat on a hot stove lid. That experience taught the cat never to sit on a hot stove lid again. But further, that cat never sat on a cold stove lid either. He took more from the experience than it had to offer. If we're going to talk about experiences, we would be wise to talk to a number of people who have faced similar decisions and extract direction from their combined counsel.

917 Motivation behind Choices

There are a great many actions which, in and of themselves, are neither right nor wrong. They are made right when we act in love. They become wrong if we act in selfishness.

It's like playing the piano. There are no right or wrong notes. There are only right or wrong notes in the context of the musical score. We many not like G or F, or be very favorable to middle C, but the note is only wrong in the context of what is being played. Likewise, choices become right or wrong based on the motivation behind them.

Witness

918 The Aroma

To just come right out and ask somebody what they think you smell like might be offensive to them (or to you—if they give you a candid answer). But most people care deeply about what others think of their particular odor. Americans spend zillions of dollars every year on perfumes (Obsession—$50 for 4 ounces) and cologne (quality gentlemen's foo-foo sells for about $10 an ounce, too). But those products just fix you from the neck up. Deodorants, special soaps, body splashes and powders, breath mints and mouthwashes are also big ticket items for the socially conscious.

If you need a good excuse to buy products that make you smell pleasant, here it is. Now there is a new branch of scientific research called "odor engineering." So far the researchers have tried odor engineering only in the work place.

According to the publication *Communication Briefings*, one Japanese firm reports that air scented with lavender cut keypunching errors by 21 percent. Jasmine-scented air dropped errors by 33 percent and lemon in the air was even better—this cut errors by 54 percent. They determined that lavender reduces stress, jasmine relaxes and lemon stimulates. Odors do make a difference.

This gives new significance to a Scripture that has always intrigued me. "For we are to God the aroma of Christ among those who are being saved and those who are perishing. To the one we are the smell of death; to the other, the fragrance of life" (2 Cor. 2:15, 16).

The odor engineers have not done any research as to what happens to people (or a community) when a true believer comes around and gives everybody a whiff of Christ. But Paul says this odor does make a difference. The believer, with the knowledge and life of Christ, emits (in a figurative way) the very smell of Christ's sweet sacrifice (note Eph. 5:2). We cannot buy it in a bottle. It does not ooze out of our pores. It comes out in our attitudes, actions and words.

That sweet smell affects everybody around us. So it might not be a bad idea to ask yourself, "What do I really smell like?" If you know Christ your life smells good. And you will naturally make a difference in all those around you.

919 Who Changed Tom Brown?

The book *Tom Brown's School Days* contains a story about a boy who had the courage to stand up to ridicule.

Tom Brown was a student at Rugby Boys School when a new boy enrolled. On his first night in a room with 12 beds and 11 other boys, he knelt to say his evening prayers. Tom turned his head just in time to see a heavy slipper flying through the air toward the head of the new boy.

When the lights went out a little later, Tom Brown thought of his mother, and the prayers she had taught him to say, which he had never done since he came to Rugby. He decided that the next time he went to bed, he, too, would say his prayers.

The next night, the other boys in the room, ready to laugh and scoff at the newcomer who said his prayers, were amazed to see Tom Brown, whom they all respected and feared, kneel down at the side of his bed and pray.

That boy's courageous prayer, in spite of the ridicule, won him the respect of all his companions. He later became one of the most distinguished men of the Church of England.

"Do not be anxious about anything, but in everything, by prayer and petition, with thanksgiving, present your requests to God" (Phil. 4:6).

920 The Real Proof of God

Keith Robinson, in *The Encourager*, writes:

"When God wanted to authenticate Himself to the ancient world, He called His nation Israel as witness. 'You are my witnesses,' He said, testimony that 'I am He. Before Me there was no God formed, and there will be none after Me. I, even I, am the Lord' (Is. 48:10). The people of God served as the undeniable proof of God.

"God's people still offer the most basic and best proof of God. A changed life is still the best testimony of God's power. Divine love reflected in a Christian heart which accepts, forgives and loves the unlovable is still the best witness of the nature of God. Hope that will not die is still the best proof of eternal life. Faith which cannot be shaken even in the face of death is still the best demonstration of the immutability of God's promises.

"We who have been granted the imponderable privilege of partaking in the divine nature (2 Pet. 1:4), are the witnesses, the demonstration, the proof of the divine presence in the world. Books and lessons and sermons and reason may have their place, but the real test is in the lives of God's chosen people. If that proof is not clear and constant, everything else is just hearsay."

921 Which Am I?

A strong horseshoe magnet may be held over an old rust-eaten, shapeless nail without meeting any response. A bright, ringing nail will leap to the magnet, attract another, and through it draw yet another, until several are attracted.

That is how Christians are. A really genuine, active, shining Christian has a tremendous attraction to Christ, is magnetized by His love and purity, attracted by His power. And through that Christian, Christ can draw others to Him to share the same power and attraction.

But a rusty, unpolished, corroded Christian, cranky, defiled and selfish, has very little attraction, and through him the power of Christ to win the world cannot flow.

God has enough power to wipe out every vice and every evil doctrine in this world, but first of all, there must be conductors. And rusty, untaught, unprepared, and unpracticed church members neither draw others near to God nor are drawn near themselves.

Our religion must be intensive before it can be extensive.

922 Every Christian Is a Missionary

One day, Mr. Wilfred Grenfell, medical missionary to Labrador, was guest at a dinner in London together with a number of socially prominent British men and women.

During the course of the dinner, the lady seated next to him turned and said, "Is it true, Dr. Grenfell, that you are a missionary?"

Dr. Grenfell looked at her for a moment before replying, "Is it true, madam, that you are not?"

923 Example and Teaching

What ingredients go into creating the environment of a truly Christian home? Some would say it is teaching our children right from wrong, belief in God, and re-

spect for their fellowman. But can one truly "teach" such fundamental truths as these? Rather we must live these truths each and every day so that our children are irresistibly drawn to the right and the good life by our continual example.

924 The Wife's Example Made the Difference

A young man finally came to Christ and was baptized after years of indiffernce. Many talked to him about the Lord, but were not able to sway him. It is not known what finally moved him, but for years his faithful wife went to every service of the churchl, Sunday morning and evening, Bible Study on Wednesday night. Sometimes he went with her. Sometimes he was working or out of town, but she went. They had one, then two and finally three children. She went on with her children rain or shine. On one instance, it was raining so hard that one could hardly see. The wind was blowing. This good Christian mother drove up, got out of her car and carried one baby into the church building and then started back for another one when a man came forward to help her out on that last trip. It was her husband who was baptized, and we all probably know the sermon that converted him.

925 Let It Shine

Benjamin Franklin wanted to interest the people in Philadelphia in street lighting. He did not call a town meeting nor try to persuade the people by talking about it. He acted upon what he considered a good idea. He hung a beautiful lantern on a long bracket in front of his house. He kept the glass polished and carefully trimmed and lit the wick every evening at the approach of dusk. The lamp helped the people see the pavement ahead; made them feel more secure at night. Others began placing lights in front of their houses. Soon Philadelphia recognized the need for street lights.

Be the one today to light up your neighborhood with the light of life. Let it shine. Let your light shine TODAY!

926 Salt Creates Thirst

At a missionary meeting some young people were discussing the text, "Ye are the salt of the earth."

One suggestion after another was made as to the meaning of "salt" in this verse.

"Salt imparts a desirable flavor," said one. "Salt preserves from decay," another suggested.

Then at last a Chinese Christian girl spoke out of an experience none of the others had. "Salt creates thirst," she said, and there was a sudden hush over the room.

Everyone was thinking, "Have I ever made anyone thirsty for the Lord Jesus Christ?"

927 Does Your Behavior Make Others Behave?

In a cemetery, a little white stone marked the grave of a dear little girl. On the stone were chiseled these words: *A child of whom her playmates said, "It was easier to be good when she was with us."* It was one of the most beautiful epitaphs ever heard of.

928 Godly Influence

Around the turn of the century in rural Tennessee an old man crippled with arthritis was very faithful in his assembling with the saints. Twice on Sunday and on Wednesday nights a little girl watched from her window as the old man with his cane painfully made his way down to the little church on the corner. One Sunday morning following a snow storm, the little girl ran to her window and looking out exclaimed, "Surely the old man will not go to church this morning." But there he was, right on schedule, plodding very cautiously through the snow.

The little girl could not contain herself any longer. She just had to visit the little church to see what possibly could be there that would bring the old man out on such an inclement morning. The rest is history. The little girl was impressed by the services there that morning and a short time later became a Christian. After high school she enrolled in a Christian college and while there she met a fine young Christian boy whom she later married. To this union a son was born who was to become one of the finest gospel preachers. This brother during his ministry has literally led thousands to Christ.

The old man went to his reward never realizing just what an impact he had made for the cause of Christ. Because of his godly influence many will go into heaven with him. There can be no greater joy than to reach heaven and to her someone say, "I am here because you have shown me the way."

929 "Thou Shalt Not Steal"

A young man, employed by a Sunday school board, was invited at the last minute to preach at a church in Nashville. On a sudden impulse he used as his text, "Thou shalt not steal."

The next morning he stepped on the bus and handed the driver a dollar bill. The driver handed him back his change. He stood in the rear of the bus and counted the change. There was a dime too much. His first thought was, "The bus company will never miss this dime." Then quickly came the realization that he could not keep money that did not belong to him. He made his way to the front and said to the driver, "You gave me too much change." Imagine his surprise when the driver replied, "Yes, a dime too much. I gave it to you on purpose. You see, I heard your sermon yesterday, and I watched in my mirror as you counted your change. Had you kept the dime, I would never again have had any confidence in preaching."

930 The Power of a Smile

One day as a woman was crossing a street at London station, an old man stopped her and said, "Excuse me, Ma'am, but I want to thank you."

"Thank me?" she exclaimed.

"Yes'm. I used to be a ticket collector, and whenever you went by, you always gave me a cheerful smile and a good morning. I knew that smile must have come from inside somewhere. Then one morning I saw a little Bible in your hand. So I bought one too, and I found Jesus."

931 Let There Be Light

A young girl once consulted with her minister. "I cannot stick it out any longer. I am the only Christian in the factory where I work. I get nothing but taunts and sneers. It is more than I can stand. I am going to resign."

"Will you tell me," asked the minister, "where lights are placed?"

"What has that to do with it?" the young Christian asked him rather bluntly.

"Never mind," the minister replied. "Answer my question: 'Where are lights placed?' "

"I suppose in dark places," she replied.

"Yes, and that is why you have been put in that factory where there is such spiritual darkness and where there is no other Christian to shine for the Lord."

The young Christian realized for the first time the opportunity that was hers. She felt she could not fail God by allowing her light to go out. She went back to the factory with renewed determination to let her light shine in that dark corner. Before long, she was the means of leading nine other girls to the Light.

932 The Chameleon

Some of you have seen a lizard called the chameleon. Certain chameleons can quickly change color, and even develop spots and streaks that seem to be part of their background. They can turn green, gray or brown if they are standing on a green, gray or brown background.

Those of us who love the Lord Jesus should "show our colors"—let others know you belong to the Lord. Do not be like the chameleon who changes color with his surroundings. If you have to be with unsaved girls and boys at school and in other places, do not act as they do and do naughty things. Let others know you are different because you have a new life!

933 The Christian's Gauge

If you visit any large foundry where the boilers are kept going at full force, you would never be able to look into a boiler to tell how much water there is in it, but you would be able to tell how much water the boiler contains by an instrument which is attached to the side of the boiler. Alongside is a small glass tube which has some fluid in it. If this glass tube is half full of liquid, then there is an indication that the boiler is half full of water; if the glass gauge indicated that there is no water in the glass, then we can depend that there is no water in the boiler. The little glass gauge is the indicator for the large boiler.

How can people tell whether we love God, our fellowman, or even ourselves? They can never look within our hearts and get the answer; it is only by our outward actions, the works that we do as Christians that people are able to tell how much or how little our religion amounts to. Our love for God is indicated by the works of love in which we engage. There are people who are constantly looking at the Christian's gauge.

934 A Youth's One-Time Visit

"I refused a date to the movies, choosing rather to go to the Wednesday night prayer meeting.

"When I arrived, I looked for several people who were important to me.

"I looked for my Sunday school teacher—but he was not there. I looked for the familiar faces of a couple of deacons whom I knew—but they were not there. I looked for several of the members who seemed to be spiritually real and who had greeted me warmly at the Sunday morning services—but they were not there.

"Perhaps, these Christian friends do not think the Wednesday night services are so very important. I guess next Wednesday night I will go to the movies."

Was this young man from your church?

935 The Way Your Child Should Go

Abraham Lincoln's comment, made when talking to a father who was chagrined and embarrassed because his 17-year-old son had begun to indulge in liquor, is most convincing: "Well, there is just one way to bring up a child in the way he should go, and that is to travel the way yourself."

936 A Christian's Reputation

The story is told of Gordon Maxwell, missionary to India, that when he asked a Hindu scholar to teach him the language, the Hindu replied: "No, Sahib, I will not teach you my language. You would make me a Christian."

Gordon Maxwell replied, "You misunderstand me. I am simply asking you to teach me your language."

Again the Hindu responded, "No, Sahib, I will not teach you. No man can live with you and not become a Christian."

Gordon Maxwell's reputation as a Christian preceded him. His very lifestyle attracted people to Christ. And so it was with the Apostle Paul and his two missionary companions, Silas and Timothy. Saint Francis of Assisi captured their philosophy of evangelism when he said, "It is no use walking anywhere to preach unless we preach as we walk!"

937 A Drunkard Speaks to a Drinking Christian

A young lady went to a rescue mission to help out with the inquirers who would respond to the Gospel. As she approached one derelict in order to help him make a decision for Christ, he said to her, "Do you play cards, or dance, or go to the theater, or drink socially?" "No, not now," she replied. "Well, then you may talk to me; but I will not listen to one word from you fine Christian folks who are doing on a small scale the very things that brought me a poor wretch to where I am." This young Christian woman later confessed that she had greater joy in leading that young man to Christ than the exercise of all the pleasures that many Christians hold on to simply because they have not yet been ruined by them.

938 Little Things Mean a Lot

Dr. W. H. Lax was a Methodist minister in the East End of London for 38 years. He learned that an old man was gravely ill, and Dr. Lax called on him. However, he was an unwelcome visitor, for as soon as the sick man caught sight of Lax's clerical collar, he turned his head and refused to utter a word.

While trying to sustain a conversation, Dr. Lax noted the dreariness of the room and the pitifully small fire; he suspected that provisions had run low. When he left the patient, Dr. Lax stopped at a butcher shop and had two lamb chops sent to the house.

He called again a few days later, and though the old man was still far from talkative, he was a little more friendly. On the way home another order was left with the butcher. By the third visit, there was a pronounced change in the patient. He was congenial and even outgoing, and before leaving, Dr. Lax was even able to pray with the man.

A preaching engagement took Dr. Lax out of London for a few days, and when he got back he was informed that the old gentleman had died. At the end when he was hardly able to speak, the patient had gasped, "Tell Dr. Lax it is all right now. I am going to God; but be sure to tell him that it was not his preaching that changed me. It was those lamb chops."

939 Who Wants to Be a Square?

In Mark Twain's day, "square" was one of the best words in the language. You gave a man a *square deal* if you were honest. You gave him a *square meal* when he was hungry. When you got out of debt, you were *square with the world*. And that was when you could look your fellow man *square in the eye*.

Then a lot of characters ran down the word. Result: A square today is a man who never learned to get away with it; a Joe who volunteers when he does not have to; a guy who gets his kick from trying to do something better than anyone else can; a boob who gets lost in his work.

This country was discovered, put together, fought for and saved by "squares"—Nathan Hale, Patrick Henry, Paul Revere, George Washington, Benjamin Franklin. We need to get back to this nation's old beliefs in such things as ideas, pride, patriotism, loyalty, devotion—even hard work.

940 The Gift He Never Received

Billy Graham relates the story of a wealthy father who provided well for his only son.

One day, the boy came to his father and said he was dropping out of school and leaving home.

Asked why, the son said, "Well, Dad, the truth of it is, I hate you."

The father was stunned and demanded, "Why, son, why? I have given you everything, have I not?"

"Well, that is just it. You have not. You may have thought you bought me everything, but you have not given me anything to believe in."

941 I Saw God Today

I saw God today—
>   As a tearful child found comfort in your arms.

I saw God today—
>   As an old man's face was lit with hope by the grasp of your hand.

I saw God today—
>   As a smile etched the lips of the stranger you greeted on the street.

I saw God today—
>   As you stopped in the midst of a busy schedule to listen to a burdened soul.

I saw God today—
>   As I spent the day with you, my friend, and
>   Though the hours have flown and night draws near,
>   Today will linger on, with memories so dear,
>   For as we shared each hour's

array,

I met God through you today.

942 If Christ Has Really Done Something for Us, We Should Tell Others

A little fellow in the hospital had had a piece of deformed bone removed from his arm. He got well, but before he left the place he sent for the doctor. "You wish to see me, Willie?" asked the doctor. The little fellow reached up his hand and laid it on the doctor's shoulder and said, "My mama will never hear the last about you." I think that if we fully realized what Christ has done for us, we would say to Him, "My friends will never hear the last about You."

943 How One Life Affects Others

The unfilled spiritual tank is an invitation to disaster, and many of us have known that awful moment when, like a car out of gas, we seem to cough and sputter and pull over to the shoulder, out of service, not able to go any farther.

We have all seen the car out of gas in a long tunnel or on a narrow bridge at rush hour. Thousands of people are potentially affected by the clogged-up mess that follows. And it can happen in spiritual life also. One empty spiritual tank can affect a score of other people. It has happened more than once.

944 Reputation

What kind of reputation do you have? When people speak of you, are they saying kind things? Jesus honored that unselfish woman who anointed him with perfume by including mention of her good deed in the gospels. She was well thought of by her Lord. She had a good reputation.

How others perceive us is usually established by our consistent behavior. We need to live such honorable lives that even when someone speaks ill of us, others will not believe it of us. We also need to conduct our lives in such a manner that it will be easy for others to say kind words to us.

There are people who make life difficult for others. One such a person lives such a life that it will be hard for the speaker at his funeral to find something about his life worthy of mentioning. Sad.

Even Christians can live such distraught lives that they are looked on as trouble makers, boat rockers and negative knells. Though we study our Bibles, worship our God, and pray fervently, just how do neighbors and friends consider us? Are we known for being faithfully involved and supportive of the church's work, or do we have the reputation of being hard to please and a terror to live with?

If someone were asked to deliver a eulogy for you, what could easily be told "in your memory"? "He (or she) was a warm, gracious, faithful, zealous, dedicated, caring, thoughtful Christian," or "He (or she) was anxious, unhappy, critical, selfish, uninvolved, bitter, unloving, opinionated and socially obnoxious"? One cannot build a noble reputation on what he intends to do some day. One's reputation is affirmed and established daily.

Witnessing

945 Word Not in Vain

A highwayman once stopped John Wesley and demanded his money or his life. Wesley, after giving him the money, said, "Let me speak one word to you; the time may come when you will regret the course of life in which you are now engaged. Remember this, 'The blood of Jesus Christ cleanseth from all sin.' " No more was said, and they parted. Many years after, as Wesley was going out of a church in which he had been preaching, a stranger introduced himself, and asked Wesley if he remembered being waylaid at such a time. He said he recollected it. "I was that man," said the stranger, "and that single verse you quoted on that occasion was the means of a total change in my life and habits. I have long since been in the practice of attending the house of God and of giving attention to His Word, and trust that I am a Christian."

946 Now Is All the Time We Have

1. *Remember that this may be the day the Lord returns.* The thought of Psalm 118:24 surely includes our rejoicing in the return of the Lord. If I really believe Christ may return today, I'll live differently than I ever have, seeking to affect others for Christ. Nobody knows when He will return, so we ought to live each day as though He will come back today.

2. *Use time wisely, make the most of every opportunity* (Col. 4:5). Don't make excuses—be involved in the lives of those outside the Lord. Pray daily that God will keep alive in your heart a picture of those who are outside Christ as being lost. Ask God to revive your loving concern that all men be taught of Him, and to help you be involved in every effort to teach them.

3. *Treat everyone as if you'll never see them again* (Acts 10:37, 38). If we don't take for granted that we'll have time in the future, surely our treatment of each other will greatly improve. Use the time NOW to share a little about Jesus, for you may not have another opportunity.

If we truly believe NOW is all the time we have, what a difference that will make in our lives. It's great to be part of the family of God.

947 Forgive Me God, I Had No Time

The year slipped by and time was spent,

And all the good things that I
meant
To do were left undone be-
cause . . .
I had no time to stop and pause;
But rushed about, went here and
there,
Did this and that, was every-
where.
I had no time to meditate
On things worthwhile. No time
to wait
Upon the Lord and hear Him say,
"Well done, My child, you have
shown the way."
And so I wonder, after all,
When life is o'er and I am called
To meet my Savior in the sky,
Where saints live on and never
die,
If I can find one soul I have won
To Christ by some small deed I
have done.
Or will I hang my head and
whine,
"Forgive me, God, I had no time"?

948 "Man Overboard!"

There is a story of an Atlantic passenger lying in his bunk in a storm,
deathly sick—seasick. A cry of "Man
overboard!" was heard. The passenger thought, "God help the poor
fellow. There is nothing I can do."
Then he thought at least he could
put his lantern in the porthole,
which he did. The man was rescued, and recounting the story the
next day, he said, "I was going down
in the darkness for the last time
when someone put a light in a porthole. It shone on my hand, and a
sailor in a lifeboat grabbed my hand

and pulled me in." Weakness is no
excuse for our not putting forth all
the little strength we have, and who
can tell how God will use it?

949 Exalting Christ

A young man entered training as
an art student in London. During
those years he thought he would
draw a portrait of Christ. He was
disappointed. In trying to reveal
tenderness and sympathy, he portrayed only weakness, and he tore
up the portrait. He tried again later
but failed to satisfy himself.

War broke out, and his work
came to an end. He went to camp
and was finally sent to France and
to the front. He was billeted in a
French chateau in a room with nine
other men. When he went to bed
the first night he was distressed to
see over the beds of the other fel-
lows horrible drawings from some
of the vulgar papers that were circulated in France in those days. He
was tempted impetuously to pull
them down, but remembered that
everyone had a perfect right to put
on his wall space anything he liked,
so instead he planned what he
should do with his space.

The only spare time he had was
in the night, and his drawing material was a plain postcard and a
pencil. He determined to try again
to draw a head of Christ. He
worked upon his drawing for several nights with only a candle to
give him light; and when it was finished, he nervously pinned it on
his wall. He did not know what the
men would say or do when they

saw it in the morning. They simply looked at it, said nothing and went out.

In a few days all the other pictures were pulled down and only his drawing remained. He had exalted the risen Christ in testimony to those around him.

950 Invite a Golfer to Church

One man came out of his house on his way to church on Sunday morning, just as his neighbor came out of his with his golf clubs. The golfer said, "Henry, come play golf with me today." Henry, with an expression of horror on his face, replied, "This is the Lord's day, and I go to church. Certainly I would not play golf with you." After a moment's silence, the golfer quietly said, "You know, Henry, I have often wondered about your church, and I have admired your fidelity. You know also that this is the seventh time I have invited you to play golf with me, and you have never invited me to go to church with you."

951 The Power of Multiplication

On a wall in the Museum of Natural Science in Chicago there is a checkerboard with 64 squares. In the lower lefthand corner is a grain of wheat. The display includes this question: "If you doubled the amount of wheat as you move from square to square, how much would you have when you reached the 64th square? A carload? A trainload? You would have enough wheat to cover the country of India six feet deep."

That is the power of multiplication. Suppose you go out and reach one person for Jesus. Stick with that person for six months. Help, encourage and strengthen him. At the end of six months there are only two. At the end of the year there are four of you. At the end of 18 months there are eight; two years, 16. Do you know how many people there would be at the end of 17 years? More than the entire population of the world—more than six billion. Stop and think about what you can do!

952 One Red Rosebud

There it was—a tiny rosebud thrown in a heap with other uprooted and discarded rosebushes. Out of the tangled mass, one long stem pushed its way upward, thrusting forth its one tiny bud.

The rosebushes had been thrown away by a disgruntled homeowner who couldn't seem to get them to grow well. As the man passed by the heap, he noticed the little rosebud, but he went on his way. The next day he noticed that the bud still seemed to have life and was trying to bloom.

Donning gloves, he retrieved the bush on which that one bud clung tenaciously to life. He planted the bush and was rewarded several days later when a beautiful rose bloomed. Before long the whole bush came alive. In fact that one bush outbloomed and outgrew other rosebushes the man planted later. Each year the bush seemed to have one especially long stem with an exquisite red rose on it.

Because one tiny rosebud was unwilling to die, the whole bush was saved. In the same way, whole families have been won to the Savior because one child came to know Him first.

May we never lose hope for the children who need to know about Jesus and His love for them!

953 A Lesson From the Palm Tree

One can readily recall the words of Exodus 15:27 which reads, "And they came to Elim, where were twelve wells of water, and three-score and ten palm trees: and they encamped there by the waters." Think what a wonderful sight a grove of palms must be to the wary and thirsty traveler on the desert! These trees not only mean shelter from the blistering sun, but water to slake the thirst. Palms grow where there is water, and they send down their trap roots to water. Thus this tree is never without its testimony.

Those familiar with this most famous of all Bible trees know that it *Bears Fruit in Old Age.* The palm never stops bearing fruit, even though it grows to a very old age. The 14th verse of Psalm 92 states, "They shall still bring forth fruit in old age." The tree is never on the retired list. Too many of us are retired Christians. We get to the place where we imagine we have done

our share, so someone else can take over and carry on the work. Recall the spirit of the old pioneers of Tombstone, who were willing to die with their boots on, working and toiling to the very last. Just as the palm grows for the ages, so should it be with all the children of God. We are not shrubs, but trees. "He shall be like a tree"—that which abides.

Who among us is not familiar with the fact that the *Branches Are Symbols of Victory.* In Revelation 7:9, the Apostle John caught the vision of the mighty multitude which no man could number, standing "before the Lamb, clothed with white robes, and palms in their hands." There were they who had come out of great tribulation, and victory was theirs in the presence of their Lord. It was a time of rejoicing. Are we symbols of victory? Do men look at us and see some blessed evidence of the power of God operative in our lives? Or must they behold evidences of defeat? God forbid!

I exhort you, be a palm-tree Christian, the praise and glory of His grace. What a blessing we can be to others by living the upright palm tree life!

954 Blossoming in Spite of Adversity

In her book, *North to the Orient,* Anne Morrow Lindberg, tells about the oriental symbolism of trees:

The bamboo stands for prosperity.
The pine tree means long life.

The plum tree suggests courage. Mrs. Lindberg asked a friend why the plum tree stood for courage. The answer: "Because it puts out its blossom while the snow is still on the ground."

The Christian should adopt the plum tree as our example. We should show our Christian attitudes at times when they are needed the most.

Be kind and forgiving to those who mistreat you.

Be understanding and open-minded to those who are prejudiced toward you.

Stand for moral ideals when it is contrary to popular custom.

Have the courage and strength to do the difficult thing by "putting out your blossoms" when it is difficult.

955 "Was That Somebody You?"

Tom Carter, the evangelist, told this in one of his messages: While he was holding meetings in a Pennsylvania town, a young man who had formerly lived next door to the parsonage committed a murder. The whole community was stirred. Mr. Carter and the pastor obtained permission to visit the young man in his cell. After telling him his own story of conversion in a prison, Mr. Carter and the pastor succeeded in leading him to Christ. Then the newly-saved man addressed the pastor and sadly said, "To think I lived next door to you for months and you never told me anything about

Jesus until I came here! If you only had, I probably never would have become a murderer."

Are we overlooking any close-by opportunities?

956 No One Ever Asked Me

In St. Louis years ago, a Christian was transacting business with a lawyer. As the Christian businessman turned to go, he said, "I have often wanted to ask you a question, but I have been a coward."

"Why," replied the lawyer, "I did not think *you* were afraid of *anything*. What is the question?"

The businessman then asked the lawyer pointblank, "Sir, why are you not a Christian?"

The lawyer hung his head. "Is there not something in the Bible that says no drunkard shall have any part in the Kingdom of God. You know my weakness."

"You have not answered my question," answered the Christian. "I am asking *why are you not a Christian*."

"Well," answered the lawyer, "I cannot recall that anyone ever asked me such a question before. Of this *I am sure*—nobody ever told me how to become one." The Christian businessman then read passages from the Bible and suggested simply, "Let's get down and pray."

Kneeling, the lawyer prayed first: "O Lord, you know that I am a slave to drink. This morning this businessman, your servant, has shown me the way to Thee. Oh, God, break the power of this evil habit in my life." Later, the lawyer with the "besetting sin" testified that "God broke that power of drink instantly."

Do you know who that lawyer was? Dr. C. L. Scofield, famous editor of the Scofield Reference Bible!

957 How the Gospel Came to Korea

Robert J. Thomas, a Welshman, was a colporteur working in China for the Scottish Bible Society. In the course of his work, he learned that the Korean language is based on Chinese and that, as a result, the Korean intellectuals could read Chinese. His main responsibility was toward the millions in China, of course. But the love of Christ for the Koreans constrained him, and he determined to push on to that country. An American ship called the *General Sherman* was sailing to Pyongyang, a large city in the north. He boarded it. As the ship drew near to Pyongyang, however, a sharp fight broke out between the officers of the American ship and the Korean coast guard. The ship was burned in the conflict, and all the passengers were killed. The death of Thomas was unusual, however. As the ship and the passengers were sinking, he struggled to reach the shore and staggered up out of the water his arms filled with books. They were Bibles. He thrust these into the hands of the Koreans who clubbed him to death. It was through such love that the gospel first came to Korea in the year 1886.

958 Gentle but Persistent Influence

Paul gave this admonition in Galatians 6:9, "And let us not be weary in well-doing: for in due season we shall reap, if we faint not."

A scientist once conducted an interesting experiment in his laboratory. From the ceiling he suspended an iron ball weighing a ton, attaching it to a cable strong enough to sustain its weight. Beside the huge iron ball, he hung a small sphere made of cork attached to a thread fastened to the ceiling. An electrical mechanism kept the little cork ball swinging slowly, pendulum-like, against the iron weight.

At length, after days of unceasing swinging back and forth on the part of the cork, the iron ball weighing a ton began to swing very gently to and fro in harmony with the little cork ball. Gradually, its motion increased until it was prescribing a wide arc, all because a tiny cork ball had kept persistently knocking against its massive side, day in and day out.

Our effort to influence people to love God, accept Christ as Savior, and live under the direction of the Holy Spirit should be as gentle as the tapping of the cork ball, but also we should be persistent and faithful. May we be so.

959 He Died for Them, Too!

Christopher D. Green recalls this incident:

"It was my gut reaction to become tense as the dark figure approached. Walking down the street late in the evening, I assumed the worst. I figured it would be at any moment that I would have a knife or a gun plunged into my side. I had to keep walking because stopping would mean certain death!

"Walking toward each other, my heart raced as I took a deep breath. He had shoulder-length hair, a ruddy beard, and wore dark clothes. Within six feet of one another, I looked into his eyes. I had vowed not to speak. It was he who spoke first. 'Good evening, how are you?' he said. After a startled pause, I managed to squeak, 'Fine, and you?' We walked on without incident, my shame growing more intense with each passing step. One hundred yards later, I began to pray. I remembered that Christ died for that man!

"Anger swelled within me as I watched the newscast. Gay rights activists had marched into a city council meeting demanding to be heard. They demanded attention and charged the city with discrimination. Charges were made that physical abuse at a recent rally had gone unprosecuted. At this point, an individual stood and shouted, 'If they hurt us again, they will have to pay. We will fight back!' My gut reaction was to think, 'Go ahead, and see who gets the beating!' Moments later, I began to pray. I realized that Christ had died for that man, too.

"When I see individuals I am afraid of or individuals I disagree with so severely I feel like 'punching them out,' I have to realize that what they need is not a poke in the nose or judgment from me. They need Jesus. They need me to tell them about Jesus! Lord, help me remember that you died for them, too!"

960 They Never Heard of Christmas!

Why have we not heard of Christmas?
Why have you denied us light;
We who long have groped in darkness
Chained by sorrow, sin, and night?

Why have you refused to tell us
Of this Son born from above?
Why have you withheld such tidings
Of God's condescending love?

When was it you learned of Christmas?
Has this story just been heard?
Can it be that God would send Him
Just for you who hold His Word?

Will you still deny us Christmas?
Will we reach out in vain?
Can it be that we must perish
Never having heard that name?

All our fathers died in torment,
Racked with anguish, fear and pain;
Never knowing of a Savior,
Never breathing Jesus' Name!

Hear the words of hopeless millions,
Dying where no light has been:
"Won't you share this Christ of Christmas,
Let Him save us from our sin?"

961 Good News Provides Opportunities

All news is not beautiful. Or had you noticed? But bad news is good news for Christians, in a sense, because we see in it opportunities to turn things around. Or, as Jesus said, to be lights in a dark world. Christians can do more than curse the darkness. We can light a candle. We can change the world.

962 Reading Your Own Obituary

It is possible to live under a delusion. You think you are kind, considerate and gracious, when you are really not. You think you are building positive values into your children, but, if you could check with them 20 years later, you really did not. What if you could read your own obituary? How do people really see you? Here is the story of a man who did.

One morning in 1888, Alfred Nobel, inventor of dynamite, awoke to read his own obituary. The obituary was printed as result of a simple journalistic error. You see, it was Alfred's brother that had died and the reporter carelessly reported the death of the wrong brother.

Any man would be disturbed under the circumstances, but to Al-

fred the shock was overwhelming because he saw himself as the world saw him. The "Dynamite King," the great industrialist who had made an immense fortune from explosives. This, as far as the general public was concerned, was the entire purpose of Alfred's life. None of his true intentions to break down the barriers that separated men and ideas for peace were recognized or given serious consideration. He was simply a merchant of death. And for that alone he would be remembered.

As he read the obituary with horror, he resolved to make clear to the world the true meaning and purpose of his life. This could be done through the final disposition of his fortune. His last will and testament would be the expression of his life's ideals and ultimately would be why we would remember him. The result was the most valuable of prizes given to those who had done the most for the cause of world peace. It is called today the "Nobel Peace Prize."

You may think you are a kind, thoughtful, gracious person. But what if today you read your own obituary? You are a businessman, what would your employees write? You are a professional person, what would your clients say? You are a parent, what would your children write? You are a preacher, teacher, whatever, what would those who listen to you say? Since we cannot read our obituary, let us rewrite it. Starting today.

963 Upsetting the World

During New Testament times those who were actively sharing the gospel met opposition. A case in point is Paul and Silas in Thessalonica. According to Acts 17:1-9, these two personal workers were persuading and converting several people. There were, however, those who were unconvinced, and they complained that the preaching was disruptive and upsetting. They took their views to the authorities and ultimately the two missionaries had to flee by night.

It might be hard for us to imagine such a thing happening today. We may believe that our beloved Bill of Rights would protect us from such outlawing of evangelism. The reality, though, is that the local newspaper recently reported on the front page an instance of religious freedoms in jeopardy. The article is about an 11-year-old in the Norm school system who was told not to discuss the Bible or pray during recess because "a parent had complained that it was disruptive." The school district further states that the girl had "infringed on the rights of other students."

Greg Clark comments, "I have seen several things take place during recesses, both while a student and later as a substitute teacher. Amongst other things I saw boys fighting, girls arguing, hair being pulled, kids being picked on, and heard all kinds of foul language. I am wondering if a girl with 'six of her friends' reading and praying could be any more 'disruptive' or could be any more infringing on personal rights?

"I can remember school days with Bibles on the bookshelf and lively religious discussions. We certainly did not consider ourselves religious fanatics and prospects for lawsuits. What has happened? Why are things like flag burning, Satan worship, and obscene materials "forms of expression" protected by the Bill of Rights, and yet an 11-year-old praying is questionable?

"What would Paul and Silas do in a similar situation? Would they agree with the idea that religion should be confined to the church building? A quick look at the text shows that in their case they merely moved on to Berea and agitated (and converted) a few more.

"It is true that there are people who purposefully set out to cause disorder. On the other hand, I have personally been threatened by a local man simply for doorknocking in his neighborhood. The thing we need to remember in both cases is that Christians have never gone through a period when everyone was encouraging them to proclaim Jesus. There have always been those who give 'strict orders not to continue teaching.' It is in response to such charges that first century proclaimers stood and said, "we must obey God rather than men" (Acts 5:28, 29). They knew that if they waited around on the majority vote they would only end up talking to each other. Such a lifestyle for a disciple was and is unsatisfactory. The command of our Lord is still: 'Go into ALL the world,' even if the world gets a little upset."

964 The Lost Boy

Once a little boy was lost in the woods. The alarm was sounded; a church meeting broke up; the whole congregation and neighborhood responded. Fishermen abandoned their nets and merchants closed their shops. Plows were left in the field and washing in the tub. Everyone turned out to hunt for the little fellow. There was a feverish haste. The night was dark and harm might befall the little fellow. After hours of search, he was found, and oh, the joy that was felt because of the rescue!

Today that boy is grown. He is lost again! But none seem to care. Mom and Dad are busy with other things. The church does not seem to care. No alarm is sent out. Yet, a far worse fate awaits him now. You see, he is now lost in sin! Do we really care? Enough to do something?

965 Better Previews Needed

In the movies and on television, previews show coming attractions. Designed to create interest, the previews always show the most dynamic and dramatic parts, such as the chase scenes, love scenes, and fight scenes in the show. The whole point of the previews is to whet our appetites for the upcoming programs.

Someday a big show will come to town, and Jesus will be the star. It will be a worldwide performance, and the cast will be sensational. But until then, He has left previews of coming attractions in the world. He has left His church to provide clips of the major production that is to come.

Unfortunately, some of the clips are so bad that people have little interest in attending the major performance. The church has been so weak in demonstrating the power and wonder of the main feature that fewer and fewer people have interest in it.

It is time for God's people—the church—to start showing previews that are worth watching: previews to the world that will prompt the questions, "Where can I buy a ticket for the show?" Then we can respond, "No purchase is necessary. We are giving the tickets away. The price has already been paid."

Works and Service

966 How to Avoid Frustration

Keep your shoulder to the wheel
Your hand to the helm
Your eye on the ball!
Your nose to the grindstone
Your ear to the ground
And you will not have time to
Put your foot in your mouth.

967 Missed Opportunity

During the first three days of July, 1863, in the midst of America's great Civil War, the armies of the North and South clashed decisively at Gettysburg. For the first three days of the battle, the fighting was inconclusive, but then the tide began to turn against General Lee and the Confederate forces. The northern troops under General G. G. Meade were winning. Lee began to retreat southward on the night of July 4, while storm clouds drenched the East Coast with rain. When Lee reached the Potomac, he found that the river was swollen with rain. He could not cross it. Behind him was the victorious Union army. Before him was the river. He was trapped.

Here was the great, golden opportunity for General Meade to end the battle. Meade could have attacked immediately, destroying Lee's army and, in effect, ending the Civil War. President Lincoln actually or-dered him to attack. However, instead of attacking, Meade delayed. He held a council, then delayed again. Eventually the water of the river receded, and Lee escaped over the Potomac. The war was extended two more years. Meade never regained his lost opportunity, and it was to General Grant that Lee eventually surrendered on April 9, 1865.

This story shows us the tragedy of having missed a great opportunity. But if this principle is true in the physical realm, as we realize, it is certainly more true spiritually. The Bible recognizes this when it says, "For what is a man profited, if he shall gain the whole world, and lose his own soul?" (Matt. 16:26). Or again, "If any man's work shall be burned, he shall suffer loss; but he himself shall be saved, yet as by fire" (1 Cor. 3:15).

968 The Yoke of God Does Not Fit Stiff Necks

Remember when farmers used a collar to harness a team of horses or mules to pull a plow or wagon? This collar was made of leather with padding to protect the animal's neck and forequarters so he would not become disabled. The collar was made with a leather strap and buckle at the top, and the bottom

403

was rounded to provide comfort to the animal. When the harness was put on the collar, it was designed to get the most even pull and least pressure on the horse. If the equipment shifted, the horse would develop a sore. Then the animal would become so stiff-necked that you could not turn him at all. He would go one way only.

Brethren sometimes get the same way. Some will not adjust to situations when they know they should but will not because of custom or tradition and become stiff-necked, instead of doing what God wants done.

Proverbs 19:20 says, "Hear counsel and receive instruction that thou mayest be wise in thy latter end." Let us wear the yoke of God with pleasure and breach not against the harness that guides us in His way. "The discretion of a man deferreth his anger, and it is his glory to pass over a transgression" (Prov. 19:11). Think long before you rebel.

969 The Second Symbol

The cross is the great symbol of Christianity. On steeples atop churches, covers of hymnals, lids for communion ware and lapel pins on Sunday jackets, it stands an awesome reminder of all that Jesus suffered. Jesus spoke of the cross as a symbol of Christian dedication. "Whosoever will come after Me, let him deny himself, and take up his cross, and follow Me" (Mark 8:34).

But Jesus also used another symbol for Christian commitment. *"Take My yoke upon you and learn of Me . . . My yoke is easy and My burden is light"* (Matt. 11:29, 30). The yoke is a wooden harness tying two animals together to pull a load. Yokes are not usually painted on church buildings, or printed on the covers of Bibles, or worn as ornaments on neckchains. Maybe they should be. The yoke as much as the cross is a symbol of commitment to Jesus Christ.

Paul W. Powell, in *The Complete Disciple* elaborates:

"The cross and the yoke symbolize for us the two different aspects of commitment. The cross is an instrument of death; the yoke is an implement of toil. The cross is the symbol of sacrifice; the yoke is the symbol of service. The cross suggests blood; the yoke suggests sweat . . . to be committed to Jesus Christ means that we are ready for either the yoke or the cross."

Let me suggest four lessons from the yoke:

SUBMISSION. "Take My yoke upon you." The Christian willingly submits to Jesus Christ as Lord and Master. "It is not in man that walketh to direct his steps." "Not my will but Thine be done."

OBEDIENCE: "And learn of me." The yoke suggests submission to a master who must be obeyed. Blessed is the man who "heareth these sayings of mine and doeth them."

SERVICE: "My burden is light." Compared to the burden of sin, the yoke of the Lord is easy. But the very idea of a yoke is that of pulling a load, of work, of service. Christians are to be ministers—servants. "Work for the night is coming."

FELLOWSHIP: "All ye that labor." We are not alone in Christ, but serving alongside those of like precious faith. Paul spoke of his "loyal yoke-fellow." A yoke harnesses two animals together so as to pull a load neither one could pull alone. "Bear ye one another's burdens."

As we follow Christ, let us take up our yoke as well as our cross, "serving the Lord."

970 My Turn in the Nursery

Last Sunday was my turn in the nursery to work.
My heart wasn't in it; my feelings were hurt.
A child from its mother did not want to part
And it cried a lot with its broken heart.
I prayed that soon the hour would end,
That I would relax—no more children to tend.
Soon the hour was over; it felt good to be free.
I said, "Once a month was too much for me!"
The very next Sunday as I sat in the pew
Heard a very good sermon, but visitors were few.
But down came a woman and her soul was saved.
She was the mother of that crying babe!
Then it dawned on me that I had been a part
Of one being saved—giving God her heart.

From that day on I would never dread
Working in the nursery while souls are fed.

971 A Volunteer's Prayer

I thank Thee, Lord, as a volunteer
For the chance to serve another year.
And to give of myself in some small way,
To those not blessed as I each day.
My thanks for health and mind and soul,
To aid me ever toward my goal.
For eyes to see the good in all,
A hand to extend before a fall.
For legs to go where the need is great,
Learning to love—forgetting to hate.
For ears to hear and heart to care,
When someone's cross is hard to bear.
A smile to show my affection true,
With energy aplenty—the task to do.
And all I ask, dear Lord, if I may,
Is to serve you better day by day.

972 Little Things

I thought to be an actress great
The toast of lords and kings.
The good Lord said, "I have need of you
To do My little things."

I thought I would be a dancer rare
To fly on gossamer wings.

The Lord smiled and said, "Stay
here on earth
And do My little things."

Now I am content to be right
here.
My heart with rapture sings
'Cause I know how important it
is to God
To do "His little things."

973 *When People Work*

"So we rebuilt the wall till all of it
reached half its height, for the people worked with all their heart"
(Neh. 4:6).

Few tragedies scar as does a raging fire. The devastation is complete. The desolation is mournful.
Such was the disaster of the city of
Jerusalem when God judged His
holy hill with the torch of Neb-
uchadnezzar. On the day Jerusalem
fell, the Edomites cried, "Tear it
down . . . tear it down to its foun-
dations!" (Ps. 137:7).

In God's mercy, at last a remnant
returned to rebuild their beloved
city. And the city began to rise from
its ashes. Yet, when some later visited Nehemiah, yet in Persia, they
told of Jerusalem's continuing anguish: "Those who survived the
exile and are back in the province
are in great trouble and disgrace.
The wall of Jerusalem is broken
down, and its gates have been
burned with fire" (Neh. 1:3). Hearing this, Nehemiah ". . . sat down
and wept" (v. 4).

The Persian monarch, Artaxerxes,
moved by Nehemiah's sorrow, commissioned him to return to rebuild
the city. After a quiet tour "by night"
with some of the local leaders to
evaluate the ruins, Nehemiah urged:
" 'You see the trouble we are in.
Jerusalem lies in ruins, and its gates
have been burned with fire. Come,
let us rebuild the wall of Jerusalem,
and we will no longer be in disgrace.' I also told them about the
gracious hand of my God upon me.
They replied, 'Let us start rebuilding.' So they began this good work"
(2:17, 18).

The task was formidable—after
70 years of abandonment. Enemies
"mocked and ridiculed" them, demanding, "What is this you are
doing . . . Are you rebelling against
the king? . . . What are those feeble
Jews doing? Will they restore their
wall? . . . Will they finish in a day?
Can they bring the stones back to
life from those heaps of rubble—
burned as they are" (2:19; 4:2).

The story of the wall's restora-
tion from rubble is a thrilling one.
Each family had its own segment
of the wall to rebuild. As enemies
threatened, some would "serve as
guards by night and workmen by
day" (4:22). And finally, "the wall
was completed on the 25th of Elul,
in 52 days. When all the enemies
heard about this . . . (they) lost their
self-confidence, because they realized that this work had been done
with the help of our God" (6:15).

When our people today, together
"work with all their heart," amazing
achievements will likewise be celebrated—to the glory of our God.

974 How Our Heavenly Father Feels about Our Uncompleted Task

It is said of one of the famous composers that he had a rebellious son who used to come in late at night after his father and mother had gone to bed. And before going to his own room, he would go to his father's piano and slowly, as well as loudly, play a simple scale, all but the final note. Then leaving the scale uncompleted, he would retire to his room. Meanwhile the father, hearing the scale minus the final note, would writhe on his bed, his mind unable to relax because the scale was unresolved. Finally, in consternation, he would stumble down the stairs and hit the previously unstruck note. Only then would his mind surrender to sleep once again.

God's labor seems never to be complete until the final note on the scale, the concluding, still time, a pause that looks backward and pronounces completion and value.

975 Avoiding the R

Jimmy had trouble pronouncing the letter "R" so his teacher gave him this sentence to practice at home: "Robert gave Richard a rap in the rib for roasting the rabbit so rare."

Some days later the teacher asked him to say the sentence for her. Jimmy rattled it off like this: "Bob gave Dick a poke in the side for not cooking the bunny enough."

He evaded the letter R.

There are many useful, committed Christians at church, but it is sad that so many others are evading the R meaning R-eady: ready to serve, sing, visit, teach and be truly committed.

These friends are saved, we believe, they are good people, accommodating, and are religious, but are just not committed.

It is possible to be so religious that we cannot be Christian.

Are you handling the letter "R" right?

976 To Need and Be Needed

"I appeal to you for my son Onesimus, who became my son while I was in chains. Formerly he was useless to you, but now he has become useful both to you and to me" (Phile. 1:10, 11).

Keith Robinson asks (for all of us):

"What use am I in the world? Has my life really made a difference in anything? Would anything be appreciably different if I were not here? What is the old saying about putting your hand in a pail of water and withdrawing it: the hole that remains is how much you will be missed when you are gone! I am not pessimistic, depressed, or tired of living, but in reality, I have to recognize that my life has not made much of an impact on the world, certainly nothing like I had intended when I was 18 years old. But I am encouraged by the fact that human worth is not measured only in terms of fame, fortune, and sociopolitical influence. Perhaps the greatest measure of our value is how much we are needed by some other human being. John Mark was important because Paul needed him in a time of extreme anxiety and distress. The once useless Onesimus became 'useful' to Paul and to Philemon.

"When the final books are balanced and closed, the greatest tribute anyone could receive would be: They were useful! Someone needed them! And what greater ambition could a person entertain than to be needed, to be useful. My input is not desired or needed for the Mid-East peace talks. It is doubtful that those involved are indispensable. But I fill a need in the lives of a few people that cannot be filled by anyone else. If there is someone who needs my love, if there is someone who looks forward to my presence, even if I can be nothing much more than just the object to someone's love, then I am not worthless. My life is not in vain. My existence is not futile. I may not be much, but I can love someone and make them feel needed. I can be the object of someone else's love and thus fill their needs and mine. No one is useless unless they give up on life and love.

" 'Onesimus' means 'useful.' "

977 *Being a Servant*

Jesus was the greatest servant who ever lived. "For even the Son of Man did not come to be served, but to serve, and to give His life a ransom for many" (Mark 10:45).

Christ came to serve and to give, and God desires the same for us. "And whosoever will be chief among you, let him be your servant: Even as the Son of Man came not to be ministered unto, but to minister" (Matt. 20:27, 28).

The finest model of serving, except Christ Himself, was the Apostle Paul. Almost without exception he begins every one of his epistles with words to this effect: "Paul, a servant. . . ." or "Paul, a bond slave. . . ." He was indeed an apostle, but he conducted himself as a servant.

Very few of us want to be known exclusively as a servant. We want to be known as a servant and a great preacher, or a famous missionary, or an outstanding elder, or a well-known business man. What we fail to realize is that true servanthood does not have hidden aspirations to be great in the eyes of men.

When we think of our relationship to Christ, can it be said of us that we want only to serve Him?

Although his religious philosophy was questionable, Albert Schweitzer was a man willing to abandon a great career in order to serve his fellow man. In 1913, he sailed for Africa, having turned his back on fame, money and prestige. His first hospital was an old abandoned hen house and his first operating table an old campboard.

On a trip to the United States, a reporter asked, "Dr. Schweitzer, have you found happiness in Africa?"

"I have found a place of service," he replied, "And that is enough for anyone."

This does not represent the feelings of many of us who are members of the church. It is not sufficient to simply have a place of service. Many of us want a place of recognition and a road to fame.

All of us need to do some serious thinking and praying about this matter of being a servant.

We need to make this prayer ours: "O God, help me to be the master of myself, that I may be a servant of others."

978 Servants Do Not Choose Tasks

Throughout the ages, God has referred to His faithful people as His servants. The Bible even calls Jesus "His holy servant."

Unlike the religious leaders who exercised unquestioned authority over the people, Jesus came not as a ruler, but as a servant. From the example of His own life He teaches, "But so shall it not be among you: but whosoever will be great among you shall be your minister and whosoever of you will be the chiefest, shall be servant of all. For even the Son of man came not to be served, but to serve, and to give His life a ransom for many" (Mark 10:43-45).

Christ ransomed us that we, too, might serve God and man. In our zeal to serve, we often overlook a critical truth: The servant does not choose his tasks. Our concept of serving God may be doing what we would like to do—for God. We tell God what we will do for Him, and what we will not do; where we will go for Him, and where we will not. We even tell Him what must not interfere with our plans. In doing this we forget He is the Master, and that the Master assigns the task. Our part is to give ourselves to Him, accepting the assignment He bestows.

A servant is not free to serve on his own terms. Jesus said, "You have not chosen Me, but I have chosen you to go and bring forth fruit" (John 15:16). So, we have been chosen to "run with patience the race that is set before us" (Heb. 12:1). The race set before us may not be on the track we would choose. Perhaps we would not choose the people God has placed around us, or the location or circumstances we find ourselves in, but a servant is not above his Master. "A disciple is not above his master, nor the servant above his lord. It is enough for the disciple that he be as his master, and the servant as his lord" (Matt. 10:24, 25).

Christ's life was one of sacrifice and doing the Father's will. Though He was rich, for our sakes He became poor (2 Cor. 8:9). He counted equality with God a thing not to be grasped but emptied Himself and became a servant (Phil. 2:6, 7). He came to do God's will (Heb. 10:5-7).

As servants following in the footsteps of Christ, we must present our bodies as "living sacrifices" and say, "Here I am—I have come to do Your will," regardless of what the task may be.

979 "I Can't Get No Satisfaction"

John Gipson shares this lesson:

"As I turned the key in the ignition my car radio sprang to life. Some popular singer was belting out the lyrics, 'I can't get no satisfaction.' I didn't care for the song and turned the dial. But the memory lingered. I wonder how many people there are in the world who cannot find satisfaction? Do they even know where to look?

"Countless people are on record to testify that satisfaction does not come in gathering up things for ourselves. As Horace said, 'Those who seek for much are left in want of much. Happy is he to whom God has given, with sparing hand, as much as is enough.'

"And satisfaction does not come in showing off a Gold Card, or bragging about one's possessions. In fact, 'If the crow had been satisfied to eat his prey in silence, he would have had more meat and less quarreling and envy.'

"I learned something last week from a commercial. Normally, I do not care for commercials. They carry about as much weight with me as a political jingle. But this one caught my attention. The man was explaining that when he was growing up he tried everything in the world to make his sister cry. Nothing worked. Then last week he decided to send her a bouquet of flowers. And you know what? She cried.

"Sometimes we get the desired results in the most unexpected ways.

"Take the young woman with a busy schedule and small children who went out of her way to minister to a family in need. After her mission was complete she said, 'I just have to do more of that. It really makes me feel good inside.'

"David knew people who were saying, 'Oh, that we might see some good!' But he confessed to God, 'Thou hast put more joy in my heart than they have when their grain and wine abound' (Ps. 4:7). Only by drawing near to God would he ever find complete satisfaction. Thus he says, 'As for me, I shall behold thy face in righteousness; when I awake, I shall be satisfied with beholding thy form' (Ps. 17:15).

"It is sad that a lot of people cannot find any satisfaction because they do not know where to look. Take out your Bible and read John 10:10."

Worldliness

980 Something to Think About

A shipwrecked sailor who had spent three years on a deserted island was overjoyed one day to see a ship drop anchor in the bay. A small boat came ashore, and an officer handed the sailor a bunch of newspapers.

"The captain suggests," he told the sailor, "that you read what is going on in the world and then let us know if you want to be rescued."

981 Painted Sticks

One Sunday a preacher told how, while sitting in his garden, he had watched a caterpillar climb a painted stick that was for decoration. After reaching the top, the caterpillar reared itself, feeling this way and that for a juicy twig to feed on, or some way to further progress. Finding nothing, it slowly returned to the ground, crawled along till it reached another painted stick, and did the same thing all over again. The preacher said: "There are many painted sticks in the world—those of pleasure, wealth, and fame. All these call man and say, 'Climb me to find the desire of your heart, fulfill the purpose of your existence, taste the fruit of success, and find satisfaction, but they are only painted sticks.' "

Solomon tried to find the purpose of his life in the world's "painted sticks." He gave his heart to seek wisdom, but learned that it was "vanity and vexation of spirit" (Eccl. 1:15).

He then turned to the pleasures of the world for meaning in life. He built great houses, and gardens, and pools. He had servants and maidens; in fact, he had all that a man could desire. Solomon's comment on pleasure as a true source of happiness, however, was, "All was vanity and vexation of spirit, and there was no profit under the sun" (Eccl. 2:11).

After trying all that the world could offer, Solomon's final decision was, "Let us hear the conclusion of the whole matter: Fear God, and keep His commandments: for this is the whole duty of man" (Eccl. 12:13).

982 The Oldest Profession on Earth

Three men, a surgeon, an engineer, and a politician, were arguing about whose profession was the oldest.

"Mine is," said the doctor. "Remember that Eve was carved out of Adam's rib."

"Admitted," said the engineer, "but remember that the earth was created out of chaos in six days. That obviously was an engineering job."

"Yes," said the politician, "but who created the chaos?"

983 Stylish Saints

Once a man attended a fair and saw another man leading a fine, well-groomed horse. He inquired, "Is that a saddle horse?" The other replied, "No sir. This horse will buck off a saddle. Nothing can stay on his back."

"Is he a driving horse, then?" the man asked. "No, he was hitched up once and made kindling wood of the vehicle he should have pulled."

"Well, what is he good for? Why is he here?" the man asked. The answer was, "Style, man, style. Just look at the picture he makes."

Once I was in a church building and saw people clad in fine clothes coming into the morning service. I asked the preacher, "Are those people workers in the church?" "No," he answered sadly. "Do they visit the sick and minister to the poor? Do they attend other services of the church?" "Never," said the preacher.

"There is that horse," I said to myself. "Nothing but style."

984 Trapped by Things

Are you trapped in the tyranny of things? A wealthy man was moving into a new house, and his next-door neighbor happened to be a Quaker. The Quakers, as you know, believe in simplicity and plainness of life. The Quaker neighbor watched as the movers carted in numerous pieces of furniture, a great deal of clothing, and many decorative pieces. Then he walked over to his wealthy new neighbor and said in his quaint Quaker way, "Neighbor, if thee hath need of anything, please come to me and I will tell thee how to get along without it." Jesus would have agreed with that advice, for He said one day, "A man's life does not consist in the abundance of things that he possesses."

985 Want to Carry the Ball?

The coach said to the quarterback, "Give the ball to George." But instead he gave it to John, and there was no gain.

Demanded the coach, "Why didn't you give the ball to George?"

"Sir," replied the quarterback, "George said he did not want the ball."

There was a player on our Lord's side named Demas. Like George, he did not want to carry the ball. He valued comfort above character, ease above effort, gold above God, self-indulgence above self-control.

Of him Paul wrote, "Demas has forsaken me, having loved the present world."

Are you willing to carry the ball for the Lord?

986 The World Will Give You Up

A man said to D. L. Moody, "Now that I am converted, have I got to give up the world?" Mr. Moody answered, "No, you do not have to give up the world; if you have a good ringing testimony for the Son of God, the world will give you up pretty quick; they will not want you around."

987 TV Exposure

Have you consciously decided to expose your growing child to 18,000 murders? That is what the average young person will view on television by the time he or she graduates from high school. Your child will have spent approximately 12,000 hours in formal classroom learning but will have watched approximately 22,000 hours of television.

Those figures explain the results of a recent *World Almanac* poll of 2,000 eighth-grade boys in the United States. The poll asked them which people they wanted to be like when they grew up. Their leading role models were, in order, Burt Reynolds, Richard Pryor, Alan Alda, Steve Martin, Robert Redford, and the late John Belushi. Traditional names such as Abraham Lincoln, George Washington, and other noted figures in American history were conspicuously absent from the published list. In fact, no one was named who was not an entertainer or a sports figure.

Whom do your children want to emulate and admire? Will they someday say, "Aw, come on," if you suggest that they should want to be like Jesus?

988 A Lesson From Nature

A man standing on the bank of the Niagara River saw a dead sheep being swept down by the current. An eagle lighted upon that sheep. The body sank for a moment under the weight and then came to the surface again. The day was bitter cold and the wool wrapped around the talons began to freeze. Meantime, the sheep was being swept more and more rapidly toward the falls. But the eagle had not the slightest fear. Had you shouted a warning, he would probably have laughed at you. He would have said, "Do not disturb yourself. Do you not see these great wings? There is not the slightest danger."

By this time, the great falls were but a few feet away. The time for action had come. The eagle spread his great burnished brown wings and fanned the air. But the wings did not lift him. The frozen wool held his talons fast, and while his great wings frantically beat the air, he was swept to his death.

Now there was a time when the eagle could have saved himself. He was not made for such a terrible death. But he held on to the sheep so long that, in the end, he could not let go.

Do not hold on to the world so long that you will not be able to let go!

989 Is Television Harmless?

Richard Nixon's book, *In The Arena*, has an attention-grabbing paragraph on television:

"Computer specialists have a saying—'Garbage in, garbage out'—which they use when they want to make the point that a computer is only a mechanism for processing information, not creating it. The same principle applies to television. Young people used to learn their lessons from McGuffey's Readers; the baby-boomers learned them from the Beaver and Gilligan. As the postwar generation came of age, it spawned a new generation of TV programmers, who in turn have put more triviality, sex, violence, and bad manners on the air than anyone ever thought possible. Trash TV could only have been created by people who were raised on the tube. 'Garbage in, garbage out.' "

Fabricated "news" programs, "re-enactments," peeping-tom journalism, heavy-metal rock music, slasher movies, and programs which glorify homosexuality as an alternative lifestyle can hardly be considered neutral as they relate to our culture. Soap operas are chock-full of unfaithfulness, vindictiveness, revenge, materialism and murder, while comedy gives way to lewd and suggestive material. Television has become more than a "vast wasteland" in recent years. It is a sinkhole of depravity with eroticism and occultism being fed to us on a daily basis.

It is certainly sub-Christian, and in many cases even sub-human. Harmless? Hardly! Dangerous? Certainly! Fatal? Possibly.

990 The Prodigal Dog

Danny Dodd tells this story:

"Theophilus Kimble was his name. He was a big-footed, clumsy, loud-mouthed mutt of a dog. Smart as he was large, T.K., as we called him, had a way of bringing many valuable lessons to life.

"I remember once he got through the fence. He thought he had invented the trash can. He ran and jumped and bounded over and into everything. He was free at last! All the things that looked so alluring to him in the far regions of the other side of the fence were now his to explore, and explore he did. There was no sign of him for days. I kept a close watch on the local news for a report of a half-crazed, bent-on-examining-the-contents-of-every-trash-can dog, but there was nothing. Just when I thought I had lost him for good to the charms of three-ply Hefties, here he came. He had his tail between his legs, whimpering, wanting to come back home. I let him, of course. He was my dog, and I did care for him regardless of the number of trash cans I had to replace. He was home.

"Does this story sound familiar? It should. T.K. was playing the canine role of the prodigal son (Luke 15:11–32). All of the elements were there: The enticement of the forbidden in a far-off country (the trash cans on the other side of the fence); the opportunity to leave (the open gate); the wasting himself in riotous living (one too many trash cans); The realization of mistake (probably when he missed his Milk Bone); and the humble return."

991 Limited Vision

The Bible tells of prophets who "err in vision, they stumble in judgment" (Is. 28:7) and of those who "find no vision from the Lord" (Lam. 2:9). Christians are too often like the little boy living in East London who made his first visit to the country. He lay on the grass in the orchard and made a chain of daisies. The swallows flew across the sky.

"Look up, Jimmy. See the pretty birds flying through the air," called his mother. He looked up quickly and in a pitying tone, said, "Poor little birds; they haven't got no cages, have they?"

East London had dwarfed Jimmy's vision. So it is with many professing Christians. They become so occupied with the paltry things of earth that they scorn those who place their affections on things above.

992 Do Not Stay with the Turkeys

There is a story about a little eagle that fell out of its nest and landed in a turkey farm. The eagle grew up among the turkeys and, although he looked a bit different, he learned to waddle like a turkey, bob his head like a turkey, and act like a turkey.

One day the young eagle looked up into the sky and saw a beautiful eagle soaring above. The little eagle in the turkey yard thought, Oh, I would love to be able to do that! As the eagle soared overhead, it looked down and saw the young eagle below. Suddenly it swooped down to the ground and asked, "What are you doing here?"

The little eagle replied, "I am just here in the turkey yard where I have always been."

The great eagle looked and said, "Spread your wings, boy. You do just what I do. Follow me." Then he flapped his wings and lifted off the ground.

The young eagle tried it, too. "Wheeee! This is all right!"

"See," the mature eagle said, "you have been living among these turkeys so long that you were beginning to believe you were something you are not! Follow me, and you will find out what you really are."

So the little eagle began to soar and fly. He loved it. But the turkeys down below called out to him and said, "Hey, little guy, what are you doing up there? You belong down here."

"No, I don't," called the young eagle. "I used to belong there, but now I am what I was created to be. I do not belong with you anymore."

993 Spiritual Kudzu Vines

In central Georgia and other parts of the South, a common sight is trees completely covered with kudzu vines. Often these lush-green leafy vines completely hide the tree and even small houses.

Although imported to be a ground cover to combat erosion, these vines are now a curse. Covering acres and acres of excellent timber and farmland, they slowly destroy other vegetation. And the kudzu begins as a little seed but is almost impossible to eliminate, once it sets its woody roots.

Spiritual and moral kudzu vines choke our world and hide our true identity. They begin as insignificant seeds of thought and grow into massive systems of destructive thinking, completely distorting and hiding our real nature, even from ourselves. In a parable Jesus warned about weeds that choke the true plant and keep it from bearing fruit. The kudzu vine is not really the tree whose exterior it covers. It is a foreign element so attached to the tree that one could easily mistake it for the tree itself.

994 Is Our Secular Wisdom Foolishness?

"Wisdom" may best describe our present scientific and cultural plateau, yet spiritually we are foolish indeed. Many men, seen as wise in the eyes of the world, are fools in the eyes of our God.

The atheist who audaciously affirms, "I know there is no God," is elevated upon the pedestal of intellectualism and wisdom by the world of pseudo-science, yet God calls him a fool (Ps. 14:1).

Humanists, who deny the existence of sin, and contend that one's conduct should best be determined by the circumstances in which he finds himself, are applauded and lauded as the wise men of our age. God, in no uncertain terms, has said, "Fools make a mock at sin" (Prov. 14:9).

The world cries out, "Do what makes you feel good; do your own thing!" God has decreed, "He that trusteth in his own heart is a fool" (Prov. 28:26).

The rich farmer in the twelfth chapter of Luke, who found comfort in his accumulation of worldly goods, would be seen by many among us today as a wise man indeed. God called him a fool (Luke 12:20).

How does God see you, my friend? Our nation seems to be floating with the tide of moral and spiritual corruption. Are you drifting with the tide, or are you willing to stem the tide? I would rather be a fool in the eyes of a foolish world, than a fool in the eyes of my all-wise Creator.

995 Junk Thoughts

Similar to junk food—tasty and fun but of little value and ultimately damaging—are the secular messages sent to our brains en masse every day. Take, for example, the message offered by a recent television ad campaign: "Success is getting what you want; happiness is wanting what you get." To the average listener (Christian or non-Christian) this pleasantly presented axiom is tasty, pithy, memorable—and classic junk food for the brain. The "principle" stated in the axiom is diametrically opposed to Scripture. Yet if we hear the message often enough, before long we may find ourselves not only believing it, but living also it out, like all the pagans around us.

This is but one example of hundreds of junk food thoughts offered us every day. In fact, if we ever hope to think correctly about the danger of receiving "junk thoughts" from the world system, we need to understand that during the past decades, North America has changed its mind dramatically. Culturally, it has moved from thinking patterns based on Scripture to a decidedly secular pattern of thought.

Intellectually, it has rejected thinking processes based on objective biblical evidence to foregone conclusions that automatically exclude the supernatural. Philosophically, it has moved away from the concepts of truth, morality, ethics, and virtue toward the belief that there are no absolutes and that everything is relative.

Unfortunately, the way Christians think has moved, too.

996 Four Woes

Maybe something does get lost in the translation, but a trained mule will stop when he hears "Whoa!" At least we might stop and listen to Jesus' four "Woes" and take them to heart.

WOE TO THE RICH! Jesus is not condemning wealth, money, or resources. His condemnation is in the trust we often put in our riches. The rich young ruler went away sorrowfully because he "had great wealth." He cared more for his "belongings" than he cared for "belonging."

WOE TO THE WELL FED! No, it is not wrong to eat. It is not even a sin to enjoy good food. But it is sinful to "live to eat" rather than "eating to live." Many are becoming gluttons. Affluence brings with it the temptation to over-indulge. Beware!

WOE TO THOSE WHO LAUGH! Is Jesus condemning a funny bone? It is doubtful. But He does remind us that life is serious business. We are not here simply to "eat, drink, and be merry." There must be time to mourn. One can rejoice in the Lord without childish levity. Christianity is solemn commitment.

WOE TO YOU WHEN ALL MEN SPEAK WELL OF YOU! Even Jesus made enemies. When everybody thinks you are "simply marvelous" you must be doing something wrong. God did not put us on planet earth to win popularity contests. We are here to serve, love and worship. Not everybody appreciates that. Satan hates it!

To the rich, the stuffed, the laughing, and the ever-popular, Jesus reminds us to remember who put us here, why we are here and where we are going.

Woe to us if we miss it!

997 Time to Think

"Will the hassle never end?" One senses that this is more and more a feeling which is becoming a way of life to the majority of us in this country. What has happened? We have let ourselves be swept along in the current of modern society and culture until we are almost swallowed up. We have been molded into place by machines, schedules, neurotic activity, peer pressures, and "little league" activities of all sorts. Family units seem to be more individual units living under the same roof. Could it be we only have a form of that which God intended and that modern society has gutted our spiritual house? It is possible! What is to be done?

First of all, it is time to take time to **think**. We do so little of that these days. No one needs to think as long as he is swept along in the stream of routine, never-ending activity. Get out of the stream, on the bank, and think. Stop right now and think.

O.K. Here I am. What am I supposed to think about? The following suggestions are offered by Gary D. Taliaferro:

1.   Think about God's love and power and how they have affected your life.

2.   Think of your family and all the natural gifts and resources He has given you.

3.   Think about and enumerate what the components of His kind of life are in your world and in the life you are living.

4.   Think about a growing tree, the birds flying south at winter, the process of a bee making honey.

5.   Think about a boy learning from his father about the wonders of life and of creative work.

6.   Think about a day without any yelling and screaming and hassle.

7.   Think about how your life in your world and family can incorporate the quiet serenity of Jesus Christ.

8.   Think and control your life in harmony with God and not be gobbled up by this present world.

Remember, Jesus said through the Apostle Paul, "Do not be conformed to this world, but be transformed by the renewing of your mind that you may prove what the will of God is, that which is good and acceptable and perfect" (Rom. 12:2).

Worship

998 Whale Songs

According to research conducted by the National Geographic Society, the 40-ton creation of God—the humpback whale—has a fascinating singing ability. Recordings have been made of the humpback whale singing in various pitches in solos, duets, trios, and choruses of dozens of interweaving voices lasting from six to thirty minutes. What an experience it is to hear, over one's own stereo system, songs from the ocean depths—sung by 40-ton whales! The passage of Psalm 148:7 comes to mind: "Praise Him down here on earth you creatures of the ocean depths."

999 The Worship Service

A small boy asked an aged sailor, "What is the wind?" The old man replied, "I don't know, son; I can't tell you what the wind is, but I can tell you how to hoist a sail."

It is not really necessary to know all about the wind if we know how to set our sails. We simply make them ready, and let the wind come.

This is what we are doing in a worship service—setting our sails for whatever gale the tomorrows may bring. Here, as it were, we adjust the wind-catching paraphernalia of our lives. Then we will be ready for life's gentle zephyrs or its howling storms. Here we align ourselves, set ourselves right with reality, and then, whatever winds may blow, we can receive their forward-thrusting force and sail on.

1000 Greeting the King

Noblemen were gathered together in London waiting for the King of Great Britain. They all knew him personally, yet they all honored him as their king. When he entered, they stood solemnly to their feet. "Take your seats, gentlemen," he said, "I count you as my personal friends." And then joking he added, "I am not the Lord, you know!" Immediately one of the noblemen, a Christian, said, "No, sir, if you were our Lord, we would not have stood to our feet; we would have fallen to our knees."

1001 Get in Tune

A sheep rancher in the remote mountains of Idaho found that his violin was out of tune, and, try as he would, he was unable to make the instrument sound the way it should. A frequent listener to a radio station in California, he wrote the station concerning his problem, asking these good people at a certain hour and minute on a certain day to strike the right note for him. This they did: stopping everything else, silencing all other sounds for a moment, they struck that note. In his shepherd's hut in the distant mountains, the shepherd heard that sound, and from that single note he put his instrument into tune again.

Thus is the hour of worship, a special time of being in touch with God. Here we listen for the signal-tone He strikes for our lives, for the pitch He gives by which our hearts may be put in tune.

1002   Sincerity in Singing

The late Dr. Peter Marshall once selected for use in a church service the familiar hymn of consecration, "Take My Life and Let It Be." He requested the congregation to give particular thought to the words:

"Take my silver and my gold,
Not a mite would I withhold."

Exacting the practical sense of the words "not a mite would I withhold," he asked that all who could not sing this line with literal sincerity, refrain from singing it at all.

The effect was a dramatic commentary on the glib, thoughtless manner in which, all too often, we sing our hymns. Hundreds of voices, with organ accompaniment, sang vigorously up to the designated point. Then, suddenly, there was only the sound of the organ music. Not a single voice ventured to so challenging a height!

1003   Worshiping the
Preacher

Henry Ward Beecher, the famous pulpit orator, once had to be ab-sent and his brother was invited to speak for him. The church house was crowded, but when it became evident the eloquent Henry Beecher was not going to appear, many started to leave. Beecher's brother was not disturbed. He stood up before the murmuring crowd, called for silence and said, "All who came this morning to worship Henry W. Beecher may now leave. The rest will remain and worship God."

What are we doing in our assemblies? Some, like the Athenians, come only to hear the preacher say "something" (Acts 17:20, 21). "Is it relevant?" "Is it positive?" Are mental guidelines used in judging sermons? Some attend to judge the singing, the prayers, or the friendliness of the congregation. These go away with a host of criticisms, perhaps, or even pride, but worship has been forgotten.

Why do we gather for worship? Some come to "get it over with for a week"; to get their tickets validated once more. But those who come because they need strength in carrying their crosses know the value of true worship.

Worship has nothing to do with the song leader or the talent of the preacher. It has to do with you and your God. Let people do what they will to please themselves. "The rest will remain and worship God."

1004   Take Our Bearings

In the old days of ocean sailing, a small boy was traveling on shipboard with his father. About once a day the boy saw the captain stand on deck with sextant in hand, and, as they used to say, "shoot the stars." The boy said to his father, "Daddy, what is the captain doing?" His father replied, "The captain is taking our bearings, seeing where we are, finding out if we are going in the right direction."

As a matter of fact, it is something of this kind that each of us is doing as we are in worship on Sunday morning. We are checking in with God; we are seeing where we are; we are finding out about our directions in relation to His will concerning our journey of life.

We can so easily become confused or lose our way out there in the weekday world of days, and we need this checkpoint. Here we touch base with the Lord of our life, and from Him we take our bearings for going on. We can deviate from the course and by winds and currents be carried far astray, unless from time to time we check in with God to set our course again.

1005 The Meaning of Worship

Worship that is accepted by God is a privilege unique to the Christian (1 Pet. 2:5). It is not a right. I am permitted to offer acceptable worship only by the grace of God.

Therefore it is disheartening when children of God deliberately reject this privilege and wantonly absent themselves from the public assembly God has ordained for His glory and our good.

Consider briefly the significance of worship:

It is obedience to a divine command.

It is a means of nourishing the spirit.

It assists in achieving spiritual growth.

It encourages others in their spiritual development.

It shows the world where my priorities are.

It is one means of expressing my love for God.

It is an avenue God has provided by which I can praise His name.

It is the offering of spiritual sacrifices.

It is a way of showing my thanksgiving to God for all He has done for me.

It is a period of communion with God with the world shut out entirely.

It is an experience that should make the heart of every Christian glad!

Will you join your fellow Christians this Lord's day as they assemble to honor His name? Your Father will be looking for you.

General Index

Scripture Index

4:9	595	**Romans**	
6:35	690	ch. 1	30
6:45	622	1:16	68
7:21–24	561	2:1–3	561
8:12	414	3:13, 14	862
8:44	749, 750	6:3, 4	225
9:4	156	6:3–7	723
10:7–9	20	6:16	748
10:10	750, 979	8:13, 26	748
12:32	485	8:18	702
12:48	351	8:28	54, 487, 769, 892
ch. 13	673	8:37	145
14:2	140	10:1	638
14:6	750	12:1	156
14:15	612	12:2	262, 744
15:5	354	12:3	763
15:13	590, 596	12:4, 5	815
15:16	978	12:11	523
19:23	97	12:16	545
		12:17	19
Acts		13:8	673
2:47	673	14:3, 4	561
3:19	733	14:7	419
5:3	748	14:10, 13	561
5:23	723	15:5, 6	156
5:28, 29	963		
10:37, 38	946	**1 Corinthians**	
13:36	639	3:6–9	187, 903
13:39	733	3:15	967
14:27	20	3:18	752
ch. 16	247, 574	4:5	561
16:31	350	6:9	752
17:1–9	963	10:1, 2	225
17:20, 21	1003	10:6, 11	19
20:35	436, 767	10:13	703, 774, 791
24:25	673	13:8	140
26:17, 18	748